Teaching
MIDDLE YEARS

3rd edition

Teaching
MIDDLE YEARS
Rethinking curriculum, pedagogy and assessment

EDITED BY

Donna Pendergast
Katherine Main
Nan Bahr

Routledge
Taylor & Francis Group

LONDON AND NEW YORK

First published 2017 by Allen & Unwin

Published 2020 by Routledge
2 Park Square, Milton Park, Abingdon, Oxon OX14 4RN
605 Third Avenue, New York, NY 10017

Routledge is an imprint of the Taylor & Francis Group, an informa business

Cataloguing-in-Publication details are available
from the National Library of Australia
www.trove.nla.gov.au

Set in 11/14 pt Minion by Post Pre-press Group, Australia

ISBN-13: 9781760292928 (pbk)

Printed in the UK by Severn, Gloucester on responsibly sourced paper

We wish to dedicate this book to all of those in the field, including the students, parents, teachers, school leaders, tertiary students, academics and policy-makers who each bring passion and commitment to the middle years.

Contents

CONTENTS

CONTENTS

Tables, figures and provocations

Tables

Figures

Provocations

Abbreviations

AAMT	Australian Association of Mathematics Teachers
ABS	Australian Bureau of Statistics
AC: HPE	Australian Curriculum: Health and Physical Education
ACARA	Australian Curriculum, Assessment and Reporting Authority
ACER	Australian Council for Educational Research
ACHPER	Australian Council for Health, Physical Education and Recreation
ACWP	Australian Child Wellbeing Project
AHKA	Active Healthy Kids Australia
AIHW	Australian Institute of Health and Welfare
AITSL	Australian Institute for Teaching School Leadership
AMLE	Association for Middle Level Education
ARACY	Australian Research Alliance for Children and Youth
ARC	Australian Research Council
ARG	Assessment Reform Group
BMI	Body Mass Index
CSCL	Computer supported collaborative learning
DEEWR	Department of Education, Employment and Workplace Relations
DET	Department of Education and Training
DETA	Department of Education, Training and the Arts
DETE	Department of Education, Training and Employment
DETYA	Department of Employment, Training and Youth Affairs
EB	expectancy benefit
ECM	Educational Change Model
FAM	Four Attributes Model of the Middle School Teacher
HASS	Humanities, Arts, and Social Sciences
HPE	health and physical education
HSMS	Highly Successful Middle Schools
ICT	information and communication technologies
IMPACT	Inspire, Model, Practise, Connect and Transform Learning Framework

ABBREVIATIONS

KLA	Key Learning Area
LSIA	Learning Sciences Institute Australia
MYSA	Middle Years of Schooling Association
NAPLAN	National Assessment Program—Literacy and Numeracy
NMSA	National Middle School Association
OECD	Organisation for Economic Co-operation and Development
OPV	Other Peoples' Viewpoint
PAR	participation action research
PAT-R	Progressive Achievement Tests in Reading
PE	physical education
PIRLS	Progress in International Reading Literacy Study
PISA	Programme for International Student Assessment
PLT	Professional Learning Teams
PMI	Plus, Minus and Interesting
PYD	positive youth development
QLSTL	Queensland Longitudinal Study of Teaching and Learning
QSRLS	Queensland Schools Reform Longitudinal Study
REACH	Reach Every Student through Differentiated Instruction
SAFE	Sequenced Active Focus Explicit
SEL	Social and Emotional Learning
STV	subjective task value
TFS	Team functioning scale
TIMSS	Trends in International Mathematics and Science Study
TPACK	Technological Pedagogical and Content Knowledge
TTF	Teaching Teachers for the Future Project
UK	United Kingdom
USA	United States of America
WA	Western Australia
WHO	World Health Organisation
ZPD	zone of proximal development

Contributors

Editors

Donna Pendergast

Professor Donna Pendergast is dean of the School of Education and Professional Studies at Griffith University, Brisbane, Australia. She has an international profile in the field of middle years education. Her work focuses on school leadership for reform, along with developing capabilities to enhance teacher efficacy. Her journey in middle years education has included leading and developing the first dedicated teacher education program in Australia, influencing state and national policy directions, conducting state and national evaluations, developing a tailored reform model, leading competitive research tenders commissioned by state and federal authorities valued at more than $3.7 million and contributing to more than 100 publications in the field.

Katherine Main

Dr Katherine Main is a senior lecturer and program leader in the School of Education and Professional Studies at Griffith University. She teaches undergraduate and postgraduate courses on middle schooling and junior secondary. Her research interests include middle school and junior secondary reform and the need for targeted professional development, and teacher efficacy, including the collective efficacy of teacher teams. She is a strong advocate for young adolescents, and her research interests also include student efficacy and student engagement.

Nan Bahr

Professor Nan Bahr is dean (learning and teaching) of the Arts, Education and Law Group of Griffith University. Nan has a strong background in schools, as a teacher educator and as an institutional leader, having held leadership positions at Queensland University of Technology and the University of Queensland. Nan has an international profile in middle years and teacher education and has an excellent track record for published work, leadership of large competitive research projects and partnerships across the education sector.

Authors

Lenore Adie

Dr Lenore Adie is a senior research fellow with the assessment, evaluation and student learning research concentration in the Learning Sciences Institute Australia, Australian Catholic University. Her research focuses on assessment and moderation practices, including online moderation, as these contribute to supporting teachers' pedagogical practices and student learning. She has extensive professional experience, having worked in schools for over twenty years as a teacher and within leadership positions in Brisbane and central Queensland.

Georgina Barton

Dr Georgina Barton is a senior lecturer in the School of Education and Professional Studies at Griffith University. She is also the program director of the bachelor of secondary education and lectures in English and literacy education. Georgina taught in schools for over twenty years, including teaching English in South India. Her research interests include English and literacy education, multimodalities, arts and music education and teacher education with a focus on international students.

J. Joy Cumming

Professor Joy Cumming is research director of assessment, evaluation and student learning in the Learning Sciences Institute Australia, Australian Catholic University. Her research into educational assessment and accountability focuses on equity and social justice, including work in education law that examines the impact of educational policy and legislation in assessment and accountability. She is leading a major Australian Research Council discovery project on working with teachers to provide adjustments in summative assessments for students with disability in mainstream subjects.

Shelley Dole

Shelley Dole is professor and head of the School of Education at the University of the Sunshine Coast. She has been involved in several research projects that focus on embedding numeracy across the curriculum and the professional development of teachers. Her research has highlighted the importance of proportional reasoning as essential to numeracy.

Tony Dowden

Dr Tony Dowden is a senior lecturer of curriculum and pedagogy at the University of Southern Queensland. He is co-editor of the *Australian Journal of Middle Schooling*. His research focuses on curriculum design and teacher beliefs in the middle years. He has previously taught in Tasmania, New Zealand and Samoa.

Glenn Finger

Glenn Finger is professor of education in the School of Education and Professional Studies at Griffith University. He was dean (learning and teaching) of the Arts, Education and Law Group at Griffith University (2011–15). He has been acknowledged through prestigious teaching and paper awards for his scholarship on technologies. Prior to his appointment at Griffith University, in 1999, he served with Education Queensland for 24 years as a health and physical education specialist, primary school teacher, deputy principal and acting principal.

Annette Hilton

Annette Hilton is associate professor in research leadership at the International Research Centre for Youth Futures at the University of Technology Sydney. Her research interests focus on development of conceptual understanding in mathematics and science and on teachers' professional growth through practitioner research.

Geoff Hilton

Dr Geoff Hilton is a lecturer in mathematics education and teaching and learning at the University of Queensland. His research interests focus on children's acquisition of mathematical concepts and teacher professional development through practitioner research.

Sherilyn Lennon

Dr Sherilyn Lennon is an academic in the School of Education and Professional Studies at Griffith University. Prior to this appointment she worked as a head of department and literacy project officer in schools across western Queensland. Currently, Sherilyn juggles her time between university life and a sheep, cattle and wheat property four hours west of Brisbane. Her various roles and life experiences have allowed her to develop a wide and deep knowledge of issues relating to boys' education, rurality and literacy.

Mia O'Brien

Dr Mia O'Brien is a senior lecturer at the School of Education and Professional Studies and coordinator of initial teacher education at Griffith University. She leads a large Australian Research Council discovery project and several school-based projects where she works in collaboration with classroom teachers to develop pedagogical practices that foster students' positive learning identities.

Sarah Prestridge

Dr Sarah Prestridge has made contributions in the area of information and communication technologies professional development and the categorisation and relationship between teachers' information and communication technologies beliefs and practices. She has extensive experience in teacher change theory and core processes of professional development and an understanding and application of digital tools and environments to engage and direct constructive discourse, reflection and investigation. Conceptualising what is considered effective pedagogy in a digital world is a major part of her research and teaching practice.

Fabienne Van der Kleij

Dr Fabienne Van der Kleij is a research fellow in the assessment, evaluation and student learning research concentration of the Learning Sciences Institute Australia, Australian Catholic University. Her main research interests are formative assessment and feedback, including feedback in computer-based assessment and reporting environments. Recent and ongoing research has focused on, for example, (formative) assessment for diverse students, formative assessment and feedback, teacher assessment identity, assessment for learning in classroom practice, and curriculum and assessment in the Australian context.

Sue Whatman

Dr Sue Whatman is a senior lecturer in health and physical education and sports coaching at Griffith University. She is a fellow of the Australian Council for Health, Physical Education and Recreation and editorial committee member for the council's national *Active & Healthy Magazine*.

Claire Wyatt-Smith

Professor Claire Wyatt-Smith is the director of the Learning Sciences Institute Australia, Australian Catholic University, and professor of educational assessment and literacy. Her research focuses primarily on classroom assessment and teachers' work and, more specifically, on professional judgement, standards and moderation. Her publications address teachers' assessment identities, large-scale standardised testing and its impact on learning, assessment adaptations for students with disabilities, and assessment and new technologies.

Preface

The middle years are increasingly recognised as a crucial stage of schooling with significant consequences for ongoing educational success and future participation in society. Middle years reform focuses on establishing and sustaining academically rigorous and developmentally responsive educational learning contexts and experiences for young adolescents. Teachers in this critical phase need specialist preparation, as they are required to teach across key learning areas and to have the skills and knowledge to understand and manage issues related to young adolescents.

This book will assist schools, academics, preservice student teachers and teachers in their quest to successfully develop middle years curricula, pedagogies and assessments to meet the needs of today's young people, in a context-specific way. The book brings together policy and evidence-based practice for middle years education contributed by leading academics and school-based practitioners. It is not exhaustive in its coverage—several books would be required to document all the relevant aspects of middle years teaching and learning.

The organisation of the book reflects the cornerstone of middle years education—that is, reform in curriculum, pedagogy and assessment. It commences with a platform about the middle years as a site for educational reform before addressing reform in practices grouped around curriculum, pedagogy and assessment. Each chapter includes provocations to engage readers in deep thinking about the field and ends with a reflection on the concepts developed in that chapter.

This third edition has been developed to reflect recent contemporary influences that are impacting across the dynamic contexts for schooling in the middle years while still capturing the essence of middle schooling principles addressed in the first two editions. In addition to meeting editorial requirements, each chapter has been peer reviewed. The result is a resource that fills a gap in the resources available to teachers, researchers, academics and school and systemic leaders around middle years teaching and learning, bringing together sound scholarly debate and practical applications.

Professor Donna Pendergast
Dr Katherine Main
Professor Nan Bahr

Part One

The middle years

Chapter One

Middle years education

DONNA PENDERGAST

Learning intentions

In this chapter we will:
- introduce the field of middle years education
- consider factors that shape middle years education
- engage in a three-step strategy to develop a school-based philosophy for middle years education.

Introducing middle years education

Why focus on middle years education?

Over the last three decades, around the world there has been a great deal of interest in effective teaching and learning for young adolescents with the impetus to provide the best learning opportunities for engagement and, in turn, student achievement. It is through the thoughtful adoption of intentional approaches to learning and teaching that take account of, and respond to, young adolescent learners in formal and informal contexts that effective middle years education can be achieved. Middle years education applies to young people aged from around eleven to fifteen years and typically in Years 5–9 in schools. The exact age range and year levels vary in different states and territories around Australia and internationally, hence there will be some variation in this book. The need for addressing the middle years separately has emerged from an increased understanding of the changes that occur in the lives of young people during this period and of the effects these changes have on student learning.

The magnitude of physical, psychosocial, emotional and cognitive changes that occur during early adolescence is second only to that of the changes experienced in the first two years of life. In addition, we can expect the most differentiation, because for each individual the journey through adolescence is unique, with changes occurring at different times and at different rates. This means classrooms are widely differentiated, not only in the usual senses of socio-economic status, ethnicity, gender, location and other generally accepted variables, but also in terms of the widest range of maturation across the developmental domains. The middle years are also typically characterised by a transition in school from a student-centred model to an increasingly subject-centred model, with accompanying structural, organisational, cultural and other aspects of the school experience coinciding with this time of change.

The quality of teaching students experience is now accepted to be the most significant factor we can focus on to improve student achievement. This challenges us to consider what quality teaching means in the context of young adolescent learners, especially because there is a predictable, measurable decline in student achievement in the middle years. Indeed, much of the research around student academic performance indicates that during the early years of secondary school, students make the least progress, the gap between the low- and high-performing students increases, and students are less engaged with education. This has been called the 'middle school plunge' (West & Schwerdt, 2012) and the 'dip' (Education Queensland, 2001), and estimates put the effect as representing a loss of between 3.5 and 7 months of learning achievement. The impact on academic achievement is most significant in students who lack literacy and numeracy capacity, especially reading and spelling. It might reasonably be assumed that this pattern is connected to the nature of the changes that occur during early adolescence, along with the challenges associated with transition between primary and secondary school. Pulling these elements together, the Australian Council for Educational Research (ACER, 2012) has captured the key challenges for education in the middle years as:

- the need to manage a heterogeneous student population without sacrificing inclusiveness
- a decline in student academic performance
- a high incidence of disengagement, disruptive behaviour, boredom and disconnection from schooling
- a knowledge gap between what is taught and the kind of content that would engage early adolescents and match their cognitive skills
- transition, which often entails major change.

Hence, the purpose of a focused approach to middle years education is to intentionally, and with a full understanding of the context, employ a range of evidence-based practices to provide the best learning opportunities to engage and improve student achievement.

Middle years education in Australia

In Australia, the middle years are increasingly the focus of education reform initiatives, and there is a growing corpus of literature and emergent theoretical perspectives regarding, and hence a growing intellectual investment and commitment to, the field. Many schools and school systems now publicly identify and name themselves or a sub-school within their organisation as middle schools, junior secondary schools or other comparable terms. For some this might be virtually a change in name only. For many others the change involves a significant re-imagining and re-culturing in order to implement teaching and learning approaches that meet the needs of young adolescent learners.

A highly influential platform for middle years education reform in Australia has been the 2008 *Melbourne declaration on educational goals for young Australians*, which identifies 'enhancing middle years' development' as one of eight areas for action. In the declaration, the importance of the action is explained thus: 'The middle years are an important period of learning, in which knowledge of fundamental disciplines is developed, yet this is also a time when students are at the greatest risk of disengagement from learning. Student motivation and engagement in these years is critical, and can be influenced by tailoring approaches to teaching, with learning activities and learning environments that specifically consider the needs of middle years students' (Ministerial Council on Education, Employment, Training and Youth Affairs, 2008, p. 10).

The need for tailored approaches to teaching and learning activities for young adolescents has now been generally accepted in Australia as well as in many other parts of the world. In Australia, the Middle Years of Schooling Association (MYSA, 2008), now named Adolescent Success, formulated and advocates for the adoption of a set of Signifying Practices that are regarded as enabling quality learning for engagement and success for middle years learners:

1. Clear philosophy relevant to the context.
2. ...
    - higher order thinking strategies
    - integrated and disciplinary curricula that are negotiated, relevant and challenging

Provocation 1.1 Understanding middle years students

You are a new middle years teacher. The sketch in Figure 1.1 shows a group of four friends who are studying Year 8 together and are within six months of age. As their new classroom teacher you have made a few assumptions about the students based on their appearance. The image is a simple depiction of the variation of physical development that exists even in a group as small as this. As you get to know the students you realise that appearance is no indicator for cognitive maturation or for other readiness aspects of learning. You also realise that these four are at very different points of psychosocial maturity.

 As a middle years educator, what are your first steps to understanding the students in your class—and not just these four, but the entire 30?

Figure 1.1 Four friends

- heterogeneous and flexible student groupings
- cooperative learning and collaborative teaching
- authentic and reflective assessment with high expectations
- democratic governance and shared leadership
- parental and community involvement in student learning.

A cursory glance at these practices confirms that the approaches are built on principles that are desirable for all learners, not just those in the middle years. It is necessary to drill down into each of these to gain an understanding of what this means in the middle years context. Hence, many of these practices are chapter topics in this book, to enable deep engagement and understanding.

The need for an approach to teaching and learning that intentionally privileges these Signifying Practices is well supported through rigorous research that reveals that the quality of teaching diminishes in the middle years and that specific strategies are better suited to middle years students' age and developmental needs and to the wide range that is typical during the adolescent years. The absence of many of these practices and other high-quality pedagogy indicators remains a challenge in many middle years educational settings. Perhaps this is why there is an abundance of evidence that points to greater incidence of underachievement, disengagement, truancy, mental ill health and problem behaviours along with declining levels of resilience and motivation for those in the middle years (M.-T. Wang & Fredricks, 2014), despite the increased awareness of the effectiveness of employing appropriate approaches to teaching and learning for these students.

Factors that shape middle years education

Middle years curriculum, pedagogy and assessment

In Australia, schools generally operate on a two-tiered system (primary and secondary), providing a very different context for middle school reform. An important aspect of the underlying philosophy of reform in the middle years of schooling in the Australian context revolves around the provision of a seamless transition from primary schooling (which is traditionally student centred) to secondary schooling (which is traditionally subject or discipline centred) leading to more effective student learning, positive experiences in adolescence and a desire and capacity for lifelong learning. These issues go beyond the traditional shift from the smaller primary school site to the larger secondary school. Difficulties are exacerbated by the different structures, the new relationships with teachers, the unique needs of adolescent learners and the different emphases students encounter in the movement from primary to secondary. Abundant evidence points to the failure of traditional structures for students in the middle years. Particularly for boys, the failure to meet the specific needs of adolescent learners can manifest in disengagement from schooling, often reflected in poor achievement and behaviour. Students also believe that they are required to deal with variable teacher responsiveness. For their part, teachers must confront and deal with the consequences of student disengagement and variable work environments (P. Hill, 1995).

However, changing school structures to reflect those more likely to be found in middle schools does not ensure that middle schooling will take place. As Chadbourne (2001, p. iii), one of the early Australian advocates for reforming middle years education, noted, an effective middle years approach 'refers more to a particular type of pedagogy and curriculum than a particular type of school structure'. Hence, generally speaking, middle years work has tended to focus on the convergence and transformation of curriculum, pedagogy and assessment to meet the needs of young adolescents and to a lesser degree on organisational elements. It does not rely on rearranging traditional schooling structures, and it is increasingly recognised that for reform to have any cogency and impact on the educational experience of students and the workplace conditions of teachers the articulation of all key aspects is required, rather than isolated change.

In terms of curriculum, it is acknowledged that a coherent curriculum appropriate to the needs of early adolescents is focused on identified needs; it is negotiated and linked to the world outside the classroom. In addition, it is explicit and outcome based: progress and achievement are recorded continuously in relation to explicit statements of what each student is expected to know and be able to do. This leads to changing views and practices surrounding pedagogy— the way we teach these students. Classroom pedagogy must match the needs and abilities of middle years students. To be effective, pedagogy must be flexible, reflecting creative uses of time, space and other resources as well as group and individual needs. It must also be learner centred, with an emphasis on self-directed and co-constructed learning. As the literature indicates, it must also be increasingly team focused for both teachers and learners, all of whom require supportive, ethical and challenging environments. Assessment must be relevant, authentic and connected to the life experiences of young people. Educational goals specific to the middle years must be determined. These are fundamental changes in terms of rethinking curriculum, pedagogy and assessment, not about reshaping existing practices. Pedagogical effectiveness is at the core of effective middle years education, as it is about 'an intentional approach to teaching and learning that is responsive and appropriate to the full range of needs, interests and achievements of middle years students in formal and informal schooling contexts' (MYSA, 2008). Extensive research evidence confirms that teacher quality is the most important factor in improving outcomes for students (Dinham & Rowe, 2007; D.H. Hargreaves, 1994; Hattie, 2003); hence, quality teaching and learning provision is the most important imperative in the middle years.

In terms of school organisation, there is a need for collaboration between teachers across disciplines and year levels; there must be administrative support for change; there must be adequate resourcing at all levels—experienced teachers and support staff supported by high-quality facilities, technology, equipment and materials; and, finally, the school must be community oriented, with parents and outside agencies contributing to productive and sustained partnerships. There are many models for middle school organisation which are proving to be effective, including pod structures, with a group of students (typically multi-aged and numbering around 70–100) and a small number of teachers (typically from four to six) who remain with the pod. Teachers may loop—that is, stay with the same group over a two- or three-year period—and then start with a new group.

Educational institutions at primary, secondary and tertiary levels have shown active responses to the emerging middle years reform agenda, with many schools around Australia experimenting with the elements of reform in an attempt to address issues of disengagement and disenchantment. The various Australian state and territory education departments along with the independent and Catholic education sectors have responded with research and development funding, the emergence of junior secondary schools and a general positive interest in this area.

Middle years research

For almost three decades in Australia there has been deep interest in middle years education and in addressing the educational needs of young adolescents as a distinct group of students in our schools. This is increasingly evident through attention in policies, programs and practices that relate specifically to students in the ten to fifteen years age group. In some cases, middle schools are being designed and established to cater specifically for the needs of this group of students (Chadbourne, 2001; Cormack, 1991; Eyers, 1992; A. Hargreaves & Earl, 1990; Manning, 1993). Cormack and Cumming's (1995) report *From alienation to engagement* was particularly influential in Australia in terms of kicking off this agenda, highlighting reform strategies for curriculum, pedagogy, school organisation and environment, as well as reinforcing the need for a multilayered approach to reform. During 1996–97, the National Middle Schooling Project developed a 'common view of the needs of young adolescents; the principles that should guide our work with them; and the practices that are regarded as most appropriate for their positive and successful development' (J. Cumming, 1998, p. 14). Since then, sectoral, state and territory and nationally based projects and initiatives inspired by the desire to motivate and engage students in the middle years have sprinkled the Australian education landscape. Similarly, around the world, attention to these years of schooling has featured prominently.

In fact, the focus on middle years education is not an Australian initiative; indeed, Australia has benefited from a considerable body of international activity and research that has accumulated over many decades. The impetus for middle schooling in other countries, however, has been quite different from the Australian scenario. In the United States, for example, issues such as population growth, racial segregation and curriculum imperatives led to the development of middle school as a tier of schooling in an already three-tiered model. Claims about the success of middle schooling in the United States have been bold, such as that made by Lounsbury (1997, p. xi), who maintains that 'the middle school movement is an educational success story unparalleled in our history. In a little over three decades the face of American education has been remade'.

Along with the growing body of research, projects and position statements relevant to middle schooling, there are other signs that the field continues to be a focus of reforms. Below is a selection of evidence-based studies that provide insight into the need for a focus on teaching and learning in the middle years. These studies have been conducted in various parts of Australia or internationally and have been selected because of their efficacy and impact on the middle years agenda.

Queensland School Reform Longitudinal Study
The Queensland School Reform Longitudinal Study found that the combination of the particular needs of the students and the teaching and learning experiences schools were providing was contributing to what it described as the dip in student achievement typical of the early years of secondary school. Researchers found from direct classroom observations that there were much higher levels of connectedness, recognition of difference and intellectual quality in Year 6 and Year 11 classes than in Year 8 classes (Education Queensland, 2001).

Beyond the Middle
The Beyond the Middle Project was commissioned by the Commonwealth Department of Education, Science and Training to investigate the perceived efficacy of middle years programs in all states and territories in improving the quality of teaching, learning and student outcomes, especially in literacy and numeracy and for student members of particular target groups (Luke et al., 2003). This report found that

> middle years programs that evidenced the greatest current and potential value for target group students tended to have developed in state policy environments that encouraged what we term a 'structural' rather than 'adjunct' approach to middle years innovations. This involves naming and defining the middle years as a distinctive and core area for specific educational focus and intervention activities.
>
> Our findings strongly suggest that the focus on middle years to date has been largely 'first generation' work concentrated on advocacy and development, with some serious definitional limitations and unfinished business . . .
>
> There is a need for a second generation of middle years theorising, research, development and practice. We argue that while this work can build upon some of the accomplishments documented here, there will need to be a stronger and more sustained focus on the intellectual engagement and intellectual demand expected of students (Luke et al., 2003, pp. 4–5).

Developing Lifelong Learners in the Middle Years of Schooling
In 2005 the results of a national project, Developing Lifelong Learners in the Middle Years of Schooling, were published, which addressed the broad question of how to ensure the engagement with learning of all young adolescent students and how to encourage a higher order of learning objectives and outcomes both now and throughout life (Pendergast et al., 2005). The project built on nationwide and international efforts at school reform intended to provide learning programs that were intellectually demanding, connected to the real world, socially supportive, community linked and engaged with the wide diversity of student abilities, preferences, circumstances and needs. The study revealed that when attention was paid to implementing pedagogical approaches that were informed by young adolescents' needs and when a focus on lifelong learning occurred, students were more resilient and demonstrated greater lifelong learning capacity. The study also mapped the reform processes for improving young adolescent learning, leading to the development

of the Educational Change Model. Details of the model are provided in the final chapter of this book.

Longitudinal Study of Teaching and Learning in Queensland State Schools (Stage 1)
The Longitudinal Study of Teaching and Learning in Queensland State Schools (Stage 1) was commissioned by the Department of Education, Training and the Arts to establish a framework for the monitoring of classroom practice in Queensland state schools across time and to create an initial data set on such practices (Goos et al., 2008). The focus was on the middle years (Years 4, 6, 8 and 9) in the key learning areas of mathematics, English, science and studies of society and environment. The study involved case studies, surveys and the analysis of existing systemic data. The data collected included observations of classroom practice; samples of assessment tasks and student work; interviews with students, parents, teachers and key school leaders, including principals, from 18 case study schools; and surveys of teachers and students from 83 schools. Data obtained from this study were also compared with data collected from the Queensland School Reform Longitudinal Study (Education Queensland, 2001). The comparison showed there were small but statistically significant improvements in the dimensions of 'intellectual quality' and 'valuing and working with difference'. There was no statistically significant change in the 'connectedness' or 'supportive classroom environment' dimensions. Hence, the pedagogical practices in Queensland schools did not improve substantially in the ten-year period under review. Interestingly, during this time there was considerable discussion about the value of taking an intentional approach to teaching and learning in the middle years, but there were no significant and funded policy initiatives.

American middle schools
A report of two national studies conducted in the United States in 2009 comprising 827 randomly selected public middle schools and 101 of the most successful middle schools (classified as 'highly successful middle schools') revealed that the highly successful middle schools followed the concept and philosophy that responded to the particular needs of young adolescents and implemented recommended middle school components such as teams, advisory programs, common planning time and flexible block scheduling. In particular:

- The percentage of students on or above grade level in mathematics and reading on standardised tests was higher in the highly successful middle schools than in schools in the random study.

- Middle schools authentically following the middle school concept and philosophy were more likely to be associated with higher scores on achievement tests and other positive student outcomes.
- The middle school concept and philosophy remained legitimate; this was the most important finding. The survey of highly successful middle schools showed that they followed the concept with more fidelity than other schools not recognised for their high levels of success (McEwin & Greene, 2011).

Western Australian Catholic Education

After much preparatory work, the Catholic Education Office in Western Australia committed to move Year 7 students from its more than 100 primary schools to secondary schools in 2009. This was the first time in the state's history that a major education system had embarked on such an undertaking. This system-wide shift presented unique opportunities to investigate the degree of success experienced when viewed through the eyes of relevant stakeholders and to obtain data that would help answer this important question. Six large secondary schools of varying contexts were involved in the study, which was conducted using mixed-methods surveys and focus group interviews (Coffey, Berlach & O'Neill, 2013). Eighty-six teachers, 506 Year 7 students and 344 parents participated and were asked about their perceptions and experiences of commencing secondary school, the transition process and the teaching and learning programs. The study concluded that the shift of Year 7 was a success and that while students experienced transitional challenges, these were not related to the year level of the transition but to generally inadequate transition practices.

Queensland state schools

In 2014 Queensland state schools underwent the cross-sectoral experience of moving Year 7 to secondary, alongside the introduction of junior secondary for Years 7–9 by the Queensland Department of Education and Training. The shift of 99,000 Year 7 students across all sectors was based on a six-month-earlier school starting age and widespread uptake of a preparatory year. The introduction of junior secondary for state school Year 7–9 students was based on knowledge that had grown over many years. Junior secondary is a narrower age range within the broad category of middle years students and draws from much of the research that has informed middle schooling initiatives worldwide. It is an intentional approach to teaching and learning in the early adolescent years to bring about improved outcomes for these students. The junior secondary model is based on identification of key challenges having a major impact on the school experiences of middle years students already noted by ACER (2012) earlier in this chapter.

The introduction of junior secondary was underpinned by six Junior Secondary Guiding Principles, which incorporated structural and philosophical aspects:

1. **Distinct identity**

    Junior Secondary students will be encouraged and supported to develop their own group identity within the wider high school. This can involve dedicated school areas and events.

2. **Quality teaching**

    Teachers working with students in the Junior Secondary years will be given the skills they need through additional professional development, so they can support young teens through these crucial early high school years.

3. **Student wellbeing**

    We will meet the social and emotional needs of Junior Secondary students with a strong focus on pastoral care. For example, schools could provide a home room to support students as they adjust to new routines and greater academic demands.

4. **Parent and community involvement**

    We want parents to stay connected with their students' learning when they enter high school. Parent involvement in assemblies, special events, award ceremonies and leadership presentations will be welcomed.

5. **Leadership**

    Schools will be encouraged to create leadership roles for students in Years 7, 8 and 9. Dedicated teachers experienced with teaching young adolescents will lead Junior Secondary supported by the principal and administration team.

6. **Local decision-making**

    The needs of each school community will influence how Junior Secondary is implemented in each school (ACER, 2012).

The principles can be conceived together to form a conceptual map of the junior secondary initiative (see Figure 1.2).

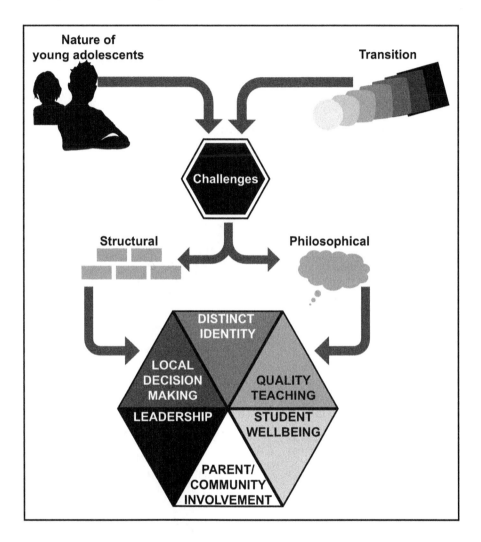

Figure 1.2 A conceptual map of the junior secondary initiative

Source: Pendergast et al. (2014a).

Provocation 1.2 Signifying Practices with the Junior Secondary Guiding Principles

Figure 1.3 aligns the MYSA's (2008) Signifying Practices with the Junior Secondary Guiding Principles (ACER, 2012).

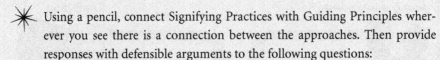 Using a pencil, connect Signifying Practices with Guiding Principles wherever you see there is a connection between the approaches. Then provide responses with defensible arguments to the following questions:

- How similar are these approaches?
- Where are the differences?
- Does either approach have a gap?

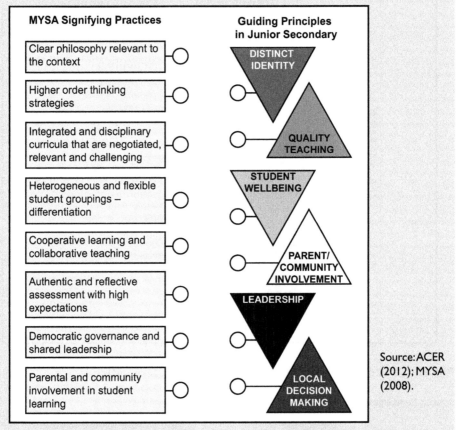

Figure 1.3 Aligning the Signifying Practices and Junior Secondary Guiding Principles

Middle years teachers

An international review of literature about teaching and learning in middle schooling by Dinham and Rowe (2007) draws the conclusions that middle schooling effectiveness is most influenced by teacher quality and instructional effectiveness and is influenced to a much lesser degree by student compositional characteristics (e.g., learning difficulties and disruptive behaviours) and structural arrangements (e.g., dedicated middle schools). Dinham and Rowe further connect the relationship between teacher quality and student outcomes by noting that teacher quality is the 'key determinant of [students'] perceptions and experiences of schooling, as well as their achievement progress and behaviours in the classroom' (pp. 81–2). To be effective requires high teacher self-efficacy—that is, personal belief in the teacher's abilities and competence and in their capacity to influence the outcomes of students. Hence, the need for effective middle school teachers with high self-efficacy appears to be incontestable.

Achieving high self-efficacy relies on preservice and continuing professional learning. This is best achieved through specialist programs and courses. In an American study of the status of middle schooling programs, three elements were deemed essential for success: clarity of mission, authentic commitment and skilful execution (George, 2008–09). The last of these fits squarely on the shoulders of teachers, and the evidence suggested that those teachers without specialist capacities were not achieving the necessary level of skilful execution required, leading to low self-efficacy and hence lack of belief in their capacity to influence the outcomes of students. We dedicate a chapter to quality teaching and learning in this book, where we deeply explore the role of the teacher in the middle years.

Specifically related to middle years teachers, Rumble and Aspland (2010) have developed a model that captures the essence of what differentiates middle school teachers from primary and secondary school teachers. Their model has four key attributes that distinguish middle school teachers. These attributes are the capacity to forge a middle school identity; be a designer of a wholesome curriculum; be a specialist in adolescence as a socio-cultural construct and have a capacity to sustain middle school reform.

It is unsurprising that these four attributes emerged from the study conducted by Rumble and Aspland (2010), as they reflect the broader context in which these teachers are located: their focus on a need to understand young adolescents and their curriculum space and on recognising themselves as distinct from primary and secondary school teachers. The attributes also mirror the current climate of reform that characterises the field (Pendergast, 2015). In order to achieve these four attributes, it is essential to hold a philosophy or set of beliefs about what it means to be a middle years teacher.

Developing a school philosophy for middle years education

In a broad sense, philosophy is an activity people undertake when they seek to understand fundamental truths about themselves, the world in which they live and their relationships to the world and to each other. Developing a middle years teaching and learning philosophy is about thinking through and taking a position on the *what*, *why* and *how*. The following questions will help when developing a philosophy, or understanding, about middle years education:

- Should middle years teaching and learning principles be adolescent specific?
- Should middle years teaching and learning principles prioritise the intellectual development of students?
- Should young adolescents be made to fit the organisation of schools or should the organisation of schools be made to fit young adolescents?
- What should the curriculum of middle years teaching and learning contain? On what concept of reality should the middle school curriculum be based?
- Should pedagogy in middle years teaching and learning be teacher centred or student centred?
- Is there one true, or pure, middle years teaching and learning model?

Step 1 Thinking through the issues

All school staff require an understanding of the justifications for middle years reform in order to make a commitment to this initiative. Consideration of the following questions can help build such understanding. The Junior Secondary Guiding Principles (ACER, 2012) or the MYSA's (2008) Signifying Practices might be used as organisers for the second and third questions.

- Why is the middle years teaching and learning agenda important in your school context?
- What practices around middle years teaching and learning has the school already in place that you believe should be kept?
- What opportunities does the middle years teaching and learning agenda provide to improve practices? Develop a list of ideas for how these can be included.

Step 2   Formulating a school-based shared understanding of middle years
         teaching and learning

School staff should develop through discussion a consolidated position for each
of the previous step's considerations in the context of the school. By formulating
a shared set of beliefs about middle years teaching and learning, staff will be more
likely to make a commitment. Middle years teaching and learning reform cannot
happen without a sharp focus on quality teaching to meet the needs of young
adolescent learners.

Step 3   Enacting the philosophy

A plan for action is necessary, including timelines and resource commitment, and
ways should be established to determine if the actions are achieved. It is important to disseminate these commitments so that actions follow the formation of the
philosophy. Statements should appear on websites, in reporting and in communications with parents and the wider community. There should be overt messages that
clearly show that middle years teaching and learning philosophy—the *what*, *why*
and *how*—is embedded in the culture of the school. Examples of how this might be
evident include:

*   naming the structure in the school—e.g., Junior Secondary School
*   stating beliefs on the school website
*   shifting structure and pedagogy to match quality teaching in middle years teach-
    ing and learning—e.g., core teachers and teacher teams, a focus on engagement
    strategies, and pastoral care looping.

Provocation 1.3 Developing a personal philosophy

Having now considered the attributes of a school philosophy of middle years
teaching and learning, we turn to considering a personal philosophy.

 Provide responses with defensible arguments to the following questions:

*   What is middle years education?
*   Why is or why isn't middle years education necessary?
*   How does middle years education look, feel and sound?

Chapter summary

This chapter makes the following key points:

- Middle years education is the thoughtful adoption of intentional approaches to learning and teaching that takes account of, and responds to, young adolescent learners in formal and informal contexts.
- During the early years of secondary school, students make the least progress, the gap between the low- and high-performing students increases, and students are less engaged with education.
- The middle years are increasingly the focus of education reform initiatives, and there is a growing corpus of literature and emergent theoretical perspectives regarding, and hence a growing intellectual investment and commitment to, the field.

Chapter Two

The adolescent learner

NAN BAHR

Learning intentions

In this chapter we will:
- examine the historical development of conceptions and characterisations of adolescence and adolescents
- consider the key constructions of adolescence from biological, social and cultural perspectives
- discuss a model for maturation and development that brings contemporary notions of development together.

Conceptions and characterisations of adolescence

Adolescence is a term that has changed over time and has different meanings to different cultures. Any sense of an exact concept is undermined by the plethora of contested ideas and theories raging in contemporary literature and media. If adolescence is a murky term, then what of young adolescence? This chapter examines some of the stable and contested views of adolescence expounded in contemporary sources. Conceptions of young adolescence as a developmental stage are problematised and explored. The aim is to provide a model for teaching the middle years student. This model will support the development of curriculum, pedagogy and assessment, and the creation of learning environments and contexts that optimise schooling for middle years students; it will also give direction to the organisational structures that frame them. The development of this type of model represents a move towards a comprehensive theory of the middle years of schooling students. That is, the middle years are characterised by dichotomy and conflict, diversity and similarity, and yet the middle years learner shares with peers unique attributes and assets that contrast with younger and older learners.

Research and theoretical literature into adolescence are fertile and prolific, but this hasn't always been the case. Formal recognition of adolescence as a distinct phase of life is first attributed to Hall, the 'father of adolescence' (Groenke et al., 2015, p. 35), in his seminal work of 1904. Hall's two-volume work *Adolescence* gave rise to attention that faltered at the demise of his rather untenable recapitulation theory (Arnett, 2006a, 2006b), which described adolescent development as being naturally evolutionary. Simply put, the idea was that young people will naturally develop through identifiable stages of maturation emotionally, cognitively, socially and physically. Hall's (1904, vol. 1) view was that we cannot interfere with this natural progression, with the implication that those working with youth should accept the maturational progression as unchanging, lock step and not responsive to environmental or educational factors. This approach predated that of Piaget (1964), who captured the imagination of researchers and teachers, but set hardline age–stage perspectives on education. The recapitulation theory was tied closely to the idea that there should be a label even for a part of life's journey that fits between childhood and adulthood. This, as it turns out, is a rather Western view of maturation.

Since the 1980s, specialist journals addressing all manner of aspects of the adolescent experience have emerged and have attracted prominent and gifted contributors. Indeed, the activity and interest level seem to be escalating in more recent times. All these scholars share an interest in, and concern for, the lot of young people. But when they use the term adolescent, are they really referring to the same thing? Just a quick scan of the most prominent journals on adolescence in 2009 and 2016 shows that authors disagree on who the adolescent is. These years are chosen to illustrate the instability of the age range considered for adolescence in two recent snapshots. The authors don't agree on age markers (see Table 2.1), boundaries for qualitative dimensions or, indeed, whether the term is even useful (Letendre, 2000).

The writings cited in Table 2.1 are empirical adolescent studies reported in 2009 and 2016 that clearly identify an age span for their research in key journals. The articles are based on a tacit assumption that their participant group aligns to some

Table 2.1 Various age spans for adolescence in contemporary literature

Author by journal	Age of adolescence (years)	Comments
Journal of Adolescence (2009)		
Albiero, Matricardi, Speltri & Toso	14–18	
Alfaro, Umana-Taylor, Gonzales-Backen, Bamaca & Zeiders	14–17	
Atuyambe, Mirembe, Annika, Kirumira & Faxelid	10–19	
Baiocco, Laghi & D'Alessio	15–19	
Begue & Roche	14–19	French
Berten & Van Rossem	14–18	Flemish
Brand, Hatzinger, Beck & Holsboer-Trachsler	12–19	
Carter, Jaccard, Silverman & Pina	11–17	
Chen & Jackson	12–19	Chinese
Connolly & McIsaac	15–18	
Corkindale, Condon, Russell & Quinlivan	15–18	
Davila et al.	(Early) 12–14	
Devís-Devís, Peiró-Velert, Beltrán-Carrillo & Tomás	12–17	
Froh, Yurkewicz & Kashdan	(Early) 11–13	
Giannotta, Ciairano, Spruijt & Spruijt-Metz	14–19	Italian
Goede, Branje & Meeus	12–20	
Holtmann et al.	15–20	
Kloep, Güney, Çok & Simsek	14–20	Welsh
Knowles, Niven, Fawkner & Henretty	(Early) 12–13	
Lajumen et al.	11–17	
Mason & Korpela	14–19	American
Mesch	13–17	
Padilla-Walker & Bean	14–17	
Petersen & Hyde	10–16	
Portzky, Audenaert & van Heeringen	15–19	
Roberts, Ramsay Roberts & Duong	11–17	*(continues)*

Table 2.1 *continued*

Author by journal	Age of adolescence (years)	Comments
Selfhout, Branje, ter Bogt & Meeus	(Early) 11–14	
Smetana, Villalobos, Tasopoulos-Chan, Gettman & Campione-Barr	(Early) 12–13	
	(Middle) 15–16	
Song, Ross, Thompson & Emilio Ferrer	(Early) 11–15	Chinese
	(Middle) 14–19	
	(Late) 17–23	
Starr & Davila	(Early) 12–15	
Sumter, Bokhorst, Steinberg & Westenberg	10–18	
Tuisku et al.	13–19	
Whitehouse, Durkin, Jaquet & Ziata	12–17	
Winstock	13–16	
Journal of Adolescence (2016)		
Alessandri, Eisenberg, Vecchione, Caprara & Milioni	12–25	Italian
Chan & Lo	14–24	Hong Kong
Kinnunen et al.	14–17	Irish
O'Connor, Dolphin, Fitzgerald & Dooley	12–19	American
Parr, Zeman, Braunstein & Price	11–15	
Adolescence (2009)		
Caglar	(Late) 11–16	
Freyberg	11–19	Taiwanese
Kavas	(Late) 17–24	
Kwok Lai & Shek	11–18	
Lee & Sun	12–16	
Niu & Wang	13–20	
Park, Kim & Kim	15–22	South Korean
Shek, Tang, Vver & Lo	(Early) 11–15	Chinese
	(Late) 16–18	

Author by journal	Age of adolescence (years)	Comments
Journal of Adolescent Research (2009)		
Dhariwal, Connolly, Paciello & Caprara	13–21	
Nalkur	12–18	
Journal of Adolescent Research (2016)		
Romo, Mireles-Rios & Hurtado	(Middle) 14–16	
Weinstein et al.	12–17	
Journal of Research on Adolescence (2009)		
Balsano, Phelps, Theokas, Lerner & Lerner	(Early) 10–12	American
Liu, Raine, Wuerker, Venables & Mednick	(Early) 11	Asian
Natsuaki, Biehl & Xiaojia	12–23	
Simpkins et al.	(Early) 10–13 (Middle) 14–17	
von Soest & Wichstrøm	13–21	
Journal of Research on Adolescence (2016)		
Deutsch & Crockett	From 15	
Guan & Fuligni	12–18	
Monahan & Booth-LaForce	9–12	

Note: If not specified, the articles did not clearly identify whether the adolescent participants were from any specific country or ethnic background.

conventional agreement on adolescent age. They do not detail the qualitative measures for determining if participants are adolescent. The selected age boundaries for adolescence are startlingly diverse. Even if we concede that the authors might simply be describing their samples, and that their participants fall somewhere within the adolescent ambit, we still do not cater entirely for the differences. There is a substantial spread of opinion shown in the comparative onset age for adolescence in these publications. If adolescence is a commonly understood term, with an agreed-upon notion of general age range, then it wouldn't be possible for a ten year old (Atuyambe et al., 2009) and a fifteen year old (Park, Kim & Kim, 2009) to equally be considered at the onset of adolescence without reference to qualitative markers.

In 2009, five articles reported ten year olds as being at the lower boundary for adolescence (Atuyambe et al., 2009; Balsano, 2009; Petersen & Hyde, 2009; Simpkins et al., 2009; Sumter et al., 2009). By 2016, fewer articles were identifying an age band for adolescence. However, the research by Monahan and Booth-LaForce (2016) lowered the age boundary further, to nine years of age, for the earliest bound for adolescence. The upper age limit for adolescence by 2009 research reports was as high as 24 years (Kavas, 2009), with several research papers setting the upper age bound for their adolescent participants at over 20 (Goede et al., 2009; Holtmann et al., 2009; Kavas, 2009; Kloep et al., 2009; Song et al., 2009). By 2016, this upper age bound had extended further, with Alessandri et al. (2016) reporting adolescent participants up to the age of 25 years. However, it is clear that fewer papers cited age boundaries for adolescence in 2016 compared with those published in 2009.

Jeffrey Arnett is a prominent American researcher who has focused attention on the distinction between adolescence and adulthood. Arnett (2006a, 2006b, 2007) identified the stage of 'emerging adulthood' that was previously consumed within the broad category of adolescence. His work has had a significant influence and has heralded greater agreement on the features of, and considerations for, identifying boundaries for adolescence for other researchers. For example, his recent work with Elisabeth Fishel, *When will my grown-up kid grow up?*, identifies the contemporary shift towards an extended adolescence and a delay for emerging adulthood (Arnett & Fishel, 2013). This notion, that adolescence may be a descriptor for people in their middle to late twenties, is reflected in the journal research profile for 2016.

The prominent approach in the more recent research has been to identify age bounds for the research but to avoid specifically labelling the participants as being adolescent. Articles from 2016 in other leading contemporary journals in the field, such as the *International Journal of Adolescence and Youth*, the *Journal of Youth and Adolescence* and the *Journal of Early Adolescence*, have noticeably avoided the definitional age bound issue by carefully reporting research without specifically categorising or labelling participants as adolescent. The journal titles would suggest that all participants studied would be adolescent, but this is not clear in the manner the research is reported. In some ways this is reminiscent of research into adolescence before the 1980s.

Older articles and texts up to the early 1980s shy away from explicit age definition. For example, David Ausubel (1954), a luminary researcher in the field of educational psychology, described physical (pubertal) and some qualitative attributes for adolescence but did not delineate ages. Even by 1985, Kimmel and Weiner avoided clearly identifying chronological age boundaries and instead cited biological age (puberty) as the mark of onset and social age (assumption of adult roles and responsibilities) as the transition point to adulthood. This early sentiment that age bounds should not be prescriptively set for adolescence is exemplified by the work of Lefrancois (1976), who most strongly contested the use of age for the definition of adolescence. He argued that 'chronological age is a notoriously bad index of social, emotional and physical development during adolescence. Changes that occur during adolescence, while highly correlated with one another in terms of sequence and rate of appearance, are not nearly as highly correlated with chronological age' (p. 124). It is, however, debatable even that the sequence and rate of appearance of maturational attributes are reliable predictors for social and emotional development. Further, in socially and culturally diverse environments, surely the notion of a consistent homogeneous developmental progression must be stringently challenged. Even though the term adolescent is well worn, adolescence as a diverse concept has not yet been coherently character- ised in the literature.

Adolescence as a construct

In the quest for qualitative markers, authors historically, and up to the early 2000s, have written of adolescence as agony, immaturity or incompleteness (Shaffer, 2002). The media were alert to this and expended significant effort demonising young people and rationalising this position through reference to the rather deficit view of adolescence that often underpinned the contemporary schol- arly literature. Media accounts of adolescents productively contributing to their communities were sadly overlooked by more inflammatory stories of adolescents disturbing the peace or engaging in violent acts. The deficit view of adolescence characterised young people as lacking certain adult attributes; indeed, they were considered adolescent by virtue of what they were not. For example, adolescents have been described as not yet fully independent of their parents and family sanc- tions (Shaffer & Kipp, 2010), not cognitively complete (Giedd, 1999; Lenroot & Giedd, 2006), not having developed a range of mature interpersonal relationships (Arnett 2007; Graber, Brooks-Gunn & Petersen, 1996) and not having completed their personal construction of identity (Marcia, 1980; Moshman, 2005; Selman, 1980; Swanson, Beale Spencer & Petersen, 1998). In line with the deficit view of youth, the terms adolescence and adolescent have become common usage, accepted labels for people who, in one way or another, cannot be considered fully

Provocation 2.1 Vertical groupings in pastoral care

You have a pastoral care class of twenty-four Year 8 students (twelve- and thirteen-year-old girls and boys). This means that of the suite of teachers that work with the students for their subject area studies, you are the key teacher specifically nominated to provide them with personal support and assistance as they engage with their schooling across the year. As their pastoral care teacher you conduct activities with the students that are designed to help them mature, work well with peers and develop a strong sense of belonging and wellbeing. You meet with them twice a day, at the start and end of their day, for a short time slot (fifteen to twenty minutes), and you have a full period of instruction with them of about an hour once a week.

At a recent school staff meeting someone asked whether it might be possible to have vertical groupings for middle school pastoral care for the next school year. This would mean having Year 7, 8 and 9 students together in the same pastoral care group (eleven to fourteen year olds).

 Consider your knowledge of adolescent development, particularly the early adolescent years, associated with the middle years. Decide whether you are supportive or unsupportive of the idea for vertical care groupings. Provide responses to the following questions:

- What is the reasoning behind your decision?
- What theoretical perspectives have you drawn on to form your view?
- If vertical grouping is adopted, what might be the advantages and disadvantages?
- How might this alter the way you plan for and conduct your pastoral care sessions?

adult. In fact, these terms still colloquially serve as insults, to designate someone as behaving in an immature or juvenile fashion.

Although it lacks clarity, educationalists have welcomed the term adolescence and use it freely. The label has provided a framework for theoretical modelling that promises answers to the question of what might be best practice in schools. As a professional community we are caught between a need for clarity and a need for flow.

Provocation 2.2 Middle years students as 'unfinished'

There is a view that young people are fundamentally unfinished. The notion of adolescence is built upon the idea that these young people are somehow deficient and are yet to be fully formed biologically, socially and culturally.

 Provide responses with defensible arguments to the following questions:

- Do you agree with the stance outlined above?
- How does and how should the concept of adolescence impact on the design of developmentally appropriate schooling?

Historical research and theory of adolescent development

To appropriately construct a view of how young people mature that assists educators of middle years learners, we must examine the purposes behind the invention of the adolescent. Hall (1904, vol. 1) appropriated a fairly old word, first found in written form in 1440 (Harper, 2001), and fashioned a science of developmental psychology. He was responding to the unique social, political and cultural climate of his time, a period of industrial revolution. The influx of immigrant adult workers to industrialised states and the enactment of laws to protect children from exploitation in the workplace had created a new *in-between* life phase. At the same time, psychology was finding its feet as a science, and the classification of people's lives into relatively neat categories was a very attractive idea. The potential to explain behaviours by creating detailed compendiums of age-related developmental attributes was openly celebrated. But, as usual, the devil was in the detail. Hall's (1904, vol. 1) theory of recapitulation built on the earlier notion of Haeckel (1868) of embryological recapitulation in prenatal ontogeny, which meant that human development was described as a process that traced a path similar to that of species evolution (Steinberg & Lerner, 2004). While this idea did not hold up to close scrutiny, the classification system remained intact as a framework for developmental research.

The distinct phase of development described as adolescence historically, is not the same as contemporary conceptions. The in-between category label has been attached to those people in their late twenties who are not yet economically independent from their parents (Arnett, 2006a, 2006b, 2007; Carroll et al., 2009; Sirsch et al., 2009). These people are clearly not the same types of adolescents imagined when the term was first applied to describe in-betweeners. Arnett (2006a, 2015) proposes a model of emerging adulthood which describes a distinct stage between adolescence and young adulthood (Carroll et al., 2009) called 'emerging adulthood' (Arnett, 2015, p. 1). Arnett (2006a, 2015) identifies five distinguishing characteristics for emerging adulthood: identity exploration, experimentation and possibilities, negativity and instability, being self-focused and feeling in between. Emerging adulthood is then a category of development that has been carved from the previous frame for adolescence.

In the late twentieth century the marketing and business industries started to recognise the emergence of something that wasn't well described by the concept of the adolescent: kidults, or adultescents. These have been described as a generation of people who sustain their buying and general interest patterns from their pre-teens well into their thirties (Cameron, 2004; Hayward, 2013). In this way they can engage in society as adults without demonstrating some of the other important markers of adulthood. Kidults have not yet assumed full responsibility for themselves as adults. For example, a kidult may have some employment and a strong sense of adult identity but may still be dependent on their parents, living in their childhood home without setting up an independent household.

Additionally, the old determination of adolescence as aligned with parenting capacities is complicated by the findings that physical capability to parent is developing in younger people in some racial and cultural groups. Krieger et al. (2015) report that some girls, particularly with low socio-economic profiles, are experiencing menarche when they are as young as eight. This compares with an average twelve years of age in the final decades of the twentieth century. Yet, conscious pursuit of parenthood is being delayed by many into their thirties (Barclay & Myrskylä, 2015; Carroll et al., 2009). Early-maturing people are neither psychologically nor emotionally ready for the responsibility of raising a family (Côté, 2000), and social contexts that are driving people to later parenthood have widened the gulf between childhood and adulthood. The concept of adolescence is not very useful at all if it doesn't clearly distinguish between an eight year old and someone in their mid-twenties or even in their thirties.

The old concept of adolescence definitely needs updating, and Arnett's (2006a, 2015) view that there needs to be further clarity and distinction across these developing years is gaining greater popularity. The most recent work of Arnett (2015) focuses on the nature and bounds for emerging adulthood and attends to the markers and conditions underpinning the graduation from an adolescent state to adulthood. A key element in the changing nature of this stage of life has been the influences of contemporary society and living.

Our changing times have brought a dramatic shift in the nature of work and career. Working hard has been replaced by a working smart ethic, allowing people of all ages to make personal economic gains without infringement of the child labour laws that curtail certain types of employment for minors. A young, enterprising individual who makes a fortune on a venture hatched and pursued in front of a computer screen in their bedroom can be far more economically independent and 'adult' than a much older person working as an articled clerk with a law firm and still financially tied to their parents. For example, Nick D'Aloisio was seventeen years old when he sold to Yahoo for $30 million an application for a smartphone that he had created. Meanwhile, Cameron Johnson built a greeting card company from his parents' home that earned him $50,000 a year by the time he was twelve. By the age of fifteen, he was earning $400,000 a month. Both these youths built their financial independence well before they were ready to leave their parents' homes (C. Anderson, 2013). Neither Nick nor Cameron can be considered adult, but they don't quite fit the notion of financial dependency that accords with a contemporary Western notion of the adolescent. Both boys were in school at the same time as they were reaping the benefits of their entrepreneurial efforts, so to their teachers they would have presented uniquely, both as adult in some respects and as adolescent in others.

The problematising of emerging adulthood has become a new field for research attention (Arnett, 2015). The concept of emerging adulthood is not quite the same as that of adolescence, but it captures the notion of *becoming* that has been a characteristic of adolescence since the term was first coined by Hall (1904, vol. 1). The idea that a person should be not yet developed or functioning is rather Western. In many world cultures, the concept of adolescence means nothing and has never been useful (Letendre, 2000). People may transition from childhood to adulthood via some sort of rite of passage or ceremony, from then on being considered part of the adult community, with no time spent in between. McMahon (2007) provides a review of the experiences of boys from Sudan who arrived in Australia as refugees. These boys are described as 'lost' in the same way as the boys in the Peter Pan story were 'lost boys'. Had they remained in Sudan, in a strong community with clear demonstrations of adulthood from men, they would have engaged in initiation practices to mark their progression directly from childhood to adulthood. Many of the boys travelled to Australia with their mothers and had no opportunity for the initiation rite of passage. They therefore could not be considered adult in their own community. Those boys who had accessed an initiation process sometimes found schooling in Australia to be a problem, because they understood schooling culturally to be for children. As globalisation hastily brings diverse cultures together, the meaning of adolescence becomes increasingly murky.

Laurence Steinberg and Richard Lerner have been prominent researchers and writers regarding child development and adolescence. Their classic text on adolescence tracks a history of scientific interest in the field (Steinberg & Lerner, 2004). They discuss the forums of the Society for Research on Adolescence, arguably one of the premier scholarly communities for research in this field. Interestingly, these forums were always held exclusively in the United States. A quick search shows contributors to the society's journal are almost exclusively American. Other contemporary scholarly societies and journals for adolescence, such as the *Journal of Adolescent Research and Adolescence*, have American affiliations on their editorial boards and content that is notably American. This is true of most societies and publications on adolescence, except perhaps the *Journal of Adolescence*, produced by the Foundation for Professionals in Service for Adolescents, which has an international editorial board and an international authorship. Steinberg and Lerner also identified an American bias in the field.

However, with increasing Westernisation across the globe, this international research profile is changing rapidly. Researchers in Austria, China, Turkey, South Korea, Taiwan and Belgium have launched large-scale national empirical studies on determining aspects of the nature of adolescence (Berten & Van Rossem, 2009; Lee & Sun, 2009; Park, Kim & Kim, 2009; Shek, Tang & Lo, 2009; Sirsch et al., 2009). The resounding finding to this point is that adolescents in these studies have very similar profiles to those of the adolescents in the earlier American studies. Although it is clear that adolescence is a socially and culturally related notion, significant Australian research is still lagging, and it really is at a point that the precise relevance of these constructs of adolescence need to be more firmly established.

Eras of research and theory

Steinberg and Lerner (2004) argued that there are three stages of research into adolescence. The first two stages overlap, and we are presently in the third. The first phase (roughly from the 1900s to the 1970s) was characterised by grand theoretical models that drew on rather descriptive and anecdotal accounts of development. The second phase (from the 1970s to the early 2000s) focused on hypothesis testing and second-order applied research and developed views on the plasticity and diversity of development. The third phase, our current venture, is characterised by a central organisational frame of scientist, policy-maker, practitioner. Research in this phase 'reflects and extends the emphases on individual-context relations, developmental systems, plasticity, diversity, longitudinal methodology, and application' (p. 52). The discussion in this chapter fits neatly in the third phase. It is hoped that attempting to deconstruct the grand theories of development that have formed a foundation for the field of scholarship will have a direct and indirect impact on policy, practice and research interest, in just the way Steinberg and Lerner predicted.

Constructions of adolescence

The grand theorists of adolescence include Hall (1904), Inhelder and Piaget (1958), Erikson (1963), Freud (1968), McCandless (1970) and, most recently, Arnett (2006a, 2006b, 2007). Each has been lauded and criticised on their unique merits. Uniting their models, however, was a conception of adolescence as conforming to a linear progression in development, characterised by direct linkages and continuity, and relying upon the assumption of individual development as a passive process. Researchers in Steinberg and Lerner's (2004) second era, with a rising concern for context, plasticity and diversity, did not directly challenge these fundamental tenets of the grand theorists. There exists a linear conception of development that appears to bring together otherwise quite divergent conceptions of adolescence.

Although not all ascribe to the deficit perspective (Benson's [1997] developmental assets view; see the work of Lerner and Benson [2003]), life development as described by these authors suggests movement towards some kind of maturational goal, in roughly a lock-step sequence. Some of the key theoretical themes present adolescence as:

- a biological event (Giedd, 1999)
- a psychosocial event (Kohlberg, 1986; Piaget, 1955)
- a social construction (Bandura, 1977)
- a cultural construction (Keith, 1985; Mead, 1935).

A brief examination of each theme provides reference points for the construction of a new maturational model.

Adolescence as a biological event

Much early discussion and theory of adolescent behaviour have centred on the storm and stress theory (Hamburg, 1974). Hormonal changes, growth spurts and development of secondary sexual characteristics are well-known markers for the stage, and the presumptions are that such dramatic physical upheaval must inevitably impact on an individual's sense of self and that an individual necessarily reflects their biological programming. All manner of connections have been notionally tied between identity development, general behaviour, family and peer relationships and puberty in these theories. From the biological perspective, individuals are doomed to a fairly predictable sequence of events by virtue of their maturational clock.

The majority of the biologically based theories are steeped in a sense of intractable inevitability. They presume that educationalists must support, inform and cope with adolescence. Adolescents are seen homogeneously and passively, and their experiences as sequentially linked and predictable. It is not reasonable to make a wholesale contestation against these biological views of adolescence. Clearly, physical and neural changes have a role in the maturational process and do deserve some professional attention by educationalists. But physicality and bodily changes are only part of the picture of who we are at any given point in our lives. They are a frame for our behaviours and self-concepts and as such are important, but models for development that are limited to physical constitution have been hotly contested in the adolescent literature (S.H. White, 1968, 1994).

Adolescence as a psychosocial event

Key theorists of a view of adolescence as a psychosocial event include Piaget (1955), Kohlberg (1986) and Arnett (1998). The Piagetian approach considers that cognitive development is influenced by maturation of the nervous system, experience, intellect and socialisation. Piaget (1955) concurred with some of the biological theorists' ideas regarding the influence of physical maturational changes of the brain on behaviour during adolescence. However, the Piagetian approach did consider that the natural maturational processes of the brain would have an underlying impact on the other three elements that contributed to cognition change.

Piaget (1955) argued that a formal operations stage characterises adolescent cognition. That is, the adolescent (from twelve years of age to adulthood) act of knowing or perceiving is qualitatively different from that of the child (from seven to eleven years), who is described as being typically a preformal thinker or in the concrete operations stage. The individual who is capable of formal operational thought exhibits a capacity for abstract logic and more mature moral reasoning. This contrasts with the earlier concrete operational thought, which is described as limited to concrete events and concrete analogies. Concrete operations include thinking activities such as classification, hierarchy, class inclusion, relations of parts to a whole and of parts to parts, serialisation, symmetrical and reciprocal relationships, substitution and rules for operations. The thinking is still linked to empirical reality—that is, the actual rather than the potential, based on real experience. According to the theory, children of the concrete operational age have difficulties dealing with more than two classes, relations or dimensions at once, while adolescents in formal operations are able to make more elegant generalisations with more inclusive laws. They think formally, but only in familiar situations, are capable of abstract thought independent of concrete objects, can consider sets of symbols for symbols (e.g., metaphoric speech and algebra) and can appreciate that words can have double or triple meanings. This makes them able to understand hidden meanings—for example, political cartoons. Piaget proposed that the hallmarks of formal operations are:

- thinking about thought—developing metacognition
- going beyond the real—abstract thought
- combinatorial thinking—combining different elements to inform understanding
- logical reasoning—cause and effect
- hypothetical reasoning—reasoning while imagining.

Neo-Piagetian researchers have interpreted Piaget's earlier work and provided some guidelines for behaviour in adolescence (Shaffer, 2002). They have attempted to draw extended implications from the foundation hallmarks. For example, they suggest that in the journey from concrete operational thought to formal operations, adolescents should gain an ability to grasp what might be and therefore may appear as idealistic rebels. Further, their developing metacognitive skills might promote time spent thinking about thoughts and increase their daydreaming, which may become more positive or wishful. Their ability to look beyond the given material may give rise to pseudo-stupidity when trying to solve problems, due to a possible tendency to approach solutions at too complex a level. They should be able to appreciate symbols in literature rather than just the storyline. Most importantly, their formal reasoning capabilities should provide a foundation for the development of long-term values.

The Piagetian and neo-Piagetian views, while still tied to lock-step and sequential age–stage conceptions of development, did consider the individual in a quite different way from that of the biological theorists. Santrock (2003), in an overview of developmental theories, describes the individual as depicted by the Piagetian and neo-Piagetian views as a 'solitary little scientist'. Basically, the Piagetian and neo-Piagetian theorists argued from a strong maturational perspective but with maturation interacting with environmental experiences. They described the individual as cognitively active and constructivist. In schools, the legacy from the strong hold of these classic views of the child has been middle years pedagogy designed on the presumption that those in their early teens are not yet capable of abstract and complex thought. As a result, intellectual rigour in the early secondary school years floundered up to the early 2000s (Department of Education, 2001) before this was recognised as a serious deficiency in the framing of learning in middle schooling. More recently, and in the light of cutting-edge research findings on brain development in young people, middle schools have been embracing the notion that young learners benefit from educational programs that are rigorous and that promote complex higher order thinking and abstraction (Collins, 2014; Schwartz, 2015). Thus, critical-thinking development has been a new consideration in the field of adolescent research (Arnett, 2014).

Piagetian and neo-Piagetian cognitive theory had a number of weaknesses. First, the expectation that all adults would be capable of formal operational thought in all areas of thought and knowledge was not universally substantiated. That being the case, the enduring question was whether older people who are not yet formally operational could be considered adult. Another point of concern centred on the development of expertise. A model that describes adolescents as cognitively unfinished does not adequately account for the observation that junior chess masters as young as eight years of age can beat adults at chess (Chi & Ceci, 1987; Chi, Glaser & Rees, 1982). Contemporary theories of cognitive development, such as schema theory, which is a theory that proposes a generalisable framework around the development of expertise and higher order thinking, better explain phenomena. These theories owe their inception to some of the Piagetian ideas but have dismantled the potency and integrity of age–stage-based theories of cognitive development. Piaget also proposed a model for moral development that derived from the cognitive development theory. This theory, like the Piagetian cognitive development theory, typically underestimated the moral capacities of children and has lost contemporary support (Shaffer & Kipp, 2010).

Kohlberg (1986), another key theorist, considered cognitive development as well as moral development (Shaffer & Kipp, 2010). This type of consideration is still extant in the literature (Malti & Ongley, 2014; Moshman, 2005). Kohlberg's (1986) cognitive development work focused on gender identity development in young children and was criticised for underestimating the strength of early gender identity, but his moral development construct initially attracted a faithful following. In this model, Kohlberg believed that moral development fell into neat, invariant stages that were sequentially ordered. The development was closely aligned to cognitive growth, but cognitive growth alone did not ensure moral development. Kohlberg's six-stage model was soundly criticised for its cultural and gender bias. Like Piaget's,

Kohlberg's theory was also contested on the grounds that it demonstrably under-estimated the morality of children (Damon, 1988; Sigelman & Waitzman, 1991). However, researchers have found that moral understanding does not predict moral conduct (Kochanska & Murray, 2000), so Kohlberg's (1986) work appears both flawed and incomplete.

These two theorists, Piaget and Kohlberg, were not the only authors advocating that psychosocial development could profitably be considered in stages linked to chronological ages. However, the criticisms their models attracted are representative of the criticisms of other age–stage models. They almost inevitably underestimate or overestimate the capacities of people at particular ages. Any model that has attempted to describe a strict template for development has drawn criticism due to the demonstrably diverse range of experiences, behaviours and capacities of people at any given age. Theorists like Halpern (2000) and Ramirez (2003) have used the term psychobiosocial to describe theories that consider the joint influence of nature and nurture, but this work gives only very limited attention to the social processes that contribute to maturation.

The influence of research into brain development

Interest in the biological template for adolescence has also considered neural devel-opment. New mechanisms for mapping the activation of the brain using magnetic resonance imaging and other highly sophisticated techniques have provided researchers with an incredible amount of new information about the way brains develop and change. For example, Giedd (1999, 2012) and others report that a proliferation of neural connections characterises childhood brain development; marking the onset of adolescence, and typical of the whole stage, are a dramatic rationalisation and pruning of these connections (Keshavan et al., 2014; Lenroot & Giedd, 2006; Shaw et al., 2006). The process is complete when the individual arrives at adulthood with a much more streamlined and less numerous set of connections than they had as a child. Educationalists work to assist students to achieve the best possible outcomes in the belief that the things they do impact upon the way their brains develop. It is not absolutely clear how behaviour and experience might effect change and development in the brain's activation. Brain scientists have been able to establish that changes can be attributed to experience. They call this plasticity. However, there is no research that shows how to make deliberate changes of any specific types.

Early on, there were two camps, or views, among educationalists about how it might be possible to positively influence the brain development of young people by carefully designing educational experiences. Some aimed to slow the pruning, preached use-it-or-lose-it philosophies and designed their practices around ideas of broadened educational experiences (Fuller, 2003). Others, convinced that the streamlined outcome was desirable, aimed to focus students on only a small number of endeavours, hoping to force the pruning through strategic neglect of some nonessential understandings. Those that did not ascribe to either view were typically gripped with a fatalistic perspective and made little or no adjustment to their practices in the light of the research.

Perhaps the most prudent approach is to enhance rigour and complexity in the learning of concepts through deep engagement with authentic complex problems. This approach would have the effect of enabling the refinement of cognitive processes while supporting the broadening of perspectives, as authentic wicked problems are rarely unilateral. However, it seems premature to design new approaches to teaching and learning based on the neural research findings. Causal relationships between behaviours and neural pruning or the reciprocal have not yet been fully explored. Research into brain plasticity continues to show that lived experiences do have an impact on the structure and functioning of the brain (Kolb, 2013), but there has been no established direct link between anatomical development and neural activation and specific experience across adolescence.

Some of the changes that have been observed in brain activation may explain the characteristics we often see in young people (Dumontheil, 2016). Changes (neural proliferation followed by pruning) have been found in the following areas of the brain in development towards adulthood:

- The amygdala (near the base of the skull at the top of the brain stem) has functions associated with emotional responses. Imaging studies have shown that young people tend to preferentially use this part of their brain when asked to interpret emotions, rather than the frontal cortex, the reasoning part of the brain, used by adults. It has been postulated that this may explain why young people might have trouble managing their emotions (Jaworska & MacQueen, 2015).
- The cerebellum (at the back lower section of the brain) is thought to be associated with coordination and movement—not only physical movement but also coordination of thought processes (i.e., moving information from the short-term memory to the long-term memory, and accessing and retrieving stored information). Dynamic growth and change in this area might explain some observations of young people appearing uncoordinated and unfocused (Sussman et al., 2016).

- The corpus callosum (a bundle of nerves connecting the brain hemispheres) has been implicated in connecting creative thought with reasoned problem-solving. It grows, thickens and changes before adulthood, suggesting that we might expect fluctuations in the efficacy of creative solutions offered to solve problems (Hummer et al., 2015).
- The frontal cortex (the front and outer surface section of the brain, roughly in the area directly behind the forehead) is the area of the brain that has been identified for planning and strategic thought. Changes in this area may explain deficits in reasoning and decision-making, and in the raised incidence of risk-taking (Ahmed, Bittencourt-Hewitt & Sebastian, 2015).

All of these areas undergo dramatic change during the middle years. It could be presumed that the middle school student, when compared to an adult, is likely to display more emotionality, weaker reasoning and planning, a lack of coordination in thought processes and less capacity to link rationalisations to creative problem-solving.

Provocation 2.3 Brain development and learning

The young brain exhibits dramatic proliferation of neuronal connections followed by honing and pruning of the connections through to the mid-twenties. It is not clear how educational experiences might be designed to impact upon the brain and its activation patterns. However, research into the plasticity of the brain has shown that experience does have an influence on subsequent unspecified brain functioning.

 How does and how should this information inform approaches to learning and teaching in the middle years?

Adolescence as a social construction

In contrast to the biologically based and psychosocial or psychobiosocial theories of adolescent development, the social constructionists asserted that development was more about social experience than age-linked hardwiring. An early, much contested view was Watson's (1913, 1925) doctrine of environmental determinism. Watson believed that people were passive reflections of their grooming by others. This notion was not popular, as it did not go far enough to describe and predict behaviour. Bandura's (1977) work, starting in the 1970s, proposed and developed a cognitive social learning theory characterised by reciprocal determinism. Bandura proposed that development depended on observational learning. He described people as active and reactive and said that cognitive development reflected a continuous reciprocal interaction between people and the environment. That is, people actively shaped their environment, which in turn reflected on them. The key criticism of the theory was its oversimplification of the cognitive developmental process. No account was taken of genetically endowed individual differences or the possible biological maturation impacts on development. The social construction views were almost the antithesis of the age–stage theories; in most cases, they mirrored the perpetual nature–nurture controversy and were soundly criticised for not attending to the very things that were hallmarks of the more nature-influenced theories.

A popular contemporary theory of development is the Vygotskian socio-cultural model. Vygotsky (1962) considered the cultural and social contextual influences for cognitive growth. He stressed that children's development was led and mediated by social dialogues with others. He proposed a process whereby social speech provided impetus for private speech, which was a key cognitive tool underpinning an individual's development. The theory described the value of skilled people leading and guiding learners based on an understanding of an individual's zone of proximal development. This process was called scaffolding. Working in the zone of proximal development was described as activity that was just beyond an individual's capacity to act independently. The skilled instructor would adapt their dialogue as the learner became more capable, and the zone extended as a result. This adaptive dialogue allowed the co-construction of knowledge.

Vygotsky's (1962) theory had a favourable reception and, as his works have been progressively translated from the Russian, has attracted close scrutiny (Shaffer & Kipp, 2010). Rogoff (1998) warned that the strength of Vygotsky's work lies in an assumed primacy of verbal interaction for cognitive development and that this may not be equally relevant for all cultures. While Vygotsky (1962) found a vital middle ground between the nature–nurture extremes, his important framework for development does not yet provide specific insight into the behaviour of the middle years learner.

Adolescence as a cultural construction

Alongside consideration of the other theoretical themes has been that of adolescence as a cultural construction. Margaret Mead's (1935) classic research in Samoa and Papua New Guinea demonstrated that culture makes an indelible impression on a person's development and may indeed be a potent element for understanding maturation. Mead's cultural analysis informed the development of biosocial theories of maturation like that of Money and Ehrhardt (1972), although theorists in this area have not provided comprehensive explanations of how the various elements impacting on development in a cultural context might interact. Mead's (1935) demonstration that some cultures do not have a discernible concept or place for adolescence between childhood and adulthood highlights the importance of ethnographic analysis when considering the nature of early adolescence and middle years of schooling in Australia.

Persistent issues

Persistent issues emerge in criticism of the key developmental theories. The most predominant are based on the nature–nurture debate, as already discussed. Other seemingly irreconcilable differences of opinion include debates on whether development should be considered as linear and sequential or diffuse, as linked to experience conforming to a principle of continuity or discontinuity, or as based on an assumption of the learner as active or passive. If development is non-linear (e.g., as according to Vygotskian theory), it is possible to imagine connections being drawn directly from one life point to another for an individual in an unpredictable way. For example, a person might have particular experiences in childhood that predispose them to certain behaviours and understandings much later in life. A one-to-one, one-to-many and many-to-many connection web may describe how experiential understandings may influence development at other life points. A non-linear model is attractive but doesn't enable consideration of the influence of those things we know to be linear (e.g., physical aging). On the other hand, the linear model, which proposes that one developmental stage necessarily leads to the next, doesn't readily account for individual, social and cultural differences. The continuity versus discontinuity developmental debate is similar to the linear versus non-linear debate. In a discontinuous model, the influence of any given experience may not take effect until much later. The effect of an experience may rest as a sleeper for some time. Indeed, some people experience a sense of epiphany when something they experienced long ago suddenly makes sense. The discontinuous model differs from the diffuse model in that it retains a one-to-one influence pattern, while the continuous model depicts development as occurring in a predictable and intractable sequence, and the debate over the learner being active versus passive centres on whether individuals have or do not have agency in their own development. Each of these debates has merit and utility for understanding some aspects of human development. They are irreconcilable, however, and perhaps it is futile to try to resolve the differences. Any new model for development should attempt to transcend the dichotomies.

One central consideration when attempting to review the veracity of any theory to describe the development of people is the fundamental impact of their inherent diversities. Any model for development can really describe only the typical sequences and alignments that seem to occur. For almost every typical sequence or alignment of maturational processes there is a non-typical demonstration. Adolescence and youth development extends from the diversity of people's own makeup (biological circumstances), through the interaction of this with their social and lived contexts (social circumstances) as they respond to the emergent live events and emotional contexts (emotional circumstances) that face them in various ways. Learners are all different, and models to describe and simplify our understanding of development are useful only in that they provide a basic map—they do not provide a prescription. Gifted and talented students may be emotionally immature, while learners with difficulty comprehending abstract concepts may be emotionally mature. Teachers are central and must tailor their approaches to ensure learning is framed most appropriately for learners.

A model for maturation and development

A model for development needs to allow for the diversity of individuality as well as the conformity of social and cultural immersion. It should draw on the most productive elements of the classic theories and depict growth as both linear and non-linear, continuous and discontinuous, with influences of both nature and nurture. The developing individual should have both agency and passivity. That is, the model should embrace the dichotomies and present development holistically. Figure 2.1 crudely presents a model for development that might accomplish this. The individual is conceived as invited into a given context that is both culturally and socially framed. They bring to any life point a set of assets that are physical, emotional and cognitive. These assets reflect their wants and developmental needs, which may be both individually unique and characteristic and typical of those experienced by others at a similar life point. The developmental needs are viewed through the characteristic wants. This is a Dynamic Life Path Model that is constantly in flux. The focus is primarily on the learner, their assets and their developmental tasks.

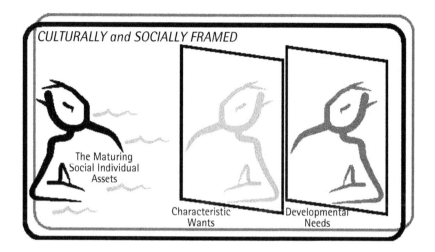

Figure 2.1 The Dynamic Life Path Model

The individual changes and matures according to this Dynamic Life Path Model, as illustrated in Figure 2.2. Depicted here is a person who might be typical of a middle years learner, according to the middle years literature, a person with a set of personal characteristics or assets including global awareness and self-orientation, as well as the unique attributes that mark them as an individual. A personal characteristic or asset can be thought of as a capability or perspective that supports a person to understand the world and engage with it. The wants and needs depicted are commonly identified in the middle years literature and are not exhaustive, for in addition to typical wants and needs the individual will have unique conceptions of their own wants and needs. These will reflect their own conception of themselves and their assets. Engagement with others, with problems and with the environment, either scaffolded or naturally occurring, will alter their assets, and from there the cycle continues.

Key aspects of the Dynamic Life Path Model are:

- the superimposition of cultural and social contexts and the dual frame for cultural and social contexts
- the depiction of an individual as a maturing person who at any given life point is complete
- an asset-based rather than a deficit-based perspective, with assets reflected in other dimensions

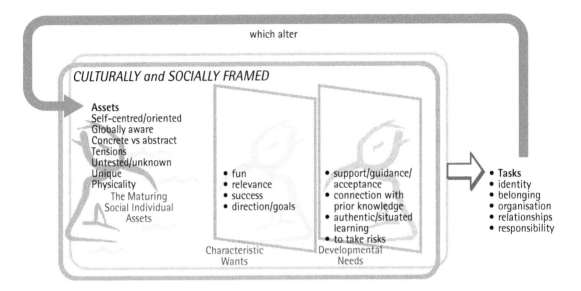

Figure 2.2 Impetus for change in the Dynamic Life Path Model

- the representation of a maturing individual adapting in response to achievement of developmental tasks
- an allowance for learning and unlearning in maturation.

The adolescent in this model exists only in social and cultural circumstances that allow them to exist or actually create a space for them. The stable and accepted elements of the classic biological, psychosocial, cultural and social constructionist developmental theories can be accommodated as descriptions of the driving forces behind the impetus for change.

The middle years learner

This life path model potentially liberates a new understanding of the middle years learner. We can embrace the anecdotal and consistent descriptions of our students from the coalface which present the shared attributes of middle years learners in our broadly similar Australian contexts. We can embrace the data available on physical maturation as giving potential insight into our middle years classrooms. We can tailor our developmental experiences for students based on our understanding of them as individuals. We can enjoy the middle years for the assets the individuals bring to us rather than entertain a deficit view of our students. We can extend and challenge our students. In short, we are empowered to take action collectively as middle years educators, individually and in teams. However, we are constantly charged with the responsibility to evaluate our own contexts for the effectiveness of our interactions with students and also for the local social and cultural frames for adolescence.

Implications for the middle years educator

There are practical implications for teachers, schools, policy-makers and funding bodies. First, the value of local action research must be emphasised. Action research is a quite common approach to researching in the field of education. It typically involves participant researchers—that is, teachers as researchers. An action research approach involves identifying a problem within a specific context, collecting baseline data, devising and implementing an intervention aimed at improvement of the problem condition and then cyclically reflecting on the impact of the intervention by progressively evaluating performance and adjusting and readjusting researcher action. Resources and funding need to flow to classrooms to support the reflective, reflexive and evaluative work of teachers as they try to discern the most appropriate developmental tasks for their students. Teachers need to network with each other to share their learning from action research cycles. These networks should provide a critical resource and professional development base to assist teachers to build their shared understanding of the impacts of their actions on the development of middle school students.

Provocation 2.4 Young adolescent development and learning

The three key areas of development in young adolescents are brain development, physical development and social and emotional development.

 Drawing from this chapter and other sources, reflect on the three key areas of young adolescents' development. What are the implications for teaching and learning?

 List four or five aspects of each of the three key areas of development, and for each aspect consider its impact on curriculum design, on pedagogical and behaviour management and on assessment (formative and summative).

Chapter summary

This chapter makes the following key points:

- The term 'adolescence' has been used in various different ways historically to describe the developmental characteristics and learning needs of young people.
- Research into the adolescent brain has given new insights to key dimensions for and on biological, social and cultural development.
- Maturation should be considered holistically with attention to the intertwining of behavioural, physical, social and cultural elements.

Chapter Three

Student wellbeing and engagement

KATHERINE MAIN and DONNA PENDERGAST

Learning intentions

In this chapter we will:

- develop an appreciation for the distinct needs of the middle years learner in relation to wellbeing
- consider the importance of social and emotional competence as an academic enabler
- examine the roles of resilience and self-efficacy as essential character traits
- explore the notion of student engagement and what it means for middle years learners.

Wellbeing needs of middle years students

Internationally, early adolescence is increasingly recognised as a crucial stage with significant consequences for ongoing educational success and future participation in society. The latest research around the young adolescent has led to a heightened focus by teachers, policy-makers and researchers on this age group recognising that this stage is also a time when young people form their values and dispositions that will direct their attitudes and behaviours into adulthood. This focus has moved beyond developmentalism to view the subject through socio-cultural, postmodern, post-structural and critical pedagogy lenses. It acknowledges and considers broader societal influences together with the physiological, cognitive, social and emotional changes that affect middle years learners and their holistic development (see Chapter 2). It is now recognised that aspects such as health, social and emotional wellbeing, physical development, resilience, efficacy, friendships, families and parents, and the community (local and global) need to be considered when planning curricula for, and teaching, young adolescents. What has become evident is the need for educators working in the middle years to understand the wide-ranging dimensions of wellbeing for middle years learners in order to engage them in learning and optimise their potential. In this chapter we will explore the importance of student wellbeing and, in particular, a number of social and emotional competencies and how these competencies support student engagement.

According to the Department of Education, Employment and Workplace Relations, student wellbeing can be defined as 'a sustainable state characterised by predominantly positive feelings and attitude, positive relationships at school, resilience, self-optimisation and a high level of satisfaction with learning experiences' (Noble et al., 2008a). The Australian government report *Young Australians: their health and wellbeing* claims that many young Australians are faring well in regard to the national indicators (Australian Institute of Health and Welfare, 2011a). However, despite positive signs overall, there are some issues that schools should be aware of in terms of their impacts on young people's wellbeing and health, such as student motivation and engagement; academic achievement; student attendance; relationships with peers, teachers and parents; and nutrition and health. Understanding the needs of students as they enter the middle years and addressing ways in which to meet these needs will help to ensure positive outcomes in each of these areas.

A scoping study into approaches to student wellbeing found strong links between student wellbeing and student learning outcomes (Noble et al., 2008a). Seven pathways to student wellbeing were identified in the literature, each of which has implications for the approaches adopted for supporting adolescents during the middle years of learning. The term Wellbeing Pathways was used to describe the empirically based guidelines that schools can follow to improve student wellbeing (Noble et al., 2008b). Table 3.1 outlines the seven Wellbeing Pathways and the associated attributes and school-based practices.

Table 3.1 The seven Wellbeing Pathways and the associated attributes and school-based practices

Pathways	Attributes	Practices
1. A supportive, caring and inclusive school community	A community that fosters school connectedness, positive teacher–student relationships, positive peer relationships and parental involvement	Adoption of school- and classroom-based strategies for developing school and classroom connectedness and sense of belonging; positive teacher–student relationships, positive peer relationships and positive school–family and school–community relationships
2. Prosocial values	Values such as respect, honesty, compassion, acceptance of difference, fairness and responsibility	Teachers (and other school staff) teaching, modelling and acting consistently with prosocial values that promote harmony—e.g., respect, honesty, compassion (caring), acceptance of differences, fairness and responsibility Provision of opportunities to put these values into practice
3. Physical and emotional safety	Safe and responsible learning environments	Development and application of Safe Schools policies and procedures to promote safe and responsible behaviour; respect, cooperation and inclusion and to prevent and manage putdowns, harassment, bullying, cyberharm and violence
4. Social and emotional learning	Coping skills, self-awareness, emotional regulation skills, empathy, goal achievement skills and relationship skills	Explicit teaching of the skills for coping and acting resiliently, optimistic thinking, self-awareness, emotional regulation, empathic responding, goal achievement, successful relationships and decision-making
5. A strengths-based approach	Valuing, catering for and extending diverse student strengths as well as collective strengths of students, teachers and parents	Adoption of a strengths-based approach to organisation, curriculum and planning which involves catering for and extending a diverse range of student intellectual and character strengths at different levels and valuing, developing and utilising (in a meaningful way) both the individual and the collective strengths of students, teachers and parents
6. A sense of meaning and purpose	Through one or more of spirituality, community service, participation in school clubs and teams, peer support, and collaborative and authentic group projects	Offering students many opportunities to participate in the school and community and to develop a sense of meaning or purpose, which may include worthwhile group tasks, community service or service learning, civic participation, contribution to the school community, school leadership, involvement in peer support, and activities that focus on an exploration of spirituality
7. A healthy lifestyle	Good nutrition, exercise and avoidance of illegal drugs and alcohol	School-based approaches that teach students the knowledge and skills needed for a healthy and self-respecting lifestyle and provide encouragement and support to apply them to their own life, including a focus on good nutrition, fitness and exercise and avoidance of illegal drugs, alcohol and other self-harming actions and situations

Source: Adapted from Noble et al. (2008a, pp. 33–43).

The list below gives seven approaches for supporting the Wellbeing Pathways and suggests questions that may be discussed when considering the implementation of the pathways in schools.

1. Implement whole-school programs—e.g., peer support and mentoring programs.
    *   Are there peer support or mentoring opportunities available to junior secondary students?
2. Provide ready access to a home room teacher, giving one teacher responsibility for mentoring and pastoral care for a subset of students within the broader group.
    *   Does the school have home groups?
    *   Do these groups meet regularly? Do the meetings provide opportunities for issues to be discussed or are they mainly for administrative purposes—e.g., marking the roll or reading out a school bulletin?
    *   How are home group teachers chosen? Are teachers with good pastoral care skills assigned to home group classes? Are subject teachers assigned to home groups regardless of their interpersonal skills or interest in helping adolescents? Is this a timetabling-related decision?
    *   What duties do home group teachers have? To what extent are they able to contribute to student wellbeing?
3. Develop and enhance competencies in effective social and emotional skills, which are academic enablers, through explicit teaching, modelling and practising.
    *   How are pro-social skills (e.g., respect, honesty, tolerance and compassion) encouraged in the junior secondary school?
    *   What curriculum, teaching approaches, policies or programs encourage this?
    *   Are social and emotional learning skills (e.g., coping skills, self-awareness, emotional regulation skills, empathy, goal achievement skills and interpersonal relationship skills) explicitly taught, modelled and practised?
4. Establish a supportive, caring and inclusive school community that fosters school connectedness, and establish an environment that is physically safe.
    *   Does the school have a clear anti-bullying policy?
5. Start from a strengths-based approach, which identifies and builds on students' intellectual strengths.
    *   Are there any vertical groupings which allow junior secondary school students to benefit from interaction with older or younger students?

6. Provide a sense of meaning and purpose through peer support, participation in school clubs and teams, and collaborative group projects.
   • Are there opportunities for students to take part in collaborative projects?
   • Do projects have real-life purpose?
7. Encourage a healthy lifestyle, including good nutrition and exercise.
   • How are students encouraged to adopt a healthy lifestyle? Is this incorporated into the curriculum?

Provocation 3.1 Supporting student wellbeing

Having reviewed the seven approaches for student Wellbeing Pathways, including the clarifying questions above, we now explore a situation you have experienced.

 Consider the following questions in relation to a school that you have attended, where you have undertaken professional placement as a preservice teacher or where you are currently teaching:

   • What are the issues affecting Years 7–10?
   • How are you addressing these issues?
   • What is working well?
   • What needs improvement?

 Work within a pair or small group and answer the questions in the list of seven approaches for supporting the Wellbeing Pathways, giving examples and descriptions where relevant.

Social and emotional skills

A critical component of student wellbeing in the middle years is the distinct social and emotional needs that require attention. There is a common misconception that social and emotional skills are naturally acquired as individuals interact with others in their everyday experiences. However, some students' everyday experiences with parents, families, teachers and peers may not provide the range of opportunities necessary or may not be regulated in a way that supports the development of such skills (Main & Whatman, 2016). Social skills are competencies and not character traits, meaning they can be taught and developed through explicit teaching and by providing opportunities for practice and reflection (Merrell & Gimpel, 2014; Noble et al., 2008a). The importance of a focused effort to teach and enhance students' social and emotional skills during the middle years cannot be understated, as these skills are 'more malleable between early childhood and adolescence' (Organisation for Economic Co-operation and Development [OECD], 2015b, p. 16); a window of opportunity opens at a time when the need to develop a more sophisticated skill set is necessary due to a range of developmental changes.

As a developmental period, early adolescence is a time of significant changes in a young person's emotional, cognitive and psychosocial levels (Steinberg, 2005). Social skills are critical during this time, as social allegiances begin to shift from being family centred towards a more peer group focus. This shift in allegiances requires young people to learn how to develop and sustain more complex relationships with peers and teachers within a school setting. To develop positive relationships involves middle years learners being able to effectively use social and emotional skills such as understanding, reflection, self-control, problem-solving and cooperation, and to know how to act appropriately in a range of social situations—for example, one on one, in small groups and in large groups. When students have not developed effective social and emotional competencies, studies have shown that poor outcomes can result in several domains (Durlak et al., 2011).

An increasing amount of research is highlighting the positive results that social and emotional learning has for students on their attitudes, sense of belonging, academic outcomes and reduced antisocial behaviour, including bullying and violence (Durlak et al., 2011; Sklad et al., 2012). In particular, the effective use of social skills, which means specific behaviours in context and therefore social competence, is an academic enabler (Upadyaya & Salmela-Aro, 2013). The inverse is also true: a lack of social and emotional skills—for example, anxiety and stress—can be a barrier to learning. Developments in neuroscience have shown that the emotional centres of the brain are intrinsically linked to areas of the brain involved in cognitive learning. Thus, when a child is experiencing a distressing emotion, the cognitive areas of the brain involved in learning are temporarily impeded (Zins et al., 2004). This can result in students underperforming in their day-to-day class activities and can create a negative attitude towards school and learning.

As mentioned above, social and emotional skills are competencies rather than character traits: they can be developed and enhanced through explicit teaching. Social and emotional learning programs should be designed and embedded within existing school curricula. All students can benefit from the inclusion of social and emotional learning, as these skills integrate the cognitive, affective and behavioural aspects of learning (Weare & Gray, 2003). Many of the competencies, such as resilience, a sense of self-worth, decision-making, self-control and relationship building, can be proactively embedded within daily classroom learning experiences. Importantly, research has shown that when students participated in social and emotional learning programs, not only were more prosocial attitudes demonstrated but an 11-percentile-point improvement in academic performance was achieved (Durlak et al., 2011).

There is still debate over the best way to teach social skills, with advocates for both an experiential approach, in which students are involved in more active methods of learning, such as role play and hands-on activities (Schulz, Kushnir & Gopnik, 2007), and a directive approach, in which students are directly taught the necessary skills (Kinder & Carine, 2001). However, in a review of social and emotional programs, Durlak et al. (2010) found that social and emotional initiatives that showed positive outcomes followed a four-step approach to implementation by using the acronym SAFE. The four steps are:

1. using a *sequenced*, step-by-step approach to skills development
2. using *active* learning that provides students with opportunities to practise the skills in real-life or life-like situations
3. ensuring there is a *focus* on social and emotional learning
4. *explicitly* targeting specific social and emotional skills (Payton et al., 2008).

Resilience

Over the last two decades, research has made a marked shift from a focus on risk to a focus on the positive—that is, resilience—noting it to be a key social and emotional skill (L. Rutter, 2012). This shift has marked the emergence of positive psychology and, as well as resilience, includes research around happiness (Layard, 2007) and the growth mindset (Yeager & Dweck, 2012). Research suggests that people who are emotionally resilient, courageous and optimistic are more likely to succeed now and in the future and that resilience can best be promoted by focusing on competence (Masten, 2003). In the face of difficulties or hardship, resilient people are able to adapt (Cefai, 2004; Fuller, 1998, 2002; Schoon, 2006).

In an analysis of the literature, resilience has been defined as 'referring to positive adaptation, or the ability to maintain or regain mental health, despite experiencing adversity' (Herrman et al., 2011, p. 258). Resilience occurs when an individual encounters stressful situations and is able to successfully adapt (L. Rutter, 2012). In

Provocation 3.2 Social and emotional development

Samuel is a twelve-year-old boy in Year 7. It is the beginning of the year, and he is new to the school. His primary school records show that he had difficulty getting along with peers and was prone to demonstrating aggressive behaviour.

You have noticed that in class Samuel tends to work on his own but quickly loses interest in the activity and tries to attract the attention of other students by making faces and trying to get others to talk to him. On one occasion, when nearby students did not respond, Samuel resorted to poking Jason with a pencil. Jason loudly yelled, 'Stop it!', which resulted in a warning from you and moving Samuel further away from others.

During lunch break when you were on duty, you observed Samuel's interactions with other students and noticed that nearly all of the interactions that he had with the other boys were negative: shouting, pushing, snatching personal items and running away so that others would chase him, and so on. The other boys rallied together to exclude Samuel from their games.

When you returned to class, you started all of the students on an activity and called Samuel to the side of the room where you could chat with him. When you asked him how he got on with other students, he became defensive and sullen and responded loudly, 'They all hate me!'

You realise that if you allow Samuel to continue along this line of behaviour, it will escalate, and the potential outcome will not be good; if the aggressive nature of his interactions with others continues, over time he will be on a sure pathway to being excluded from school.

 Provide responses with defensible arguments to the following questions:

- What do you think Samuel is trying to achieve?
- What approach do you take as a teacher?
- How can you help Samuel to interact with others more effectively?

this sense, resilience cannot be discussed in the absence of adversity. Indeed, research suggests that exposure to moderate risks is beneficial in developing both the skills and the confidence to cope (Garmezy, Masten & Tellegen, 1984; Masten, 1999; M. Rutter, 1985). However, the exposure to the moderate risk must be authentic enough to provoke a genuine response.

It is now well accepted that resilience is not so much a personality characteristic as a competence, something that can be taught and enhanced (Luthar & Zelazo, 2003; L. Rutter, 2012; Ungar, Ghazinour & Richter, 2013; Windle, 2011). Resilience is a dynamic process that is reliant on the ongoing interactions between the individual and their environment to support positive adaptations when faced with adversity (L. Rutter, 2012; Ungar, Ghazinour & Richter, 2013; Windle, 2011). There are strong commonalities between the attributes that enhance resilience and the behaviours and attitudes of lifelong learners, which would suggest that the middle years of schooling present a time of unique opportunity for teachers and schools to develop these capacities in their students (Main & Whatman, 2016). Deliberate educational action targeting the competencies that promote resilience is possible, and arguably ethically demanded, in the middle years of schooling.

The developmental journey of middle years learners (as outlined in Chapter 2) includes aspects such as the search for identity alongside seeking to understand themselves as having independent and multiple identities, and the development of formal operational thought and a personal understanding of more adult relationships. As adolescence is a time of transition occurring alongside cognitive, emotional, physical and social development, it is important that individuals have the skills to face these new life situations with a sense of optimism and confidence. While most young people do move from adolescence to adulthood without major problems (Offer & Schonert-Reichl, 1992), around 14 per cent of Australian adolescents develop mental health issues (Australian Institute of Health and Welfare, 2011a). Therefore, it is important that middle years learners be given multiple opportunities to develop the self-reliance and personal resources needed to effectively approach life challenges and to build and reinforce their own capacity for resilient behaviours.

Resilient attributes, attitudes and behaviours will assist middle years learners as they navigate a complicated social world. Middle years learners face complex issues within their social development that include establishing friendships with peers, gaining more independence from parents and making decisions about school subjects and career pathways. Growing uncertainty about the future, the ready availability of alcohol and drugs, powerful media messages, divorce, socioeconomic adversity and violence in relationships all serve to increase adolescents' vulnerability and exacerbate the healthy achievement of these life tasks (Ungar, Ghazinour & Richter, 2013). But resilience reaches beyond the immediate world of the middle schooler. A person who has a well-constructed set of life skills and attitudes emanating from quality middle schooling is more likely to cope in the face of negative personal events throughout their whole life. In this way, middle schooling is inextricably connected to each life point of the individual.

It is widely recognised that socio-economically disadvantaged students will experience high levels of risk. Students who experience social disadvantage early in life often face lifelong consequences—even the most resilient individuals. Most critically, these risk factors and issues are at their greatest intensity during the middle years, when long-term 'decisions about future educational and occupational careers are made' (Schoon, 2006, p. 70). In light of this, it can be argued that it is imperative that schools meet their social and ethical responsibilities to this specific cohort of students and ensure that there are appropriate opportunities for building competencies of resilience in their programs. It is impossible to predict which individuals will experience adversity throughout their life, and so middle years educators should look to build and enhance all students' self-efficacy and capacity to be resilient and not just those identified as being at risk.

Self-efficacy

Self-efficacy is the belief held by the individual about the probability of their being successful in certain situations (Bandura, 1977, 2001). An individual's sense of self-efficacy is highly influential on the way they view new situations and life challenges. A person with high self-efficacy will be more likely to attempt new activities, feel confident in their abilities and their chances of achievement, strategise their approach and have increased levels of persistence (Bandura, 1977, 2001). Individuals who have high self-efficacy tend to attribute their misfortunes or failures to external causes rather than internal factors (similarly to optimistic individuals).

Attribution theory, which is the process of attributing success or failure to ability, effort, luck or task difficulties, can either encourage or discourage students (Covington & Omelich, 1992). Students who attribute their potential success to their ability and effort, and consider that they have the ability and if they work hard are likely to succeed, are motivated to continue trying. Students who attribute their potential success to luck or task difficulty can be unmotivated to continue trying if they feel the task is too difficult or they need an element of luck to be successful. Students who have developed a strong sense of self-efficacy and have more resilient behaviours tend to have a positive view when attributing success or failure in their work. That is, if they find a task challenging, they will be more persistent, attempt to problem-solve and seek help. Success is generally attributed to effort and ability, and failure is attributed to the need for greater effort rather than a lack of ability.

An important contingency identified by Dweck (2006) is the belief that abilities are developed and not innate. Learners who believe that abilities are innate or inherited are more likely to interpret setbacks and failure as evidence of a natural or unchangeable lack of ability (negative attribution). Dweck argues that learners need to cultivate a growth mindset for learning, whereby they learn to believe that their ability is a reflection of strategies and effort, rather than inherited or innate, and therefore become more resilient and more adaptive in their learning.

Dweck's (2006) mindset theory suggests that how students think about their own intelligence has a significant effect on their attitudes towards their work. She posits that people can have one of two mindsets (or personal theories of intelligence): either a fixed or a growth mindset. Those students with a fixed mindset believe that their intelligence is static and cannot change. When a student has a fixed mindset, their overarching goal is to appear good. That is, they want to be seen to be able to do their work successfully as well as being seen in a positive light by their peers. As a result, students with a fixed mindset avoid work they feel is too hard (in an attempt to avoid failure), do not align success with effort, tend to be grade or mark oriented (seeking an extrinsic goal or reward) and do not display the characteristics of a lifelong learner.

A growth mindset (or an incremental theory of intelligence) is held by students who believe that intelligence can change and grow with effort (Dweck, 2006). Students with a growth mindset put in effort and work towards achieving learning goals and are focused on understanding and concept mastery. As such, students with a growth mindset see challenging work as the exercise they need for their brain to get smarter and failure as a way of learning. There is a growing body of research that has clearly shown how different mindsets can positively or negatively affect academic performance across the middle grades (Blackwell, Trzesniewski & Dweck, 2007; Romero et al., 2014).

The research around mindsets has also shown that mindsets can be changed. That is, with continual feedback, guidance and encouragement, students with a fixed mindset can develop a growth mindset towards their work (Blackwell, Trzesniewski & Dweck, 2007). This highlights the important role of the teacher in helping students develop and sustain a growth mindset. Teaching students explicitly that effort is critical to improved outcomes requires modelling and opportunities for practice. When students see gains in their academic outcomes through their own efforts, they in turn become more motivated to work hard.

Engaging the middle years student

The middle years have been identified as a period when students' motivation and engagement decline, and this can be manifested in a range of ways, including indifference and disinterest in classroom tasks, disruptive behaviour and non-attendance and eventual school drop-out (Carrington, 2006). The higher incidence of alienation and disengagement from schooling in this age group has been the impetus behind the research around the middle years in Australia. Further, student disengagement has also resulted in a noticeable decrease in student achievement, with middle years students reportedly making the least amount of progress in their learning and with the gap between low and high achievers widening (Hascher & Hagenauer, 2010). A number of significant reports have also noted a decline in quality teaching practices in this age group, bringing quality teaching into focus as a means of addressing the declines in student engagement and resulting academic declines (Hayes et al., 2006; Luke et al., 2003; Pendergast et al., 2005).

The causes of alienation are multifaceted and complex. However, in a summary of research on student alienation, Hascher and Hagenauer (2010) found that the literature consistently reported several predictors of student alienation that need to be considered to improve student motivation and engagement, including:

- Individual characteristics—Gender, socio-economic status, ethnicity, socio-cultural context and geolocation are each individual characteristics that influence student alienation (White, Wyn & White, 2013).
- Decline in student academic motivation—Students who experience a decline in their motivation towards academic work are more likely alienated during adolescence (Jacobs et al., 2002).
- Students' self-efficacy as learners—Students with a low sense of efficacy as learners are more likely to struggle with the demands of school and give up. E. Skinner et al. (2008) found that competence was a strong contributor to behavioural engagement and motivation to learn. It should be noted that these negative effects build up over time (Walker & Greene, 2009).
- Student–teacher relationships—Supportive relationships that involve positive interactions with students are important for students to feel challenged and motivated (Legault, Green-Demers & Pelletier, 2006). Research has shown that positive student–teacher relationships were significantly and positively correlated with both engagement and achievement, with engagement being the stronger association (Roorda et al., 2011).
- Positive learning environments—When environments provide students with

autonomy in which they have a voice and choice in their learning (Toshalis & Nakkula, 2012), they are less likely to be alienated. E. Skinner et al. (2008) found that students who experienced low autonomy were more likely to withdraw, not attempt or participate in tasks and become bored, frustrated and disengaged.

- A positive connection to the school and school community—When connections including peers and parents are evident, positive attitudes, personal learning goals and educational values have a positive influence on student motivation (Legault et al., 2006).

The link between engagement and student learning and achievement

Gibbs and Poskitt (2010) have identified eight factors that influence student engagement and the subsequent learning and achievement of students. They have also provided an insight into the strength of these eight factors' effects on student learning, by assigning a value to each of the factors, ranging from strong, through moderate, to some evidence of effect. The eight factors are presented in Table 3.2 grouped in their levels of importance; the table also lists a range of pedagogical approaches that can be employed to address each of the areas. Importantly, all eight engagement factors are interconnected and operate in a dynamic manner within individual students.

Student motivation and engagement

Recognising the negative long-term effects of student disengagement and aliena-tion, teachers try to understand what student engagement is and what it looks like in a classroom. However, this is a topic of great debate, as student engagement is a complex and multifaceted construct, and finding a universal definition is a work in progress. Earlier studies around student engagement focused on active learning and participation as being indicative of student engagement, but further studies have shown that identifying student engagement is far more complex than observing students doing something in a classroom. In a meta-analysis around student engagement, Fredricks, Blumenfeld and Paris (2004, p. 60) noted that engagement has been defined as '[being] actively committed', 'to involve oneself or become occu-pied; to participate' and to 'attract or involve'. According to an extensive literature review conducted by Gibbs and Poskitt (2010, p. 10), engagement is

a multi-faceted construct that encompasses students' sense of belonging and connectedness to their school, teachers and peers; their sense of agency, self-efficacy and orientation to achieve within their classrooms and in their broader

Table 3.2 Student engagement factors, the strength of their effects on engagement and learning outcomes and/or achievement, and pedagogical approaches to achieve them

Factors	Strength of evidence of a positive effect	Explanations	Pedagogical approaches
Relationships with teachers and other students	Strong, compelling	Good relationships between teachers and students promote wellbeing and enhance the academic lives of students.	Nurturing trusting relationships
Motivation and interest in learning	Strong, compelling	Motivation is what compels learners to invest time and effort. Fostering motivation is crucial for short-term learning and for equipping students to be lifelong learners.	Engaging students in fun learning activities Making learning meaningful
Goal orientation	Strong, compelling	One of the most potent ways to encourage students to be academically self-regulated is to involve them in planning and assessment related to their own learning. Goals influence the effort students put into learning tasks and direct future action.	Making learning meaningful
Academic self-regulation	Strong, compelling	Self-regulation affects the degree to which students are motivated to learn, think about their own learning (use metacognitive processes) and proactively use self-regulatory processes to improve their learning.	Making learning meaningful
Self-efficacy	Strong, compelling	Students who are cognitively engaged possess a sense of confidence about themselves as capable learners. Self-efficacy influences aspirations and commitment to goals and the use of metacognitive strategies.	Making learning meaningful
Relational learning	Moderate	Relational learning provides opportunities for students to participate in classroom activities that encourage them to work together.	Nurturing trusting relationships

(continues)

60

Factors	Strength of evidence of a positive effect	Explanations	Pedagogical approaches
Personal agency	Some	The perceived and actual control students have over their learning affects outcomes. Instructional behaviours that support autonomy enhance personal agency.	Making learning meaningful
Disposition to be a learner	Some	Attitudes acquired by students make them inclined to work in certain ways. Being resilient and having a propensity to challenge themselves have roles in cognitive engagement.	Engaging students in fun learning activities

Source: Adapted from Gibbs & Poskitt (2010).

extra-curricular endeavours; their involvement, effort, levels of concentration and interest in subjects and learning in general; and the extent to which learning is enjoyed for its own sake, or seen as something that must be endured to receive a reward or avoid sanction. Further, engagement is a variable state of being that is influenced by a range of internal and external factors including the perceived value or relevance of the learning and the presence of opportunities for students to experience appropriately-pitched challenge and success in their learning. As such engagement is malleable by the actions of teachers.

In this definition, student engagement is a multidimensional and interconnected construct and includes both outcomes and processes that contribute to engagement. Gibbs and Poskitt (2010) identify three key engagement dimensions: behavioural, emotional and cognitive. Table 3.3 outlines the ways in which these dimensions are exemplified.

The engagement continuum
In an attempt to define student engagement and to understand what engagement looks like in a classroom, Schlechty (2002) argued that there are five different levels of engagement that students exhibit in the classroom. These levels are presented below, along with particular characteristics students were observed to display.

1. Engaged—The student gives high attention and high commitment to the task. They see the work as valuable to them and persist when obstacles occur. The

Table 3.3 The engagement dimensions and the elements in which they are exemplified

Behavioural	Emotional	Cognitive
Participation Presence Engagement Behaviour Compliance with rules Effort, persistence Concentration, attention Rates of quality contribution Involvement in school-related activities	Reactions to teachers, classmates, academic activity, school Attitude Perception of the value of learning Interest, enjoyment Happiness Identification with school Sense of belonging within school	Level of volition learning (learning by choice) Investment and willingness to exert effort Thoughtfulness (applying the processes of deep thinking) Self-regulation Goal setting Use of metacognitive strategies Preference for challenge Resilience, persistence Mastery orientation Sense of urgency

Increasing levels of investment in, and commitment to, learning

Source: Adapted from Gibbs & Poskitt (2010, p. 12).

student is likely to move beyond the set task and begin to demonstrate the characteristics of a lifelong learner (i.e., learning for the intrinsic benefits of learning). The student retains what they have learned, and they are likely to be able to transfer the skills to different contexts.

2. Routine—The student may put in effort due to the nature of the task and its intrinsic value (i.e., grades, a necessary skill for future goals or being placed in a group and working with peers). However, in general, the student has low commitment to the work so does not persist when the task gets difficult and is not likely to be able to transfer the skills to different contexts.

3. Ritual—The student is seen to exert the least amount of effort possible to meet the requirements of the task. They do not move beyond the set task. The student will learn at low levels. Interestingly, it is at this level that most classroom teachers

appear satisfied that a student is learning, as their behaviour is compliant and they complete the set task.

4. Retreatism—The student is not paying attention or completing tasks, but their engagement level differs from rebellion in that they are not disruptive and do not display overtly negative attitudes towards school and learning. Work avoidance is typical, in which a student will be unprepared to commence work by either not having the relevant resources or finding excuses as to why they do not commence the work. The student will learn little or nothing from the task.

5. Rebellion—Rebellion is characterised by a student's refusal to complete work or their acting in a disruptive manner which affects other students. The student also exhibits no commitment to work and negative attitudes about school, and generally learns nothing from the task (Schlechty, 2002).

What is interesting about the work of Schlechty (2002) is that it demonstrates that there are times when a teacher may feel that their students are engaged in the work, but in reality they are being compliant, which is not the same as being engaged. How teachers respond to the different levels of student engagement has been highlighted in a year-long study in Australian schools by Angus et al. (2009). The study found that, over the year, 20 per cent of students were considered disengaged (displaying compliant and non-aggressive behaviours), 12 per cent were low-level disruptive and 8 per cent were uncooperative (displaying aggressive, disruptive and disengaged behaviours). It revealed that those students who were identified as disengaged reached only marginally higher achievement levels than the uncooperative group. However, in the day-to-day activities in the classroom, students who were identified as being uncooperative and displaying disruptive behaviours received the greatest amount of teacher time and resources, while the compliant and disengaged students were often left unnoticed (A. Sullivan et al., 2014). These results align with the findings of Willms (2003), who noted that the correlation between engagement and achievement is moderate, suggesting that students can be high achievers but disengaged.

In a study of student engagement across a large, diverse high school, Cooper (2014) surveyed 1132 students with a factor analysis, highlighting three main types of engaging teaching practices: connective instruction, academic rigour and lively teaching. Cooper noted that although these practices individually and collectively engaged students, connective instruction was by far the most effective strategy for engaging students. Connective instruction practices help students to make personal connections to the content, meaning they emotionally connect with the content and the teacher. Martin and Dowson (2009, p. 367) theorised that, as one of the primary goals of middle years learners is identity formation, connective instruction 'honors *who* the students are—acknowledging that they are particular people with particular interests, points of views, personalities, and experiences'. Cooper's (2014, p. 382) study found that 'connective instruction and engagement were more than seven times higher than the relationships for rigor or lively teaching'. Table 3.4 shows key pedagogical approaches to promote student engagement linked to the three engaging teaching practices.

Table 3.4 Three pedagogical approaches to promote student engagement

Approaches	Explanations	Example strategies
Connective instruction (individual orientation—i.e., students can personalise)	Students perceive the relevance of learning when it is made meaningful for them.	Indicate why learning is important and relate content to students' lives Enable students to learn better and help them take responsibility for their own learning Emotionally connect learning to students
Lively teaching (collective orientation)	Students are more actively engaged when learning is perceived to be fun, inspiring and challenging.	Encourage discussion, cooperative learning, peer tutoring, problem-based learning, hands-on work, demonstrations, and video games and technology
Academic rigour (collective orientation)	The academic dimensions of the classroom practice are promoted by demanding high levels of cognition and focus.	Provide challenging work Convey passion for the content Maintain high expectations of students

Source: Adapted from Cooper (2014).

The second of these engaging teaching practices, lively teaching, engages students in fun learning activities. It also highlights the need for activities to be challenging and links to academic rigour. According to recent research, academic rigour is a key element for ensuring student engagement but is frequently missing from middle years classrooms (Nitzberg, 2012). Hence, student engagement sits squarely within the ambit of quality teaching and, importantly, quality instruction that meets the needs of students where they are currently located in their learning.

Provocation 3.3 Connective learning for middle years learners

We now look at student wellbeing and engagement in order to facilitate connective learning.

 Consider a range of common topics in the content areas you teach. Working with another colleague list at least five topics and develop a range of teaching and learning activities that facilitate connective learning for middle years learners. Remember to ensure other elements of quality teaching for middle years students are considered, such as higher order thinking.

Chapter summary

This chapter makes the following key points:

- Student wellbeing is an important focus for students in the middle years and is pivotal to their academic success.
- There are empirically based pathways that can guide wellbeing programs for young adolescent learners.
- A critical component of student wellbeing is social and emotional competence.
- Student disengagement can result from a number of factors, and the incidence of disengagement and alienation is heightened during adolescence.
- Student engagement is a multifaceted construct that comprises the interconnected dimensions of behavioural, cognitive and emotional engagement.
- Connective learning, lively teaching and academic rigour are critical to engaging middle years learners.
- Resilience is a key to building self-efficacy in students.

Chapter Four

Quality teaching and learning

DONNA PENDERGAST and KATHERINE MAIN

> **Learning intentions**
>
> In this chapter we will:
> - explore the concepts of quality teaching and learning and best practice in middle years education
> - consider the signifying practices that are regarded as enabling quality learning for young adolescent engagement and success
> - compare and contrast upper primary, middle and secondary pedagogy with a view to proposing a best education practice model which is appropriate for the age and developmental stage of middle years students.

Middle years teaching and learning

The key teaching and learning challenges in the middle years are closely linked to the nature of the changes that occur during early adolescence, along with the challenges associated with transition between primary and secondary school. As we have seen in earlier chapters of this book, adolescence is a distinct, significant and unique period of life characterised by physical changes related to puberty, and to psychosocial and cognitive changes, including the following:

- psychological—acquiring independence and autonomy
- social—dealing with changing family and peer group relationships

- emotional—shifting from narcissistic to mutually caring relationships
- cognitive—moving from concrete to abstract thought (supported by brain development)
- moral—developing a set of moral beliefs and standards.

Later in this book we will consider the effects of transition. Taken together, in the middle years these changes often result in students disengaging from their learning opportunities, evident in a shift in learner disposition away from volition learning, and in increases in absenteeism and truancy, suspension and expulsion rates. Coupled with this there is strong evidence that students with low engagement and low academic skills are more likely to drop out of school and are at risk of a range of mental health problems. It is now well understood that the process of disengaging from school begins early in a student's journey through schooling and increases in the middle and secondary school years (Willms & Friesen, 2012).

There is an abundance of advice around what teachers, parents and the wider school community can do to provide the best opportunities to engage students in learning during the middle years, taking into consideration this multifaceted context of age and stage. There is also an abundance of research that points to the importance of quality teaching as a major factor impacting on student achievement. Further, many studies have shown that age- and stage-appropriate pedagogies— that is, what teachers know, do and value for different age groups and for students with various developmental needs—are more significant in influencing student achievement than structural arrangements (Dinham & Rowe, 2007). This chapter will consider the idea of best pedagogical practice in learning and teaching, and ways to enhance student engagement through quality teaching. It will also compare and contrast upper primary, middle and secondary pedagogies. This will be done with a view to proposing a best education practice model which is age appropriate and accommodates the differentiation typical of the wide range of development in young people in the middle years.

Best education practice can be used to describe what works for a particular situation or application. When data support the success of a practice, it is referred to as an evidence-based practice. According to A. Hargreaves and Fullan (2012), existing practices that already possess a high level of widely agreed effectiveness should be accepted to be best education practices, but the problem is in determining what is effective and when wide agreement is reached. There is no doubt there is an appetite worldwide for evidence-informed practices in education, and the field of middle years education is no exception.

In Chapter 1, some insights have been shared into what is known about the effectiveness of pedagogy for the middle years in the Australian context. However, as Dinham and Rowe (2007) identified a decade ago, the evidence base around the effectiveness of middle years education, by whatever name, has not been produced in Australia in ways that provide the rigorous and deep insight needed. Indeed, they endorse Pendergast (2005, p. 19) when she notes that 'middle schooling has a legitimate place in our education system. Regardless of this however, champions of middle schooling are needed at all junctures in schools, in systems, and especially in universities, where academic, research-based evidence is required'.

Little has changed since 2005 when Pendergast and others called for high-quality research in the field of middle years education. However, there is an abundance of evidence that points to increases in underachievement, disengagement, truancy, mental ill health and problem behaviours, along with declining levels of resilience and motivation (M.-T. Wang & Fredricks, 2014). Taken as a whole, this evidence builds a strong case for focusing on middle years schooling as a high-priority area for research. Given that quality teaching rates so highly as a factor impacting on students' learning, it makes sense to further refine the focus to quality teaching in the middle years.

In other parts of the world, there is a slow trickle of research that points to the benefits of adopting pedagogies that are responsive to the classrooms typical of the middle years. For example, a study by McEwin and Greene (2011) in the United States in 2009 comprised 827 randomly selected public middle schools and 101 of the most successful middle schools (called 'highly successful middle schools'). The highly successful middle schools followed the concept and philosophy that responded to the particular needs of young adolescents and implemented recommended middle school quality teaching components (e.g., teams, advisory programs, common planning time and flexible block scheduling). The findings revealed that in schools following the middle school concept and philosophy authentically and with fidelity, the percentage of students on or above grade level in mathematics and reading on standardised tests was higher, and the school was more likely to be associated with higher scores on achievement tests and other positive student outcomes.

The dilemma concerning the paucity of evidence base continues to restrain the possibilities for truly understanding which facets of middle years pedagogy are the most valuable, especially as the approach argues for a combination of pedagogical approaches taken together. The type of evidence needed is both at the large, system scale and at the small, individual student and classroom scale. Many of the important data in relation to schooling outcomes are quantitative—that is, measured and represented in the forms of numbers. National Assessment Program—Literacy and Numeracy scores are probably the most talked about form of schooling outcomes data, and they are numerical. Truancy figures, class sizes, numbers of parents who attend school concerts or swimming carnivals, marks on exams, ages of the students in a particular year, gender balances among students and teachers and a huge number of other things yield quantitative data. Quantitative data, particularly with large sample sizes, can be subjected to statistical tests so that means and standard deviations can be compared, percentiles and quartiles calculated, and significance and effect size measured.

Crucially, however, not all of the important data in relation to schooling can be measured in numbers. Morale of staff, student perceptions of wellbeing, severity of bullying, quality of teaching: all have dimensions that can meaningfully be expressed and discussed only in words. It should be possible to make credible, accountable claims about a school and to support those claims, in part, with carefully collected qualitative evidence. Such evidence may include interviews, focus group discussions, conversations or observations. It is important to use strategies such as randomly choosing classes to observe or students to interview in order to ensure that the data gathered are representative of what is being measured.

Provocation 4.1 Evaluating classroom practices

Evaluating the effectiveness of teaching and learning in classrooms is not new. There are many ways to evaluate what happens in classrooms to determine if quality teaching is evident.

 Investigate a range of methods for evaluating classroom practices to determine if the teaching and learning are of high quality. Select one method for evaluation. Provide a justification for your choice and, if possible, apply it in a middle years classroom setting.

Principles and practices of quality teaching

Pedagogical effectiveness is at the core of effective middle years education, as it is about 'an intentional approach to teaching and learning that is responsive and appropriate to the full range of needs, interests and achievements of middle years students in formal and informal schooling contexts' (Middle Years of Schooling Association [MYSA], 2008). With research evidence showing that teacher quality is the most important factor in improving outcomes for students (Dinham & Rowe, 2007; D.H. Hargreaves, 1994), quality teaching and learning provision is the most important imperative in the middle years.

Hattie (2003) has achieved international prominence as a researcher by being among those who urge educators to focus on the quality of teaching in their classrooms. His synthesis of over 500,000 studies of the effects of influences on student achievement revealed that although almost all things teachers do in the name of education have a positive effect on achievement, the effect of quality teaching accounts for around 30 per cent of student achievement, being the most significant factor after the students themselves (50 per cent). In line with this position, according to the Grattan Institute:

> Improving teacher effectiveness outweighs the impact of any other school education program or policy in improving student performance.
>
> A student with a great teacher can achieve in half a year what a student with a poor teacher can achieve in a full year. And because the impact of highly effective teaching is cumulative, relatively modest increases in effectiveness can make a big difference to student learning. (Jensen, 2014)

So what is high-quality teaching for the middle years? As mentioned in Chapter 1, after undertaking close analysis of the evidence and following the lead of international movements, the MYSA (2008), now named Adolescent Success, formulated and advocates for the adoption of a set of Signifying Practices that are regarded as enabling quality learning for engagement and success for middle years learners. The MYSA argues that there is a need to ensure the following practices are intentional and collectively apparent in middle years classes:

- higher order thinking strategies
- integrated and disciplinary curricula that are negotiated, relevant and challenging
- heterogeneous and flexible student groupings
- cooperative learning and collaborative teaching
- authentic and reflective assessment with high expectations
- democratic governance and shared leadership
- parental and community involvement in student learning.

Many of these practices are reflected in the chapter topics in this book, to enable deep engagement with each of them. Along similar lines, the recent introduction of the new junior secondary phase of education in Queensland is based on the six Junior Secondary Guiding Principles developed by the Australian Council for Educational Research (ACER, 2012). These principles are intended to provide challenging educational offerings that engage middle years learners while at the same time giving them a sense of belonging and support during the changes they face. One of the principles, quality teaching, is explicit to the topic of this chapter, serving as a firm commitment for quality teaching approaches that enhance student learning.

Within the quality teaching practices it is acknowledged that there are generic qualities that make all teachers at all year levels effective, such as good interpersonal skills and skills in communication, collaboration, problem-solving, decision-making, organisation and time and classroom management (ACER, 2012). Importantly, in addition to these generic qualities, it is suggested that teachers of middle years students also require a range of specific skills, including:

- the ability to forge a middle school identity
- proficiency in integrated curriculum design
- the capacity to working collaboratively within a small learning community for team planning and team teaching
- an in-depth understanding of the concerns and needs of adolescents
- a willingness to develop positive relationships with students, families and the community
- a capacity to sustain middle school reform (ACER, 2012, p. 14).

This list is generated largely from 'The four attributes model of the middle school teacher', elicited from interviews with principals, teachers and students by Rumble and Aspland (2010). They set out to explore the question 'What differentiates the middle school teacher from primary and secondary school teachers?' Their model represents a new image for secondary and middle school teachers in Australia in a time of curriculum reform. Their study found that the four key attributes that differentiate middle school teachers are the capacity to forge a middle school identity; be a designer of a wholesome curriculum; be a specialist in adolescence as a socio-cultural construct; and have a capacity to sustain middle school reform.

The alignment between the Signifying Practices (MYSA, 2008) and the Junior Secondary Guiding Principles (ACER, 2012), which is a further development of 'The four attributes model of the middle school teacher', is unmistakable, with the MYSA focusing on quality teaching strategies while ACER uses a wider lens to present characteristics of quality teachers. Some of the growing evidence of the impact and effectiveness of employing these approaches will now be considered.

A best practice model

Linking together the available evidence and informed by frameworks such as the MYSA (2008) Signifying Practices and the ACER (2012) Junior Secondary Guiding Principles, Table 4.1 presents elements related to middle school subject-matter, pedagogical response to student characteristics, teacher characteristics and physical teaching space for teaching. By way of contrast, upper primary and senior practices are also presented.

From the comparisons presented in Table 4.1, it is evident that, in the four key areas discussed, for middle years students:

1. The curriculum should be challenging, relevant and connected to the lives of students.
2. A pedagogical response to student characteristics should direct attention towards adolescent-centred learning, which means knowing and understanding the characteristics of young adolescents and how this impacts on teaching and learning.
3. Whatever learning activities teachers use, they need to promote higher order thinking, facilitate flow of learning for the diverse range of students, encourage deep understanding of knowledge, allow opportunities for collaborative learning, be fun and exciting and provide students with some choice in, owner-ship of and responsibility for their learning.
4. The teaching space should provide a sense of connection, safety and distinct-iveness and should enable flexibility for group work and collaboration and for reshaping groups according to need.

Table 4.1 A comparison of upper primary, middle and senior secondary quality teaching and learning practices in four key areas

Elements	Upper primary[a] Years 4–6 Child centred	Middle years[b] Years 7–9 Young adolescent centred	Senior[c] Years 10–12 Subject centred
		Curriculum	
Knowledge	Commonsense knowledge reshaped into schooled knowledge Comprehensive and structured, but flexible enough to address individual learning needs Holistic approach Explicit teaching in order to gain high-level learning outcomes	School knowledge increasingly differentiated into curriculum areas, becoming more abstract as attitudes and expressions expand Content with rigour and practical application explained in terms of the overall subject discipline knowledge Significant and meaningful tasks outside school	Curriculum-specific knowledge characterised by increasing abstraction, generalisation, value judgement and opinion Knowledge development often focused on assessment or matriculation but connected to life and citizenship Learning the conventions of the discipline
Higher order thinking	More concrete operational than abstract, although setting discrete tasks in which students find solutions to problems is recommended Learners developing more abstract thinking skills by the end of primary Clear examples provided to assist students to understand complex concepts	Engagement of young adolescents in relevant, meaningful and challenging learning through higher order thinking processes, which still require scaffolding throughout junior secondary	Development of skills in critical and creative thinking that is informed by knowledge of discourses within the discipline Focus on skilled evaluation of concepts and own work
Relevance	Reliant on curriculum expectations as well as relating to students' own experiences through use of everyday language Learners beginning to relate personal experiences to broader contexts	Relevant curriculum, drawing from students' backgrounds, interests and academic needs Value of learning to students' lives made explicit Learning experiences taken into wider community	Relevance ideally linked to developing global perspective on issues and ideas Connecting disciplinary knowledge with students' developing world views

(continues)

Table 4.1 *continued*

Elements	Upper primary[a] Years 4–6 Child centred	Middle years[b] Years 7–9 Young adolescent centred	Senior[c] Years 10–12 Subject centred
Connectedness	Connections made between information and students' own experiences, particularly in regard to family and community life	Connections made between information taught and real life, especially everyday concerns of the particular age group Social awareness developing	Connections between and within domains of disciplinary knowledge (school subjects) Links to ethical, moral and social issues
Pedagogical response to student characteristics			
Physical	Varied activities provided, often with clear learning expectations, including group tasks and hands-on activities	Focus on active learning—e.g., interactive group tasks, hands-on activities, differentiated instruction and opportunity for discussion	Hands-on, engaging activities and collaborative tasks still important Students developing skills in long periods of focused work alone
Social	Supportive grouping structures designed with students of similar ages and interests	Strong emphasis on collaborative, cooperative and peer-assisted learning Most adolescents learn well in a mixture of patterns—e.g., alone, with a partner, in a small group of peers, in a team or in teacher-directed activity	Increased emphasis on individual results and achievements, albeit often in the context of group tasks Ideally a wide range of learning activities rather than a single mode
Emotional	Supportive, safe environment Building self-worth and self-confidence	Safe, supportive environment in which students feel safe, valued and listened to Students encouraged to experiment and take risks with own learning, express own ideas and challenge ideas of others	Safe environment in which students feel able to actively participate and free to share ideas
Intellectual	Learning provides opportunities to be curious and accept differences—e.g., compare and contrast, imagine and experiment	Learning provides challenge and differentiation to cater for wide range of intellectual development in the class Students encouraged to set goals, make choices in learning, experiment with new ideas and self-regulate learning	Trends from middle years continue with increased focus on individual learning, responsibility and autonomy Challenging activities and differentiation still important

Elements	Upper primary[a] Years 4–6 Child centred	Middle years[b] Years 7–9 Young adolescent centred	Senior[c] Years 10–12 Subject centred
Teacher characteristics			
Subject approach	Integrated approaches to content knowledge Making connections between subject areas and focusing on big ideas	Subject and generalist role Flexible and adaptable, prepared to teach outside subject specialisation Making links between discipline areas	Strong emphasis on subject specialisation, teaching in isolation from other subjects Lecture style a more frequent but ideally not universal tool
Teaching style	Explicit approaches enhancing learning outcomes in general Constructivist approaches with strong support and structured scaffolding Modelling appropriate behaviour, learning attitudes and language	Focus on constructivist learning through active learning and hands-on activities Unique teaching style	Focus on high-level engagement with concepts that requires building on existing knowledge New learning experiences challenge assumptions and develop understanding
Teacher focus	Generalist	Generalist with subject specialist knowledge	Subject specialist role with deep content knowledge Pedagogical content knowledge of how students engage with content
Relationship with students	Supportive, encouraging and nurturing Makes students feel valued Strong pastoral care role	Encouraging and supportive to students Meaningful pastoral care role Students value and seek authentic interactions with teachers outside classroom environment	Encouraging and supportive to students Senior students wish to feel known as individuals by teacher
Teacher learner knowledge	Expertly prepared to teach children	Expertly prepared to teach young adolescents	Expertly prepared to teach subject specialisation, with deep content knowledge and skills to teach young adults

(continues)

Table 4.1 *continued*

Elements	Upper primary[a] Years 4–6 Child centred	Middle years[b] Years 7–9 Young adolescent centred	Senior[c] Years 10–12 Subject centred
Teachers working together	Teachers plan together Mostly responsible for majority of one-class teaching Team teaching in some contexts	Strong emphasis on teacher collaboration and teacher teaming	Teachers plan together Usually responsible for separate subject delivery
Teacher expectations	Students expected to do their best Students expected to experience learning as high skills and high challenge for flow in learning	Students expected to do their best Students expected to increasingly take responsibility for own learning Students expected to experience learning as high skills and high challenge for flow in learning	Students expected to do their best Students expected to increasingly take responsibility for own learning Students expected to experience learning as high skills and high challenge for flow in learning
Assessment practices	Clear and directed setting of tasks that can also allow for flexibility in introducing student choice Comprehensive feedback	Formative feedback given on a range of tasks to help students with current learning Authentic assessment used to ensure relevance and to focus on engagement Opportunity to negotiate assessment when appropriate	Determined by the nature of the discipline and government or system requirements Individual performance focus
Working with data	Teachers are data literate and work with data beyond classroom assessment Deep knowledge of individual student achievement for class across all learning areas	Teachers are data literate and work with data beyond classroom assessment Deep knowledge of student achievement across a number of learning areas	Teachers are data literate and work with data beyond classroom assessment Deep knowledge of individual student achievement limited to discipline area for many classes and year levels
Physical teaching space			
Feeling of belonging	Safe and supportive environment created for all children Designated space (classroom) is 'theirs'	Ownership of learning space promoted by provision of designated learning areas and display of student work	Space becomes more functional Appropriate if effective and efficient for learning

Elements	Upper primary[a] Years 4–6 Child centred	Middle years[b] Years 7–9 Young adolescent centred	Senior[c] Years 10–12 Subject centred
Flexibility	Guided flexibility to make students aware of expectations, learning outcomes to be met and consequences	Flexible space created that can be easily adapted to suit different learning experiences—e.g., lecture style and cooperative learning	Spaces designed to reflect subject-specific requirements
Cater for learning styles	Differentiated approaches required for optimal learning outcomes for all children	Learning styles identified with learning spaces catering for differentiation—e.g., quiet individual work and small-group work	Space reflects dominant learning style associated with subject
Movement around the classroom	Cooperative learning groups in the classroom Flexible options during the school week recommended	Learning pedagogies varied to allow and facilitate movement around the classroom	Little movement around the classroom Students may be asked to present work to or complete work with whole class
Resources	High-quality resources that enhance educational content and focus	Access to practical resources for relevant application of learning	Reflect the subject requirements Ideally include additional textbooks and other complementary information sources in addition to information and communication technologies (ICT)
Technology	Technology embedded in learning Access enabled	Technology resources provided Access to mobile technology facilitated	ICT tools including workstations or laptops in classrooms Can use 'bring your own device' to give students access ICT may be used for composition

Source: Adapted from Pendergast et al. (2014a).

Provocation 4.2 Comparing upper primary, middle and senior school teaching and learning

You have been invited to present a session at school to your colleagues who are keen to explore the differences and similarities between upper primary, middle and senior school quality teaching and learning practices.

 Select one of the four areas of practice: curriculum, pedagogical response to student characteristics, teacher characteristics or physical teaching space. Drawing from Table 4.1, list ways in which the various elements might be enacted in a classroom.

It is our contention that the imperative of quality teaching and learning provision is the most important part of middle years education. Ensuring the teacher workforce is equipped with capabilities to enable quality teaching and learning remains an ongoing challenge for education sectors, especially given the lack of an evidence base that predictably points to practices that maximise student engagement, learning outcomes and achievement. Nevertheless, if teachers are equipped with a clear set of quality teaching and learning practices, the task then is to ensure that teacher self-efficacy—that is, teachers with both the confidence and the competence to employ pedagogies for young adolescents—is a central feature of teacher preparation and professional learning.

A teacher's sense of efficacy is their belief or perception of their capabilities to bring about desired outcomes of student engagement and learning, even among those students who may be difficult or unmotivated (Guskey & Passaro, 1994; Tschannen-Moran & Woolfolk-Hoy, 2001). Teacher self-efficacy forms within the beginning years of teaching and, according to theory, once developed is resistant to change (Hoy & Spero, 2005). Teacher efficacy can be categorised into two types: general teacher efficacy (teachers' beliefs in the ability of teachers in general to influence student outcomes) and personal teacher efficacy (teachers' beliefs about their own ability to affect student outcomes) (Tschannen-Moran & Woolfolk-Hoy, 2001).

A teacher's sense of efficacy, or their belief that they have the capacity to affect student performance, is directly linked to their enacted practices. A growing body of literature reveals that when teachers have stated a high level of self-efficacy, improved student outcomes have been reported (Klassen et al., 2011). This causal link has been attributed to a range of behaviours connected to classroom practice, including the level of teacher effort invested in planning and organisation, goals and aspirations, risk-taking with new pedagogies to meet the needs of students and persistence and resilience when things go awry (Bandura, 1993). For teachers to operate in self-efficacious ways to deliver quality teaching, they must develop mastery of the skill sets required. This calls for development of both competence and confidence, and hence a focus on quality teaching and learning requires a focus on teacher professional learning, such that teacher self-efficacy can be enhanced and student achievement levels will parallel these improvements.

The self-efficacy beliefs teachers hold about their ability to teach subjects shape their competence in teaching. Measuring the self-efficacy of teachers is a useful process to gain insight into their levels of confidence and competence to deliver quality teaching in junior secondary. When teachers have high levels of self-efficacy, with high levels of both confidence and competence, then they have mastery and, therefore, are more likely to have a positive effect on student achievement. If they have low self-efficacy in confidence, competence or both, then they are likely to be misinformed, doubt their ability or be ignorant of appropriate quality teaching practices. In all of these circumstances they will not operate effectively to enhance student achievement potential. Bandura's (1977, 2012) social cognitive theory posited that teachers' self-efficacy beliefs are developed from four main sources:

1. mastery experiences—actual teaching accomplishment
2. vicarious experiences—observe teaching modelled by someone else
3. verbal persuasion—feedback from others
4. physiological arousal—feelings experienced when teaching.

Of these sources, mastery experiences are the most effective in increasing a teacher's sense of efficacy.

According to Mourshed, Chijioke and Barber (2010), who investigated the factors that enable systems to improve, teacher self-efficacy through the building of the instructional skills of teachers and the management skills of principals is one of six essentials. So, to ensure quality teaching and learning provision, it is important to work with teachers both at the initial teacher education stage and through ongoing professional learning to ensure they are equipped with pedagogical capacity and the self-efficacy to employ this capacity. Quality teaching and learning provision, hence, is a vital focus.

Provocation 4.3 Teacher peer reflection activity:
quality teaching

One of the strategies known to support teachers as they reform their pedagogical practices is to collaborate with other teachers. This activity provides you with the opportunity for ongoing collaboration and could form the basis of a learning community as teachers reflect on their approach to teaching and learning for young adolescents.

 Working with one or more of your colleagues, observe each other's classes and provide feedback on what you observe, using as guides the elements described for the middle years in Table 4.1 and the suggestions listed below:

- For each element described in the middle years column of Table 4.1, note whether it is a typical element of this class, by rating its occurrence frequency using the following scale: 0 = not observed, 1 = occasionally observed, 2 = frequently observed.
- If any of the elements are observed, give examples of those which occurred in each lesson.
- Suggest changes that could be made to increase the quality of the teaching and learning, then list the actions that might be necessary to implement these changes.

Chapter summary

This chapter makes the following key points:

- The provision of quality teaching and learning is the most important aspect of achieving effective education for young adolescents.
- There remains a paucity of high-quality research into the effectiveness of middle years practices, yet the literature is consistently increasing the awareness of the challenges of young people disengaging from learning and of the potential effects on achievement.
- A comparison of upper primary, middle and secondary pedagogies highlights ways of being responsive to the changes experienced by middle years students and the wide range of developmental stages typical in these classes, with a view to proposing a best education practice model which is appropriate for the age and developmental stage of middle years students.

Chapter Five

Catering for individual students

KATHERINE MAIN

Learning intentions

In this chapter we will:
- understand what is meant by differentiation and differentiated instruction
- explore the importance of differentiation in a middle years classroom
- identify the key principles and processes that underpin differentiation
- discuss a range of strategies that teachers can use to differentiate the curriculum in a middle years classroom
- introduce the concept of personalised learning and consider its value for teaching and learning in the middle years.

Student diversity

The literature defines differentiation as a pedagogical approach to meet the diverse needs of all students (Tomlinson, 2005). Differentiation emphasises the needs of each individual learner and has the overarching goal of creating a learning environment that enables all students to succeed through accessing a meaningful curriculum. As students enter the middle years (Years 6–9), a number of factors combine to increase the student diversity. As with all classes, differences in abilities, genders, cultures, linguistics, family structures, socio-economic backgrounds and racial and religious backgrounds mean there is wide heterogeneity in any student population. However, in addition to these factors, as young adolescents transition into a new educational setting, they are also experiencing a time of significant physical, emotional, social and cognitive change, with dissimilar rates of growth being experienced by each individual in all areas of development (see Chapter 2). Further, national and state anti-discrimination acts call for equitable access for all students and have resulted in inclusion policies that have added to the heterogeneity of classes by increasing the numbers of students with special needs who are educated within general or main-stream classrooms (Haager & Klingner, 2005). The combination of these factors has resulted in significant diversity and a range of instructional levels within general classrooms that has been estimated to be, on average, 5.4 grade equivalents (Jenkins et al., 1994).

The Organisation for Economic Co-operation and Development (OECD, 2000) acknowledged the significant changes that students experience during their middle years of schooling. The differences in onset and rapidity of the physiological changes linked to puberty further increase the effect on students with diverse and differen-tiated learning needs, and many of these students, without additional support or an adjusted educational program, are at greater risk than the general population of not achieving their full potential at school. The OECD defined three broad categories of students with specific learning needs that would place them at greater risk:

1. students with identifiable disabilities and impairments
2. students with learning difficulties that are not attributable to a specific disability or impairment
3. students who are disadvantaged due to environmental factors (such as socio-economic status, and students from linguistically or culturally diverse backgrounds).

In the past, a deficit view of these students blamed them for the challenges and obstacles they needed to overcome to be successful learners. However, additional support mechanisms within the schooling system help those students with identifi-able disabilities, impairments and learning difficulties to participate more effectively within the classroom (Ashman, 2015). But for those students who experienced diffi-culties due to social disadvantage and marginalisation during the latter part of the twentieth century, the notion of cultural capital and the mismatch between home environments and positive schooling experiences have been clarified. The changing view of these students has resulted in a more socially just approach to learning and teaching and the implementation of a number of 'key laws, policies, and directives to better inform and frame' how teachers cater for their diverse learning needs (Garrick & Keogh, 2010, p. 73). For middle years students with special support needs, it is important to note that they are young adolescents first, and this should shape teaching and learning alongside their special support needs (Pendergast & Garvis, 2015).

As a consequence of the increasing diversity in student populations, the biggest challenge for middle school teachers is to provide a developmentally appropriate curriculum that meets the educational needs of all students within their classroom (OECD, 2011). The scope of this challenge has been reinforced through position and policy statements published by the National Middle School Association (2001, 2010), now called the Association for Middle Level Education; by the Middle Years of Schooling Association (MYSA, 2008), now called Adolescent Success; and through the *Melbourne declaration on educational goals for young Australians* (Ministerial Council on Education, Employment, Training and Youth Affairs, 2008). These all argue that meeting the unique learning needs of students in the middle years is an essential tenet of effective middle school practice. In order to meet the educational needs of such a diverse student population, teachers cannot use a one-size-fits-all approach without marginalising a large number of their students. Therefore, teachers must utilise a wider range of curricula and pedagogical approaches to differentiate their instruction.

Differentiated instruction

Carol Tomlinson (2005), who is recognised as a leading researcher in the area of differentiated instruction, explains that differentiated instruction or differentiation is an approach to, or philosophy of, teaching rather than a set of hard and fast rules and, by its very nature, is a dynamic process within every lesson in every classroom. Indeed, most, if not all, teachers differentiate their instruction through subtle and not-so-subtle means without ever putting a label on their practice: they just see it as good pedagogy and as being responsive to their students' learning needs. Differentiation by definition is being responsive to students' needs and is demonstrated when a teacher changes the pace, level or kind of instruction to provide students with a range of different ways to access or learn the required curriculum. It is an instructional model that supports teachers' efforts to improve student outcomes by addressing variations in students' readiness, interest and learning profiles (Tomlinson, 2005; Tomlinson &

Provocation 5.1 Differentiating the curriculum

The following statements have been drawn from national and international position statements or recommendations for teaching middle years learners:

Middle schooling is an intentional approach to teaching and learning that is responsive and appropriate to the full range of needs, interests and achievements of middle years students in formal and informal schooling contexts. (MYSA, 2008)

Teaching [and learning] approaches should . . . accommodate the diverse skills, abilities, and prior knowledge of young adolescents, cultivate multiple intelligences . . . draw upon students' individual learning styles [and utilise digital tools] . . . When learning experiences capitalize on students' cultural, experiential, and personal backgrounds, new concepts are built on knowledge students already possess. (National Middle School Association, 2010)

Australian governments commit to working with all school sectors to ensure that schools provide programs that are responsive to students' developmental and learning needs in the middle years, and which are challenging, engaging and rewarding. (Ministerial Council on Education, Employment, Training and Youth Affairs, 2008, p. 12)

Braggett (1997, p. 26) noted that 'when we recognise the diversity of the learners in our classrooms and provide for their diverse learning needs in our planning and instruction, we differentiate the curriculum'.

 Consider the students in a middle years classroom. Make a list of the personal and contextual differences that would influence their learning needs. Describe how difficult it is to cater for such a diverse group of students.

Imbeau, 2010). This approach to teaching involves teachers making modifications to the curriculum, teaching structures and their teaching practices, either as individual modifications or in combination, to ensure that the teaching and learning experience is responsive, relevant, promotes student success and assists students in becoming self-regulated learners (van Kraayenoord & Paris, 1997).

Definitions and misconceptions

Kluth and Danaher (2010) noted that there can be confusion around what differentiation is and is not. The lists below provide definitions of, and the most common misunderstandings about, differentiation.

- Differentiated instruction is:
  - an approach that supports the learning of all students
  - student centred
  - a specific way to think about and plan instruction
  - curriculum, pedagogy and assessment that are carefully planned and aligned to meet the needs of all students
  - a range of approaches provided to content, process and product
  - a dynamic blend of whole-class, small-group and individual instruction
  - engagement of all students in respectful and challenging tasks.
- Differentiated instruction is not:
  - a new teaching strategy or fad
  - an approach designed to help students with disabilities
  - individual instruction
  - tinkering with parts of a lesson for just one or a few students
  - more work for good students and less and/or different work for struggling students
  - lowered expectations for struggling students
  - just changing the way students' assessment is marked.

Differentiating

Differentiation is a key element in the curriculum, pedagogy and assessment triad within the classroom environment. Teachers can differentiate in:

- content—what students should know
- process—what students should be able to do
- products—how students demonstrate their learning
- learning environment—both the physical and affective domains of a classroom.

An adjustment to any of these elements is based on student needs (Tomlinson, 2005; Tomlinson & Imbeau, 2010). As well as these classroom elements, there are three student characteristics that can affect how teachers design their curriculum: each individual student's readiness, interest and learning profile (Tomlinson & Imbeau, 2010).

A student's readiness is their preparedness to learn. This readiness consists of each student's individual innate ability, which can be positively or negatively influenced by many factors, including their life experience, language skills and socio-economic status. For example, Voltz and Fore (2006) noted that the high poverty rates that exist in urban school districts have increased the readiness gap among children.

A student's interest is unique to each individual and dynamic and can include particular topics, subjects that spark their curiosity and ways of learning that they enjoy, find interesting and motivating and are prepared to invest time and energy in. Understanding students' interests and linking those interests to the curriculum is how teachers implement connective instruction, which creates the links necessary between the curriculum and the students' world to make their learning more meaningful, which is highly motivating for students (Cooper, 2014).

A student's learning profile is developed over time and comprises the individual characteristics of each student concerning how they learn best. Thus, a teacher's overarching aims are to increase the academic and social success of all students and to decrease student disengagement, alienation and marginalisation. The challenge for teachers is to understand and attempt to respond to the diverse range of interests and abilities within a classroom to ensure opportunities are provided for all students that enable them to reach their potential.

Meeting students' needs

Many teachers are familiar with the concept of scaffolding a student's learning. The term scaffolding as used by Wood, Bruner & Ross (1976) is linked with the socio-cultural theory of learning proposed by Vygotsky (1978). Vygotsky promoted the concept of the zone of proximal development to explain the difference between what a learner can do without help and what they can do with the help of a more capable adult or peer. The term scaffold is borrowed from the field of construction and, as such, creates a picture of temporary structures used to support a building, renovation or restoration of another structure. Within education, scaffolding refers to the *temporary* support given to learners to enable them to successfully complete a task that they might not otherwise be able to do on their own. Scaffolding can take a variety of forms, such as accommodations or differences in the initial task being set, prompting, questioning, modelling and other forms of direction. When a student encounters an obstacle in their learning process, a teacher can provide support to scaffold the student through that obstacle. This input will be differentiated based on the individual student's needs, skills and knowledge, as well as the task being undertaken. Also, students may need more frequent scaffolded support at the beginning of a project and less towards the end. Hence, differentiation supports the scaffolding process, and scaffolding supports differentiated instruction.

There is a growing body of evidence that suggests differentiated instruction improves students' outcomes (Reis et al., 2008; Rock et al., 2008; Van Tassel-Baska et al., 2002). In a focused study of 58 Year 7 students placed in an extended curriculum program that combined curriculum differentiation with acceleration and ability grouping, students self-reported being more intrinsically motivated than their peers in mixed-ability classes, with their resulting motivational orientations being associated with positive outcomes (Kronborg & Plunkett, 2008). However, while educators acknowledge that their classroom populations are becoming increasingly diverse, studies have shown that few teachers implement differentiated instruction in their classrooms (Tomlinson et al., 1997).

Key to being able to differentiate are knowing each student's learning needs and ensuring each student is appropriately challenged. In short, differentiation is a teacher's response to learners' needs guided by general principles at the instructional level. When teachers design and deliver curricula in a way that matches teaching and learning experiences with the students' needs and readiness, they are able to support students' positive outcomes in the classroom. Therefore, differentiation is a critical part of the lesson-planning process.

For middle years learners there are polarised motivational states that disrupt learning—namely, anxiety and boredom. Anxiety occurs when teachers expect too much (the task is too difficult), and boredom occurs when the teacher expects too little (the task is too simple) (Willms & Friesen, 2012). Thus, the diversity of the readiness, interests and learning profiles of students needs to be reflected in the diversity of the educational response, through differentiated instruction.

Traditional classroom instruction has seen teachers teaching to the middle, which has resulted in a large number of students' educational needs not being met. However, even when attempting to differentiate, teachers may become discouraged or disillusioned if they have found their efforts to be ineffective. In many cases, teachers have been ill prepared and untrained in how to differentiate (Schumm & Vaughn, 1995). In a focused study of 99 teachers concerning the facilitators of, and barriers to, implementing differentiated instruction in their classrooms, Rodriguez (2012) identified a number of reasons for a lack of differentiation, which included the teacher being overwhelmed by the range of diversity in the classroom; the scarcity of time to plan adequately, of support from other staff and school leadership and of available resources to implement a range of activities; insufficient training and knowledge about pedagogical practices; and parents' expectations. However, despite the truism that 'teaching is hard, and teaching well is fiercely so' (Tomlinson, 2000, p. 6), teachers have a responsibility to embrace the diversity within their classrooms and to cultivate learning environments in which all students can succeed. Such learning environments are those in which the teacher differentiates instruction.

Differentiation in practice

To differentiate, teachers must consider the knowledge, interests and abilities of the students together with the key or necessary knowledge and skills of the content area, the most effective way to organise the students for learning (i.e., different types of groupings) and how the content will be assessed (K.M. Anderson, 2007; Rock et al., 2008). Universal Design for Learning, Reach Every Student through Differentiated Instruction (known as REACH) and Response to Intervention are examples of curriculum models of differentiation. These models support the aim for students not just to gain a specific knowledge or set of skills but to become *learners*. The overarching goal for such learners is to develop three general learning characteristics—namely, to be goal oriented, to be knowledgeable and to be self-directed and motivated to learn more: in effect, to be lifelong learners. Designing and delivering curricula through such models enables teachers to remove many of the would-be barriers to learning that students must overcome. The models use differentiation as the lens that is looked through when using any materials, programs or instructional strategies. Thus, differentiation is the key element in the curriculum, pedagogy and assessment triad within the classroom environment in which high-quality curricula and materials are selected. It is not so much what is used but how it is used to meet the varying readiness, interests and learning profiles of students that creates an effective learning environment. The key questions to be asked are 'What do I want all students to know and be able to do?' and 'How am I going to meet this learning goal for all students in my class?'

Differentiating content

Differentiating content does not mean that the teacher is varying the objectives or lowering the standards or expectations of student achievement. This has been shown to be counterproductive for struggling students and results in the knowledge gap between the more capable students and the weaker students widening (Balfanz, 2009). Content differentiation can be achieved through tiered instruction, which requires varying either what is taught (the content) or how students are able to access the content (the process) (K.M. Anderson, 2007). Tiered instruction is one way to teach a concept or piece of content and meet the different learning needs within a class. There are five main steps when tiering instruction:

1. Select the content or a concept from the curriculum that students should know or understand. At this point, the teacher should make decisions around

how to tier for the students in their class—i.e., readiness, interest or learning profile.
2. Assess students' readiness, interest or learning profile.
3. Create an at-level activity that is focused on the content or concept.
4. Adjust the activity to provide different levels of difficulty—i.e., through process, product, resources or outcome.
5. Match students to an appropriate tiered activity.

Through tiered instruction each student can be appropriately challenged, as the focus is on the content or concept and not on the learning differences. In tiered instruction, pre-assessment is used to correctly match students with an appropriate activity. Post-testing is then used to ensure students have achieved the required standard.

When differentiating the content through tiered activities, it is important to note that the actual content is not changed or modified but is represented in multiple ways. Changing or modifying the content would be considered only when there is a large gap in one student's readiness compared to the readiness of the majority of the class (e.g., a student with disabilities).

Differentiating process
When differentiating the process, a range of strategies can be used. Tomlinson (2000) identified eight points of differentiation that can be applied to a range of learning tasks, which involve moving from:

1. simple to complex
2. concrete to abstract thinking
3. straightforward to transformational
4. a single facet or few facets to multiple facets
5. small increments to larger increments
6. very structured to open ended
7. dependent to independent
8. slow to rapid.

The key is to design tasks that have multiple entry points along the process continuum to ensure the content is accessible to all students and that all students are appropriately challenged.

Provocation 5.2 Tiered activity

The process for creating a tiered activity is illustrated below, using for an example a class learning about contour lines in geography:

- Class context:
  - Year 8, Term 2, 27 students
  - high school, rural community, hub of the region
  - range of socio-economic statuses, from low to high
  - mix of abilities, including two students who require additional support, one student who has English as a second language and three students who consistently produce A-standard work.
- Learning intent:
  - learning to calculate scale, interpret contour maps and connect information on contour maps to the real world.
- Success criteria:
  - identifying key information on a contour map
  - using a contour map to visualise a landform
  - creating a physical representation of a landform using scale and a contour map
  - moving from abstract concepts to concrete concepts.
- Possible barriers to learning:
  - boredom and frustration from top three students, mirrored by other students who don't understand
  - students have focused on this for two lessons already.
- Solutions to barriers to learning:
  - three-tiered activity using contour maps and play dough
  - all students attempt any level they wish
  - if students meet the success criteria for one level, encouraged to attempt the next level.
- Tiered teaching plan:
  - Level 1: students provided with a simple contour map (e.g., a round hill) and need to make an approximate model of the landform using play dough and teacher support for building strategies
  - Level 2: students provided with a contour map of a well-known landform (e.g., Uluru) and asked to make a scale model using play dough with limited teacher support

— Level 3: students provided with a contour map of a region with a variety of landforms and asked to make a scale model of the region using play dough and label it.

 Review the process for creating a tiered activity. Then, using the example, create a different tiered activity for the class. The following questions can be used as guides:
- What is the context of the school or class?
- What do I need to modify to make this lesson relevant and accessible for students?
- What do I need to do to maintain a safe and supportive classroom environment?
- What strategies can I use to ensure that students are developing their skills to relate effectively to me and the other students in the class?
- What do I know about middle years learners and their need for relevant, engaging, challenging, integrated and hands-on curricula?
- How do I put all this together with what I know of quality effective classroom pedagogy and practice?

Differentiating products

Tomlinson (1999, p. 10) argued that assessment is 'today's means of understanding how to modify tomorrow's instruction' and the lynchpin of differentiated instruction. To determine the effect of instruction, teachers use:

- assessment *for* learning—formative and diagnostic assessments
- assessment *of* learning—tasks or activities used to measure, record and report on the level of achievement
- assessment *as* learning—tasks or activities that allow students to use assessment to further their own learning.

To differentiate effectively, teachers must use multiple methods of pretesting as well as formative and summative assessment before, during and after instruction. Pretesting, or pre-assessment, is used as a diagnostic tool to gauge students' levels of readiness for or interest in the content and skills. Ongoing informal and formal assessments ensure that the teacher is constantly aware of students' progress and when and how to adjust instructional strategies to support or extend students' learning (McTighe & O'Connor, 2005).

Differentiating learning environment

Changes can be made to the learning environment to support differentiation. One strategy is to use different student groupings. However, a range of different group configurations should be used, as the overuse of any one grouping pattern can have negative consequences for some students. Teachers can differentiate through flexible grouping arrangements in which students are given opportunities to work with a variety of peers through whole-group activities or a number of different configurations of small groups. If teachers do not use flexible grouping within their classroom, it is almost impossible to differentiate instruction for all learners. Radencish and McKay (1995) also argued that the grouping arrangements, including group membership, within a classroom needed to change frequently. The key to differentiating through student grouping is to be flexible. Students are placed or choose to work in different groups depending on the activity.

Prior to instruction, the teacher needs to match the appropriate grouping strategy to the instructional objectives and students' needs. For example, a whole-class group would be appropriate for sharing common information and instructions with all students, and small, teacher-facilitated groups would be suitable when there is a need to focus on specific skills or content for particular students. Other grouping configurations range from independent learning centres and pairs to small same-ability, mixed-ability or interest groups. All different groupings have value, but for their value to be realised they must be linked to the goals of the instruction and to students' needs. Groups should be fluid in both composition and membership. It should be noted that ability groupings without differentiation have been shown to have little or no influence on student outcomes (Tieso, 2005).

Effective instructional practices that support differentiation

From a meta-analysis of over 900 studies that examined effective curricula and instructional practices for diverse student populations, Kline (1995) extracted a list of thirteen instructional strategies:

1. cooperative and collaborative activities
2. real-life or life-like (reality) based learning
3. inclusion of thematic, interdisciplinary or integrated curricula that integrate knowledge and skills across subject areas

4. a constructivist approach that includes active learning
5. awareness of each student's literacy levels
6. modelling appropriate cognitive and affective behaviours
7. promotion of critical- and creative-thinking skills
8. a multicultural approach to teaching that recognises and celebrates difference within the classroom
9. alternative assessment opportunities
10. strong home–school partnerships
11. accelerated learning techniques
12. questioning techniques that promote exploration and elaboration
13. multifaceted teaching that considers brain-compatible instruction.

All students benefit from a variety of instructional methods, and these evidence-based strategies provide a foundation framework for differentiating instruction to cater for the diversity within a middle years classroom. It is not surprising that these practices align very closely with the signature practices promoted as best practice for quality teaching and learning in the middle years.

Each student in a middle years classroom is unique, with a wide set of influences from their own innate dispositions to the environmental influences they have experienced to date. Quality teaching is key to supporting their diverse needs and supporting their academic growth.

Provocation 5.3 Differentiating activity

Use a rubric and checklist to develop an activity that is differentiated.

 Select a lesson, activity or project that you have taught or will teach. Look for ways to differentiate it for your class using the questions below as guides:

- What range of learning needs are you likely to address?
- What should students know, understand and be able to do as a result of the lesson?
- What is your starting point lesson? How will you hook the students?
- What are your first, second and third cloned versions of this activity?

The personalised learning paradigm

The shift from individualised to differentiated instruction, both of which are teacher-centred pedagogies, has dominated approaches to catering for diversity in classrooms for more than two decades. More recently, personalised learning has been posited as the next frontier in rethinking classrooms to meet the range of diverse needs of learners in parallel with the changing nature of the education landscape (Garrick, Pendergast & Geelan, 2017). This shift is consistent with the ideas of leading thinkers such as Sir Ken Robinson, who, as long ago as 2006, in his TED talk 'Do schools kill creativity?', contended that the industrial age, factory model of schools that served our education systems well in the twentieth century is no longer relevant. Along with Robinson, there is a growing group of researchers who argue that education systems need to be more learner centred and prepare young people for a post-industrial society (Darling-Hammond, 2002; Fullan, 1999, 2003; Prensky, 2014; Reigeluth & Karnopp, 2013; Schlechty, 2001, 2002). In a review of literature focused on personalised learning, Reigeluth and Karnopp (2013) noted that a learner-centred paradigm would require a number of adjustments in our approach to education that would include changes to:

- the role of the teacher—being more of a guide and facilitator
- the way that curriculum was presented—providing more authentic learning
- assessment—allowing for more competency-based student progress, criterion-referenced tests and authentic assessment
- teachers' perceptions of students—promoting and supporting students as active and self-directed learners, including providing a personal learning plan for every student.

Indeed, Reigeluth and Karnopp (2013) argued for a move away from a standardised education to a personalised education.

Personalised learning aligns well with the middle years philosophy, as it recognises the unique attributes of each individual learner and acknowledges that a one-size-fits-all approach will not meet the needs of all students. Personalised learning is not new. It was an approach to teaching and learning that was formally described by Keller in 1968 and used in higher education psychology courses. Keller (1968) argued that personalised teaching differed from conventional teaching in that it placed the student at the centre of their learning. They were self-directed, the teaching focused on competence, and teacher direction was minimised.

After a decade of implementation, Kulik, Kulik and Cohen (1979) conducted a meta-analysis of 79 programs using personalised instruction. The results of their analysis showed an average increase of 10 percentage points in student outcomes when personalised instruction was used. As its potential to improve student outcomes is realised, personalised learning is gaining momentum as an instructional method in school classrooms. The tenets underpinning personalised instruction and its potential to improve student outcomes suggest closer consideration of a more universal application should be explored. Table 5.1 shows the alignment of the features of personalised learning with the signature features of effective middle schooling.

Table 5.1 Middle school signature features aligned with personalised learning features

Middle school	Personalised learning
The focus is on each student as a unique individual, and teachers support all individuals to reach their full potential as learners.	Each learner is unique and learns in different ways.
Learning is active.	Students are co-designers of the curriculum and learning environment.
Curriculum is relevant, challenging, integrative and exploratory.	Curriculum is relevant, challenging, integrative and exploratory.
Students and teachers hold joint responsibility for their learning.	Students have high-quality teachers who are partners in learning.
Teachers are responsive and reflective, value young adolescents and are prepared to teach them.	Teachers are responsive and reflective, value young adolescents and are prepared to teach them.
Multiple learning and teaching approaches are used that are dynamic and allow students to ask questions, make predictions, design investigations, collect and analyse data, make products and share ideas.	Students design their own learning path; they have a voice and choice about their learning.
Students become increasingly independent and self-directed as learners.	Students self-direct and self-regulate their learning.
Formative and summative assessments are varied and ongoing, and, in particular, assessment *as* learning is used.	A competency-based model is used to demonstrate mastery.
Students have a sense of belonging that is positively correlated to their self-concept as learners.	Students are motivated and engaged in the learning process.

Sources: Anfara et al. (2008); Bray & McClaskey (2013).

In some instances, personalised learning has been confused or used in conjunction with individual instruction. However, there are distinct differences between the two. Individualised learning is teacher centric, and the work to be undertaken is 'paced to the learning needs of different learners', whereas personalised instruction is student centred and 'tailored to the learning preferences, and . . . specific interests of different learners' (Bray & McClaskey, 2013, p. 13). Furthermore, individualised instruction puts all of the responsibility on the teacher to direct and prepare work for each student, placing an overwhelming workload on teachers. In contrast, personalised instruction is the next step for teachers to improve student outcomes as they understand how to cater for the diverse student populations that are found in middle years classes and provide choice and challenge to meet the individual needs of each student, regardless of where the student currently is in their learning. However, differentiation is teacher centric, and although it provides instructionally appropriate learning experiences for students, the next step is for the students to take more control and choice over their own learning through personalised learning.

A cautious approach should be taken to the implementation of personalised learning in a middle years classroom. As with any new approach to teaching and learning, the implementation process takes time. Teachers need to be able to engage in a staged approach to implementation to avoid the boom-to-bust cycle that is often experienced when initial enthusiasm for a new and promising pedagogy fails to deliver immediate results. The inevitable *dip* that can occur after the initiation phase of a reform strategy can be reduced in its severity and duration if certain guidelines that support its implementation are employed (Pendergast et al., 2005). In the case of personalised instruction, a number of recommendations have been provided. In a meta-analysis of learner-centred programs, Reigeluth et al. (2015, p. 2) described four major functions necessary to support learner-centred education and, more specifically, personalised instruction: 'record keeping for student learning, planning for student learning, instruction for student learning, and assessment for and of student learning'. Bray and McClaskey (2013) recommended a staged approach to implementation that aligns with a gradual release model in which the teacher hands more responsibility to the students progressively. They recommended three stages: teacher centred with learner voice and choice, learner centred with teacher and learner as co-designers and learner driven with teacher as partner in learning. The introduction of personalised learning would be a significant paradigm shift for teachers and learners; however, its potential to meet the needs of the diverse student population in middle years classrooms makes it worth further investigation.

Chapter summary

This chapter makes the following key points:

- There is a wide heterogeneity within middle years classrooms due to the differences in the onset and rapidity of the physiological changes linked to puberty as well as other factors, including individual abilities, genders, cultures, linguistics, family structures, socio-economic backgrounds, and racial and religious backgrounds.
- Differentiated instruction is a pedagogical approach that aims to meet the diverse needs of all students and to create a learning environment that facilitates students' access to a meaningful curriculum.
- Teachers can differentiate the content, the process, the product or the learning environment. How a teacher adjusts one or more of these elements of their curriculum, pedagogy, assessment or classroom environment is based on the needs of the student.
- Key to being able to differentiate is to know the students. Differentiation starts with the planning process and considers students' readiness, interests and learning profiles.
- Examples of what differentiation looks like in practice are provided and emphasises that differentiation is not just a set of knowledge and skills that each student is required to gain but is more about students becoming self-directed in their own learning to achieve their own learning goals.
- A range of effective instructional practices that support differentiated instruction have been drawn from the literature and provided to guide classroom practice.
- The personalised learning paradigm is introduced and explained. This approach recognises the unique attributes of each individual learner and places the student at the centre of their learning.

Chapter Six

Transition

DONNA PENDERGAST

Learning intentions

In this chapter we will:
- develop an understanding of the complexities of transitioning from primary to secondary school for young adolescent learners
- discuss the academic decline often experienced by young adolescents during transition
- formulate strategies and practices that can support students through transition in the middle years.

Transition for the young adolescent

Students experience change in schooling constantly, whether they are shifting from school to school, from one sub-school to another within a school, from one year level to the next, from teacher to teacher or from class to class. Each of these shifts requires adjustments by the students involved as they move from the familiar to the unfamiliar, and some changes are more likely to be disruptive to the flow of learning than others. Major changes, including those when students move from one sector of schooling to another, such as from preschool to primary school or from primary to secondary school, are so complex and multidimensional that they are labelled as transitions.

When transition is mentioned in the middle years it typically relates to the shift from a primary school setting to a middle or secondary school setting, and it may also involve many of the other shifts mentioned. The transition may be internal (within the same school environment) or external (moving to a different school). The latter is the more common transition experienced by students in the middle years. Such transition is a time of considerable change and may lead to negative effects on students' engagement and achievement and broadly impact negatively on their wellbeing.

The transition from primary to middle or secondary school is often associated with a drop in academic achievement regardless of the age and year level at which transition takes place. In fact, the very nature of a transition through which students move from being the oldest to being the youngest grade in a school is a major catalyst for these negative effects, coupled with changes in class size and number of teachers, increased expectations of, and desire for, independence, and greater workloads, both in school and in the form of homework. The metaphor 'Big fish, little pond to little fish, big pond' is regarded as accurately representing the experience of students involved in this transition (Marsh, Craven & Debus, 2000), and as it implies, there is a major change in the status of those students, which impacts on their self-esteem. Also, the timing aligns with the vulnerabilities experienced during early adolescence, especially those involving identity formation and peer group acceptance. Therefore, transition in the middle years is an important aspect in the teaching of, and learning considerations for, young adolescents.

Because transition is typically disruptive, it is more likely than not to lead to negative effects, even though not all students experience this and many have neutral outcomes or positive gains. The negative transition effect has been labelled the middle school plunge, and it is estimated that the drop in academic achievement can represent a loss of between 3.5 and 7 months of learning achievement (West & Schwerdt, 2012). The effects are widespread and typical, rather than the exception. The impact on academic achievement is most significant for students who lack literacy and numeracy capacity, especially reading and spelling, and transition challenges are also likely to be magnified for children with disabilities, including those with attention deficit hyperactivity disorder (Langberg et al., 2008).

The effective transitioning of young adolescents to high school underpins a number of the education principles that provide a quality school environment for young adolescents; hence, it is an important topic to explore in the context of middle years learners. Schools working towards developing a distinct identity for these young people as they enter the middle years, through specific spaces, programs, support staff and other strategies, assist in creating an environment that is conducive to minimising negative transition effects. Quality teaching also forms a critical key to transition, as it engages and motivates students to reach their potential and helps to minimise the negative effects of transition.

In general, students moving from primary to high school, regardless of the structure of the environment, are transitioning from a familiar, generally smaller primary school environment, which is student centred, to a secondary school much larger and generally unfamiliar in terms of physical space, curriculum and programs. These larger secondary schools are also generally less student centred and more focused on subject learning. Much of the research around student academic performance indicates that (as noted in Chapter 1) during the early years of secondary school, students make the least progress, the gap between the low- and high-performing students increases, and students are less engaged with education. Furthermore, the key challenges in these middle years are closely linked to the nature of the changes that occur during early adolescence, along with the challenges associated with transition between primary and secondary school. According to the Australian Council for Educational Research (ACER, 2012), transition therefore can be regarded as one of the key challenges in the middle years. Schools can sometimes mistakenly think that an orientation day is the only event or accommodation necessary to help students transition from primary to secondary school. However, orientation is an event, whereas transition is an ongoing process that takes time; indeed, for some students, it can continue long after they enter their new environment.

The transition from primary to junior secondary coincides with physical, social, emotional and cognitive growth and development which occur during the adolescent years. The adolescent brain is undergoing huge reconstruction, and the tendency towards impulsive behaviour, experimentation and risk-taking can be confronting for teachers and parents alike. Difficulties typically encountered by young adolescents during times of transition occur due to swings between extremes. R. Arnold (2000), for example, points to swings of emotions, progressions and regressions in thinking and learning and swings between self-centredness and altruism, dependence and independence, and social behaviour and isolation. There are several difficulties that are typically encountered during transition in the middle years, including:

- lower self-esteem
- fears about new social situations involving older students
- difficulty managing time
- problems coping with increased academic stress

Provocation 6.1 Experiencing transition

Best friends Beth and Caera attended a small primary school in a rural area of South Australia. They both enjoyed primary school and had positive reports across the range of subjects. Their teacher, Miss Thomas, was well loved and respected by the students in the class and was popular with and well connected to the parents and wider members of the community. To help prepare her Year 7 class for transition to the large secondary school, she shared information available to her about the school and prepared student folios for each student to take with them to their new school. Although most students were transitioning to the same secondary school, some were moving to other secondary schools.

There was considerable support and encouragement for the Year 7 students and great anticipation among them. Some students were excited and looking forward to the new school, new teachers, new subjects and new uniforms. Having been the leaders in the primary school, they felt ready to move to this more mature learning environment. Some of the students, however, were a little frightened about what the new school would be like and of being around much older students. They were also worried about changing between subjects and getting times and resources right for each class. They were not familiar with the new school and so were nervous as the last day of primary school passed by.

When they arrived home, Beth and Caera discovered their parents had received an email from the secondary school welcoming them to the community and providing their uniform requirements, book list and class list. While they were still very excited, there was some disappointment when Beth and Caera discovered they were not in the same class together or with anyone they knew well from their school.

 Provide responses with defensible arguments to the following questions:

- What clues does this account contain that transition might not be entirely smooth for Beth and Caera?
- What changes do you suggest might lead to a smoother transition for these students?

- disruption of previous peer relationships
- disruption of familiar routines and procedures.

These stressors may result in anxiety and frustration and may lead to negative or disruptive behaviours. Such behaviours can be problematic and can make the transitioning process even more difficult for the young person. Many of these problems have been linked to lower levels of academic achievement in school students.

While there is considerable research into the factors that may influence a successful transition for middle years students (Hopwood, Hay & Dyment, 2016), in this chapter we will consider, as a convenient way of bringing together the range of themes, the three-factor model proposed by researchers Evangelou et al. (2008):

1. social adjustment—the degree to which students adjust to their new social environment
2. institutional adjustment—the degree to which students adjust to their new physical surroundings and new patterns of behaviour
3. curriculum interest and continuity—the degree to which students are engaged by the curriculum and perceive a continuity in curriculum, pedagogy and assessment between primary and junior secondary.

Table 6.1 provides a summary of the types of activities that foster each of these forms of transition adjustment.

Table 6.1 Aspects of transition adjustment to be fostered in the middle years

Adjustments	Aspects	Example activities
Social	Social and personal skills, so students can expand their friendship networks, self-esteem and confidence	A pastoral care program that focuses on the development of social and personal skills Student use of the growth mindset (Dweck, 2010) to set social and personal development goals Student training in becoming reflective learners and periodic establishment of new learning goals Mixing of older and younger junior secondary students—e.g., peer mentoring programs between Year 9 and 7 students, student representative councils and Year 7 students promoting junior secondary to Year 6 at their alma mater
Institutional	Student independence in managing time, equipment, commitments and assignments	Well-structured pastoral care programs Scaffolded support where required and removal of supports as students mature

Adjustments	Aspects	Example activities
Institutional *continued*	Close links and coordination with primary schools	Induction programs Taster days Teacher exchanges Data sharing
Curriculum interest and continuity	Student understanding of the expectations of them in junior secondary with regard to level and style of work and level of effort required	Talks in assembly Parent-focused articles in newsletters outlining expectations Discussion of expectations in pastoral care classes
	Staff understanding of the differences between primary and junior secondary practices and the implications for their own practice	Staff evaluation of current thinking of junior secondary student capabilities, seeking information from primary schools Professional development around the growth mindset (Dweck, 2010)
	Teacher refining of programs to further engage students in deep learning	Periodic review of unit and lesson plans to ensure curriculum goals are met
	Teacher understanding and ability to apply different learning approaches that enhance student learning	Teacher reflection on their pedagogical strengths and weaknesses Use of learning approaches that cater for the diversity of learners Creation of personalised professional development programs
	Emphasis on teaching the tools of learning to enhance student independent thinking and learning	Student training in note-taking, analysing, report-writing, revising, studying Reminders given to students of the importance of sleep

Source: Adapted from Evangelou et al. (2008).

In recent studies regarding transitions to secondary school, in particular in the Western Australian Catholic Education sector (Coffey, Berlach & O'Neill, 2013), insight was gained regarding the main concerns for young adolescents before they move into high school. In 2009, the Catholic Education Office in Western Australia moved Year 7 students from its more than 100 primary schools to secondary schools. This was the first time in the state's history that a major education system had embarked on such an undertaking. Aligned with this shift, six large secondary schools of varying contexts were involved in a study which used a mixed-methods approach, including surveys and focus group interviews. Eighty-six teachers, 506 students from Year 7 and 344 parents participated. They were asked about their perceptions and experiences of commencing secondary school, their overall perceptions of the transition process, and their teaching and learning programs. With respect to the main concerns of students prior to transitioning, the following issues were most reported by students:

- making new friends
- getting lost
- arriving late to class
- having too much homework
- adapting to different teachers and their expectations
- remembering their timetable
- being bullied.

These concerns reflect the social and institutional adjustments and to a lesser degree curriculum interest and continuity. The parents of these students had concerns mostly in the domain of social and institutional adjustments, about their children being influenced by older students and issues around rites of passage. Following the shift, Year 7 teachers reported that students settled well into the junior secondary school setting and appeared ready to commence secondary school; however, they felt that being organised was the biggest hurdle for these younger students. Importantly, Coffey, Berlach and O'Neill (2013, p. 12) noted from their unique and extensive study that 'what has emerged from this research is that many of the issues encountered by students and parents are those that, in the past, had been faced by Year 8 students and their parents. The issues discussed in this paper are, thus, not unique to Year 7 students. Rather, they relate to the transition of any cohort of students from a primary to a secondary school environment.' The study highlighted the following factors related to transition that need to be considered in order to reduce the middle years plunge:

- Inattention to little things, such as locker and timetable protocols, causes the greatest anxiety.
- Using primary-trained teachers in Year 7 may add a dimension of familiarity and, thereby, make the transition smoother for students.

- Providing a grace period in the early weeks helps students develop greater confidence and settle more quickly.
- Placing children in classes with others they already know helps to reduce the anxiety associated with being new.
- Affirming expectations early (e.g., unacceptability of foul language) has the potential of strengthening appropriate behaviour at a later date.
- It should be realised that, regardless of the feeder school, student ability will differ markedly not just because of general individual differences but because of current curriculum interpretations.
- Housing the Year 7 students in a separate block provides them with a territorial home.
- Streaming by ability for Year 7 students may be appropriate, even if the rest of the school is not streamed (Coffey, Berlach & O'Neill, 2013, p. 13).

The shift of Year 7 permanently into high schools in Queensland in 2015 and the introduction of junior secondary for Years 7–9 also specifically identified transition as a key factor to be mindful of as part of that major reform (Department of Education, Training and Employment, 2014a). The introduction of this new junior secondary phase of education was based on the six Junior Secondary Guiding Principles developed by ACER (2012), with transition challenges being part of the underpinning rationale for these principles. The need to focus on transition emerged as one of four key insights from a review that took the form of 60 hours of interviews with principals, teachers, students and parents in twenty pilot schools selected ahead of the state-wide move. The findings confirmed that successful transition was a process that involved a series of events over an extended period beginning months ahead of the new school year and continuing months into each school year.

This was affirmed yet again by Hopwood, Hay and Dyment (2016) in a study of Tasmanian schools that investigated twelve teachers' perceptions of best practices to prepare students for a successful transition to secondary school. Their findings identified three key methods that, taken together, might provide a framework for essential, best practice, these being curriculum continuity and awareness, communications between primary and secondary schools and adequate teacher support. Startlingly, they reported that 60 per cent of primary and 42 per cent of secondary teachers did not do anything to prepare their students for transition. Again, the researchers noted that successful transition is not a point-in-time event but a process occurring over time, and it involves primary and secondary teachers collaborating and communicating together alongside other stakeholders.

Academic decline during transition

Why is transition such an issue? One of the major concerns about transition challenges is that students may experience an academic decline. ACER (2012) noted that the following factors contribute to transition challenges for middle years students:

- onset of adolescence
- student perceptions of secondary school
- social adjustment
- teacher perceptions of transition
- socio-economic status
- cultural factors
- family support
- links and communication between schools
- curriculum and pedagogy
- relevance.

From these factors and from an analysis of the research around transition, nine key factors have been identified that may lead to academic decline during transition. At the centre of each of these is the key to transition: building effective relationships. Fundamental to the effective implementation of transition are relationships between teachers in primary and secondary schools, between teachers and transitioning students and between parents and teachers, to name a few. Table 6.2, developed for school leaders to help them better understand transition and its possible effects, provides a description of the factors contributing to academic decline and some examples of approaches to reduce the effects of these factors (Pendergast et al., 2014a). It is evident from these examples that relationships are by far the most important facets of effective transition.

Table 6.2 Factors causing academic decline during transition

Factors	Description	Approaches to reduce factor effects
Onset of adolescence	This is the most significant factor. Developmental effects include increased cognitive capability, heightened importance of friendships, search for independence and autonomy, and decline in academic self-concept and interest in school.	Students need to develop strong feelings of identification with their school environment or they will withdraw from school; increased absences lead to decreased academic achievement.

Factors	Description	Approaches to reduce factor effects
Student perceptions of secondary school	Students with positive perceptions of transition are more likely to have positive academic outcomes.	Students need to develop realistic perceptions of the school they are entering. Early visits and familiarising students ahead of time are effective strategies. Locating students in a separate building is advantageous, as navigating a large campus is easier from a secure home base. This place also contributes to increased feelings of safety and an identity for the year level.
Social adjustment	Students are searching for social acceptance and belonging, while the secondary setting disrupts social relationships and friendship groups, often fragmenting them over several schools. Relationships with care teachers are lost, and teacher–student relationships in general decline in secondary school. Students may experience anxiety and loneliness.	Students should have a care teacher and a care or pastoral class where they connect on a frequent basis, especially in the early stages of transition. Where possible students who are known to each other should be located together to assist in ameliorating the negative effects of social isolation. Peer support and pastoral care programs, especially with older students, are highly effective.
Teacher perceptions of transition	Students who feel supported by their teachers are more likely to have success in their academic achievement.	Individual teacher support is crucial, in the formal centralised methods such as form teachers and also attitudinally to assist in scaffolding students into a secondary learning environment. It is important that teachers acknowledge there are transition challenges for most students and to actively look for signs of transition challenges.
Links and communication between primary and secondary schools	Sharing information about the nature of the move is an important factor in helping to reduce levels of anxiety. So too is sharing student data and information so that teachers are able to immediately attend to the needs of individual students, rather than waiting for, typically, up to the end of the first term to get to know their students.	Primary teachers can help prepare students for junior secondary, and high school teachers can support the transition process with their new Year 7 students, through more discussion between primary and secondary teachers.

(continues)

Table 6.2 *continued*

Factors	Description	Approaches to reduce factor effects
Socio-economic status, cultural factors and family support	Students of low socio-economic status or different cultural backgrounds are most at risk of academic failure during the transition phase. Effective and supportive parents who are knowledgeable about education lead to better student adjustment.	Familiarising students, along with their parents, with the high school setting and providing clear details so that expectations can be shared are key strategies. Employing specific familiarisation events for defined cohorts of students is beneficial, particularly when these events appear to strongly exemplify the culture of the school.
Curriculum and pedagogy	A shift from child-centred, activity-based or experiential classrooms to a didactic approach informed by a different pedagogical ideology leads to a discontinuity of curriculum content and a failure to build on knowledge established in primary years. A 'fresh start' ignores years of effort and contribution in the primary setting.	Approaches to curriculum and pedagogy should build from where the students are and the approaches to learning they have experienced and developed confidence in, and incorporate new methods over time. This alignment of practices between primary and secondary schools takes time, as the two sectors need to share, plan and implement approaches.
Responsibility	One of the most important developmental tasks for adolescents is to learn how to take responsibility for decisions, actions and consequences. In terms of personal responsibility, research suggests that increased anxiety and confusion and decreased motivation are direct responses to the stripping of responsibilities from incoming students.	It is beneficial to provide students with responsibilities aligned with their personal learning and relevant to their class and year level. Leadership opportunities should exist at all year levels, including those engaged in transition.
Resilience	The 'everyone is a winner' approach in schools does not support resilience. Student resilience levels decline from Year 5 to Year 9, so opportunities to build resilience are crucial.	Young adolescents need well-scaffolded academic and non-academic tasks to build self-esteem and self-efficacy. Promoting goal-setting and open communication, and recognising individual learning styles and learning differences, are all ways to support students to develop resilience.

Provocation 6.2 School transition plans: an example

Midlands High School, a fictional site, has established a transition plan designed to minimise the middle school plunge experienced by some students during their transition from primary to secondary school. It is constructed in collaboration with five primary feeder schools, and a cluster model is implemented around three areas of action: institutional strategies involving teachers, strategies implemented with students prior to commencing secondary school and actions continuing after the students have begun Year 7. The school is keenly involved in digital information sharing, and so the school website is regularly updated to include information for past and future students and their families. Daily messages posted on Facebook and Twitter and reminders sent by SMS keep the school actively communicating with relevant stakeholders in the transition process. The school's key actions are described below.

Prior to transition: institutional strategies focusing on teacher involvement

Formal links are established with all members of the cluster—that is, the five primary feeder schools and the secondary school. This is characterised by:

- Key personnel meeting at least twice per term during the final year of primary school. Topics for each meeting are designed to engage key personnel from feeder schools and the high school and include improving literacy, enhancing student wellbeing and developing organisational skills in students.
- Establishing and consistently using shared terminology with a view to improving personnel and student familiarity.
- Conducting ongoing meetings including personnel information and enrolment events at each of the feeder schools to establish early the numbers of students and return of enrolment forms.
- Year 6 teachers providing advice in Term 4 about class groupings and making recommendations to maximise student engagement and minimise conflict and disruptions. This includes sharing of academic data, recommendations on ability grouping and considerations for allocating teacher aide time.
- Conducting an information-sharing event for cluster primary school Year 6 teachers and secondary Year 7 teachers. Based on now-established class groups and using the model of speed dating, Year 6 teachers rotate with future teachers of each student, including their core Year 7 teachers, with the purpose of sharing

information about students to ensure student folios and other key information are shared with Year 7 teachers.

Prior to transition: strategies with students

Enrolment information nights are conducted in Terms 2 and 3, first at each of the feeder primary schools and then at the secondary school. The latter includes tours of the school. Information about the events is promoted widely, including primary school newsletters, visits by secondary school personnel to primary schools, website information, reminders via SMS and banners on the fences of primary and secondary schools.

Students commence one-day visits to the secondary school in Term 2 and repeat two to three times until the official transition program starts, in Term 4. On these day visits, students meet current Year 7 students and hear stories of their journey. They engage in activities which take them around the physical facilities of the school and participate in selected class experiences. This is repeated with minor adjustments in each visit so that students about to transition gain a sense of place and space and increase their familiarity with the secondary school.

All Year 6 students from feeder schools attend a transition day at the end of November. During this day they receive their draft timetable, are grouped in their care classes for the day with their care teacher and become familiar with the school layout and some policies.

At point of transition: into Year 7 and beyond

The first week of Year 7 is conducted as a transition and orientation program. Students are based in their care class with their care teacher for the entire first day and then for the first half of each day for the rest of that week. Students participate in get-to-know-you activities in care class, familiarisation with school policies, Amazing Race team-building and finding their way around the school. In the afternoon they commence a small number of classes which are designed to introduce the subjects for the first semester. Where possible the principle is applied that a small number of teachers deliver more than one subject.

After the first week students participate in a purpose-designed wellbeing program which is delivered by their care teacher for two hours each week during Term 1. It focuses on organisational skills, safety and wellbeing and developing leadership skills. Transitioning students participate in sporting and pastoral events fortnightly, and these align with care classes.

Provide responses with defensible arguments to the following questions:

- Reflecting on the experience of Beth and Caera, who were introduced in Provocation 6.1, what differences might you predict for their transition if they had been enrolling at Midlands High School?
- What social, institutional and curriculum interest and continuity adjustments are evident in the Midlands High School transition plan?

Auditing transition strategies

In order to ensure middle years students are provided with a transition plan rather than a simple series of orientation events, it is recommended that schools annually conduct an audit of their transition plans. The list below provides a framework with which schools might conduct an audit of their current strategies and embedded practices (explicit and implicit) that support the transition of young adolescents from primary into high school. This audit tool was developed by Pendergast et al. (2014a) to assist school leaders in the processes related to transition effectiveness. It can be used to identify gaps and then build an action plan to implement strategies that can minimise the effects of academic decline during transition. For each question, transition adjustments should be considered in three areas: social, institutional, and curriculum interest and continuity.

1. Where are we now as a school? What are we doing well?
2. Where do we want to be? How can we improve?
3. How will we get there?
4. How will we know we're there?

Provocation 6.3 Application of the transition audit tool

Effecting transition has the potential to impact significantly on the experiences of middle years students.

 Reflecting on the key messages in this chapter and using the transition audit list, imagine you are employed at Midlands High School. Answer question 1 in the audit list using the information supplied, and then work through the rest of the list questions to build a plan for enhancing the approach to transition at the school.

Chapter summary

This chapter makes the following key points:

- Middle years students moving from primary to high school are transitioning from a familiar, generally smaller primary school environment, which is student centred, to a secondary school much larger and generally unfamiliar in terms of physical space, curriculum and programs, less student centred and more focused on subject learning.
- There is a need to ensure that orientation is not mistaken for transition. Transition is an ongoing process, with some elements extending well after students have moved into a new environment, whereas orientation is short term.
- Transition for middle years students is often associated with declines in academic achievement, regardless of the age and year level at which transition takes place.
- The transition for middle years students occurs at a time of major physical, social, emotional and cognitive growth and development, which makes this a unique phase.
- Schools can implement a range of adjustments to facilitate positive transitions in the middle years.

Part Two

Curriculum practices in the middle years

Chapter Seven

Literacy

GEORGINA BARTON and SHERILYN LENNON

> **Learning intentions**
>
> In this chapter we will:
> - discuss contemporary theories and definitions of literacy and multi-literacies and how they relate to middle years students
> - examine literacy practices of, and for, diverse middle years students
> - present some useful models and ideas for the teaching and learning of reading and writing in the middle years classroom.

Expanding definitions of literacy

Literacy is a highly contested term. 'Becoming literate is not simply about knowledge and skills ... [It] include[s] students managing their own learning to be self-sufficient; working harmoniously with others; being open to ideas, opinions and texts from and about diverse cultures; returning to tasks to improve and enhance their work; and being prepared to question the meanings and assumptions in texts' (Australian Curriculum, Assessment and Reporting Authority [ACARA], 2012). In this chapter we unpack some of the shifts and complexities surrounding this highly contentious and slippery term with a particular focus on literacy's implications for middle years students. We do this by examining the definitional quandaries and theoretical underpinnings associated with the term before moving on to explore what contemporary literate middle years classrooms might look like, sound like and feel like. In doing so, we draw on useful frameworks for reading and writing in the middle years, our own personal experiences as literacy educators and the experiences of others.

In recent years political and mainstream media discourses have been responsible for fuelling polarising debates regarding literacy and literacy standards in Australia. These have worked to portray an educational system in need of saving from imminent decline or left-wing radicals hell-bent on peddling 'ideological claptrap' rather than focusing on the basics of learning to read and write (*The Australian*, 7 January 2015; *The Daily Telegraph*, 20 June 2015). Two distinct camps seem to have emerged: those wanting a return to the basics—a skills-and-drills approach to literacy—and those who wish to reframe literacy as a dynamic and context-specific social practice. In this chapter we put forward a case for adopting a merger of traditional and nascent understandings of literacy as the best way ahead for middle years teachers, students and their classrooms.

As has already been established, the term literacy is a slippery one, shifting with the ways in which we adapt to, and adopt, a range of technologies and communicative devices across diverse contexts and for diverse purposes. Much research over the past few decades acknowledges that, as we move further into the 21st century, our methods of communicating with one another across the globe will continue to intensify and evolve (Barton, 2014; Jewitt, 2008; Mills, 2015). The consumption and creation of new and emerging texts for this future world will require students' literacy practices to be nimble, transferrable and increasingly sophisticated. Globalisation and the advancement of information and communication technologies (ICT) have influenced and created different platforms, processes and social structures for communicating (Jewitt, 2008). Understanding the implications of this for literacy teaching and learning is vital. Students' capacities to navigate both traditional and emerging forms of communication are directly related to their ability to survive and thrive in an increasingly complex and connected world.

We therefore adopt the following definition of literacy, with the caveat that we understand literacy to be both a moving and a contested feast: literacy is 'the flexible and sustainable mastery of a repertoire of practices with texts of traditional and new communications technologies via spoken language, print and multimedia, and the ability to use these practices in various social contexts' (Anstey, 2002, p. 15).

The idea of reframing literacy as a complex social practice is relatively new. In the first half of the twentieth century a skills-and-drills approach to literacy (sometimes euphemistically referred to as the three Rs) was sufficient in order to navigate a world that relied largely on oracy and print-based texts. This approach understood literacy learning as a linear progression of oral and written skills involving such things as recitations, spelling, traditional grammar, phonics and reading skills linked to the phonemic awareness and literal understandings of predominantly linguistic texts. However, the post-industrial and highly technologised worlds of the late 20th and early 21st centuries are requiring new ways of thinking about the teaching and learning of literacy, including 'a critical engagement with the popular, community and virtual cultures that students inhabit' (Department of Education, 2000, p. 9). One approach to addressing these new and emerging understandings of literacy has been to reconceptualise literacy as multiliteracies.

Provocation 7.1 New and emerging literacies

Over the past few decades literacy education research has highlighted the increasingly complex notion of 21st-century literacies. These new and emerging literacies, or multiliteracies, if you like, have been influenced by the exponential growth in digital technologies, greater access to communication platforms across the globe and a significant shift in transmobility. For middle years students, this means that the ways in which they communicate and interact have changed. These changes have impacted on their literacy practices.

 Provide responses with defensible arguments to the following questions:

- What do you think are the implications of new and emerging literacies—including understandings of the term literacy—for teaching and learning in the middle years?
- How will or do your teaching practices reflect these changes?
- What tools and resources will you need to draw on to bridge outside-school literacies with inside-school practices?

The concept of multiliteracies

Multiliteracies is a term devised by Cope and Kalantzis in the year 2000 that acknowledges the impact of different social and cultural contexts on a diverse range of text types, including print, non-print and hybrid forms. Cope and Kalantzis's work in this area focuses on the various literate practices required to read and produce a range of texts for a diversity of purposes as well as incorporating a refined pedagogical approach to the teaching of literacy. A multiliteracies approach to learning and teaching acknowledges that text consumers and producers need to be proficient across a diversity of design elements that extend beyond traditional notions of literacy as language only. When literacy practices are positioned as social practices, rather than as a set of skills to be learned, students are required to understand both the *how* and the *why* of the choices readers and authors make when composing and comprehending diverse text types. Language modes such as aural, gestural, spatial and visual need to be considered alongside the written word. Understanding when and how to interpret, construct and merge these diverse language modes is vital if students are to become effective communicators in a rapidly transitioning and highly technologised world (Department of Education, 2000; Luke, 2002). Evidence of these new and emerging multimodal texts can be observed in the recent unprecedented rise of social media sites such as Facebook, Instagram, Snapchat and Pinterest (Barton, 2014). For middle years students these platforms provide real-time access to information, friends, family and the social world. They also provide alternative platforms for middle years students to constitute and perform their literacy identities.

Provocation 7.2 Diverse literacy needs and practices

Students come into our classrooms from diverse backgrounds with diverse literacy knowledge and practices. When Peter Freebody (2016, p. 2), co-author of the Australian Curriculum: English, visited classrooms across the country he noted that 'the differences, the cultural and language differences . . . across the whole of this nation are just staggering compared to most other countries'.

 Knowing this, how do we go about engaging middle years students while supporting and extending their diverse literacy needs and practices?

Literacy practices for diverse middle years students

Viewing literacy as a social practice emphasises the reciprocity of texts in mediating individuals' literacy practices, just as texts are being mediated by the social practices of their users (Moje et al., 2009). A case in point is the recent rise of fanfiction websites—online sites extremely popular with teenage authors where readers of popular fiction can extend and transform original literary works using the genre, characters and settings of the original texts (Magnifico, Lammers & Curwood, 2015). These websites, and the practices they encourage, showcase the relational nature of literacy. Here, being literate is entangled with professional and novice fiction writers' and readers' identities; traditional, multimodal and hybrid texts; and time, digital interfaces and shifting contexts.

Researchers emphasise the importance of acknowledging middle years students' prior knowledge and experiences when teaching them, and how students come to understand their literacy identities emphasises the importance of acknowledging their prior knowledge and experiences throughout the learning process (Moje, 2002; Moje et al., 2004; Moll et al., 1992). This research posits that all students enter the classroom with diverse literacy skills and deep knowledge about personal areas of interest. Commonly referred to as 'funds of knowledge', these previously developed skills and interests can be used by teachers to focus on students' strengths rather than constructing students' literacy abilities using a deficit discourse (Moll et al., 1992). Students' personal literacies, or out-of-school literacies, play an important role in preconfiguring and shaping their future literacy practices and learning. They are particularly useful points of reference for teachers when students are being encouraged to read, discuss, plan and write in new ways, for new purposes and with unfamiliar content. Teachers who fail to acknowledge or draw on students' already constituted literacy practices and their associated funds of knowledge might, unwittingly, be complicit in constructing or perpetuating students' understandings of their literacy identities as poor readers or failing students.

In some contexts, students may be highly literate. In other contexts—where the texts, language modes and required social practices are less familiar—they may struggle. When positioning literacy as a social practice, the fluidity and plurality of students' literacy practices and identities are foregrounded, and the concept of becoming literate as a lock-step linear progression towards obtaining a set of preconfigured and predetermined skills is backgrounded. This means a one-size-fits-all, skills-and-drills approach to improving literacy outcomes for middle years students is no longer sufficient. At worst, if overly emphasised, it can lead to the devaluing of some students' literacy practices and identities while reifying those of others.

In resisting a purely skills-based definition of literacy, we acknowledge the need to reframe literacy as a social practice. Such thinking recognises the necessity of teaching and learning particular literacy skills while also appreciating the primacy of diverse literacy practices and contexts. Students' capacity to select the appropriate literacy practices from a repertoire of social and skills-based practices is key to their ability to communicate with others and make sense of the world.

Provocation 7.3 Catering for diversity

It is important for middle years teachers to understand that students have diverse learning needs and different funds of knowledge on which to draw.

 Provide responses with defensible arguments to the following questions:

- When developing and planning for literacy learning and teaching how do, or how can, you consider and include the prior knowledge of your students?
- Which literacy practices and identities do you value? Which do your students value?
- How can you incorporate a range and balance of reading and writing pedagogies in your middle years classrooms?

Strategies for teaching reading and writing in the middle years

When considering appropriate models of literacy learning and teaching for middle years students it is critical that students are placed at the centre. It is also important to ensure that a range and a balance of approaches are considered. As we have made clear, literacy is a complex beast, and one particular strategy or approach will not suit all students or cater for everyone's needs.

Teaching reading to middle years students

Teaching reading to middle years students has to be different from teaching reading to children in the early years. Even though some of the skills needed by less fluent readers are the same, pedagogies need to be appropriate for this developmental phase of learning. The teaching of reading to middle years students can be particularly complex, meaning that there is not one quick-fix approach that can be applied to all. What do work are explicit, targeted and personalised approaches that value students' literacy practices and identities by acknowledging their prior literacy experiences and interests.

While we may not be able to identify the exact mode (e.g., written, spoken or multimodal) from which the following lines emanate, many of us would be able to draw on our prior knowledge to discern a likely context wherein they would appear:

- Dearly beloved, we are gathered here today . . .
- Once upon a time, there was a beautiful girl named . . .
- In the late fourteenth century, King Richard had charge of the lands from the English Channel to the Irish Sea . . .
- Unbelievable, yes! But wait! There's more. If you ring right now you will get two Supa Chef Cutters for the price of one . . .

We may even be able to go further and predict, with a high degree of accuracy, some of the content and language features to be found in the rest of the text. How are we able to do this? What cueing systems are we using when we recognise patterns across texts despite having access to only very brief sections of them? One answer to these questions is that we have effective reading resources upon which to draw. For successful readers, these are often implicit and intuitive. We cannot say how we know; we just do! However, for some middle years students who identify as struggling readers, it is important to use—and make explicit—cueing systems and reading resources.

The Four Roles of the Reader

One useful framework for supporting middle years students to read texts is Luke and Freebody's (1999a, 1999b) Four Roles of the Reader. This model acknowledges that readers have four roles, or resources, that they can draw upon separately or together when trying to make sense of a text. These roles, along with questions for scaffolding learners in each of them, are included in Table 7.1.

Teachers using this framework to engage students in reading texts move adeptly between the various roles and their associated questions. The roles are not intended to be hierarchical or sequential. However, they do make explicit for teachers and students the different ways in which a text can be read. Code breakers use the semiotics of aural, linguistic, visual, gestural and spatial texts to begin unlocking texts. The semiotic systems they tap in to include letters, numbers, symbols and static or moving images. Meaning makers understand the literal and inferential meanings of texts. They achieve this by combining code-breaking resources with meaning-making resources, such as prior knowledge of words and syntax and previous social, cultural and reading experiences of and in the world. Text users have broken the text's codes, made meaning of it and are now involved in using the text in a real or realistic context. This may be at home, school, work or play. Text users interact with texts using any combination of spoken, written, visual, spatial and gestural modes. Finally, text analysts have broken the text's codes, made meaning of it, are perhaps

Table 7.1 Sample questions drawing on the Four Roles of the Reader

Code breaker	Meaning maker
How do I crack this text?	How are the ideas in this text sequenced?
What language or languages is this text using?	Do they connect with one another?
How many semiotic systems are operating in this text? What are they?	Is this text linear or non-linear, interactive or non-interactive? How does this affect the way I make meaning?
How do the parts relate singly and in combination? (i.e., letters—phonemes—words)	Is there anything familiar in this text?
	What prior knowledge and experiences might help me make meaning of this text?
	How will my purpose for reading, and the context in which I am reading, influence my meaning making of this text?
	Are there other possible meanings and readings of this text?
Text user	**Text analyst**
What is the purpose of this text? What is my purpose in using it?	What kind of person, with what interests and values, produced this text?
How have the uses of this text shaped its composition?	What are the origins of this text?
What should I do with this text in this context?	What is this text trying to make me think, believe or do?
What might others do with this text?	What might be some alternative or resistant readings of this text?
What are my options or alternatives after reading this text?	Whose values, attitudes and beliefs might be being privileged by this text?
	Whose values, attitudes and beliefs might be being silenced or marginalised by this text?
	Having critically examined this text, what action am I going to take?

Source: Anstey, 2002, pp. 30–6.

interacting with it and are also critically analysing it to understand who might benefit from, and who might be marginalised or silenced by, the way the text is constructed.

While some students perform these reading roles intuitively, others need support and scaffolding when reading increasingly complex and discipline-specific texts. This support can take the form of targeted questions that assist in making the language, meaning, uses and ideologies implicit in the text explicit for the reader (see the list in Table 7.1).

At the risk of oversimplification, Figure 7.1 depicts the thoughts of a reader as they shift between Luke and Freebody's (1999a, 1999b) Four Roles of the Reader to decode, make sense of, use and critically analyse a well-known, everyday text: the Home icon on the computer.

Figure 7.1 The reader in four roles

Provocation 7.4 Using the Four Roles of the Reader to conduct a critical reading of a text

A Year 10 teacher working in an isolated rural community that had a history of racial tension used the Four Roles of the Reader to step her students through a reading of Australia's national anthem. As part of a whole-class discussion, she asked her students if there were any words that they did not understand—for example, girt. Next she asked them in which contexts they had heard, or were likely to hear, the anthem being played—for example, in an Olympic stadium. She followed these questions up by asking the students what they usually thought, did or felt when they heard the anthem—for example, stand, sing along, feel proud. After this brief introductory discussion, the teacher drew a continuum across the board and wrote the statement 'Our national anthem is a fair representation of who we are as Australians' above it. She then asked her students to position themselves along the continuum with regards to whether they agreed, partially agreed or disagreed with the statement. Nearly all the students agreed with the statement. The text below is her description of how the lesson and subsequent lessons evolved from this point:

> After a brief discussion about the intended meaning and uses of the anthem we re-read the text with our Text Analyst lenses on. This allowed us to critique the lyrics and prompted some very interesting discussions. The students identified that Aboriginal people would have been one of the groups marginalised by such lines as 'we are young and free', 'in history's page', 'this Commonwealth of ours', 'we've boundless plains to share' and perhaps even the words 'Advance Australia Fair'. Students were curious to know what Indigenous people might think about it. This encouraged me to show the students an episode of *Redfern Now* where an Indigenous boy wins a scholarship to a prestigious Sydney private school but refuses to sing or stand for the national anthem. Consequently, he faces expulsion for his continued 'defiance'.
>
> After viewing this, a great debate on how Indigenous people feel about the anthem was opened up so I asked our Aboriginal aide at the school if she would come and talk to the kids about how she felt about it all. She ended up filling an exercise book with her life story and sharing it with the students. It was amazing. She was so awesome and the class asked some pretty full-on questions. She shared some personal stories about the racism she and her family have experienced and also talked about the fact that she didn't even know the words of the anthem until ten years ago. They don't sing it at her mission now.

We then finished by doing the continuum activity again and this time every single one of the students disagreed with the original statement. It was one of those moments we sometimes get as teachers where I truly felt we had transformed thinking.

In making use of the Four Roles of the Reader, the teacher used the text analyst role to come up with resistant and alternative readings of the text and, in the process, transform her students' thinking (Luke & Freebody, 1999a, 1999b). By conducting a critical reading of the national anthem with her students she tapped in to one of the Australian Curriculum's cross-curriculum priorities: Aboriginal and Torres Strait Islander histories and culture. She also managed to connect the classroom to local and national issues, capitalise on students' interests and engage them in reading related texts. Her reading pedagogies drew on critical theory and the principles of social justice to encourage students to conduct multiple readings of texts and, in so doing, transform their thinking around an important issue for all Australians.

The text analyst role has its roots in critical theory and transformative pedagogies (A. Freire & Macedo, 2000; P. Freire, 1971; Giroux, 2001, 2003; Giroux & McLaren, 1989). Critical and transformative pedagogies seek to challenge the status quo by promoting teachers as transformative, classrooms as political and students as agentic. The great Brazilian philosopher and literacy educator Paulo Freire claimed that 'when men and women realise themselves as the makers of culture ... they become literate politically speaking' (quoted in A. Freire & Macedo, 2000, p. 7). He encouraged educators to create classrooms as dialogic and democratic spaces where representations of reality and social injustices could be tabled and problematised so that students could rethink and resee their worlds. He argued that, by doing so, educators created classrooms that had the potential to be transformative. Freire claimed that, in reading the word, students could be empowered to 'read the world' (P. Freire & Macedo, 1987). If we were to reflect on the approach used by the teacher in this scenario, at no time did she tell her students how to think or interpret the text. She allowed them to come to their own conclusions through a combination of highly structured questions, engaging pedagogies, human and non-human resources and a reading of the word to read the world. In this way the teacher's approach was skilfully able to embrace all four roles of Luke and Freebody's (1999a, 1999b) reading model.

Reading for students who need extra support

It is commonly accepted that reading at a decoding and comprehending level is accomplished in the early years of learning and that children can read a diversity of text types by the time they begin the middle years of schooling. However, issues relating to reading in the middle years, and in particular decoding and comprehension, are still clearly identified in the research (Freebody, Chan & Barton, 2013; J. Rennie & Ortlieb, 2013). Struggling readers tend to cluster in two main groups: students who identify (or are identified) as finding reading difficult and students who identify (or are identified) as needing support when reading in the content or curriculum areas.

When middle years students have trouble reading it can be for a range of reasons. It is important to identify what is inhibiting students' reading so that they can be supported with appropriate and tailored reading strategies. For early years readers there is a set of skills known as the Big Six of reading instruction (Konza, 2014): comprehension, fluency, oral language, phonemic awareness (including phonics and word recognition), phonological awareness and vocabulary. However, these can also apply to middle years students who have been identified as struggling readers.

Phonological awareness is the ability to mentally manipulate words, syllables and sounds in spoken language (Goldsworthy, 2010). It is an umbrella term, as it involves intonation and stress in words as well as the use of phonemes. Phonemic awareness is the ability to focus on small units of sound that affect meaning (S. Hill, 2012), such as the three phonemes in the word cat: c–a–t. Decoding relates to the alphabetic principle and spelling. If students have failed to understand the concept of the alphabet—that each letter corresponds to a number of sounds and that these sounds can be joined together to create words (including the concept of word derivations—e.g., Latin, French and Greek roots)—then reading can be a difficult and frustrating task for them.

Fluency is the flow of students' reading when reading aloud. It includes phrasing and pausing at punctuation and is enhanced by automaticity in word recognition, particularly with the high-frequency words (S. Hill, 2012). Children who are not fluent in reading often have the additional challenge of not understanding what they have read, because the cognitive system is limited in its capacity to simultaneously decode and extract meaning from words (Silverman et al., 2013).

S. Hill (2012, p. 21) states that 'oral language provides the base and foundation for written language because it is the beginning of using language as a symbol for meaning'. If students struggle with reading and writing in the adolescent years it can be linked to the development of their oral language. If they have limited vocabulary or word banks upon which to draw, their reading proficiency can be impacted. If they have a well-developed vocabulary upon which to draw, they are often more successful readers. Vocabulary and comprehension skills are closely linked. While research has not shown one best way to teach vocabulary, the National Reading Panel (2000) suggests direct and non-direct methods should be used and age and ability should be considered when planning interventions (Woolley, 2011). Oral vocabulary is regarded as being fundamental to reading, academic growth and school success (Blachowicz et al., 2006).

Reading is an active and complex process. When making sense of texts, readers draw on the Big Six, their life experiences, their purposes for reading and the contexts in which they find themselves. Limited life experiences and a failure to build links to prior knowledge are both significant contributors to reading comprehension difficulties.

Teachers can enhance students' abilities to decode and make meaning from texts by strategically using approaches such as previewing, predicting, summarising, inferring, imagining, questioning and monitoring for meaning making. When learned systematically, these comprehension strategies become important skills upon which middle years students can draw as they are exposed to increasingly diverse and challenging text types in their secondary years.

Teaching reading across the curriculum and content areas
Also important to remember is our adopted notion of literacy as a social practice. This means that social and cultural factors, as well as ineffective reading strategies, can impact on students' ability to read successfully. For instance, some boys may present as having literacy issues at school, but further investigations might reveal that this has more to do with cultural and discursive constructions of hegemonic masculinity within the media, sporting clubs or local community than it has to do with these boys' linguistic skills and development (R. Henderson & Lennon, 2014; Keddie & Mills, 2007; Lennon, 2009, 2015). Such understandings draw on socio-critical theories that position students' literacy practices and performances as socially and discursively constructed (Alloway et al., 2004; Dillabough, McLeod & Mills, 2008; Francis, 2008; Keddie & Mills, 2007). When working with middle years students, teachers must recognise the literacy strengths that students bring with them to the classroom as well as the ways in which their literacy identities are being socially and culturally constructed by such things as gender, class, ethnicity, family values, rurality and socio-economic status.

Provocation 7.5 A collaborative, community approach to support middle years readers

A high school situated in a low socio-economic area where many families faced unemployment recognised the need to develop a reading support program. The school found that up to 25 per cent of its students commenced schooling with reading difficulties. The identification of the students needing support was a result of Progressive Achievement Tests in Reading testing, conversations with the feeder primary schools and information from the students' National Assessment Program—Literacy and Numeracy scores. As a consequence, at the beginning of the school year these students were placed in a learning support class where they participated in learning through commercial phonics and comprehension programs. The phonics approach was seen to be appropriate for these middle years students because the students themselves identified it as assisting them to be able to decode and read more fluently, although the students felt the comprehension program was repetitive and uninteresting. However, the students commented positively on the opportunities when they were able to 'teach' and support their peers in leadership roles and were asked about what they could do or already knew.

Later in the year, the school was able to take some risks around the students' literacy learning which resulted in more positive outcomes. For example, the staff realised that focusing purely on curriculum goals was not necessarily the best option for these students. They therefore created an English–literacy bridging program that the students participated in after they had completed the phonics and comprehension interventions. The administration also recognised the need for more assistance once the students re-entered their general curriculum classes. Therefore, they employed a volunteer coordinator who organised more volunteers from the community. The volunteers came and supported the students in their regular classrooms. Taking a collaborative, community approach was beneficial for all involved.

> When I was in primary I couldn't read or spell at all, so when I came here it was just like a big jump saying I can do this now and . . . come to school every day and learn everything and like they helped me.
>
> Student

> It's consolidated in our current school environment. You can see that with the breadth of teachers accessing the resource of volunteers . . . these children are

> getting supported with their reading then they're getting supported in their classroom environment.
>
> Head of department, humanities
>
> All of a sudden, they're kind of like, yeah. They're just starting to beam. So in terms of resilience, they're trying a little bit harder, whereas before they might have given up.
>
> Volunteer

Teaching writing to middle years students

As students move through their school years, texts and assessment expectations begin to match the disciplinary areas of study. Christie and Derewianka (2008) note that the purpose of language also changes across the school years. For example, in early childhood (six to eight years) commonsense knowledge is expressed in everyday language through a grammar matched to generalised categories of experience and simple attitudinal expressions such as simple sentences with lower level vocabulary. Following on from this, late childhood to adolescence (nine to twelve years) deals more with commonsense knowledge reshaped into schooled knowledge as grammatical resources expand, and grammatical metaphor emerges to express knowledge and attitude. Short chapter books and the language used in such texts are examples of this. Mid-adolescence (thirteen to fifteen years) begins to move into school knowledge that is increasingly differentiated into curriculum areas, becoming more *un-commonsensical* as demands on grammatical resources are amplified and attitudinal expression expands, such as in historical and scientific texts. And late adolescence (sixteen to eighteen years and beyond) refers more often to curriculum-specific knowledge characterised by non-congruent grammar expressing abstraction, generalisation, value judgement and opinion (Christie & Derewianka, 2008, cited in Freebody, Chan & Barton, 2013, p. 311). It is important for teachers to understand how this increasing complexity of language in use impacts on middle years students' literacy learning.

A typical day in the life of a middle years student may see them variously reading and writing stories, descriptions, reports, biographies, analyses, reviews, arguments, expositions, explanations, procedural texts and critiques—and this list is by no means exhaustive. Adding to the complexity of their school day is the practical report they are writing in science having a very different schematic structure from the descriptive report they are writing in the same subject. A practical report may contain sections covering the introduction, hypothesis, methods and apparatus, results and conclusions. On the other hand, a descriptive report may have sections concerning species name, classification, appearance, habitat, food, communication and threats. Different text types sequence their information according to highly structured, nuanced and underlying taxonomies. They also draw on specialised and technical vocabulary. Advocates of explicit genre theory believe that student understandings of such taxonomies and language features cannot be left to chance.

Freebody, Chan and Barton (2013) show how languages' and texts' schematic structures become more technical and sophisticated as students progress through school and offer ideas for how teachers might deal with these changes when supporting students' understanding of discipline-specific texts. One suggestion is for teachers to shuttle back and forth between everyday language and the technical language of the subject area when making meaning. This is an important strategy, as students link new learning to their previous experiences or knowledge about particular topics.

Another key strategy for teaching the literacies of curriculum discipline areas is to explicitly deconstruct the salient features of the text types associated with the subjects. For example, in science, students will most likely be expected to write scientific reports, while in history, they might be asked to construct biographical recounts. Teachers need to make explicit the language features of these texts at the schematic, paragraph, sentence and word levels. This approach draws on the tenets of explicit genre theory, as it encourages teachers to support students to think carefully about word and language choices when producing discipline- and genre-specific texts.

Related to this approach is the Context-to-Text Model, through which students explore the context in which texts have been written and understood (Halliday, 1973). As students comprehend and compose texts it is important that they understand the text at a macro and a micro level, working through paragraph, sentence and word levels, as displayed in Figure 7.2.

In relation to a text, Halliday and Hasan (1985) note three areas to consider: the text's field, tenor and mode. The field of a text focuses on its subject-matter. In a narrative text this would include its characters or participants, their experiences and the setting. The tenor of a text is expressed in the relationships created by the text between the author, the reader and the participants in the text. Tenor 'encompasses such matters as how the status, level of expertise, age, ethnic background, and gender of the participants can have an impact on the language used' (Derewianka, 2012, p. 132). The mode of a text concerns the channels of communication used to communicate the content. Modes can be linguistic, visual, aural, gestural and spatial. Field, tenor and mode therefore contribute to the register of the text—or how language, across all modes, has been used to create meaning.

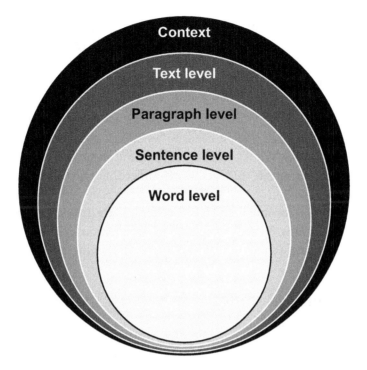

Figure 7.2 The Context-to-Text Model

Moving to the paragraph and sentence levels, it is important for students to have an understanding of such elements as theme and rheme, nominalisation and coherence and cohesion. What might this mean for students in the middle years of schooling? Consider the following two sentences:

- As the afternoon drifted lazily into the night, Ebony's eyelids weighed heavily.
- The breeding season for the whistling tree duck varies depending on a number of climatic and regional factors.

The first sentence is likely to belong to a narrative story. One clue to this is that it has a circumstance of time located in theme position with the subject, or participant, of the sentence and what she is sensing located in rheme position. It is highly likely the next sentence in this story would begin with the word *She*. This pronoun would function as a cohesive bridge between the two sentences by linking the new theme to the previous sentence's rheme—a familiar pattern with sentences belonging to the narrative genre. In the second sentence the subject has been placed in theme position. The fact that the sentence has been written using the simple present tense and the use made in it of specialised language give the reader some clues that the sentence is likely to have been taken from a descriptive science report.

Australian schools appear to have been particularly influenced by aspects of explicit genre theory in their approach to the teaching of writing (J. Arnold, 2016; Ryan & Barton, 2014). While a genre approach does ensure a certain degree of quality control in students' written texts, it needs to be used in considered and purposeful ways (Barton, Arnold & Trimble-Roles, 2015). Some argue that the use of recipes created out of genres causes students' work to become repetitive, superficial and disconnected (Ryan & Barton, 2014). This can lead to busywork, in which students' writing is presented as formulaic and text innovations are discounted. While explicit genre theory has its uses, it needs to be used in conjunction with other approaches. This may mean incorporating more liberal approaches to the teaching of writing.

Chapter summary

This chapter makes the following key points:

- Literacy is an open-textured concept that needs to take into account not only the diverse range of texts we might engage with but also the diversity of literate practices or multiliteracies that exist across socio-cultural contexts.
- It is important to therefore recognise the distinct literate practices related to middle years students.
- If middle years students need to read more effectively then approaches to teaching reading need to be different to when teaching reading to early years learners, as middle years students have distinct learning needs and styles.
- A useful model, the Four Roles of the Reader, is appropriate to utilise for teaching distinct curriculum or content area reading exercises.
- In relation to teaching writing, it is important to consider a number of theories.
- Taking all of the above into consideration, the chapter has shown what today's middle years classrooms might look like, sound like and feel like in terms of literacy learning.

Chapter Eight

Numeracy

SHELLEY DOLE

Learning intentions

In this chapter we will:
- consider definitions of numeracy and analyse a new model of numeracy for 21st-century learners
- interrogate approaches to teaching middle years mathematics for numeracy
- explore authentic and meaningful classroom examples for promoting numeracy in the middle years of schooling that engage and challenge middle years students as corporate and reflective citizens.

Defining numeracy and being numerate

Promoting numeracy is a high priority in the middle years to ensure students are sufficiently prepared for life beyond the compulsory years of schooling. Numeracy is inextricably linked to school mathematics but is a shared responsibility of all teachers, not just those who teach mathematics. In this chapter, definitions of numeracy and a new model of numeracy for 21st-century learners are presented. Approaches to developing numeracy through the teaching of mathematics in the middle years of schooling and issues associated with such practices are discussed. Suggestions and ideas for promoting numeracy in a manner that aligns principles and practices of middle years of schooling philosophy are shared. Provocation 8.1

is presented as a starting point to thinking about the importance of numeracy and how it differs from school mathematics, and to provide a context for the discussion that follows.

The word numeracy is believed to have made its first appearance in the Crowther (1959, p. 269) Report, in which it was presented as the 'mirror image of literacy'. This report, commissioned by the government in the United Kingdom, documented an inquiry into the perceived lack of capacity in young adults upon leaving compulsory schooling to apply their school mathematics learning to real-life situations—for example, being able to calculate change, budget for groceries or manage personal finances. Defining numeracy as a mirror image of literacy causes one to pause to consider a definition of literacy, which at one point was described by the Australian government as the capacity to 'read, write and spell' (Department of Education, Training and Youth Affairs, 2000, p. 7). These limited definitions of numeracy and literacy resulted in widespread discussion and debate aiming to establish definitions that encompassed the richness of what being numerate and being literate actually meant. Early definitions of numeracy in the United Kingdom associated it predominantly with knowledge and application of number: 'Numeracy is now generally understood as the competence in interpreting and using numbers in daily life, within the home, employment and society' (M. Brown, 2005, p. ix). In Australia, a broader and richer definition of numeracy was proposed by the Australian Association of Mathematics Teachers in 1997, acknowledging the importance of being able to apply mathematical concepts and skills from across the discipline as well as having a positive disposition to use mathematics in the real world. It also provided a reason for the importance of numeracy:

To be numerate is to use mathematics effectively to meet the general demands of life at home, in paid work, and for participation in community and civic life.

In school education, numeracy is a fundamental component of learning, performance, discourse and critique across all areas of the curriculum. It involves the disposition to use, in context, a combination of:

- underpinning mathematical concepts and skills from across the discipline (numerical, spatial, graphical, statistical and algebraic);
- mathematical thinking and strategies;
- general thinking skills; and
- grounded appreciation of context. (Australian Association of Mathematics Teachers, 1997, p. 15)

The word numeracy, however, is not a universally recognised term. Other terms, such as 'quantitative literacy' (Dubinsky, 2000; Steen, 2001) and 'mathematical literacy' (J. Kilpatrick, 2001; Organisation for Economic Co-operation and Development [OECD], 2004), are often used. Each tends to provide a new nuance and serves to enrich our understanding of the term numeracy. The OECD (2004, p. 15) described mathematics literacy as 'an individual's capacity to identify and understand the role that mathematics plays in the world, to make well-founded mathematical judgments, and to engage in mathematics in ways that meet the needs of that individual's life as a constructive, concerned and reflective citizen'.

Steen (2001) viewed quantitative literacy as being more than an expanded list of topics within the mathematics curriculum and as being evident in how naturally a person used their mathematics knowledge in context. He discussed the importance of a rich mathematics knowledge that included a deep appreciation for the nature and history of mathematics and its significance for understanding issues in society, how it includes logical thinking and decision-making, and using mathematics to solve practical everyday problems in different contexts. Quantitative literacy as empowerment and the provision of tools for enabling people to think for themselves also featured in Steen's description.

Foremost in definitions of numeracy is an emphasis on the application of mathematics in life situations. In this sense, definitions of numeracy must be continually revisited to ensure students are sufficiently numerate for an ever-changing and technologically advancing society beyond compulsory schooling. With new technologies, numeracy for future worlds requires considerable imagination. A futures-focused view of numeracy recognises that definitions of numeracy will continually evolve (Noss, 1998); therefore, numeracy is an elastic term (Doig, 2001).

A model of numeracy for the 21st century first proposed by Goos (2007) has been elaborated by Goos, Dole and Geiger (2012). It draws on key aspects of definitions of numeracy and encapsulates them into a visual model (see Figure 8.1). The model identifies the importance of numeracy on three fronts—personal and social, work and citizenship—which are all echoed in other definitions of numeracy. The model then presents five key elements that comprise numeracy: contexts, mathematical knowledge, dispositions, tools and critical orientation.

The model is represented by a triangle consisting of four nested triangles. Contexts are squarely placed in the middle triangle. This highlights the real-world nature of numeracy, in that numeracy capability is context dependent, and numeracy

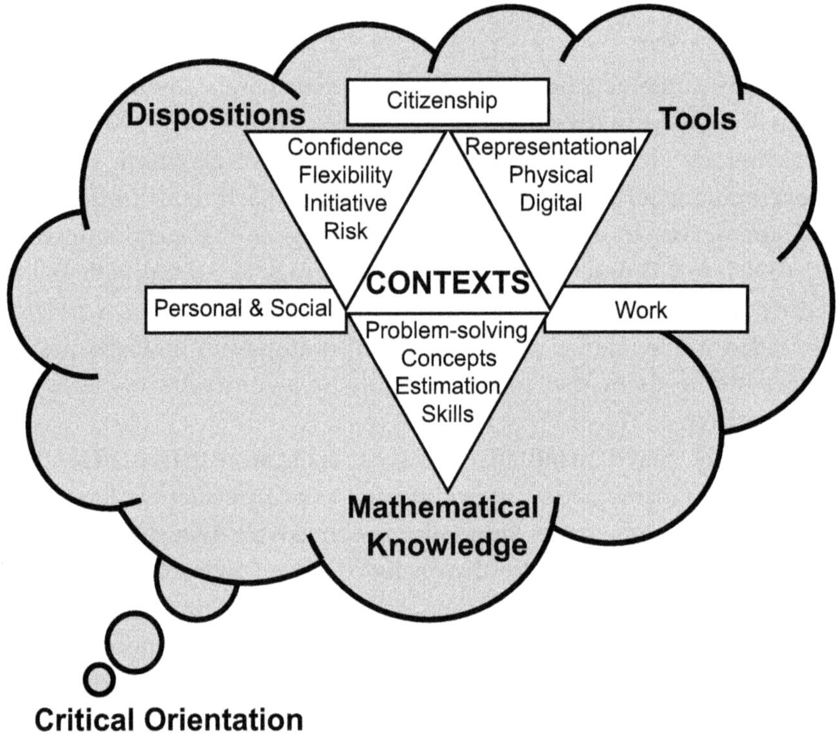

Figure 8.1 A model of numeracy for the 21st century

Source: Goos (2007).

occurs in real, authentic contexts in the real world and not in contrived situations as may occur in school classrooms. Mathematical knowledge is presented in the model as including such elements as problem-solving, concepts, estimating and skills. This serves to emphasise that the mathematics required for numeracy is about more than skills and procedures; it is about understanding and applying knowledge and skills. Dispositions include confidence, flexibility, initiative and risk. Being able to use mathematics in the real world requires confidence, and this is a fundamental requirement for numeracy. Other important dispositions for numeracy include the capacity to be flexible and to consider situations from varying points of view. This means being able to change a line of inquiry or solution process when it is clear that it is not leading to fruitful outcomes. Being numerate also requires a degree of initiative and risk-taking typified by a willingness to engage in ill-structured and ill-defined problems for which there is no immediate pathway or known procedure for solution.

The capacity to use and adapt to new tools is an element that brings Goos' (2007) model of numeracy into the 21st century. In the model, tools are physical (measuring devices, ready reckoners), representational (drawings, graphs, tables, symbol systems) and digital (computers, software, calculators, internet). Digital tools, as elaborated by Geiger, Goos and Dole (2015, p. 1122), are 'mediators of meaning making, reasoning and action in relation to mathematical learning'. Digital tools influence and serve to raise questions about mathematical skills required in the 21st century but can also enhance the development of mathematical knowledge that may be otherwise unavailable to particular learners. In the real world, specific tools are often associated with workplace contexts. A numerate person must be able to learn how to use new digital tools through applying the necessary mathematical skills. The changing nature of numeracy in the 21st century becomes more prominent through consideration of this component of the numeracy model.

Goos' (2007) model groups the numeracy elements of contexts, mathematical knowledge, dispositions and tools in the four outer triangles. The fifth and final element of the model, critical orientation, is depicted as a cloud that encompasses the other four elements to give a sense of its pervading nature. Critical orientation in numeracy involves empowerment and the capacity to make well-founded judgements and decisions. It is about using mathematical skills and knowledge to make informed decisions and to become aware of underlying and covert messages that may be enveloped in mathematical terms, texts, diagrams or jargon, particularly in a 'data-drenched' society (Steen, 1999). It is about interpreting situations and not relying on face-value presentation of facts. It is also about taking action to reduce inequality. Ernest's (2000, p. 85) call for a critical mathematics education underscores critical orientation as an essential component of numeracy: 'Complex mathematics is used to regulate many aspects of our lives, e.g., our finance, banking and bank accounts, with very little human scrutiny and intervention once the systems are in place. Only through a critical mathematics education can future citizens learn to analyse, question, challenge these systems that can distort life chances and reduce freedoms'.

Teaching numeracy and mathematics in the middle years

The study of mathematics is regarded as the foundation for the development of numeracy: 'Mathematics ... develops the numeracy capabilities that all students need in their personal, work and civic life.' Yet, promoting numeracy is not the sole

Provocation 8.1 Who is numerate?

A party of seven is dining on tacos and burritos at the local Mexican restaurant. Towards the end of the evening, the bill for the meal arrives, totalling $198. It happens to be placed next to Melanie, who quickly passes it on to the next person, saying, 'You work it out. I was never any good at maths.' All the other diners then focus on the bill, asking how much it is, and they proceed to perform various mental actions.

Kim estimates that each diner must pay between $20 and $30 (because 7×20 gives $140, and 7×30 gives $210). Margaret expresses surprise that the bill is so high, while Robyn feels that the bill is appropriate for what was ordered. Lisa is annoyed, because she ordered less food than everyone else and drank only water for the whole night and does not think it fair that the bill should be split evenly. Laura takes out her mobile phone and divides 7 into 198.

Renae rounds the bill to $200 and multiplies 2×7 to get 14, which she then changes to $140 and subtracts from $200. Focusing on the remaining $60, she recalls the 7-times table (7×7 is 49—too low; 7×8 is 56—okay) and then adds $8 to the $20. Upon reaching this figure, she states that everyone must contribute a bit more than $28, further suggesting that they all pay $29 to leave a tip. At that same moment, Laura (who was using the mobile phone) announces that everyone must pay $28.29, or $28.30, to cover the bill.

 Reflect upon the numeracy scenario described above. Who is the most numerate of the diners in the numeracy scenario? Make a list of the diners, note each of their responses, and rate them on their level of numeracy. After considering who is the most numerate, reflect upon the criteria you applied.

Renae had the strategies, skills and disposition to mentally divide 7 into $198 and to contextualise the result to ensure the total bill was covered and even provide a tip. Did you consider Renae to be the most numerate because of her mental computation skills? What about Laura, who used the calculator on her mobile phone? Is she less numerate because her instinct was to reach for technology? What about Margaret, who thought the bill was too high, or Robyn, who thought it was fair? Are they any less numerate because they did not perform a calculation to split the bill, although they obviously contextualised the bill to the situation and to their experiences and expectations? And what about Melanie, who quickly avoided contributing anything to solving the problem? Is she innumerate because her reaction was a combination of avoidance and fear?

Write a list of important characteristics of a numerate person to assist you in thinking about definitions of numeracy.

The answer to the question of who is numerate in the scenario described is, of course, that all the members of the party may be numerate, but to varying degrees. It may appear that Renae is the most numerate, as she clearly has skills and confidence. Yet Laura, who reached for the mobile phone, also demonstrated numeracy required in a technological world. Melanie, who avoided the situation, may have the skills but clearly does not have the confidence. And this is a cause for concern, although it appears to be an overly acceptable state in our society. As noted by Battista (1999, p. 426), 'Many adults readily confess, "I was never any good at mathematics" as if displaying a badge of courage for enduring what for them was a painful and useless experience. In contrast, people do not freely admit they can't read.' In saying this, however, we must not reduce numeracy simply to the ability to perform calculations and literacy to being able to read. Numeracy is a state of being along a continuum, and confidence is a strong determining factor in a person's applying mathematics skills to life situations.

responsibility of teachers of mathematics. In the Australian Curriculum, numeracy is a general capability, and every subject area has its own inherent numeracy requirements (Australian Curriculum, Assessment and Reporting Authority [ACARA], 2016a). Thus, every teacher is a teacher of numeracy, and teachers of every subject area must be aware of the numeracy demands of their discipline and teach for numeracy accordingly. This is elaborated in the next section of the chapter.

The Goos (2007) model of numeracy highlights a positive disposition as an integral element of being numerate. It has been well documented in the literature that mathematics anxiety, aversion and fear are unfortunate by-products of school mathematics (Dossel, 1993; Hembree, 1990; J. Maxwell, 1983; Meyer & Fennema, 1992; Williams, 1988). Teaching for numeracy in subject areas other than mathematics may assist mathematics-anxious students to overcome their fear of mathematics. However, in the middle years of schooling, school mathematics, and thus the development of numeracy, is challenged by students' dispositions towards the study of mathematics, and often schooling in general. The middle years literature describes adolescence as a time when students undergo immense physiological, social and emotional development and growth. Adolescent behaviour in the classroom is typified by terms such as disengagement, disinterest and disruptive behaviour.

Taking typical adolescent characteristics into account, consider the following description of a traditional mathematics classroom: 'Every day is the same: the teacher shows students several examples of how to solve a certain type of problem and then has them practise this method in class and in homework' (Battista, 1999, pp. 426–7). Such instructional approaches can readily be seen to lead to student disengagement, disinterest and disruptive behaviour, most probably exacerbated by a large majority of the class feeling confused about a subject that lacks meaning, giving rise to further feelings of frustration and boredom. Alarmingly, visits to some middle years mathematics classrooms indicate that such a traditional approach to mathematics instruction still occurs. To promote numeracy, teachers of mathematics need to consider their approaches to instruction to ensure students develop rich conceptual understandings of all mathematics topics, thus ensuring that a solid foundation for numeracy is laid.

A further factor impacting upon mathematics instruction in the middle years is the wide variation in student performance and achievement in mathematics. In a comprehensive study, Siemon, Virgona and Corneille (2001) found that, typically, in any one middle years classroom, there was as much as a seven-year gap between the highest and lowest performing students. With such a range in performance, catering for the needs of all is difficult.

Provocation 8.2 Challenges in numeracy teaching

There are many challenges to the effective teaching of numeracy in the middle years.

 Provide responses with defensible arguments to the following questions:

- How do you cater for the individual numeracy learning needs in the middle years mathematics classroom?
- What are the pros and cons of streaming (allocating students to specific classes) based on their mathematics performance and teaching them accordingly?
- If you were the teacher of the lowest performing class for mathematics, how would you plan for numeracy teaching?

Withdrawal

One of the common approaches to promoting numeracy is to withdraw students from the regular mathematics classroom and provide them with a program to promote knowledge and understanding of the basics. Such programs may be structured as self-paced modules and individualised programs. Often, instruction is via drill-and-practice exercises and completion of seemingly endless worksheets. A major Australian study into literacy and numeracy programs for at-risk students in the middle years found that this was the approach to numeracy in many cases (Luke et al., 2003). Such programs are questionable in terms of their effectiveness in promoting numeracy required for life beyond school and their relevance to the lifeworlds of adolescents (Dole, 2003).

The withdrawal approach appears to be predicated upon beliefs that numeracy is about computational skills (T.C. O'Brien, 1999) and that a back-to-basics approach is required to improve numeracy. Battista (1999, pp. 425–6) describes the folly in this approach by using a medical analogy: 'How would you react if your doctor treated you or your children with methods that were 10 to 15 years out-of-date, ignored current scientific findings about diseases and medical treatments, and contradicted all professional recommendations for practice?'

The withdrawal approach does suit some learners, however, as they begin to experience success through repetitive practice of algorithmic procedures with consequent reduction in mathematics anxiety. But in a withdrawal mode, the individual is missing out on the mathematics lessons being undertaken by the rest of the class. Thus, being selected for withdrawal classes often becomes a perpetual state of schooling for mathematics instruction. This approach does little to prepare students for problem-solving in real situations in which solution pathways are not immediate or obvious. In relation to the Goos (2007) numeracy model, such approaches would appear to focus narrowly on the mathematical knowledge and skills aspect of numeracy, with little regard for the other elements.

In 1993, Bell undertook a major comparative study of two middle school mathematics classrooms in which two different modes of whole-class instruction were implemented. Both classrooms underwent a rigorous diagnostic assessment of mathematics conceptual knowledge prior to instruction. Both classes scored similarly on the pretest. Individualised, self-paced instruction was provided for Class A. Class B engaged in whole-class rich learning tasks that challenged mathematical thinking. There were marked differences in the two classrooms during the teaching experiment.

Class A students experienced few difficulties with their individualised learning modules and were quiet and orderly during lessons. The interactions between students were infrequent, because everyone was completing different tasks. The lower ability students found security in the self-paced nature of the activities. They were working from booklets, and this generated artificial enthusiasm: 'I'm on Book 3; what about you?' Over the course of the instruction there was increasingly noticeable change in students' attitudes towards mathematics learning—from highly energetic to lethargic.

In Class B, the teacher was very active. The teacher's expertise for guiding discussion, encouraging shy speakers and knowing misconceptions was noted. The classroom was noisy. Some of the students discussed the problems they were working on in class at home with their parents. Students reported that they found the work interesting but hard.

At the end of the teaching experiment, the post-test results showed little difference in scores. The delayed post-test results, however, showed remarkable retention for those in Class B but only minimum retention for those in Class A and only slightly above scores for the post-test.

This study highlights many issues about teaching and learning mathematics in the middle years of schooling, including the limited capacity of individualised and self-paced learning modules and the necessary expertise of teachers of mathematics to engage and interest students in deep learning of mathematics. Apart from assessment outcomes, the question of how the teaching of mathematics is preparing students for numeracy is evident. Dispositions towards mathematics are of vital importance for numeracy. Any approach for supporting students in mathematics must always be considered in relation to the affective domain of the students.

Streaming

Another way of catering for the mathematical needs of students in the middle years is to stream classes—that is, to allocate students to particular classes based on performance on a particular measure or series of measures. Zevenbergen (2005) highlighted the impact of such school practices on students depending upon the stream to which they were allocated. Students in the lower stream openly admitted that they were in the 'dummy' class and expressed feelings of low self-esteem with respect to their potential achievement in mathematics. These students also presented more challenging classroom behaviours (disinterest, disengagement and disruptive behaviour). Although streaming is potentially a beneficial means for promoting mathematics understanding through a better paced curriculum, the reality often is that once students have been classified, they find that movement between class groupings occurs only infrequently and that instruction in the bottom stream typically reverts to a skills-and-drills program.

Integrated curriculum

Middle years principles advocate an integrated curriculum. With respect to mathematics, the promise for students is that the study of mathematics may occur in a repackaged and more palatable form. As stated by Brennan and Sachs (1998, p. 21), 'An integrated curriculum gives multiple pathways to different traditions and bodies of knowledge, even for those who might not usually "fit" themselves into those disciplinary areas.' A whole-school approach to numeracy has been found to be successful for learners in the middle years, particularly those deemed at risk (Perry & Fulcher, 2003; Perry & Howard, 2000). The features of such programs are their alignment with middle years philosophy: meaningful activities linked to the lifeworlds of the students, mathematical skill and conceptual knowledge development embedded in life-related problem-solving tasks, group work, encouragement of student discourse and a team approach to planning and teaching. To illustrate what vibrant middle years mathematics classrooms should look like, Schoen et al. (1999, p. 446) described recommendations that

> instruction should be focused on student investigation of substantial mathematics problems; that the classroom teacher should act as a stimulant, sounding board, and guide in that student problem solving; that students should be encouraged to discuss mathematical ideas and discoveries with classmates and with the teacher; that the classroom activity should include frequent challenges to students to develop justifications for their ideas and discoveries; and that students should be encouraged to use calculators and computers in their mathematical explorations.

In whole-school approaches to numeracy, teachers are in a position to reflect more critically upon their practice and to question the positive and negative aspects of traditional methods while trialling new ideas and strategies.

An integrated approach was a key focus of the New Basics reform in Queensland schools in the early 2000s (Education Queensland, 2000). Rich tasks were the focus of investigations by students, necessitating an integrated and team-based approach to be undertaken by teachers. New Basics can be seen to sit comfortably within middle years philosophy and principles, in that it involves students in authentic tasks designed to link to their lifeworlds, encourages students to take control of their own learning, focuses on promoting integrated and connected knowledge and necessitates group work and collaborative problem-solving. Critics of an integrated approach typically bemoan a watered-down curriculum with little focus on discipline knowledge through breakdown of traditional subject demarcation lines. However, an integrated curriculum has the potential to provide students with a new avenue for developing mathematical understanding and thus to develop confidence.

Reframing practice for numeracy

Within the Australian Curriculum, numeracy is a general capability that is integral to the teaching of all subject areas. Like literacy, it is the responsibility of all teachers to support the numeracy development of students so that they can deal with the numeracy demands inherent in the subject areas. However, being a teacher of numeracy is not a simple task. Teachers need guidance and support not only to identify the numeracy demands of their subject area but to plan for numeracy teaching (Goos, Dole & Geiger, 2012). The rich model of numeracy proposed by Goos (2007) is a valuable supporting structure for raising awareness of the multi-dimensional nature of numeracy and for assisting in numeracy planning and teaching (Goos, Geiger & Dole, 2014).

Teachers must look within every subject area they teach and identify the numeracy demands inherent within them. There is a need to deliberately plan for numeracy teaching in all subject areas to ensure that students are not denied access to core curriculum due to poor numeracy. For example, when creating artworks, students may be directed to consider the proportions of the subject-matter. A focused lesson on ratio and proportion would assist here. When creating a piece of music, fraction knowledge will assist in composing in relation to note values and the time signature. When studying history, timelines are useful representations for conceptualising events in the past in relation to our own lives. Assisting students to create timelines requires explicit teaching of scaling. When analysing persuasive elements in a text, an opportunity arises to discuss text versus diagrams as percentages. For example, a percentage is given, but there is no reporting of the sample size for meaningful comparison (e.g., '90 per cent of people agreed'—but there is no mention of how many people were surveyed or whether they were randomly selected). Similarly, diagrams can be used to exaggerate a percentage by truncating or elongating the scale. All of these examples highlight the pervasiveness of numeracy across curriculum areas and the importance of considering the mathematical knowledge and skills required in various tasks and of planning for teaching.

In all subject areas, including mathematics, numeracy moments will arise, and these teachable moments should be seized and used to promote students' numeracy. When considering the impact of disease outbreaks, pause to consider that the Spanish flu in 1918–20 claimed approximately 22 million lives (although reported figures vary). How does this compare to the populations of some countries? When students are researching the populations of some countries, compare those figures to the population of their own country. Is it ten times bigger? Ten times smaller? A hundred times bigger? What does a number look like that is ten times bigger? If you have an occasion to group approximately 100 students in a venue at one time, ask one student to stand. Then ask 10 students to stand, and compare the single person to the group that has been multiplied by 10. Then compare the single person to the whole group of 100. This helps students to contextualise the sizes of numbers when we say they are 10 times or 100 times the initial amount. It certainly has more meaning that the oft-repeated phrases when students multiply or divide by powers of 10, 'Just add zeros' or 'Just move the decimal point'.

Provocation 8.3 The teaching of numeracy

All teachers are teachers of numeracy.

 What are the implications of the statement above for beginning and experienced teachers, for mathematics teachers and for teachers of other disciplines?

 Study the examples of authentic numeracy activities presented in the investigations described in the final section of the chapter. Analyse them against the elements of the Goos (2007) numeracy model. Provide responses with defensible arguments to the following questions:

- What elements are evident in these activities?
- How would you rate their capacity to promote students' numeracy capabilities?

The philosophy and principles of the middle years of schooling associated with an integrated curriculum and emphasis on authentic investigations provide a valuable means for framing numeracy teaching. The following three examples of numeracy investigations were collected from visits to middle years classrooms.

Investigation 1

The impetus for the first investigation was the students' view that the school tuck-shop did not sell a wide enough range of food, with the result that many students were breaking school rules and buying food at a shop across the road. The students developed surveys to determine what food most students would prefer. They also conducted interviews with staff and tuckshop management. They collated the data and developed an argument for the tuckshop revising its menu. In their final report, they took into account costs to tuckshop management to increase the size of the menu and provide greater choice.

Students also visited a range of websites to find information on nutritional value of particular foods and food combinations. As a result of their investigation, the tuckshop menu did alter, and there was a consequent decrease in students leaving the school at lunchtime.

From this investigation, the students became aware of the need to have supporting evidence on which to base their demands for change. They also developed an awareness of the nutritional value of particular foods, which resulted in their creating a series of posters to display around the school and near the tuckshop outlining the nutritional value of the foods sold through the tuckshop.

Investigation 2

The second investigation undertaken by students in the middle years was in response to teachers' concerns about the amount of food wastage occurring every day in students' lunches. The school brought in a rule that all uneaten food, as well as food wrappings, must be taken home each day. To promote students' awareness of wastage and of the nutritional value of food, a lunchbox audit was conducted for a week, in which students analysed their lunches in terms of their representation on the food pyramid categories (fruits and vegetables, grains and nuts, meats, dairy, fats and oils) and also rated the packaging of their lunch through a rubbish scale. The rubbish scale assigned units to particular pieces of packaging, with recyclable material having the lowest score and prepackaged containers the highest score.

Students also investigated the costs of prepackaged containers of food, which led to broader investigations of pollution, recycling and buying in bulk and considera-tion of the time and efficiency factors that influenced decisions about single-serve portions.

From this investigation, students developed an awareness of consumerism and began to discuss nutrition and recycling in a broader sense.

Investigation 3

The third investigation was undertaken by students from an inner-city school who explored a real situation impacting upon them daily: how they travelled to and from school. This investigation differed from others of a similar nature in that the students considered school travel from the perspective of city bus routes and peak-hour traffic, which they experienced on a daily basis. The majority of students from this particular school lived in locations a considerable distance away. Their investigation included traffic surveys of numbers of passengers in the buses and cars that passed the school gates, surveys of students' transport methods, analysis of bus routes in accordance with the majority of students who attended the school and the adequacy of bicycle tracks from various locations to the school. The students also measured traffic noise through assigning levels of noise pollution to traffic at different times of the day. This extensive investigation also led to research into fossil fuels and air pollution and alternative modes of transport. From council databases, the students located information about population increases in the city, road usage increases in and around their school over the previous decade and proposals for new transportation routes. The investigation also extended to the study of energy, particularly the production of electricity and the cost of running various electrical appliances around the home.

Over the course of the investigation, students collected newspaper articles on new road proposals and followed government and council discussions on the future of roads to address peak-hour traffic delays that were a daily occurrence. Learning about the costs of transportation and use of fossil fuels allowed students to develop greater awareness of their place in the world and the impact of such usage upon the environment. Their discourse became peppered with suggestions for reducing energy consumption, and they began to question the efficiency of the methods by which they travelled to and from school. In one instance, the students mapped out a new bus route to increase efficiency for the greatest number of pupils in the school, supporting their proposal with evidence based on their research findings.

The three extensive numeracy investigations outlined above occurred in primary school settings. The teachers who supported the investigations were taking part in a numeracy project and met regularly with project members and teachers from other participating schools. The primary school settings provided flexibility of timetabling to enable lines of investigation to continue according to students' interest and engagement. Junior secondary settings that have adopted a middle years of schooling philosophy would be ideally placed to support and guide students' numeracy development through integrated curricula in a similar fashion to the examples outlined here. Promoting students' numeracy is a natural outcome of rich tasks and authentic investigations that are meaningful to the lives of students in the middle years of schooling.

Chapter summary

This chapter makes the following key points:

- The middle years of schooling are essential years for consolidating students' numeracy capabilities to ensure that students are prepared for life beyond compulsory schooling.
- Numeracy is more than skills and mental computation.
- Numeracy is the application of mathematical knowledge, tools, dispositions and a critical orientation within context.
- Numeracy has its foundations in school mathematics.
- Teaching of mathematics for successful numeracy outcomes aligns middle years philosophy and practice.
- Numeracy is the responsibility of all teachers of all subject areas.
- Teachers must identify the numeracy demands of their subject areas and plan for numeracy teaching to ensure successful student learning outcomes.
- Whole-school numeracy programs have a shared vision and common goal.
- Engaging students in real investigations develops skills, knowledge and dispositions necessary for success beyond school.
- All teachers in the middle years must work together to support and strengthen numeracy growth and development.

Chapter Nine

Physical activity

SUE WHATMAN

Learning intentions

In this chapter we will:
- define and characterise contemporary understandings of physical activity for middle years students
- problematise the often conflicting needs, learning intentions and expected outcomes for middle years students with regard to designing a physical activity curriculum
- look at innovative ideas from actual cases to inform the design of physical activity learning experiences in health and physical education (HPE) curricula and more broadly within schools.

Physical activity for middle years students

Physical activity in schools serves many purposes, not least as an important focus of learning, known as 'movement and physical activity' within the Australian Curriculum: Health and Physical Education. Understandings about the role and learning potential of physical activity for middle years students are many and manifested in different ways in school settings across Australia and around the world. The Australian Council for Health, Physical Education and Recreation (2014) notes that there is consensus around the amount and intensity of physical activity that is generally required for health-related fitness benefit. During the middle years, students are forming their learner and social identities (Main & Whatman, 2016; Pendergast & Bahr, 2010; Wright et al., 2005), so promotion of physical activity as a normal, daily part of their lives is a good aspiration. However, despite agreement by all state education authorities on the importance of the middle years (Pendergast & Main, 2013), systematic planning for this cohort is rare and often up to the individual school community (Bahr & Crosswell, 2011). Thus, planning and delivering learning experiences through physical activity for middle years students are not as straightforward as they appear.

This chapter fulfils three purposes, as outlined above in the learning intentions. Scoping what is physical activity and what it typically looks like for middle years students at school is the starting point. From there, the competing ideologies and agendas for the promotion of physical activity are outlined, and subsequent conflicting outcomes that are experienced are problematised. Finally, innovative cases of how HPE teachers and researchers have successfully addressed the promotion of physical activity with diverse students and tackling youth disengagement from physical activity are presented. These cases serve to illustrate how teachers can design effective physical activity via HPE curricula and how schools more broadly can consider their role in promoting physical activity with middle years students.

Physical activity in the HPE curriculum

Physical activity is sometimes confused with physical education (PE) and vice versa. One way to avoid confusion is to think of Australia's version of HPE as the key learning area in which you will find 'movement and physical activity' as well as 'personal, social and community health'. In the Australian Curriculum: Health and Physical Education, physical activity is intended to be taught from one of five key propositions that students will learn to value movement by learning in, through and about movement (Australian Curriculum, Assessment and Reporting Authority [ACARA], 2015a; T. Brown, 2013). Physical activity features prominently in the rationale for HPE in schooling:

> At the core of Health and Physical Education is the acquisition of movement skills and concepts to *enable students to participate in a range of physical activities*—confidently, competently and creatively. As a foundation for *lifelong physical activity participation* and enhanced performance, students acquire an understanding of how the body moves and develop *positive attitudes towards physical activity* participation. They develop an appreciation of the *significance of physical activity, outdoor*

recreation and sport in Australian society and globally. Movement is a powerful medium for learning, through which students can practise and refine personal, behavioural, social and cognitive skills. (ACARA, 2015a, emphasis added)

Haerens et al.'s (2011, p. 322) review of HPE programs in many Western countries, including Australia, noted that physical activity in schools is delivered via a traditional multi-activity sports-based curriculum. In other words, HPE is traditionally taught with a focus on sport education, sometimes with tactical or games-based approaches, but always with the objective of content and motor skill performance mastery, usually based around popular sports like basketball, football, athletics and swimming. Student expectations that HPE is like sport are established early in the primary years of schooling, during which children's experiences of organised physical activity become more prevalent and they are exposed to the '"justifying" practices of PE as sport' (Petrie, 2016). Ward and Quennerstedt's (2016, p. 142) analysis of actions in context in PE in United Kingdom primary schools found that physical activity usually comprised a 'smorgasbord of looks-like-sport', highly controlled, stage-managed tastes of different sports which ultimately required the same learning outcomes of certain motor skills performance and cooperative learning behaviour from students. They found the main exception to be in gymnastics, where students could creatively develop and implement their learning in supportive and non-competitive ways.

Despite this long history and prevalent norm of sport-centric PE, in recent critiques of curriculum reforms in Australia various researchers have moved to suggest more attention should be paid to the health-promoting potential of physical activity in HPE. While its form may be argued as a models-based approach (Haerens et al., 2011; Layne & Hastie, 2015), a strengths-based or critical approach to pedagogy and curriculum design (Leahy, O'Flynn & Wright, 2013; McCuaig, Quennerstedt & Macdonald, 2013) or curriculum reform in response to a 'defining political/economic paradigm' (Macdonald, 2014, p. 494), there is agreement that sport-centric HPE does not meet the needs of all students and most certainly does not ensure that students adopt or continue with physical activity across the lifespan.

Physical activity levels and lifelong physical activity

In attempting to answer the question of whether students' physical activity levels as teenagers bear any relationship to their activity levels as adults, Engström (2008, p. 320) compared the physical activity levels of adults aged 53 years in Sweden in

Provocation 9.1 Physical activity for middle years students

There are clearly wide-ranging beliefs and practices around what physical activities should be made available to students.

 Provide responses with defensible arguments to the following questions:

- Do teachers understand what is appropriate or effective physical activity for students aged from ten to fifteen years, the typical age range of middle years students?
- How does teachers' understanding of what is appropriate or effective physical activity for middle years students impact upon curriculum design and student engagement in learning?

2007 to their own physical activity levels which were first documented in 1968, when they were 15 years old. Engström also collected their grades in PE and other subjects and calculated their sport, cultural and social capital, combined with their education levels (pp. 327–34). His findings challenged any assumption that the amount of time spent on physical activity, particularly sports, in the middle years was significantly associated with adult physical activity levels. It was found instead that students' breadth of sports experience (their sport 'habitus') and grades in PE (which were linked to students' social capital) were far better indicators of their participation in physical activity in the future. Engström thus concluded that social position and educational capital were greater predictors of future participation in physical activity than the amount of time spent playing sport in the school years.

Similarly, another study in Sweden focused upon the characteristics of students who participated in out-of-school (club) sports at thirteen and sixteen years of age and compared them with non-participants at the age of sixteen (Jakobsson et al., 2012). Like Engström (2008), Jakobsson et al. (2012) found that young people who remained in club sport had specific cultural capital (i.e., socio-economic status and a family orientation towards sport) that enabled them to continue with it.

Data available from the Australian Bureau of Statistics (2012) show that sport and physical activity (recreation) participation among Australian middle years students is at its peak between nine and eleven years of age, with boys significantly outnumbering girls (73.3 per cent versus 59 per cent respectively). The twelve to fourteen years cohort is the next most active, with fifteen years and over considered in adult participation statistics (refer to Table 9.1).

Table 9.1 Numbers (000s) and participation rates (%) of children aged five to fourteen[a] engaging in organised sport in Australia, by gender

	Numbers			Participation rates		
	Male	Female	Total	Male	Female	Total
Age (years)						
5–8	354.7	273.8	628.5	61.4	50.1	55.9
9–11	309.5	237.3	546.9	73.3	59.0	66.4
12–14	284.8	215.9	500.7	66.3	52.9	59.8
State/territory of usual residence						
New South Wales	308.5	230.4	538.9	67.2	52.8	60.2
Victoria	227.1	182.5	409.6	65.4	55.4	60.5
Queensland	192.0	142.0	334.0	63.2	49.4	56.5
South Australia	65.2	56.9	122.1	66.1	60.2	63.2
Western Australia	110.6	78.4	189.0	72.3	54.4	63.6
Tasmania	21.1	16.2	37.2	63.8	51.9	58.0
Northern Territory[b]	7.8	5.6	13.4	60.7	46.3	53.7
Australian Capital Territory	16.8	15.0	31.8	76.0	70.5	73.3
Area of usual residence						
State capital cities	608.2	453.0	1061.1	68.4	53.6	61.2
Balance of state or territory[c]	340.8	274.1	614.9	63.0	53.6	58.5
Total	949.0	727.0	1676.0	66.4	53.6	60.2

a   Children aged five to fourteen years who participated in organised sport (excluding dancing) outside school hours during the twelve months prior to interview in April 2012.

b   Refers to mainly urban areas.

c   Includes all of the Australian Capital Territory and the Northern Territory.

Source: Australian Bureau of Statistics (2012).

Table 9.2 Numbers (N, 000s) and participation rates (PR, %) of children aged five to fourteen[a] in the top ten organised sports and recreations in 2006, 2009 and 2012 in Australia, by gender

Sports and recreations	2006		2009		2012	
	N	PR	N	PR	N	PR
Males						
Soccer (outdoor)	268.5	19.6	277.8	19.9	309.7	21.7
Swimming, diving	225.7	16.5	240.1	17.2	235.2	16.5
Australian Rules football	188.5	13.8	223.7	16.0	212.7	14.9
Basketball	101.7	7.4	118.7	8.5	131.3	9.2
Cricket (outdoor)	137.8	10.1	135.7	9.7	123.1	8.6
Tennis	109.3	8.0	131.6	9.4	119.6	8.4
Martial arts	83.4	6.1	105.2	7.5	111.2	7.8
Rugby League	107.6	7.9	97.2	7.0	107.4	7.5
Rugby Union	53.5	3.9	53.7	3.8	57.9	4.0
Dancing	32.5	2.4	41.9	3.0	50.7	3.5
Athletics, track and field	36.0	2.6	42.4	3.0	45.9	3.2
Females						
Dancing	300.1	23.1	348.5	26.3	367.4	27.1
Swimming, diving	236.8	18.2	262.8	19.8	256.9	18.9
Netball	224.1	17.3	225	17.0	220.4	16.2
Gymnastics[b]	–	–	–	–	109.8	8.1
Basketball	74.6	5.7	83.2	6.3	88.9	6.6
Soccer (outdoor)	82.6	6.4	82.7	6.2	87.8	6.5
Tennis	85.8	6.6	83.2	6.3	85.6	6.3
Martial arts	37.0	2.9	49.5	3.7	49.8	3.7
Athletics, track and field	41.5	3.2	47.0	3.5	42.7	3.1
Horse riding, equestrian, polo	36.1	2.8	31.5	2.4	27.5	2.0
Hockey	28.9	2.2	31.8	2.4	26.6	2.0

a   Children aged five to fourteen years who participated in organised sport (excluding dancing) outside school hours during the twelve months prior to interview in April of the survey year.

b   In 2009, callisthenics was included in the gymnastics category. In 2012, callisthenics was excluded from organised sport altogether, and cheerleading was included in the gymnastics category. Therefore, the data are not comparable.

Source: Australian Bureau of Statistics (2012).

The Australian Bureau of Statistics (2012) study found that children on average spent five hours per fortnight either playing or training in organised sport outside school hours. While this could be a positive feature of students' lives, it is nowhere near the required aggregation of recommended daily physical activity or proof that they actually spend the entire five hours per fortnight being physically active—that is, huffing and puffing.

The three most popular organised sports for boys (evident in Table 9.2) were outdoor soccer, swimming and diving, and Australian Rules football, with participation rates of 22 per cent, 16 per cent and 15 per cent respectively. In this list, only dancing stands out as something that does not correspond with typical sport-centric PE offerings in Australian schools. For girls, two sports were predominant: swimming and diving, with 19 per cent, and netball, with 16 per cent of girls participating. Both of these sports had double the level of participation than the third-placed gymnastics, with an 8 per cent participation rate. On this list, gymnastics, dancing, martial arts and equestrian activities are less typically offered in school HPE. In other words, nine out of ten sports on the boys' most popular list and six out of ten sports on the girls' most popular list are typically offered during school and curriculum time in sport-centric PE programs in Australian schools. That middle years students continue to participate in most of the same sports outside school as those that dominate the HPE curriculum is unsurprising.

The trend towards recreation has continued to grow, however, with the Australian Bureau of Statistics (2012) taking note of non-traditional physical activities from 2009 onwards. In particular, it has documented the rise in popularity of participation in bike riding, skateboarding and rollerblading (see Table 9.3).

The most recently available statistics of adult Australians' participation in physical activity and recreation show that 4.7 million Australians (or 26 per cent of people aged fifteen years and over) were involved in playing sport in 2014 and that the most popular forms of physical activities that people aged fifteen years and over continue to take part in include walking, at 19 per cent, and working out at a fitness gym, at 17 per cent (Australian Bureau of Statistics, 2015). The Australian Institute

Table 9.3 Numbers (N, 000s) and participation rates (PR, %) of children aged five to fourteen[a] engaging in selected physical activities in 2006, 2009 and 2012 in Australia, by gender

	2006		2009		2012	
	N	PR	N	PR	N	PR
Males						
Bike riding	1003.0	73.4	922.5	66.1	999.8	69.9
Skateboarding, rollerblading or riding a scooter	–	–	780.4	55.9	857.8	60.0
Females						
Bike riding	803.2	61.9	721.1	54.4	770.6	56.8
Skateboarding, rollerblading or riding a scooter	–	–	562.2	42.4	640.0	47.2

a   Children aged five to fourteen years who were involved in selected activities outside school hours in the last two weeks of school prior to interview in April of the survey year.

Source: Australian Bureau of Statistics (2012).

for Health and Welfare (2014) recommended that adults accumulate 150–300 minutes of moderate-intensity physical activity, or 75–150 minutes of vigorous-intensity physical activity, or an equivalent combination, each week. The institute also noted that 58 per cent of women and 53 per cent of men over eighteen years do not meet these guidelines. Thus, there is no statistical equivalence between the percentages of ten to fifteen year olds who are physically active and the percentage of adults who are physically active. The amount of time spent doing physical activity in schools in the middle years does not translate into similar levels of physical activity in adulthood. So, ensuring lifelong participation in physical activity is not guaranteed by simply keeping students active for a certain period of time at school.

The literature is clear that HPE and physical activity are not just sport and that any amount of physical activity experienced by students during HPE at school, regardless of whether it is sport-centric or not, does not ensure that they will maintain or improve their physical activity levels into adulthood. There are more complex intersecting factors that impact upon whether students will learn to value movement and gain confidence and competence in movement skills to facilitate participation in and enjoyment of lifelong physical activity.

Provocation 9.2 Learning in, through or about physical activity

As we've seen above, there are many agendas associated with physical activity in schools.

 Provide responses with defensible arguments to the following questions:

- What learning outcomes should be associated with physical activity for middle years students?
- How do we know what students learn in, through and about physical activity?

A health-promoting approach to HPE

A health-promoting approach to HPE is typically shaped around the World Health Organization's (1986, p. 1) *Ottawa charter for health promotion*, which states, 'Health promotion is the process of enabling people to increase control over, and to improve, their health. To reach a state of complete physical, mental and social wellbeing, an individual or group must be able to identify and to realize aspirations, to satisfy needs, and to change or cope with the environment.' This definition introduced a notion of health that extended beyond simple absence of disease and brought into focus the relationship between the individual and their environment. It stresses a whole-of-community approach, which is clearly evident in the successful cases presented later in this chapter. Quennerstedt (2010, p. 8) notes that focusing on mental, emotional, spiritual, cultural and environmental aspects in addition to physical, social and behavioural aspects enables PE to be conceptualised more holistically and inclusively. It provides the basis for a salutogenic (strengths-based) approach to curriculum design for middle years students, focusing on what students already have and what they need to live well (McCuaig, Quennerstedt & Macdonald, 2013).

Designing the HPE curriculum

Lifespan development

Middle years learners are typically aged from ten to fifteen years, which means their bodies are entering the phase of puberty. Disruption to the learner's perceptual motor skills, sense of balance and coordination corresponds with periods of rapid growth in long bones, such as the femur in the upper leg, the tibia in the lower leg and the arm's humerus, radius and ulna. Hand–eye coordination that has gradually developed in the early years needs rapid adjustment, as the body's proprioceptive neural pathways need reprogramming to account for relative body position changes and increased strength (Haywood & Getchell, 2009). Accounting for changes to the body over this period and planning appropriate curricula are important to ensure that middle years students are given learning opportunities to improve and refine their motor skills, as these are essential for successful partic- ipation in a wide range of physical activities. Opportunities to relearn or adjust hand–eye coordination, improve balance, build strength and maintain flexibility are affordances that students need. Confidence and competence in movement skills need to be reaffirmed in this period of rapid change, as these are directly related to students' sense of self-efficacy and enjoyment of physical activity.

Furthermore, this age group experiences the development of social competen- cies and learner identities (Hoffnung et al., 2010). Students start to see themselves in particular ways—'I like PE because I am good at it' or 'I am hopeless at sport'— and this affects their interests, peer groups and subject choices at school. Main and Whatman's (2016, p. 3) research with disengaged learners showed that engagement in learning is intrinsically linked to the perceived value or relevance of the learning and the opportunities to experience success. HPE is compulsory until the end of Year 9 in Australia, and there are many factors impacting upon students' senior schooling choices, such as considering relevant subjects for university entry or life after school. But how confident and competent middle years students feel in move- ment at the end of Year 9, and particularly how much they enjoyed their learning experiences (Wallhead & Buckworth, 2004), will play an important part in their decisions regarding whether to continue studying HPE in senior schooling or to be physically active outside school.

Politicisation of health in HPE

Educators concerned with developing enjoyable, appropriate and engaging phys- ical activity for middle years learners must also consider public health political agendas impacting upon the discipline. Governments have long been concerned with the biopolitics of health, which Francombe-Webb, Rich and De Pian (2014, p. 471) describe as 'a contingent form of governmentality [over] what it means to be healthy and which bodies are worth protecting'.

Biopolitics is played out in many ways in school curricula, not least in response to the obesity epidemic, which will be discussed shortly. More often than not, biopolitics is realised in the form of government recommendations for healthy eating, avoiding risky behaviours and daily physical activity. The Australian government's most recent guidelines for daily physical activity suggest that ten to fifteen year olds need to complete 60 minutes of moderate to vigorous physical activity per day for health-related fitness benefits (Department of Health, 2014). This intensity can be understood as huffing and puffing throughout the daily session or reaching a heart rate that is between 50 and 75 per cent of maximal rate (calculated by a generalised norm of 220 beats per minute minus the participant's age). This level of effort is required to have what is known as a training effect, meaning that the participant's body steadily becomes more efficient at performing the same physical load—that is, getting fitter. Many physical activities, whether they are the multi-activity sports-based variety described by Haerens et al. (2011) or some other form of aerobic activity, have the potential to meet curriculum outcomes such as developing motor skills and coordination and contributing to the development of aerobic fitness.

However, is putting middle years students through a regime of physical activity to make them fit and have the 'right body' the main health outcome that we should be striving for in HPE? Quennerstedt (2010, p. 10) noted that PE in New Zealand and Swedish schools was potentially bad for health, in that in order to take part, students might experience marginalisation, decreased self-confidence relative to their capability to perform, fear of the tasks and concerns about body image. In short, their wellbeing could be at risk from participation.

Curriculum planning for a holistic, critical, health-promoting approach to HPE needs consideration of how to develop students' social skills, enable informed decision-making and encourage democratic participation, creativity and joy, or pleasure, in movement (ACARA, 2015a; Quennerstedt, 2010). Penney and Chandler (2000) argued that HPE also needs to break down some of its strongly reinforced boundaries and norms (i.e., sport centricity) to facilitate valued connections between what students are learning in HPE and their real lives. No matter what underlying philosophy or rationale is enacted for the health-promoting HPE curriculum, middle years students cannot and should not be spending their available learning time simply trying to meet daily physical activity guidelines.

Physical activity and the obesity epidemic

Gard and Wright (2005), Wright and Harwood (2009) and Gard (2009) thoroughly critique the obesity epidemic, as it is routinely called in mass media and politics, noting that few people consider how 'strategically alarmist [it] is, examples of hyperbole designed to shock people into changing their behaviour' (Gard & Wright,

2005, p. 18). In this critique, the authors are not disputing that rates of obesity have increased, including in the ten to fifteen years age group, but rather are positing that the alarmist projections that are repeated by the media and subsequently taken up in health and education political portfolios, becoming the biopolitical discourse, are not substantiated with sufficient evidence. Furthermore, hasty and arbitrary assumptions are made that schools, and by natural extension HPE teachers, will somehow fix the obesity epidemic through HPE programming. Some recent statistics on obesity rates of ten to fifteen year olds show that the proportion of students now considered overweight or obese (according to body mass index) has increased (Australian Institute of Health and Welfare, 2014), but this is also countered by research that shows the same age group is just as fit as, albeit heavier than, its peers from earlier decades.

A crude body mass index measure compares the weight of an individual to their height but does not actually measure the percentage of body fat or the weight of lean body mass (i.e., muscles and bones) or water; nor does it indicate cardiovascular fitness. Research shows that Australian children across all school age groups have more sedentary screen time and less incidental physical activity now than in previous decades, but their participation in organised physical activity has actually increased (Australian Bureau of Statistics, 2012, p. 1).

Middle years students (in this study grouped as twelve to seventeen year olds) are the most incidentally active cohort of students; 60 per cent use active transport, such as cycling or walking to school at least once a week, and 35 per cent actively travel every school day (Active Healthy Kids Australia, 2015, p. 10). Students may be less likely to be running around in the backyard or playing with neighbours, but they are taking up martial arts, dance, gymnastics and other tailored after-school sports and recreation programs like never before (see Table 9.2). The biopolitical discourse both shaping and emerging from public perception of an obesity epidemic, formed around the perception of lazier, less active children, is not borne out by evidence.

So, how should schools and HPE teachers respond to the so-called obesity epidemic? Clearly, physical activity is an important part of mandated school curriculum time through the Australian Curriculum: Health and Physical Education, so schools need to ensure those essential 120 minutes are allocated to HPE each and every week. This is already a challenge for many schools preoccupied with using curriculum time to prepare students for national testing regimes (Macdonald, 2011). Schools should also resist the trend of body weight fascism, a by-product of public health intervention in schools where standardised norms such as body mass index, compulsory body tracking (i.e., use of pedometers) and other forms of digital surveillance (Lupton, 2012) become part of the learning experience, which, as Gard and Wright (2005) and Quennerstedt (2010) warn, can become an experience in body shaming for many students in HPE.

Gard (2009, p. 43) concludes that 'obesity is an utterly plastic social issue and one's orientation to it is much more a matter of visceral belief than cerebral truth'. In other words, how huge the obesity epidemic is imagined by schools and teachers to be in regard to their own student populations is what will galvanise and shape their response to it. Critical to designing effective HPE curricula and broader school-based health-promoting initiatives is understanding the reasons why middle years students may opt out.

Provocation 9.3 Who is accountable for students' physical activity?

We have learned so far that access to and enjoyment of physical activity is a key driver for participation.

 Provide responses with defensible arguments to the following questions:

- Are HPE teachers accountable for the actual levels of physical activity that middle years students achieve during their middle schooling years?
- Are they accountable for levels of physical activity achieved by those students into adulthood?

Decline in participation in physical activity
Competing interests
In examining reasons why young people withdraw from physical activity as they move into the senior years of schooling, Wright et al. (2005) noted that this age group experiences rapid changes in many other areas that compete with available time for physical activity, including seeking relationships, getting part-time jobs, having a heavier study load and taking on increasing responsibility in other areas of their lives. In other words, it is entirely reasonable that a young person may decide that the amount of time devoted to an enjoyable physical activity has to be sacrificed in order to achieve another objective in life at that point in time. The researchers claimed that discourses that continue to blame young people for dropping out of sport and consequent government policy responses are misdirected, as

it is already evident that what young people do at one time in their lives is not necessarily predictive of forms and amounts of physical activity at other times, nor what they will do for the rest of their lives. Their priorities are continually changing, as social relationships and their interaction with institutions and social structures change. It is these rather than personal interests in physical activity that we suggest influence the 'decline' in physical activity. (p. 20)

The two enduring messages from Wright et al.'s (2005) research are that, first, what middle years students are doing today, which might be participating less in physical activity, does not mean that they will never increase their participation in the future; and, second, piquing students' personal interest in physical activity now, and giving them the opportunity to develop confidence in movement, are more likely predictors of their long-term participation in the future.

With the Australian government recently announcing more funding to be made available to schools through the Sporting Schools policy initiative to combat sport drop-out (see www.ausport.gov.au), it is possible to see the influence that powerful vested interests have in keeping the nature of physical activity in schools as sport-centric as possible. In 2013, the Australian Sports Commission published a report called *The future of Australian sport*, which noted that sport participation was threatened by the rising popularity of gym fitness, recreational running and extreme or adventure sports. However, it also noted that 'the sports that Australians play today are the result of cultural evolution over the last two centuries. The desire to play and watch sport is fundamental to Australian culture, and this is *not likely to change* in coming decades. In 2040, Australians will most likely still follow and participate in AFL, cricket, rugby, touch football, netball, sailing, soccer, swimming, basketball, lawn bowls and other sports in large numbers' (Hajkowicz et al., 2013, p. 36, emphasis added). As male-centric, colonial sports continue to typify the physical activity opportunities of middle years students in their sport-centric HPE curriculum and their physical activity and club sport choices outside school, the potential to marginalise certain cohorts of students remains.

Conflicting social and cultural expectations
Recent investigations into the physical activity of middle years Chinese Australian students have revealed that HPE teachers' expectations do not account for their students' social and cultural backgrounds (Pang, 2014; Pang & Macdonald, 2016). This impacts upon student participation, in their questioning, first, 'Do I want to do this task and why?' which is known as subjective task value, and, second, 'Can I

do this task?' which is known as expectancy benefit (Pang, 2014, p. 386). Subjective task value and expectancy benefit of activities as interpreted by students are considered to be the main drivers of their participation, and this applies regardless of whether these are academic or physical activities. Pang (2014, p. 387) noted that young people will evaluate their physical activity competence in terms of the likely success of the outcome and in comparison with others. Thus, exposure to the types of physical activities on offer and opportunities to develop competency, both individually and collectively, impact upon how Chinese Australian students evaluate their physical activity competence and their propensity for physical activity.

Pang (2014) and Pang and Macdonald (2016) also found participation rates of Chinese Australian girls in physical activity to be lower than those for boys and that girls in particular felt parental pressure not to participate in physical activities, lest they interfere with their academic achievement (Pang, 2014, p. 388). Participating in physical activity for social, collective reasons was found to be more motivating for Chinese Australian students than individualistic influences and resonated with cultural expectations, such as satisfying interpersonal harmony in social interactions. Having a diverse variety of physical activities to choose from also resulted in more students engaging with physical activity in HPE lessons.

In the United Kingdom and Australia, the poor participation rates of Muslim girls in physical activity have been investigated by a small number of HPE teachers and researchers (Chown, 2013; Stride, 2014), although this number is growing. In the United Kingdom, Stride (2014) investigated ways in which fourteen middle and senior years Muslim girls aged from eleven to eighteen years from a large, urban, coeducational local authority (council) school drew upon the resources available to them to participate in physical activity within the boundaries of their family expectations and cultural obligations. Rather than starting from a point of resistance, or 'blame the family/culture/religion', Stride carefully reconstructed narratives to illustrate that Muslim girls are not anti-HPE but need to work within constraints that are not considered in the planning and delivery of typical or normative mixed-sex or male-centric, sport-centric physical activity offerings. Her study revealed that the girls would take part in sport, including football (soccer), whenever their specific requirements, such as girl-only teams and practice sessions and uniform needs, were catered for. She also found that girls readily and regularly embraced physical activity in safe spaces, such as at home or at friends' places, for playing exergames such as Wii Fit and Wii Dance, and ladies-only gyms (p. 407).

Chown (2013) outlined his experiences with implementing HPE lessons in a Muslim school in Australia. Constraints to girls' and boys' participation in HPE were attended to as his professional responsibility and included taking care of the staff resourcing implications of single-sex teaching, sourcing companies to make appropriate uniforms for physical activity and working closely with school and community leaders in selecting curriculum offerings (p. 14). He found that

> there were real barriers to negotiate in order to present a program that would engage students and respond to their needs and interests ... It was also very important to me that parents supported the development of this program ... and I had to try and put myself in every individual stakeholder's shoes. Depending on which stakeholder I was addressing, after I presented the vision and before the first 'but' I would table Exhibit A—Here is how it relates to the syllabus; Exhibit B—Here is what the Qur'an says; Exhibit C—Here is how Prophet Muhammad handled this situation; Exhibit D—This is what has been done in an Islamic school in Melbourne or the UK; Exhibit E—Here is what a sample of parents think about the proposed unit; Exhibit F—This is what students will gain and this is how they feel about it.

Chown's (2013) professional commitment to meeting the needs and interests of his students is evident in the quote above, which also illuminates how tailoring HPE curricula to meet the needs and interests of students with diverse cultural backgrounds is involved, challenging and absolutely necessary professional work.

Engaging middle years students in physical activity

Sport-centric HPE has been implicated in the disengagement of middle years students over the last quarter-century (Tinning & Fitzclarence, 1992), and yet this problem is still in the sights of contemporary researchers (Enright & O'Sullivan, 2012). Policy-makers, curriculum writers, school leaders and teachers of HPE must take note that sport-centric PE is still potentially responsible for discouraging many middle years students from participating in physical activity both within school time and across the lifespan (Engström, 2008; Jakobsson et al., 2012). The following cases look at how schools, HPE teachers and researchers both in Australia and around the world have tackled the issue of students' low participation rates or disengagement from physical activity with innovative approaches to designing and teaching HPE.

Girls and physical activity in Ireland

Girls' disengagement from physical activity in Ireland was the subject of investigation by Enright and O'Sullivan (2012, p. 255). A key aim of their participation action research project was to help students understand their self-identified barriers to physical activity participation in order to transform them. They commenced from a standpoint that students often struggle to engage in classes in which pedagogies fail to recognise their lived experiences of physical culture—that is, what they are used to out of school—especially in low-challenge classroom environments.

The purpose of the project was to highlight transgressive, student-led pedagogies, empowering students to connect with their existing physical culture. In the study, girls from one Irish school applied for sports club partnership funding with the assistance of the researchers to create an after-school girls' physical culture club, located away from school grounds. The girls selected physical activities such as boxercise, aerobics, walking, swimming, Khai Bo and going to the gym as preferred club activities. Enright and O'Sullivan (2012) found that the girls reported a greater sense of connection between their real lives and PE as a result of participating in the club and made clearer connections between what the point of learning is in PE. As one student participant explained:

> It's the first time I've seen any purpose to PE. Sad but true ... it's not nothing like before ... It's more about trying to help us be smart, active and confident to use stuff like gym around where we live. Basically it's helping us be active more than once a week in class and we're helping ourselves be active actually and PE [used not to] do that. (pp. 259–60)

Enright and O'Sullivan's (2012) findings resonated with the contemporary rationale for Australian Curriculum: Health and Physical Education that students should develop competence and confidence in their movement capabilities and take these competencies forward in their lives outside school (ACARA, 2015a). Empowering students to consider options and make choices and facilitating their ability to pursue those options were key features of the design of physical activity in this case.

Physical activity in the digital age

Öhman et al. (2014) recently completed a large national study into the prevalence and purposes of exergaming in HPE in Swedish schools. They found that the mostly fitness games, particularly Wii Fit Plus, are becoming increasingly popular with both girls and boys as physical activity choices and with HPE teachers as the pedagogy of choice for delivering HPE classes. The authors' main concern with exergames as HPE was teachers' uncritical consumption of the task designs within the programs that centred on naming and measuring an ideal body. As another form of bio-politics, exergaming relies on

> an overall logic [which is] about producing results, by means of points, gold stars, graphs, diagrams, bar charts and assessments of various kinds and each player receives a measurement and a value of his or her body and its physical status ... Measuring every aspect of performance also constitutes the idea that the able body is always a calculable body ... and individuals are thus invited to compare themselves against these ideal norms. (Öhman et al., 2014, p. 204)

The physical activities contained within exergames have great potential to be enjoyable and to invoke aesthetic feeling that could motivate students to continue to play, but the games end with calories consumed as the key takeaway message (Öhman et al., 2014, p. 206). The authors concluded that playing exergames as a learning activity in HPE had potential but could be unhealthy for the many students whose less-than-ideal bodies were continually negatively evaluated by the default program.

Meckbach et al. (2014) then unpacked the movement qualities of Wii teaching in one case study school as a means of exploring the learning potential of exergames in HPE. In addressing the questions of what exergames should solve in HPE practice and how exergames go beyond being just another way of throwing a ball, the authors adapted the four aspects of the Laban Movement Framework: body, effort, space and relationships (Meckbach et al, 2014, p. 245). The aspects are expanded below:

- Body (what):
    - body parts—arms, legs, trunk
    - body actions—balance, weight transfer, flight, rotation, stepping, jumping
    - body shapes—extending, bending, twisting, swinging, stretching.
- Relationship (with whom and what):
    - body parts to each other—in front, behind, far, near, above, below
    - with others—in front of, behind, far, near, over, under, copying, contrasting
    - with apparatus or equipment—far, close.
- Space (where):
    - space—personal, general
    - direction—forward, backward, up, down, sideways, round
    - pathway—straight, circular, curved, zigzag

- extensions—wide, narrow, long, short
- levels—high, medium, low
- planes—frontal, horizontal, sagittal.
- Effort (how):
  - time—sudden, sustained, fast, acceleration
  - weight—strong, or form, light or fine
  - space—straight, direct to flexible, indirect
  - flow—free, ongoing, bound (Laban-Eurolab, n.d.; Langton, 2007; Meckbach et al., 2014).

Meckbach et al. (2014, p. 241) classified the movement qualities of Wii teaching within three general categories—sport, exercise and dance games—through video analysis of lessons and the use of an adapted movement analysis chart. They found that the movement qualities of sport games 'can be said to be specific, elementary, straight with low intensity in some games, like in archery, and relatively high intensity in others, like boxing' (p. 252). Exercise games were found to be restricted in body movement and stationary in terms of use of space, with a focus on balance and body control (p. 255). Dance games were found to be most socially interactive, with movement qualities that 'varied in space, direction, level and plane, and developed using large movements in different planes involving also rhythm and interaction' (p. 258).

So the variety of movement qualities, particularly in the dance games, was argued to provide greater movement learning opportunities in the critical use of exergames. The results showed higher student interaction with each other in the dance games, allowing opportunity for social and pleasurable feelings to be associated with physical activity. Like any choice of physical activity, this case of exergaming in HPE should be grounded with a clear purpose. The authors here stressed that exergames should not replace HPE, 'but rather, be seen as a potential addition to other pedagogical practices' (Meckbach et al., 2014, p. 259).

Connecting migrant students with their local community

Youth Action is a pilot project for middle years students which has been trialled in four Victorian schools (Years 6 to 10) since 2012 (see monash.edu/news/show/youth-action-for-health; www.achper.org.au/blog/blog-putting-the-propositions-into-practice). It is a unit of work operationalised with critical inquiry pedagogy, designed to explore movement-based opportunities (including sports) that are meaningful to students from a migrant background (J. O'Connor, 2015). Teachers and students critically identify, discuss and challenge important influences upon health and movement, such as personal, social, cultural and environmental factors.

J. O'Connor (2015) stressed that it is essential for students to think more critically about movement—what is it, how it makes you feel and who is normally included and who is not—to move beyond seeing disengagement from normative physical activity as an individual's deficiency. For example, students are encouraged to challenge gender stereotypes related to school-based physical activity, including disproportionate access of boys over girls to playing spaces at lunchtime, creating supportive change rooms and lobbying for a broader range of physical activities than just sport, with dance, skating, yoga and Pilates being some of the activities trialled so far.

A key feature of this program is the involvement of community stakeholders as expert mentors who are elicited from within the school (existing staff or students) or from the wider community (local government departments or university, parent and volunteer groups). A three-way partnership is ideally intended to facilitate co-construction of ideas and meanings and to extend resources and strategies to enhance movement opportunities. The research team agreed that this is the most difficult aspect of the pilot program to establish, with professional time, time-tabling and other logistical constraints affecting the establishment of such triads (J. O'Connor, 2015).

For assessment, through a critical inquiry approach, students must collect evidence about the identified issue that impacts upon their participation in movement, with the intent to develop actionable outcomes. J. O'Connor (2015) notes that these outcomes are ideally developed in consultation with stakeholders who have the capacity to support the initiative.

There was some resistance by HPE teachers and students who were already content with normative, sport-centric HPE, but this sentiment was offset by an acknowledgement that students could see that their efforts resulted in greater student access to movement and health-affirming practices outside class. Such acknowledgment had far greater impact on promoting physical activity across the lifespan than the normative 120 minutes per week of teacher-directed, games-based HPE. At the very least, Youth Action is an applied example of a critical inquiry approach to HPE with the middle years, resulting in consciousness raising, potential or actual change and, importantly, students learning that their actions really can make a difference to their lives and the lives of others.

Chapter summary

This chapter makes the following key points:

- We have critiqued contemporary understandings of the aspirations for, and the types and learning purposes of, physical activities for middle years students. We have considered how past, normative, sport-centric approaches to physical activity through school HPE curricula have not always achieved their intended roles or outcomes for many students, resulting in their disaffection from HPE and declining interest in being physically active.
- There is no dispute that physical activity is central to quality HPE. Learning in, through and about movement is the basis for acquiring the necessary movement capability and confidence to apply movement skills to any future physical activity setting.
- Teachers of middle years students must remember that how their students feel about themselves at this critical time of forming their learner identity during, and as a consequence of, the physically active learning experiences offered to them in school will have a significant impact on how they perceive their own physical capability and apply it in the future.
- The cases presented at the end of this chapter show that increasing physical activity choices alone are not the answer to promoting physical activity levels in the middle years and across the lifespan. Empowering students to make choices, offering choices that increase learning about movement, seeking input from diverse community stakeholders and taking care of the school-based constraints that otherwise prevent students from taking up physical activity are essential to quality HPE planning and delivery. These are actions within the control, and are the professional responsibility, of teachers in designing quality curricula and consequent learning experiences.
- School leaders are implicated in the promotion of physical activity in the middle years by ensuring that minimum curriculum time for HPE is met each and every week and that resourcing and other structural considerations are enabled to expand choice in physical activity. Students would also benefit from schools sharing the responsibility for increasing opportunities for physical activity beyond the disciplinary confines of HPE lessons. Promoting physical activity across the lifespan is a privilege that all educators should embrace.

Chapter Ten

Curriculum

TONY DOWDEN

Learning intentions

In this chapter we will:
- develop a strong rationale for middle years curriculum design and implementation
- discuss elements of curriculum theory relevant to the middle years, including tensions between subject-centred and student-centred curriculum models
- consider a range of approaches to middle years curriculum design and evaluate them in terms of responsiveness to students' diverse learning needs.

A rationale for curriculum design in the middle years

We all learn best when we understand what we are learning and why it is relevant to us, but research tells us that it is especially important for the classroom curriculum to be meaningful and relevant to middle years students. Middle years teachers should have specialist subject knowledge in two or more fields and a sophisticated level of pedagogical content knowledge that specifically caters for the learning needs of young adolescent students (Australian Council for Educational Research [ACER], 2012). It might seem valid for a teacher to adopt a default position and just implement the official curriculum without additional thought to curriculum design, but, as we will see, this approach is too simplistic, because it fails to consider the diverse learning needs of middle years students.

Middle years curriculum design should be oriented towards personalised learning so that it meets the needs of students who have special needs, addresses student diversity and caters for students who are gifted and talented (Australian Curriculum, Assessment and Reporting Authority [ACARA], 2015a). Accordingly, good middle years curriculum design aligned with appropriate approaches to teaching and assessment is prerequisite to successful learning outcomes in high school. The ideal middle years curriculum design places both the student and key disciplinary knowledge at the heart of the curriculum, but, as we will discover, barriers to implementation need to be overcome before this can be achieved. This chapter emphasises the need for teachers to consistently exercise curriculum mindfulness; that is, as teachers design their classroom curriculum, they must be sure about what they are doing and understand why they are doing it.

Meeting students' diverse learning needs

The Australian Curriculum states that 'all students are entitled to rigorous, relevant and engaging learning programs drawn from a challenging curriculum that addresses their individual learning needs' (ACARA, 2015a). Unfortunately, statements of universal educational entitlement such as this are often poorly implemented by school systems and, in the case of the middle years, have given rise to a thriving middle years movement that has strongly criticised traditional approaches to schooling for frequently failing to cater for the developmental and educational needs of students. Indeed, a strong commitment to meeting the diverse learning needs of students is a key driver of the middle years movement.

Middle years experts have long argued that curriculum design in the middle years should be informed by students' developmental and educational needs. The *Position paper* of the Middle Years of Schooling Association (MYSA, 2008) in Australia, now known as Adolescent Success, states that students need 'integrated and disciplinary curricula' that are 'challenging, integrated, negotiated and exploratory'. Similarly, the National Middle School Association (2010) in the United States, now the Association for Middle Level Education, states that the middle years curriculum should be 'relevant, challenging, integrative and exploratory'.

Despite wide agreement among experts about desirable features in the design of middle years curricula, teachers often struggle to construct a coherent curriculum that authentically supports classroom learning. While several factors probably contribute to this problem, the most important factor is likely to be that teachers have not developed a sufficiently strong rationale for middle years curriculum design. Assuming relevant professional development on the middle years is accessible, most teachers intuitively recognise the educational benefits of developing a rich range of pedagogies and authentic assessment items, but they can struggle to understand what middle years curriculum design should look like and how to align the classroom curriculum with pedagogy and assessment. The likely reason for this is that curriculum design is complex, with several components that need to be addressed in order to achieve a successful outcome. The Association for Middle Level Education recently reaffirmed that schooling in the middle years should be 'developmentally responsive, challenging, empowering and equitable' (Levin & Mee, 2016). Let us unpack the implications of these four points for middle years curriculum design.

Developmentally responsive

Middle years curriculum design that is developmentally responsive positions the student at the heart of the curriculum. It recognises and understands that the developmental stage of young adolescence is a time of significant change that leads to many personal challenges, some of which occur simultaneously (Caskey & Anfara, 2014). Middle years curriculum design also recognises that students are in the early stages of learning how to become independent learners and they are still in the process of acquiring and developing a range of learning skills, including working with others and accepting increasing levels of responsibility for personal academic progress. Good curriculum design accordingly interweaves subject content from the disciplines with the development of important social skills for effective learning. Done well, middle years curriculum design creates the right conditions for catalysing a love of learning that will ensure students become committed lifelong learners (Pendergast et al., 2005).

In the middle years, students undergo significant maturational changes as they move from childhood to young adolescence (Brighton, 2007). Brains are still under construction (Carrington, 2006; Nagel, 2014). Emotions increase in strength and play an important role in mediating motivation and engagement. Indeed, we now know that emotion has a major influence on cognition (Damasio, 2005; Duncan & Barrett, 2007). For example, when students like a teacher and enjoy a class, they think more deeply and concentrate for longer periods. Due to brain immaturity, students are prone to making black-and-white judgements, such as 'I hate science', 'I hate my teacher' or 'I love English'. Many of these snap judgements have a negative impact on the quality of teacher–student relationships, and, if reinforced by evidence arising from negative perceptions of a teacher's management of classroom behaviour, such judgements are soon reified and become the accepted mythology within student peer groups. This can create significant barriers to academic progress for some students, especially those who are affected by low self-confidence or stress (Nagel, 2007).

Developmentally responsive curriculum design in the middle years should specifically aim to teach students how to operate effectively in the social context (Beane, 1990, 2013). Healthy and respectful peer relationships are a prerequisite to working together effectively. The social skills of middle years students are still developing, so the curriculum needs to make specific provision for teaching important life skills, such as respect for others and tolerance of differences, and key interpersonal skills, such as negotiation and conflict resolution (Beane, 1990, 1997, 2005; Brighton, 2007; Caskey & Anfara, 2014). Curriculum designs that include collaborative work should include specific strategies for teaching students the essential skills for working successfully as a team.

In summary, the middle years curriculum should be developmentally responsive and specifically designed to enhance the growth of interpersonal skills. For further information on this topic, see Chapter 2 for a general discussion of human development in the middle years.

Provocation 10.1 A developmentally responsive curriculum for Year 7

Bernard has been a secondary teacher in Queensland for five years. His main teaching subjects are senior mathematics, senior physics and junior science. His principal has invited him to take charge of the school's Year 7 curriculum and make it developmentally responsive. At first Bernard is confused. He thinks to himself, 'The curriculum is just the curriculum, especially for senior mathematics and physics', but, as he ponders some more, he realises he has already modified a junior science unit to make it more engaging and challenging for his students. He realises he doesn't fully understand what developmentally responsive means but decides to accept the invitation anyway.

 Bernard needs your help. What advice can you give Bernard about designing a developmentally responsive curriculum that will ensure his school puts its Year 7 students at the heart of the curriculum?

Challenging

Middle years students are motivated to investigate topics that are personally relevant and meaningful to them (Beane, 1991; Nagel, 2014). In contrast, academic subjects are often foreign to students and, unless the teacher can find a way to make a topic or subject relevant, students may show little interest. Middle years students have the developmental need to move towards gaining the locus of control for their learning and the need to accept increasing levels of responsibility (Caskey & Anfara, 2014). Curriculum design should therefore work in harness with these needs, not against them. Middle years students are motivated to 'make a difference' within their own social context, so curriculum designs including challenges which involve solving real-life problems in the community context are likely to be popular with students (McLaine & Dowden, 2011). The idea of negotiating the curriculum in collaboration with students is powerful and, in some cases, can hold the key to engaging otherwise unmotivated students (Beane, 1997; Boomer et al., 1992; Hunter & Forrest, 2010).

Most middle years students are in the process of moving from concrete thinking to abstract thinking but are usually unable to operate at a purely abstract level of thinking (Caskey & Anfara, 2014). Curriculum design in the classroom should therefore imply the use of a range of pedagogies with plenty of rich sensory input, such as learning from hands-on experience (Carrington, 2006; Darling-Hammond, 2008; Hayes et al., 2006). Middle years curriculum design should also set high expectations and encourage students to perform at increasingly higher levels of intellectual development (J. Arnold, 1997; Beane, 1997, 2013; Caskey & Anfara, 2014). Authentic assessment might include multimedia presentations of what students have learned or curations of relevant learning artefacts, and, where possible, it should involve parents and community members (ACER, 2012; Beane, 1990). In summary, challenging middle years curriculum design should aim for appropriate cognitive loading within a familiar and supportive social context.

Empowering

Middle years curriculum design should be empowering, but all too often we see the opposite. The transition from primary to secondary schooling tends to result in relatively shallow and impersonal teacher–student relationships and an increased emphasis on teacher control and discipline (ACER, 2012). In high school, students have many subject teachers, which decreases the number of opportunities for teachers and students to have meaningful conversations and to get to know each other properly. Indeed, the dip in student achievement in the first years of secondary education is explained in part by the remnants of an unsympathetic kind of schooling from the past that used principles of behaviourism, in which students were expected to master subject content from the disciplines or accept negative consequences. It did not matter if content was irrelevant to students. For instance, a generation or so ago it was the norm in Australian classrooms for students to have to recite English poetry, learn Latin and memorise key dates associated with the kings and queens of England. As it is, disengagement, alienation and boredom from schooling tend to peak in the middle years (Dinham & Rowe, 2007; MYSA, 2008), so unsympathetic schooling following a transition can have a negative impact on academic progress (ACER, 2012; Main & Whatman, 2016). It is now generally understood that attempting to force middle years students to learn curriculum content when they do not have good relationships with teachers or other students and lack a sense of connectedness to subject content increases the risk that they will disengage from schooling and develop a generalised dislike for formal learning (Gibbs & Poskitt, 2010; Main & Whatman, 2016).

A safe and supportive learning environment that empowers students and meets their emotional needs must be built on the quality of relationships (Main, Bryer & Grimbeek, 2004; Main & Whatman, 2016). A key to achieving warm teacher–student relationships is when the student perceives that the teacher cares for them personally (Poskitt, 2011). The classroom curriculum and associated pedagogy need to unequivocally communicate and engender this. In the case of Aboriginal and Torres Strait Islander students, teacher–student relationships that are built on a foundation of cultural competence are a prerequisite for classroom engagement (Buckskin, 2015).

The quality of teacher–student relationships can be enhanced by being mindful of the developmental characteristics of students. For example, students in the middle years respond well to teachers who use gentle humour and who are easygoing and relaxed, but they respond poorly to teachers who use sarcasm ('Miss B. says nasty things about us') and to those who they perceive as needing to be the centre of attention ('Everyone knows Mr C. loves himself'). When teacher–student relationships are well established, students are willing to try harder, take risks and accept challenges. Over time, students learn to accept increasing levels of responsibility, they become increasingly motivated and self-directed, they make meaningful connections between the classroom and the outside world, and they become aspirational about future educational opportunities. In summary, empowering middle years curriculum design builds positive teacher–student relationships, acknowledges that students need extra support during transitions and promotes emotional wellbeing.

Equitable

The middle years curriculum should be equitable and value each student's emerging personhood. Students should be specifically taught to tolerate, value and celebrate difference in the classroom. The quality of peer relationships and the nature of peer influence are important aspects in the social environment of the middle years classroom that must be factored in to curriculum design (Beane, 2013; P. Nolan et al., 2000). While it is not possible within the scope of this chapter to discuss diversity in the depth it deserves, this is an important aspect of middle years curriculum design that must not be ignored. Catering for diversity in the middle years curriculum is particularly important, because these are the years that shape students' self-concepts, personal beliefs and values (Caskey & Anfara, 2014). Every teacher can tell us that the classroom is defined by individual differences, but the wide range of maturational variation in the stage of early adolescence means that the middle years classroom has an extra dimension of diversity that is not present in other levels of schooling. Some students are vulnerable and need extra levels of support. Experienced middle years teachers know that some students are very sensitive to the social context and are easy targets for teasing, whereas other students are comparatively phlegmatic and remain unruffled even by robust banter. In addition, students are often diagnosed with learning or behavioural disorders in the middle years. A middle years teacher with a non-judgemental, gentle and caring disposition can make a big difference to students who face difficult personal struggles (Rumble & Aspland, 2010; Rumble & Smith, 2016). In summary, equitable middle years curriculum design ensures that every student feels included and valued within the classroom learning community.

Political considerations

All the elements discussed thus far are vital components of our rationale for middle years curriculum design, but, by itself, this is not enough. Middle years teachers also need to understand the political context and recognise that the middle years curriculum does not always receive unqualified support from other curriculum stakeholders.

The content and design of school and classroom curricula are always political processes, because knowledge is one of the keys to attaining and holding on to power. Politics has a major influence on curriculum content, meaning the subject content that is accepted into the official curriculum consists of carefully chosen knowledge which reflects the politics of the dominant group (Apple, 1990).

The curriculum is a convenient scapegoat for perceptions of underperformance in education. For instance, a common response to lower than expected results from mandatory testing regimes, such as the National Assessment Program—Literacy and Numeracy, is the call for back to basics from commentators who, nostalgic for the past, want a curriculum with greater emphasis on reading, writing and arithmetic that implies stricter classroom discipline. Curriculum designs that are perceived to have an emphasis on catering for the developmental needs of students at the apparent expense of a rigorous treatment of disciplinary content knowledge are especially likely to be at risk. Indeed, history shows us that designs for middle years curricula have been targeted by powerful decision-makers who do not always understand what happens in the middle years classroom (Beane, 2013). For this reason, teachers need to be able to discern whether their curriculum design will be accepted by their community and then act accordingly. One of the keys to attaining insight into this issue is to understand the tension between subject-centred and student-centred approaches to curriculum design.

Curriculum theory

In order to understand contemporary designs for middle years curricula, it is helpful to take a brief detour via some relevant curriculum theory. This section discusses the subject-centred curriculum model, the student-centred curriculum model and Dewey's theory of integration.

The subject-centred model

The subject-centred model, also sometimes referred to as the separate-subject approach or single-subject approach, is based on the idea that specific fields of knowledge should be arranged into discrete disciplines of specialised learning and inquiry. This model, which has dominated secondary schooling and tertiary education in Australia for more than a century, is descended from an elitist approach based on social class that served the needs of the industrial revolution: beyond the years of compulsory schooling, students who are successful graduate to increasingly higher levels, while those who fail either repeat a level or exit the education system and join the labour force. In the purest form of the subject-centred model, the needs of students are subservient to what is deemed to be the ideal organisation and pacing for teaching the subject. It is also tacitly assumed that all students will use the same learning resources.

The subject-centred model has its champions, but they are likely to be politicians or businesspeople with specific agendas rather than educators. Certainly, they are unlikely to be educators who are catering for the educational needs of the full spectrum of middle years students. Sustained academic progress in the middle years is very important, because it provides the foundation for successful understanding of disciplinary knowledge for the senior years of high school and the workplace. Thus, the notion that all students in the middle years must have a solid grounding in the disciplines is not up for debate, but it must be understood that a solid grounding, on its own, is not enough. In fact, when this notion of a solid grounding in the disciplines within the middle years is subjected to closer scrutiny, it breaks down, because the relatively high proportion of irrelevant subject content in any subject-centred curriculum means that many students disengage from learning and fail to make progress. This phenomenon is especially salient when students make the move to high school (ACER, 2012).

The student-centred model

The student-centred curriculum model is based on the idea that the subject content of the curriculum should be subservient to the needs of the learner. In its purest form, there is no formal curriculum and no prescribed subject content, because the curriculum is constructed according to the curiosity and whims of the child.

A famous example of a radical student-centred curriculum was implemented at Summerhill, a small private school in England that was founded in 1924 (Neill, 1960). The school's philosophy allowed students to construct their own curriculum, relevant and meaningful to each individual, and free from what was then seen as adult coercion. Of course, a radical curriculum such as this is untenable when there is an official curriculum that is mandatory.

Integration

Philosopher John Dewey (1916) developed a theory of education based on data gathered in his Laboratory School at the University of Chicago. Dewey believed that education is the primary means of ensuring social continuity between generations. He thought that a recurring problem of education in a democracy was harmonising students' individual traits with the values of their communities; therefore, he identified the student and their local context as the focus for curriculum design (Dewey, 1936, p. 465). Three notions of integration were embedded in Dewey's theory: personal integration, social integration and the integration of knowledge.

Personal integration

Dewey's (1931, p. 424) notion of personal integration lay at the heart of his theory of learning:

> The mentally active ... [student's] mind roams far and wide. All [subject-matter] is grist that comes to the mill ... yet the mind does not merely roam abroad. It returns with what is found ... [with] constant judgment to detect relations, relevancies [and] bearings on the central theme. The outcome is a continuously growing intellectual integration ... [This] is the process of learning.

Dewey's insight was that when people learn, they do their own integrating. The implication is that students should not be taught parcels of knowledge that are pre-integrated by teachers or textbooks. To facilitate personal integration, Dewey (1900, p. 120) explained that teachers should ensure that their students actively engage in the stuff of different subjects; thus, he emphasised the importance of learning by doing.

Social integration

Dewey's (1916) notion of social integration concerned the process of inducting students into society; he thought the outcome of schooling should be that students become fully functioning citizens. He promoted social integration by engaging students in learning activities that developed skills and attributes needed in wider society, such as working collaboratively, solving real-life problems and building self-discipline. Dewey explained that social integration is achieved via active participation in a democratic learning community, in which all students complete a common core of general studies, gain social experience and actively develop and hone the skills needed for responsible citizenship.

Integration of knowledge

Dewey (1936) believed that the curriculum should be personally meaningful to the learner and valuable to society. He argued that subject content should consist of the specific knowledge that is uniquely important to each individual within their community context. Although Dewey did not specifically make the link between subject content and curriculum integration, his point was clear: integration of the curriculum must provide for personal integration, which requires subject content related to the local context, and social integration, which requires subject content that promotes the development of responsible citizenship.

Provocation 10.2 A curriculum that develops social skills in Years 5 and 6

Kate and Jessie are mid-career teachers who have become increasingly concerned about bullying in Years 5 and 6 within their primary school. They talk to their principal about it, and she asks them to design a local curriculum for Years 5 and 6 that emphasises the development of social skills.

 Kate and Jessie need your advice. What key ideas do you think they should include in their middle years curriculum design?

Curriculum design

Middle years curriculum design must include several elements. The design process is not straightforward, but, with the benefit of the clarity provided by our rationale for middle years curriculum, it is evident this process does not need to be excessively complex either. This section discusses some pragmatic issues relevant to middle years curriculum design before going on to discuss and evaluate extant middle years curriculum designs.

Pragmatic issues
Developing a curriculum framework
Any middle years curriculum design must be multifaceted if it is going to be 'challenging, integrated, negotiated and exploratory' (MYSA, 2008). Accordingly, when the official curriculum is limited to an exposition of subject content to be delivered at each level—as it is in the case of the Australian Curriculum—it is necessary to develop a curriculum framework with links to pedagogy and assessment that will ensure the learning needs of students are met.

For instance, Tomlinson et al. (2002) recommended a framework that they called 'parallel curriculum' for educating gifted and talented students. Their framework entailed four curriculum strands:

1. core—derived from subject content of the official curriculum
2. connections—expands on key concepts within the core
3. practice—focuses on developing students' disciplinary expertise
4. identity—focuses on helping students relate to the discipline.

Although this framework does not attend to important aspects of the middle years curriculum such as diversity, it illustrates the necessity for curriculum design to include several facets.

Curriculum models

As revealed in the previous section, the student- and subject-centred models of curriculum are at odds with each other. Neither is appropriate, in its pure form, for the middle years curriculum, but a hybrid of the two models that focuses on meeting students' needs and ensuring that the curriculum includes substantive subject content is an ideal model for the middle years; thus, we should expect to see these two elements in contemporary designs for middle years curricula.

Curriculum models only approximate real life, so no application of a given curriculum model will be implemented perfectly. Indeed, in the middle years it is often preferable for the teacher to pragmatically and mindfully choose to implement just one part of a model or an amalgam of models that suits the classroom context, rather than attempting to implement a model in its entirety. The key is to operate mindfully—that is, always being able to justify every aspect of classroom curriculum design.

Evaluating curriculum design

Many different curriculum designs have been utilised in the middle years. Some are purpose designed for the middle years, but others have been borrowed from other fields. Some make a significant difference to student learning outcomes and are well worth the effort spent in preparation, but others have little or no impact on learning outcomes and may represent wasted effort. The middle years teacher needs to be able to discern which curriculum designs are most suitable for use in their context; thus, we will utilise our middle years curriculum rationale as a lens for evaluation. The rest of this section discusses and evaluates some contemporary middle years curriculum designs.

Middle years curriculum designs

Curriculum integration

Middle years experts are close to unanimous in their support for middle years curriculum designs that move beyond the single-subject approach. In particular, curriculum integration has been repeatedly recommended as especially suited to the middle years. Curriculum integration has appeal in the middle years because it holds the potential for students to gain a holistic or big-picture view of topics under investigation, so it harmonises with real life and avoids artificial divisions between subjects (Beane, 1990, 1997). In his review of more than 100 studies of curriculum integration over a 70-year period, Vars (2000, p. 87) concluded, 'Almost without exception, students in any type of interdisciplinary program do as well as, and often better than, students in a conventional [departmentalised] program'.

Although curriculum integration has been implemented with notable success in Australia (Pendergast, Nichols & Honan, 2012; L. Rennie, Venville & Wallace, 2012), there have also been some instances in which it has been implemented in the middle years without a sound rationale, with the result that the educational benefits to students have been regarded as dubious at best. For this reason, middle years teachers should be well informed before they decide to go ahead and implement curriculum integration.

Curriculum integration has a long and illustrious history, but in the last decade or so its reputation has suffered due to confusing terminology and a literature of indifferent quality (Dowden, 2007). Current understandings of curriculum integration derive from two separate traditions originating in the United States more than a century ago (Gehrke, 1998). One tradition is subject centred and is mainly concerned with correlating different subjects according to a common theme. This approach does not involve Dewey's (1916) notions of personal and social integration and is commonly referred to as multidisciplinary curriculum. It is closely related to the traditional single-subject curriculum and, in the middle years at least, has little to recommend it, because it does not include student-centred elements and thus fails to align with our middle years curriculum rationale, which places a premium on developmentally responsive curriculum design. A common approach to the design of multidisciplinary curricula in middle schools in the United States is for teachers to get together as a team and write a unit typically involving the Big Four subjects of mathematics, English, science and social studies but omitting the creative arts. This approach has led to the biggest single criticism of curriculum integration in the literature: planning for multidisciplinary curricula is time consuming and frustrating for teachers, and all too often the outcome is that middle years students are uninterested in the multidisciplinary unit and are reluctant to engage in classroom learning (Dowden, 2014).

The second tradition is student centred and has its roots in democratic schooling (Apple & Beane, 2007; Dewey, 1916). In its pure form, student-centred curriculum integration and the kind of school culture that is necessary to support it are far removed from the single-subject curriculum. Accordingly, both primary and secondary teachers can struggle to understand elements of student-centred curriculum integration, and they may not easily make the transition to implementing the kinds of curricula, pedagogies and assessments that are implied by a student-centred approach.

A definition of curriculum integration that is relevant to middle years curriculum design is 'a collective term for curricula where meaningful learning activities are designed by crossing discipline boundaries and/or utilising multiple disciplinary perspectives with the purpose of helping students to create and enhance knowledge and understanding' (Dowden, 2014, p. 18). This broad definition includes any curriculum design that straddles one or more subject areas, but, as we apply our middle years curriculum rationale, we can appreciate that creating 'meaningful learning activities' implies the need for student-centred elements, which moves curriculum design beyond the subject-centred focus of multidisciplinary curricula. In particular, middle years curriculum design for curriculum integration should include coherent alignment of subject content, meaningful cross-curricular connections, relevant pedagogies and authentic assessment (P. Nolan et al., 2000; Pendergast et al., 2005).

Beane's model
Twenty-five years ago, James Beane's (1990) book *A middle school curriculum: from rhetoric to reality* gave the American middle years movement a new curriculum design. This model of student-centred curriculum integration, sometimes referred to as integrative curriculum, was superbly sensitive to the developmental needs of middle years students and marked a sharp change from traditional subject-centred curriculum designs. Drawing from Dewey's (1916) ideas about democratic education, the model invited students to collaborate with their teachers and engage in curriculum making. Beane's model utilised Dewey's notions of integration discussed earlier. Beane (1997, p. 19) defined his model as 'a curriculum design theory that is concerned with enhancing the possibilities for personal and social integration through the organisation of curriculum around significant problems and issues, collaboratively identified by educators and young people, without regard for subject-area lines'. The notions of personal and social integration are central to Beane's model. These notions build students' knowledge and skills as well as preparing them for active citizenship. The process of negotiating the curriculum via collaborative teacher–student planning facilitates social integration and teaches middle years students valuable social skills.

Beane's (1997) integrative model is based on dynamic interplay between themes generated from students' personal and social concerns, disciplinary knowledge needed to explore the themes and the concepts of democracy, dignity and diversity. Students are asked two questions: 'What questions or concerns do you have about yourself?' and 'What questions do you have about your world?' As these questions are addressed, the subject content of the classroom curriculum emerges, and a particular problem or project is negotiated. In this student-centred curriculum design, students actively seek particular knowledge within the disciplines, because they are motivated to learn, as opposed to students following a subject-centred curriculum design, in which they would be expected to passively learn decontextualised disciplinary knowledge for its own sake. Beane grounded his curriculum design in the concepts of democracy, dignity and diversity. These concepts underpin his model by ensuring that subject content is relevant and meaningful for the diverse range of middle years students and dignifies them as learners by ensuring their experience of schooling is a democratic and inclusive process.

Beane's (1997) model is especially suited to the middle years, because, as we apply our middle years curriculum rationale, we can see it is attuned to a range of student developmental needs. High on the list are the important social skills developed while negotiating the curriculum, an approach to including students in curriculum making that also has a history in the Australian context (Boomer et al., 1992). Beane's (1997) model lends itself to a range of real-world contexts beyond the school gate, such as service learning (Theriot, 2009) and community-based projects that will make a difference—for example, determining the sustainable use of a water supply for local public amenities.

Although Beane's (1997) model is elegant and no doubt beguiling to teachers who are predisposed to democratic education, it is a radical curriculum design that is distinctly different from most other curriculum models, and it may struggle for acceptance in some school communities. Key political questions for the teacher to address, then, are whether Beane's model is an appropriate means of delivering mandated subject content and whether this form of curriculum integration will be accepted by local community stakeholders.

Lessons from the past

The following recommendations for the design and implementation of curriculum integration are indicated for the middle years and are drawn from hard-won lessons from the past when curriculum integration was less than successful (Dowden, 2012, 2014).

The status of the single subject

When designing curriculum integration for the middle years it is wise to respect the status of the single-subject curriculum within the Australian education system. The traditional single-subject curriculum model increasingly dominates as students progress from the middle to the senior years. Each subject has specific pedagogical content knowledge associated with it that defines subject-specific approaches to teaching. In the case of mathematics, for example, the subculture of specialist mathematics teachers validates particular ways of teaching mathematics and rejects others. The single-subject approach is conservative and resistant to change. It is reinforced by subject experts and scholars, by school cultures and by traditional assessment such as exams. Indeed, most secondary teachers define themselves by the subject they teach, rather than by the students they teach.

In many contexts, then, the high status of the single-subject curriculum explains the origin of resistance to curriculum integration. Subject teachers may be genuinely worried that the result of implementing curriculum integration will be that students will have diminished content understanding and will not develop subject-specific skill sets to the expected standards. Parents and caregivers may be concerned about curriculum integration because they want their children to be prepared for senior high school.

Accordingly, curriculum integration must comply with normal checks and balances. It is essential to be able to clearly demonstrate what middle years students have learned and the new skills they have mastered. In a traditional unit of work, the scope, sequence and learning outcomes are determined by the teacher beforehand, but this is not possible when the design of curriculum integration is negotiated by the teacher and students. An effective solution is to back-map learning outcomes from the unit against required standards or skills (Nesin & Lounsbury, 1999). Back-mapping can also include authentic assessment items, such as exhibitions of students' work and performances of students' skills (Beane, 1997).

Clarity of purpose

In order for middle years students to make substantive academic progress, the teacher must utilise the full range of curriculum, pedagogy and assessment tools to develop strategies that motivate students to actively engage in classroom learning activities. When curriculum design is done well, middle years students have an emotional and intellectual investment in it. Good design supports effective learning, and students soon build a portfolio of learning skills and develop a disciplined approach to their studies. The following points are especially relevant when planning curriculum integration in the middle years:

- Establish a clear and unambiguous rationale for implementing curriculum integration.
- Design student-centred curriculum integration that helps students achieve personal developmental goals and build social connections (especially in Years 5–7).
- Ensure that all teachers understand developmental needs in the middle years when implementing student-centred curriculum integration.
- Implement subject-centred multidisciplinary units in instances in which two or more disciplinary perspectives are desirable and this leads to deep learning, but avoid subject-centred multidisciplinary units unless the inclusion of each subject can be justified on a case-by-case basis.

Community stakeholders and pragmatism
When implementing student-centred curriculum integration, the teacher should make sure it is understood and supported by the community. In particular, the teacher must be certain that they have the unequivocal backing of the school principal (Snapp, 2006).

Teachers should be constantly aware of the need in the middle years to rigorously prepare students for academic success in high school; therefore, when implementing curriculum integration, teachers should be prepared to act pragmatically when necessary. For example, it often makes sense to temporarily suspend a curriculum integration program in order to teach standalone lessons for subjects such as mathematics (Dowden, 2014).

A doctrinaire approach to the implementation of curriculum integration for ideological rather than educational reasons is unacceptable. A likely outcome is that students will be disadvantaged and the wider community will not welcome future proposals to implement curriculum integration. In particular, it is important to always remember that student-centred curriculum integration is not a mainstream curriculum design; thus, in order to maintain a good reputation, it is vital to implement it well and to get the politics right.

Provocation 10.3 A negotiated curriculum that makes a difference

Penelope recently read an article in a teacher magazine about service learning. She thinks that her Year 6 class would greatly benefit from service learning if it were implemented in their local community. She is keen to get underway but is unsure where to start, especially since she knows her principal will want a sound argument before he will allow any of her students to go into the community.

 What advice can you give Penelope that will help her to enable her students to authentically engage in negotiating the content of the local curriculum and achieve learning outcomes that will make a lasting difference to the local community?

Chapter summary

This chapter makes the following key points:

- Middle years teachers must have a strong rationale for curriculum design.
- Middle years teachers should understand that curriculum is always political and that the curriculum enacted in the classroom is often the result of compromise.
- The middle years curriculum is the site of a political struggle between the interests of the subject-centred model, which emphasises a challenging curriculum that focuses on a robust understanding of the disciplines, and the student-centred model, which aims to harness the energy and enthusiasm of students by ensuring the curriculum is relevant and meaningful to them.
- Good middle years curriculum design is integrative, because it utilises elements of both the subject-centred and the student-centred models.
- The student-centred curriculum integration model offers exciting potential for the middle years, because it has the potential to maximise student engagement. But, because it is not a mainstream design, the political context tells us that teachers should implement it respectfully and pragmatically.

Part Three

Pedagogical practices in the middle years

Chapter Eleven

Cooperative and collaborative learning

KATHERINE MAIN

Learning intentions

In this chapter we will:
- examine the characteristics of cooperative and collaborative learning and the theories underpinning these as teaching strategies
- explore the benefits of collaborative learning for middle years students
- consider strategies that enhance the success of collaborative learning
- unpack the important role of the teacher as facilitator in collaborative learning and the implications for teaching.

What is cooperative and collaborative learning?

There is a significant amount of literature focused on cooperative learning and collaborative learning which explores their effectiveness and guides their use as pedagogical strategies to support student learning. However, the terms cooperative learning and collaborative learning tend to be used interchangeably, without a universally applied or accepted definition for each. Rather than focus on the semantics of the terms, some researchers have attempted to highlight the benefits of the social approach to learning and have worked using a conceptual understanding of cooperative and collaborative learning as being any activity in which two or more people work together to learn (see, e.g., the extensive work of Johnson and Johnson [2002, 2009]). While some researchers have argued that cooperative learning and collaborative learning are at opposite ends of the group work spectrum (Nagata & Ronkowski, 1998), others have sought to clarify the nuanced differences between them through a meta-analysis of literature around the two terms (Schoor, Narciss & Körndle, 2015). In a review of the terms and concepts surrounding cooperative and collaborative learning, Schoor, Narciss and Körndle (2015) argued that there were indeed distinct differences between the terms that could be summarised in relation to the amount of student ownership of the learning process. The results of their review described cooperative learning as a structured and teacher-directed activity involving the social interaction of groups of two or more students in the learning process and collaborative learning as involving a more interrelated learning experience in which students worked together to construct a common or collective understanding through the total combined efforts of the group.

Using the broad definitions drawn by Schoor, Narciss and Körndle (2015), in practice, we can say that cooperative learning is where students work together in small groups and help each other to learn. Research around cooperative learning has described the teacher as setting the task so that students still individually either complete a piece of work or find a solution to a problem (R. Brown, 2010; Johnson, Johnson & Smith, 2007; McInnerney & Roberts, 2004). Furthermore, cooperative learning activities generally have a specific focus and are usually content specific, placing the teacher in a position of authority and control over the learning (R. Brown, 2010; McInnerney & Roberts, 2004). Expert Jigsaw and Think, Pair, Share (see p. 204) are examples of cooperative learning activities. So, although the students work together, the work is directed and filtered through the teacher.

Collaborative learning has been described as students working together to co-create and co-produce a product or a response to a problem (Schoor, Narciss & Körndle, 2015). In contrast to cooperative learning, collaborative learning places the student at the centre of the learning (McInnerney & Roberts, 2004; Schoor, Narciss & Körndle, 2015). When given a collaborative task, students take ownership and responsibility for their learning by directing the exploration of the content, comparing and evaluating their findings, sharing and challenging new under-standings and being jointly responsible for the final product or solution to the problem (Gillies, 2008). Therefore, collaborative learning places the responsibility for learning on the students as they reflect and challenge their current thinking and beliefs to build a common understanding with others.

The focus of this chapter is on the purposeful use of social learning activities within the classroom for their recognised benefits. However, a majority of the literature on social learning activities has used the terms cooperative learning and collaborative learning interchangeably. McInnerney and Roberts (2004, p. 206) note that 'the title of a paper may use the word cooperative, while the body of the paper discusses collaborative learning, or vice versa'. However, many have argued that the differences in meaning are of real benefit only when reporting empirical results of studies. Thus, for ease of reading, the term used in this chapter will be collaborative learning.

Collaborative learning draws on the social constructivist theories of Vygotsky (1978), who argued that knowledge, values and attitudes are internally constructed through interpersonal interactions (conversations and communications) with others within learning contexts. Vygotsky's social constructivist theory recognises a number of other interrelated learning theories that shape how we understand the use of social learning activities. Johnson and Johnson (2002) examined a number of theories that support the use of collaborative learning strategies. These include social interdependence theory, cognitive development theory and behavioural learning theory. Together, these theories build our understanding of the under-pinning principles that guide and support students working together effectively to realise the benefits of group interactions.

Social interdependence theory posits that a positive interdependence among students encourages learning, as it supports and facilitates the learning environment (Johnson & Johnson, 2002). This positive interdependence occurs when group members perceive that achieving their individual goals is intrinsically linked to the other members of the group achieving their goals as well. In effect, collectively they can either succeed or fail (Johnson, Johnson & Smith, 2007). No interdependence exists where individuals believe that they can independently achieve their goal despite the success or failure of others. Thus, unity and a supportive network are developed in the group in which a common goal is aimed for. Without a positive interdependence, a competitive environment is created, which is at odds with the overarching aims of collaborative work.

Cognitive development theory claims that collaboration is essential for cognitive growth. Vygotsky's (1978) theory of cognitive development argues that social learning is the foundation for cognitive growth. During collaborative work, students experience peer tutoring, extended discussion and guided learning. They also are required to negotiate, plan and build on each other's ideas to solve a common problem. That is, as students work towards a common understanding, they experience and are exposed to multiple perspectives, thus broadening and challenging their current understanding far beyond what could be achieved on their own (Johnson & Johnson, 2002).

Collaborative learning creates an interdependence that aligns with the behavioural learning theory assumption that students will be motivated to learn and work towards an outcome if they perceive the result (reward) to be worth the effort. In a collective environment, the social aspects of learning and the interdependency created through the group tasks link to the classic work of B.F. Skinner (1963, 1984), who demonstrated that people can be conditioned through rewards or punishments. The collective and social rewards experienced through working collaboratively or the social sanctions experienced by not contributing effectively to the group can provide the rewards and sanctions argued for by behavioural learning theorists.

Provocation 11.1 Collaborative learning as a strategy

You are in your first year of teaching and have been assigned a Year 7 class. You really want to use some of the different teaching strategies that you learned through your teacher training program to bring some variety into your classroom, and you like the idea of group work. You know that middle years students enjoy working together and so are considering using a group work task for their history assessment. However, you are a little unsure whether to have the students do a task in small groups or whether it would be better to have them do a task individually.

 Consider your own experiences with cooperative or collaborative learning. It may have been in pairs or in a small group. Provide responses with defensible arguments to the following questions:

- What is your understanding of the reasons behind using these strategies for that subject?
- What benefits do you think you gained by doing the task with others?
- What, if anything, could have enhanced that experience for you?
- Does reflecting on your experiences change your thoughts about using group work in your own class?

The benefits of collaborative learning

For some teachers, whole-class teaching is almost exclusively the way that they teach. A review of studies of collaborative activities in mathematics and science teacher-centred strategies represented the method of instruction used most often in schools, with direct instruction dominating over 80 per cent of the talking in the classroom (Effandi & Zanaton, 2007). This historically entrenched approach to classroom teaching has been consistently reinforced through its replication over generations of classroom experience and a sense that a teacher (the fount of knowledge) teaches and students (vessels to be filled) practise, repeat and memorise information to be reproduced for assessment purposes. This polarised position of what teaching should look like has been challenged by a more student-centred approach since the 1970s (Vygotsky, 1978). Indeed, earlier theorists such as Piaget 'recommended group learning as a standard means of classroom learning' (Palmer, 2001, p. 41). Yet, Gillies and Boyle (2011) found that there is still a reluctance shown by some teachers to adapt to this more progressive form of education. Some teachers who are reluctant to adopt a group learning approach believe that direct teaching is the most effective or appropriate way to teach the content in their particular subject. Others have reported concerns around the organisation of the students as well as worries that behaviour management may be more challenging when using different pedagogical approaches. However, whole-class teaching does have a place in a middle years classroom and is particularly effective when teaching new and complex concepts and skills, introducing a new unit and requiring whole-class discussion to generate ideas, conducting demonstrations and creating an atmosphere in the classroom through music or narratives (Main, 2016a).

As a teaching strategy, collaborative learning aligns with the ethos of middle years education and is uniquely suited for middle years learners, as it meets the developmental demands and readiness of middle years students to interact with each other and engage in a challenging curriculum (Braz et al., 2011). Indeed, in a meta-analysis of research around 'cooperative, competitive, and individualistic goal structures', it was found that 'the more early adolescents' teachers structure students' academic goals cooperatively . . . (a) the more students will tend to achieve, (b) the more positive students' relationships will tend to be, and (c) the more higher levels of achievement will be associated with more positive peer relationships' (Roseth, Johnson & Johnson, 2008, p. 238).

Collaborative learning also aligns with Bruner's (1996, p. 84) statement that 'learning should be participatory, proactive, communal, collaborative, and given over to the construction of meanings'. Through this, Bruner, the definitive leader in cognitive psychology, argued that when learners work collaboratively they are proactive, in that they accept responsibility for their own learning through active involvement, they participate actively in their own learning, and they construct their own knowledge and learn through meaningful interactions and communications with their peers, their teachers and others beyond the classroom.

Over time, a number of meta-analyses have been conducted to examine the effects of collaborative, competitive and individual learning on a range of variables across students' academic, social and personal attributes: Johnson and Johnson (2002) reviewed 117 studies, Johnson et al. (1981), 122 studies and Roseth, Johnson and Johnson (2008), 148 studies. Each of the meta-analyses has consistently shown the use of collaborative learning strategies resulting in positive effects on students' achievement, socialisation, motivation, peer relationships and personal development. In particular, Johnson and Johnson's (2002) meta-analysis of collaborative learning found that the strength of the relationship between the dependent and independent variables for collaborative learning was significant and concluded that collaborative learning makes a positive impact on student outcomes.

Social benefits

The personal and social benefits of collaborative learning have been widely reported (Johnson & Johnson, 2002; Johnson et al., 1981; Roseth, Johnson & Johnson, 2008). The very nature of group work activities provides opportunities for students to interact with others and build a learning community. In a two-year study on science achievement, students reported that working together was fun and had the added benefit of improving students' social skills and social inclusion within the class (Thurston et al., 2010). Many researchers have found that, when working together, students are able to discuss their knowledge and thoughts with others, enabling them to clarify and exchange ideas as well as to gain knowledge through the varied explanations, views and perspectives of others (Ajaja & Eravwoke, 2010; Gillies, 2003; Gillies & Boyle, 2010). Collaborative learning strategies not only support different learning styles (Hennessey & Dionigi, 2013) but also enhance learners' acceptance of cultural diversity and openness to diversity in thinking (Cabrera et al., 2002; Sultan & Hussain, 2012). The intrapersonal and interpersonal skills developed when working with others are among the transferable soft skills necessary to negotiate the adult world, including self-management, self-awareness, social management and social awareness (Australian Curriculum, Assessment and Reporting Authority [ACARA], 2015d).

Achievement and cognitive benefits

Collaborative learning has been reported to improve students' academic outcomes (Gillies, 2016). Studies found that when students were actively engaged in the learning process through group activities, their reasoning, critical-thinking and problem-solving skills were enhanced (Ajaja & Eravwoke, 2010) and they attained higher academic results (Alghamdi & Gillies, 2013). During group learning tasks, students also showed greater ownership over their learning, with an improved quality of output in their academic work (Shachar & Fisher, 2004).

For the benefits of collaborative learning to be realised, consideration must be given to how students are grouped, and the task must be designed in a way that challenges students to use higher order thinking strategies (Gillies & Boyle, 2008). A meta-analysis of within-class grouping found that a group size of three or four was most effective and that how students were grouped in terms of ability had differing effects on student achievement gains. Gillies (2016) found that, when placed in heterogeneous groups, low-ability students learned more, while a homogeneous group configuration produced better outcomes for average-ability students. High-ability students performed equally well in any group configuration. This data would indicate the need for teachers to be aware of each student's ability level across different subject areas and to incorporate a range of different group configurations to support student learning. Importantly, though, higher academic results were reported for all different student ability levels and across a number of different subjects when collaborative learning was implemented (Ajaja & Eravwoke, 2010; Gillies, 2003).

There are numerous examples of studies that have demonstrated improved student outcomes in specific subjects through the use of collaborative learning strategies. For example, in an investigation of the effects of collaborative learning on students' attitudes and achievements in science, Thurston et al. (2010, p. 506) found that achievement gains, positive attitudes towards science and the 'range and nature of social connections persisted over time'. Other studies in science also found that working collaboratively not only improved students' attitudes, under-standing, scientific thinking and interest in science but also decreased their anxiety towards the subject (Hong, 2010; Kose et al., 2010; Lin, 2006). In health and physical education (HPE), collaborative activities were found to improve students' physical and communication skills as well as building positive relationships. Collaborative work also increased students' participation in active lessons (Bayraktar, 2011). And a meta-analysis of the benefits of collaborative learning in English classrooms found improvements in students' understanding of complex material through the discussion of ideas as well as gains in students' vocabulary, reading and comprehension levels (Puzio & Colby, 2013).

With the brains of middle years students reconfiguring and maturing, the use of teaching strategies that assist in building and developing cognitive ability can have a marked effect on how and what these students learn as well as on their academic gains (Atkins et al., 2012). Thus, for middle years students, group activities provide opportunities to use a range of higher order thinking skills, such as analysing, evaluating and creating (L.W. Anderson et al., 2005). As middle years students interact and work together, a range of other skills are also developed which help to support the young adolescent's brain development, such as negotiating, interpreting, organising, applying learning to new situations, clarifying information with others, discarding irrelevant information, reviewing and revising, reflecting on the product and process, abstract problem-solving and time and task management skills (Willis, 2007).

Provocation 11.2 Challenges of working collaboratively

Maree is a visual arts teacher in your team and, as a team, you have attended a professional development session about students working collaboratively. You all agree with the principles and understand the benefits for students in your classes and have made a commitment that students should experience group work in every discipline. However, Maree just doesn't see it working in her class and argues that visual art, particularly creative pieces, is an individual and personal expression of each student's skills, interests and creativity. She concedes that her students could work together on some of the theory-related tasks but is concerned that this is where the 'less creative and artistically talented' students tend to excel and 'catch up' their marks. Maree feels that making these tasks a group effort would disadvantage them.

 How would you respond to Maree?

Psychological benefits

The psychological benefits attributed to collaborative learning include trust, which students begin to develop as they express their ideas and experience a sense of being understood, and confidence that their ideas will be accepted without sanctions even if an answer or idea is incorrect (Hamada & Ebrary, 2013). For middle years students, the ability to contribute to a group increases motivation and helps to maintain a positive attitude even if a task is challenging (Laal & Ghodsi, 2012).

Furthermore, when students work together, the social interaction helps to promote self-esteem and a sense of belonging, as well as promoting interpersonal relationships resulting in improved attitudes towards school and peers (Ajaja & Eravwoke, 2010). Students working collaboratively also have reported an increased sense of autonomy, independence and achievement (Sultan & Hussain, 2012), which further promotes student engagement (Tinto, Goodsell & Russo, 1993).

Through collaboration, students are also able to improve their self-regulation skills. These are experimented upon and honed when situations arise that are difficult and require the individual to develop coping mechanisms that in turn reinforce positive behaviours and promote self-management skills (Atkins et al., 2012). Being able to regulate emotions is an important part of social and emotional learning in this critical developmental period.

Implementing collaborative learning strategies

Although research has shown a range of potential benefits from collaborative learning, it is important to note that placing students in groups will not always realise those benefits. To realise the benefits, the learning needs to be structured in a way that incorporates the key elements necessary for effective group learning. Johnson and Johnson (2009) developed a list of five key components that should be considered when establishing groups:

1. positive interdependence
2. individual responsibility and accountability
3. interpersonal and group work skills
4. face-to-face substantive interactions
5. group processing.

These interrelated components work together to promote effective group work.

Positive interdependence

Positive interdependence occurs when all the members of the group understand that the successful completion of the task can be achieved only through the combined efforts of the group. Students need to know not just how to do the task (task processes) but also how to work as a group (group processes) and how to get along (relationship processes) (Main, 2012). When working with others, students have two key responsibilities: first, to help each other complete the task, and second, to maintain positive working relationships in the group. Tasks that promote positive interdependence include inquiry- or problem-based projects.

Individual responsibility and accountability

Individual responsibility and accountability can be created through a range of recording and reporting processes that track and create responsibility for individual contributions and effort throughout the group task. Tracking the assignment and completion of tasks ensures that students take their individual responsibility seriously. During longer term projects, students should keep minutes of meetings, with action sheets for future tasks, as well as individual reflective journals around their group work experience, making their contribution easy to identify (Gillies, 2016).

Interpersonal and group work skills

Students need to be taught the interpersonal skills necessary for collaborative learning in order to maximise its effectiveness. The required skills include taking turns, communicating through active listening and speaking, making decisions, managing conflict, presenting as a group and running a meeting (Li & Lam, 2013). Reflecting on the group experience individually and collectively is also important for members of the group in order to understand what went well, where they could improve and what they are going to do next time they work in a group (Gillies, 2016).

Teachers should focus on explicitly teaching individual skills. One method to teach collaborative skills is to use a T-chart for each skill (i.e., a chart with two columns, the left headed 'Looks like' and the right headed 'Sounds like'). Through a teacher-led discussion around a particular skill (e.g., how to be encouraging), the class discusses and charts what this would look like and sound like in their classroom. The teacher then models the skill and provides students with opportunities to role play and practise the skill. The T-chart is displayed as a reminder of the skill and as a reference point for students.

Face-to-face substantive interactions

Through face-to-face substantive interactions students learn to contribute ideas and build upon the ideas of others. They also learn how to criticise or critique the ideas presented while not criticising others. Through these exchanges students are able to ask questions to clarify ideas and provide feedback to others, as well as 'helping, assisting, supporting, encouraging and praising each other's efforts' (Johnson & Johnson, 1999, p. 71). Working closely together helps students get to know one another better and builds the foundation for strong relationships with peers (Johnson & Johnson, 2009).

Group processing

Group processing involves group members evaluating the different aspects of their group, including assessing their progress as a group, summarising ideas and information and checking that their decision-making processes and problem-solving strategies are supported by all members of the group. Li and Lam (2013) reported that groups who worked through group processing (i.e., evaluating progress and processes) had higher achievement scores than groups who did not evaluate their group's processes and than students working independently. The process provides students with an increased understanding of the group process skills that are necessary for completing tasks, and the reflective nature of the process encourages students' metacognition and helps them develop an understanding of what works and what doesn't (i.e., social skills and group processes) when working in a group.

Once these five core elements have been considered and structured into collaborative activities, the respective roles of the teacher and students will be changed considerably. The activity changes from being teacher directed to being student directed. The role of the teacher becomes one of a facilitator who is involved only when students need clarification or instructions or to provide positive feedback on the students' work or the use of their interpersonal skills (Van Dat, 2013).

Provocation 11.3 Facilitating group projects

You have assigned student groups for an inquiry-based project that will run for the entire term. The students are in mixed-ability groups of four, and you are quite pleased with the progress that is being made by most groups. However, you are concerned with one group and, in particular, one student. Jerry is a bright student but tends to coast in all of his work. Learning comes easily, and he excels in almost every aspect of his work with seemingly very little effort. Two of his group members have come to you at different times in the last week complaining that Jerry isn't helping with the group project. You have noticed that he tends to sit back and watch the others work rather than becoming involved in the project.

 Provide responses with defensible arguments to the following questions:

- What are your first thoughts about what might be going on with Jerry?
- How will you approach this problem?

The role of the teacher

The first question that needs to be asked when considering using collaborative learning is 'What is the best way for students to learn this concept or skill?' Teachers must carefully consider how students will engage in material prior to setting the task, as the type of task being set and clarity around the task will determine whether students gain the full benefit from working together (Hu & Liden, 2011). However, placing socially unskilled students in a group and expecting them to work together effectively to complete a task is unreasonable. Many students are unaware of the processes they should follow to help them work together, and teachers need to explicitly teach a number of key skills to facilitate student collaborative learning. Understanding the process of working together to solve a problem or complete a task is also important. The requisite complexity of the task means that there is often a backward and forward flow through the stages of design, trial and final solution. Understanding the stages of the cycle helps a teacher know the best type of support to provide at each stage. A process cycle of group work tasks is outlined in Figure 11.1.

There are a number of factors that can affect the effectiveness of groups. When using collaborative learning strategies in a classroom, teachers need to ensure that they consider each of these factors to support the best possible outcomes for students:

- Group size: The optimum group size has been noted as three or four (Gillies, 2016).
- Group configuration: The best type of grouping for the activity—homogenous, heterogeneous or something else—should be considered.
- Task clarity: The task must be clearly defined and understood by all, so that students spend their time actively engaged in the task and not trying to understand what the task is actually asking them to do.
- Task complexity: The task needs to be stimulating and challenging, necessitating the use of the collective skills of the group.
- Rules: Setting guidelines and reminding students of the social skills that are important for effective collaborative learning at the beginning of every session helps set high expectations for the work to be completed.
- Roles: Clearly defined roles are needed for each member of the group.
- Facilitation of the group work process: Teachers need to continually monitor and support groups, but they also need to be careful not to offer too much advice or support, as one of the key benefits of collaborative learning is that students work together to complete the task.

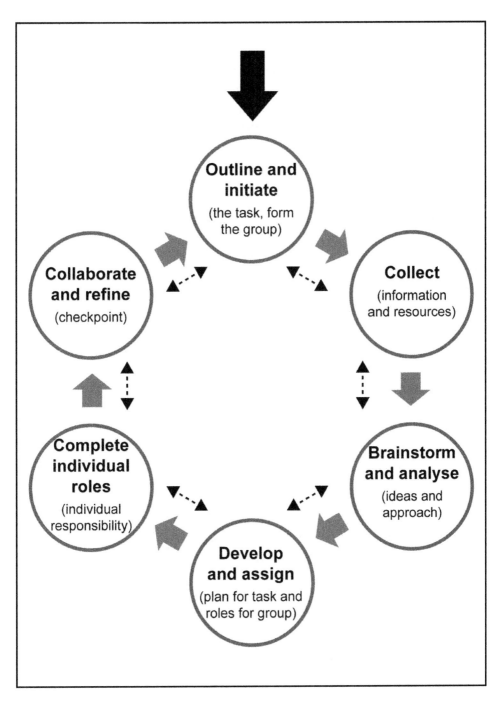

Figure 11.1 **A process cycle of a group work task**

Using collaborative learning strategies in the classroom

Teaching the skills necessary to undertake collaborative work effectively takes time and practice. Teachers begin to attune students to their roles and responsibilities when working together through the use of a range of teacher-directed collaborative learning strategies. There are many varied strategies; it is important for teachers to have a repertoire of these to meet the varied needs of the classroom and to remember that one strategy will not be appropriate for every activity. Below are a few well-known collaborative learning strategies taken from the *Productive pedagogies strategies kit*:

- Think, Pair, Share: Students engage in individual and paired thinking before they are asked to answer questions in front of the whole class. This is an easy first step to teaching group work and collaborative learning. It also helps to build the confidence of students who normally may be reluctant to offer answers in class.
- Expert Jigsaw: Members of the class are organised into jigsaw groups, and each member is given a different element of the material or problem to be solved, so that each group as a whole holds all of the material or problem to be solved. The jigsaw groups are then split into expert groups, so that all students holding the same part of the material are in the same group. The members of the expert groups work together to learn their part of the material or solve their part of the problem, then they reform into their jigsaw groups to share their learning one at a time. In this way, the work of the expert groups is quickly disseminated throughout the class, with each person taking responsibility for sharing a piece of the puzzle.
- Academic Controversy: Groups of four students engage in a process that challenges them to justify their beliefs on a specific issue.
- 1:2:4: Students engage in individual and small-group thinking before they are asked to answer questions in front of the whole class. This builds on the Think, Pair, Share strategy and helps students to build strong communication skills and the confidence to formulate and express an opinion on a topic or issue.
- Group Crossover: Students form into groups of three. Two of them complete the task, and the third plays a supporting role by observing and feeding back on their group's efforts (Day, Hazzard & Locke, 2002).

Computer-supported collaborative learning

Computer-supported collaborative learning is a method of collaborative learning that is increasingly being recognised as a pedagogical tool to engage learners

(So & Brush, 2008). Web 2.0 technologies such as wikis enable students to generate and share ideas and content (A.M. Kaplan & Haenlein, 2010) and build their critical-thinking and communication skills (Wheeler, Yeomans & Wheeler, 2008). Working collaboratively, students are able to review, question and refine the work of others, with classroom teaching continuing to facilitate the learning and skill development processes.

There is strong evidence that middle years students benefit in a number of ways when they are able to work collaboratively as opposed to when they work competitively or individually. Specifically, middle years students enjoy the social aspects of collaborative learning, and there are well-documented cognitive and psychological benefits gained through working together. However, the responsibility for the effectiveness of collaborative work rests with the teacher. The role of the teacher is to explicitly teach the skills necessary for students to collaborate effectively, including the skills necessary to complete tasks and work as a group, as well as effective intrapersonal and interpersonal skills. A critical component of facilitating collaborative activities is to promote extended dialogue among students, to scaffold problem-solving strategies and to model the skills necessary for effective collaboration.

Chapter summary

This chapter makes the following key points:

- There is a nuanced difference between cooperative and collaborative learning in relation to the amount of student ownership of the learning process. Working definitions for both constructs are provided, with cooperative learning being a more structured and teacher-directed activity and collaborative learning being a more interrelated learning experience that is student directed.
- Collaborative learning is underpinned by principles drawn from a number of learning theories, including the social constructivist theories of Vygotsky (1978), social interdependence theory, cognitive-development theory and behavioural learning theory.
- A range of benefits are realised when collaborative learning is used within a middle years classroom. There is strong empirical evidence demonstrating the social, psychological and academic benefits that students gain from working collaboratively.
- To realise the benefits of collaborative learning, a number of key elements must be considered when establishing student groups and setting group tasks. These

205

key elements include promoting positive interdependence, ensuring each student has individual responsibility and accountability within the group, explicitly
teaching interpersonal and group-work skills and providing opportunities for
substantive face-to-face interactions and group reflective processes.

• The role of the teacher is critical to the success of collaborative learning activities.
The structure of the task and student groupings must be carefully considered
and students must be explicitly taught the art and science of working together.

Chapter Twelve

Teams and teaming

KATHERINE MAIN

Learning intentions

In this chapter we will:
- define and characterise middle school teaching teams
- explore the skills and processes necessary for implementing effective teams
- consider the importance of self and group reflection and evaluation as ongoing improvement processes for teams.

Teaching teams in middle schools

Effective teaming practices continue to be a focus of much research (Erickson et al., 2015; Main, 2012; Vangrieken, Dochy & Raes, 2015; Vangrieken et al., 2015). In particular, an historical overview of the middle school movement in the United States noted that during the first decade of the 21st century the focus was on research-based practices of the middle school movement which highlighted teacher teaming as a critical component of middle school practices (Schaefer, Malu & Yoon, 2016). In 1989, the ground-breaking Carnegie Report was released, which outlined the imperatives for improving education for young adolescents. Elaborations to this report were developed with specific guidelines on what these imperatives would look like in action and were subsequently published in Jackson and Davis' *Turning Points 2000*. With teacher teams being an early structural component of middle schooling, they are also recognised by some as the keystone of middle years education (Felner et al., 1997; Mertens et al., 2010). Additionally, research has shown that the successful implementation of teaming practices appeared to 'have a significant effect on the degree to which other elements of the *Turning Points 2000* reforms may be accomplished' (Felner et al., 1997, p. 534). In Australia, a study of innovative Australian schools showed that during the implementation of middle school reform the typical trajectory of reforming schools' implementation efforts experienced a major dip, which occurred during the crossover between the initial implementation phase and the developmental phase of the reform (Pendergast et al., 2005). One of the key factors identified that could reduce the severity and duration of this dip was effective team practices, particularly consistency in team membership; congenial, philosophically aligned dynamics among team members; and a strong emphasis on posing and solving problems as a team (Pendergast, 2006). Thus, how well teacher teams function has a direct influence on both the level of implementation and the effectiveness of other components of a middle years philosophy (Felner et al., 1997; Pendergast et al., 2005).

The rationale underpinning teaching teams in middle schools is that teams create small learning communities of teachers and students. Teams also support other fundamental components of a middle schooling philosophy, including an integrated curriculum and strong teacher–student relationships. In a recent large-scale study of teacher collaboration, Vangrieken et al. (2015) identified almost 190,000 articles published from 2000 to 2012 which were synthesised to 82 studies that focused on teacher collaboration in mainstream schools. This review collated a large number of benefits reported for students and teachers, as well as for the whole school as an entity, when teachers collaborated. The benefits reported are presented below:

- Student benefits:
  - improved learning and understanding
  - greater social bonding
  - increased attendance.
- Teacher benefits:
  - increased opportunities for professional learning
  - heightened innovation, communication and problem solving
  - initiated and improved professional learning
  - improved technological skills
  - increased collective efficacy

- increased quality teaching, including more student-centred instruction
  - higher morale and motivation
  - greater moral support and reduced sense of isolation
  - improved collegiality and sharing of ideas and resources
  - more flexible environment
  - better alignment of written, taught and tested curricula.
- School benefits:
  - consistent adaptation and innovation
  - effective vehicle for restructuring and reculturing schools
  - cultural shift to more equity within schools
  - planned school-wide focus on students' needs
  - movement towards a flattened power structure (Vangrieken et al., 2015).

As team practices have positive implications for both teaching and learning when teachers team effectively, understanding how to form, develop and then sustain effective teams is important (Main, 2007). Thus, assigning teachers to teams is the beginning; getting teachers to team effectively is the key to improved teaching and learning outcomes in middle school classrooms.

Implementing teaching teams

Many schools embarking on a middle schooling reform recognise the importance of creating teaching teams. Team teaching can be described as two or more teachers taking responsibility for teaching the same students, irrespective of group stage or community building. Teaming may include all or any of the following activities:

- sharing of physical space
- joint planning of curriculum
- collaboratively teaching, either as a whole class or with each teacher taking different combinations of students across the classes for specific lessons
- establishing common rules across classes
- sharing of resources
- collaboratively planning and administering assessment tasks (Chadbourne, 2004; Main & Bryer, 2005a; Vangrieken, Dochy & Raes, 2015).

These joint responsibilities can create a positive interdependence between the members of a teaching team, in which each member of the team has specific

Provocation 12.1 Teacher teams and middle years practices

The signature practices of middle schooling include the following:

- integrated and disciplinary curricula that are negotiated, relevant and challenging
- heterogeneous and flexible student groupings
- cooperative learning and collaborative teaching
- small learning communities that provide students with sustained individual attention in a safe and healthy school environment
- emphasis on strong teacher–student relationships through extended contact with a small number of teachers and a consistent student cohort
- authentic and reflective assessment with high expectations (Middle Years of Schooling Association [MYSA], 2008).

 Consider some of the signature practices of middle schooling and provide responses with defensible arguments to the following questions:

- How does organising teachers into teams support the implementation of these signature practices?
- Which practices could not be implemented effectively if teachers worked in isolation?

responsibilities in relation to the planning, teaching or assessing of classes. However, 'placing teachers in teams does not guarantee that teaming will take place' (Main, 2007, p. 277). Research on teaching teams has shown that the most salient difficulties facing teams are members' uncertainty about their roles within the team (Thomas, 1992) and, indeed, what teaming is all about (Main, 2007). Teachers enter into a team with enthusiasm and optimism about its potential, but without adequate training the team's progress can be slow and uncertain. In both the United States and Australia, research has identified a number of team skills that need to be explicitly taught, including skills in problem-solving, conflict management and team processes, and interpersonal and intrapersonal skills (Erb & Doda, 1989; Main, 2007).

How teachers work together in teams varies widely, and current descriptions of team teaching can provide starting points but not prescribed texts for those embarking on a team teaching experience. Each new team must accommodate differences among team members (e.g., levels and types of expertise, personalities and understandings of team practices), students (e.g., age, year level and class configurations), the physical layout of classrooms and the school programs under which the team will be operating (e.g., interdisciplinary team or interdisciplinary curriculum, primary school, middle school or senior school). Taking into consideration these differences, team teaching can look very different across year levels, within year levels and from setting to setting across schools. However, there are also a number of commonalities that can be identified in any team's development.

Formation, development and maintenance

In a similar fashion to business teams, teaching teams have been shown to go through a life cycle with a beginning, middle and end. One of the most popular theories of small-group development—the Stages of Group Development Model, which comprises the stages of forming, storming, norming and performing—was proposed by Tuckman (1965). Although teams do not necessarily progress through the stages identified by Tuckman in a sequential pattern, there are particular characteristics and tasks associated with each stage that team members should recognise and work through if the team is going to progress on an upward trajectory. Understanding the characteristics and tasks associated with each stage is important, as a team's effectiveness is improved by team members' commitment to reflection and ongoing evaluation of their practices and progress.

J.E. Jones and Bearley (2001) proposed the Group Development Assessment Model. This model also proposes a staged approach to group development, however there is both a task and a process dimension to it. In this model, the task stages (orientation, organisation, open data-flow and problem solving) refer to how the group completes the task and the aligned process stages (dependency, conflict, cohesion and interdependence) refer to the interrelationships of the group members at each stage. Further, Jones and Bearley argued that groups may resolve their task structure and group dynamic concerns at different rates. For example, a group may have won its way through to the problem-solving task stage but remain arrested at the dependency process stage. While Jones and Bearley further argued that task structure and group process combinations are interdependent, J.K. Ito and Brotheridge (2008) noted that in natural work settings the starting point in the task behaviours may be well advanced (i.e., group members have had a similar experience) but the process stage still be in its infancy (i.e., group members have not worked together before).

Table 12.1 highlights the relationships between Tuckman's (1965) Stages of Group Development Model and J.E. Jones and Bearley's (2001) Group Development Assessment Model (Main, 2012).

Table 12.1 Aligning two models of effective team processes

Stages of Group Development[a]		Group Development Assessment[b]		
Stages	Characteristics	Task	Process	Relationship
Forming	Immature	Orientation	Dependency	Formal
Storming	Fractionated	Organisation	Conflict	Antagonistic
Norming	Sharing	Open data flow	Cohesion	Artificial collegiality
Performing	Effective	Problem-solving	Interdependence	Authentic collegiality

a   Tuckman (1965).
b   J.E. Jones & Bearley (2001).

A teacher teaming method

The two models described above are incorporated in this section into a further suggested model of effective team processes, with guidelines summarising some of the characteristics of effective teams during each stage of development and the associated processes.

As a team progresses through its life cycle, Main (2012) argued, team members must manage three different processes simultaneously:

• task processes—the job to be done
• team processes—how the team functions
• relationship processes—how team members get along with each other.

How teams negotiate each of the processes can determine how quickly a newly formed team becomes a performing team. Typically, newly formed teams are in the forming stage for approximately two to three months. If conflict management is addressed effectively, the storming stage may last only a month or two before teams move into the norming stage. Teams settle quickly in this stage, which can be very transient, also lasting only a month or two, before becoming a performing team. In optimal conditions, a team can move through the cycle from forming to performing in approximately six or seven months. This means a team that has been newly formed at the beginning of the school year can be working as a performing team by the beginning of Term 3. Members of performing teams have reported a greater sense of efficacy, and their students' outcomes are improved (Wheelan, 2005).

Stage 1 Getting started: forming
Normally, once teams have been formed, they jump straight into the task and attempt to hit the ground running. This is often done without team members taking the time to get to know each other, to learn and understand each other's strengths and weaknesses or to gel as a team. The main tasks in the forming stage of a team's development are to establish ground rules for the team, set in place team goals, assign roles, agree upon rules and set common expectations. Some of the most common reasons teams fail are disorganisation, unclear or conflicting goals and expectations, competing commitments (time management), lack of motivation and conflict (Katzenbach, Smith & Douglas, 1993; Main, 2007). It is during the initial forming stage that team members can set the boundaries and avoid a number of the pitfalls common to teams.

It is important to note that team members do not have to be the best of friends to work effectively together. In an Australian study, Jarzabkowski (2001) explored the extent to which a genuine collegiality is necessary to the success of a team's goal. Her intensive case study showed that positive personal relationships in which teachers socialise outside school hours can be advantageous but are not a necessary component of collegiality. However, strong professional relationships are important.

Stage 2 Moving along: storming
Conflict is an inevitable and important aspect in any team's development, and it can either help or hinder a team's performance. It is the key element in the storming stage and is then an ongoing feature throughout the team process. Van de Vliert (1997, p. 5) described conflict as a situation in which a person or a group is 'obstructed or irritated by another individual or a group and inevitably reacts in a beneficial or costly way'. Thus, any issue that creates discord within an individual member of the team is said to cause conflict.

A conflict can be broken down into two parts: the actual cause of the conflict or issue and the team members' behaviour responses. A conflict issue can include anything from a different idea about how to complete a task to incompatible beliefs or philosophies; disagreements about goals, expectations or actions; perceptions about the quality or quantity of another person's work; roles and resources; lack of contact or communication; poor planning resulting in doubling up, misinterpreting or missing key aspects of the task; unfair distribution of the workload; external work or personal commitments; and dominance of the team by one or more members. J. Brown and Duguid (2000) argued that many conflicts are caused by misunderstandings during communications; that is, the message or idea received is not the message or idea intended. The range of issues causing conflict when working together have been condensed into the following list:

- goals—fuzzy or unrealistic
- roles—unclear or unacceptable
- resource allocation—insufficient or inefficient
- leadership—weak process for task and relationship management
- accountability—not in place; team members can feel there is an unequal distribution of work
- values—different priorities (turf wars)
- communication—poor communication skills, miscommunication
- personalities—not recognising the value of and building on differences (Sallis, 2014).

Conflict behaviour is an individual's 'intended or displayed outward reaction to the conflict issue' (Van de Vliert, 1997, p. 6). Conflict can 'provoke anger, anxiety, distress, fear, and aggression. It often breaks down relationships, hinders communication, and obstructs problem solving' (Tillett, 1999, p. 15). Nevertheless, these negative factors are more likely to be the results of the conflict behaviour than those of the conflict issue. Hoover and DiSilvestro (2005, pp. 4–5) maintained that the differences between conflictual and constructive conflict are in the timing and in an individual's ability or inability to use conflict constructively. Thus, to manage conflict effectively, getting the timing of the response right can be as important as the response itself.

It has been widely assumed that for teams to function effectively great emphasis should be placed on harmonious collaboration (Callanan & Perri, 2006). However, while it is important that team members do not let conflict escalate to the point that the team becomes dysfunctional, conflict is an important and positive feature of all teams, as continually deferring to a collaborative style and avoiding conflict can result in a 'contrived collegiality' (A. Hargreaves & Dawe, 1990).

How team members manage conflict will largely determine whether the team progresses towards becoming a performing team. It has been recognised that conflict does not remain confined within the storming stage but continues to be an important facilitator throughout the team's norming and performing stages. Tillett (1999) identified an extensive list of constructive functions of conflict, including:

- preventing the stagnation of ideas and enthusiasm
- encouraging members to examine problems more closely
- promoting personal growth and development by challenging the individual
- promoting the team's identity and cohesion
- encouraging critical self-reflection
- improving interpersonal communication
- building trust among team members as thoughts, feelings, needs and opinions are shared and explored.

Stage 3 Pulling it together: norming

In the norming stage, the team has begun to be more effective. Focus has moved from the individual towards an attitude of 'How can I help the team?' Team goals, rules and expectations are accepted and adhered to. Trust begins to be more evident, and team members have learned to work together in order to complete the task at hand. Differences among team members are recognised and appreciated, and team members begin to feel a sense of belonging to the team and confidence that the team is heading in the right direction. As the team works and grows together, there is a balance between being focused and getting the task done and maintaining and supporting relationships between members of the team. As confidence grows within the team, team members can begin to evaluate, and implement ways to improve, the team's performance.

Stage 4 Working as a cohesive team: performing

Over time, as a team manages and solidifies the task, the team and the relationship processes involved in working together, it moves into the performing stage of its life cycle. It takes time to reach this stage of team development. Team members are generally satisfied with the team's progress, roles are more fluid, and there is a history developing between team members. Often a number of inside jokes have developed, and there is a common language and accepted code of behaviour. Individuals are all working together to reach the optimum outcome for the team. There is a sense of reward in the team achieving well.

For permanent work teams such as teaching teams, performing is the last stage in their development (Robbins, Millett & Waters-Marsh, 2004). During this stage, commitment to the team is high. Once teams reach this stage their output is at an optimal level. Teams can continue as performing teams for a significant period of time, until they become stale and need new ideas (from five to seven years) or there is a change in the team composition or dynamics that causes them to regress to an earlier stage in the developmental cycle.

Provocation 12.2 Teacher teams

Beck has just graduated and is excited about her first teaching position. She has been placed in the middle school of a Prep to Year 12 school. She excitedly goes onto the school's website and her excitement quickly dissipates as she realises that the middle school has a very strong emphasis on teacher teams. Beck's experiences in group work in her university studies were not good. She worked hard and often discovered she was doing a large proportion of the work. She found group work difficult, yet she was keen to work with more experienced teachers because she knew she would need support as a newly graduated teacher.

 Describe how you would approach this new appointment if you were Beck. How could you ensure a different experience from that of the disappointing group work projects?

Knowledge, skills and processes in effective team practices

The success of a teaching team depends on a combination not just of the aggregated skills, talents and resources of the individual members, but also of the processes team members use to interact with one another to complete the task. Understanding the interrelationship between team processes has increasingly been recognised as critical to developing theoretical models of team effectiveness (Marks, Mathieu & Zaccaro, 2001).

Team effectiveness depends on more than productivity (task completion) or performance (the team working together). It also involves different levels of each individual's self-efficacy, satisfaction and commitment to the team (relationships) (Marks, Mathieu & Zaccaro, 2001).

Certain knowledge, skills and processes are important throughout the teaming process, from the team's formation to the maintenance of a performing team. A range of skills associated with some of the collaborative tasks undertaken by teachers was identified by Main (2007). However, the importance of some of the skills and knowledge is heightened during certain stages of a team's progress. For example, a newly formed team will need to utilise organisational, decision-making and team process skills to set up the team, while a team entering the storming stage will have a heightened need for communication, negotiation and conflict management skills. The aggregate of each team member's assessment of their feelings, behaviours and task focus may enable teams to identify where the team is predominantly sitting. This in turn may allow targeted professional development to be undertaken in the predominant skills associated with that stage to help the team progress.

In addition, the effects of the relationship processes must be factored in. These are particularly salient for teaching teams in which poor interpersonal relationships may adversely affect professional relationships. For example, if group members have had negative experiences in team work or with another member of the team, they may enter a work group with a negative attitude and cause the group to falter, and sometimes stay, within the antagonistic stage of the relationship process model. Specific skills and resources relating to each set of processes are essential to the successful functioning of a team. Lag effects of task behaviours on process behaviours have been identified, and process behaviours can also cause lag effects on task behaviours (J.E. Jones & Bearley, 2001, cited in J.K. Ito & Brotheridge, 2008). If the team is to progress, issues in the stage that is lagging need to be resolved. Factors necessary to move teams effectively and efficiently through each process can be identified at an individual, team and whole-school level.

Barriers to effective team practices

The expectation that collaborative practices will result when teachers are placed in teams has not always been realised. Collaborating on some tasks has not always been effective in classrooms, beneficial for teachers or students or useful to teaching practice. A number of barriers to effective team practices have been identified, and several, such as balkanisation, groupthink, wasted collaboration and lack of staff continuity, are particularly salient in middle school teaching teams.

Balkanisation

When a team is formed and there is a strong emphasis on commitment to the team, it can be effectively isolated from other teams and staff within the school. This has been called balkanisation. Fullan (1997) argued that creating an insular climate within teams, in essence isolating team members from other staff, can lead to the burnout of individuals within these teams. In an Australian study by Main (2007), a sense of being isolated from other teams and staff was expressed by at least some of the members in all teams within the study. However, when team members were involved in ideas and issues or were able to seek help or advice outside the immediate setting of the team, and yet maintained sight of the core goals of the team, the sense of isolation and burnout was reduced (Fullan, 1997; Main, 2007).

Groupthink
Groupthink occurs when individuals within a team attempt to avoid conflict, or to keep the peace, by agreeing with team decisions. Groupthink can negatively affect teams in a number of ways. First, it may result in team members sabotaging the team's effort (e.g., agreeing with a decision and then refusing to follow through). Second, deferring to a groupthink decision-making style can suppress the exploration of ideas. Third, groupthink can result in one person dominating or directing the team, which in essence negates any positive effects of the team's original purpose. Numerous ways to avoid groupthink have been suggested, including creating an open climate of communication within the team, occasionally drawing on the expertise and opinions of others outside the team and the rotation of leadership roles within the team (Fullan, 1993).

Wasted collaboration
Wasted collaboration occurs when team members believe that everything done within the parameters of the team needs to be done collaboratively. Chadbourne (2004, p. 9) argued that collaboration can be 'counterproductive or inconsequential'. There are some aspects of a team's work that can best be done by one person, particularly tasks that require specialist expertise that one team member holds. This is not to say that others cannot comment on, or have input into, what is being undertaken, but that the lion's share of the task may be best done by one person. Finding the balance between collaborating on everything and identifying tasks that are more effectively completed by individuals is important, as a better or greater result cannot be achieved in every aspect of a team's work by collaborating.

Lack of staff continuity
Having a stable core of people has been argued to be a key attribute in successful teaching teams, while a lack of staff continuity has been shown to be a regressive step in a team's development (Erb & Doda, 1989; Main, 2007). Effective working relationships take time to develop and mature. Teaching partnerships and teaching teams become good only after teachers have had the opportunity to work together

for a sustained period of time (Sandholtz, 2000). Every time a new member of the team is introduced, bringing changes to the core teaching staff of a team, the team regresses to the forming stage. It takes time for team members to get to know one another and for the team to renegotiate its rules and expectations. If team membership is constantly changing, it may result in a lack of coherence with learning pathways for students and in difficulty for teachers in establishing strong relationships with students.

Evaluating middle school teaching teams

One of the dangers when establishing a teaching team is to create a list of all the key collaborative tasks that can be undertaken by the team, together with a list of the key attributes of team members, and to check off these practice indicators as rigid orthodoxies for an effective team. That is, 'if all these tasks are undertaken collaboratively by all team members and all team members possess all these key attributes, effective team practices will be a natural result'. However, teams that are implementing new practices require optimal structures and processes to progress from a forming to a performing team. Regardless of the level of team skills that individuals possess, teams cannot function effectively within an inhospitable environment (i.e., where they are not supported), and teams will not function effectively if individuals do not have sufficient training in order to commit to and invest in the team. Alexander, Murphy and Woods (1996) noted that without adequate training or support, teachers tended to revert to what they knew and understood in practice (i.e., working in isolation) despite any innovations (e.g., middle schooling) implemented by the school.

Just as research into Australian middle schools has shown that there is not one true model or ideal of middle schooling (Chadbourne & Harslett, 1998; Luke et al., 2003; Main, 2007), nor is there one ideal model of a middle school teaching team. Differences in school contexts, such as location, physical setup and organisation of classes, can affect the functioning of teams. Also, the personality, experience, expertise, gender, race, age and so on of individual team members can affect the way a team looks. Indeed, teams can look very different within and across year levels within a school, as well as from context to context. Thus, while the implementation of middle years teams may have overarching guidelines as to the knowledge, processes and skills that support effective team practice, ideal teams will and should look different from within and across year levels and from school to school.

Provocation 12.3 Building effective teacher teams

You are working in a highly effective school teaching team with three motivated and energetic teachers. You all get along well and regard each other as friends as well as colleagues. Things just seem to work. You are looking forward to staying together as a team. Other teams in the school look to you as the lighthouse team. Although it seems like serendipity, the team hasn't just happened. You have worked hard to set the common rules and expectations and to be considerate of each other. You have been asked to summarise what it takes to make a team work to all staff on the first day back in the new year. You consider the benefits of working together and are also aware of the difficulties that can occur.

 Imagine that you have to give a ten-minute summary of effective middle school teaching teams. What would be the five main pieces of advice that you would give to other staff?

How are effective teaching teams measured?

The difficulty in defining and identifying good or effective teams has become the focus of a new wave of research, including the development of the Team Functioning Scale (Erickson et al., 2015). A summary of the literature on team practices has identified six indicators of good practice that are present in effective teaching teams:

- each member having a clear role with a definite purpose within the team, creating a positive interdependence between team members
- equitable distribution of responsibilities among team members
- flexibility of team members and ability to adapt to changes in both pedagogy and curriculum
- strong communication evidenced by regular open and honest communication among team members, including conflict being dealt with quickly
- clear and attainable team goals
- each member's expertise being valued and utilised to produce the best outcome for students (Flowers, Mertens & Mulhall, 1999, 2000, 2002; Pounder, 1999).

Effective teams are also measured against a number of qualitative indicators, including team members':

- positive attitude to teaming
- perceived effectiveness in teaching
- positive perceptions about relationships with students, other staff, parents and the wider community
- improved student outcomes (Flowers, Mertens & Mulhall, 1999).

The Team Functioning Scale (TFS) was designed for teams to self-audit their current practices and identify areas that are in need of improvement. It has been tested and validated for reliability by almost 5500 respondents representing 365 schools across three American states (Erickson et al., 2015). A self-audit tool such as the Team Functioning Scale would be useful in helping teaching teams evaluate and reflect on how well they are utilising the range of practices of effective teams and as a starting point to support their improvement efforts.

Teacher teams in the middle years

The research strongly supports teacher teams for the benefits afforded to teachers, students and the school as a whole. However, a number of difficulties face schools as they attempt to implement teaching teams. Although teaching teams may initially find the approach challenging, effective team practices are critical to the successful implementation of a number of the underpinning principles of middle schooling.

Effective team practices in middle school teams start with the need for schools to improve team establishment processes—that is, looking at the requisite skills and supports necessary to help teams form and develop on an upward trajectory. When assigning members to teams, experience (i.e., in teaching, in the school or year level and in working in teams) has been shown to be just as important as achieving balance with other variables such as teaching areas (Main 2007; Pounder, 1999). Experience counts! Teachers who have experience in team practices are able to guide other less experienced team members through the challenges of developing a strong team. Teachers who have experience within a school are able to provide the team with expertise about how the school functions. Team members who have a number of years of teaching experience are able to guide other team members more effectively through the task processes, avoiding some pitfalls.

Barriers to good team practices have been easy to identify—for example, lack of explicit training in team knowledge, skills and processes, and staff turnover. Bridging the gap between research and local practice will require ongoing professional training and support for teams and, in some instances, exploring local education policy to find ways to keep teams together.

Chapter summary

This chapter makes the following key points:

- Effective team practices underpin a number of the signature features of middle schooling practice, including the creation of small learning communities. There has been a large research agenda around effective team practices and the benefits for students, teachers and the school community.
- Team teaching and teaming are broad umbrella terms for a range of activities that can be undertaken by two or more teachers who are responsible for the same group of students.
- All teams experience a 'life cycle' that commences when teams are formed and continues throughout the life of the team. Different models for the life cycle of teams have been presented but all propose a staged cycle that includes either tasks or processes to be achieved at each stage.
- At each stage of a team's development there are certain types of knowledge, skills and processes necessary for effective team practices. Teams must also simultaneously negotiate the three interrelated processes relating to the task, the team's functioning and interpersonal relationships.
- Where teams do not have clear goals, roles and rules, or team members do not possess the requisite skills to progress the team's goals, a number of barriers to effective team practices can arise.
- Although all teams are different, as they consist of different team members and are operating within different contexts, there are certain common characteristics that are present in effective teams.

Chapter Thirteen

Higher order thinking

ANNETTE HILTON and GEOFF HILTON

Learning intentions

In this chapter we will:
- explore the components of higher order thinking
- develop an understanding of the importance of higher order thinking for students
- explore ways to explicitly focus on the development of higher order thinking in classrooms.

The components of higher order thinking

In today's competitive society, it is vital that all citizens are able to think critically and creatively. It is important that they are able to collaborate, communicate effectively, engage in lifelong learning and function in a society that is data rich and increasingly visual. If the job of educators is to prepare students for their futures in this rapidly changing world, it is imperative that deliberate actions are taken to ensure that those students are equipped with experiences and skills that will allow them to function effectively through the use of higher order thinking.

An easy and workable definition of higher order thinking was offered by Geertsen (2003), who identified it as an appropriate umbrella term for all types of extraordinary (not ordinary) thinking. He went on to say that higher levels of thinking are distinguished from ordinary thoughts by the amount of control exercised by the thinker and the degree of abstraction required.

Teachers, schools and school systems must identify practices that appropriately address the unique needs and characteristics of middle years students. These characteristics are evident in middle years students' physical, social, emotional and intellectual development (Centers for Disease Control and Prevention, 2016). The intellectual characteristics of middle years students include:

- greater capacity for abstract thinking
- intense curiosity and interest in intellectual pursuits
- high achievement when challenged and engaged
- ability to be self-reflective
- increased ability to engage in metacognition and self-regulation
- increased ability to express themselves verbally (Effeney, Carroll & Bahr, 2013; M.-T. Wang & Eccles, 2011).

These characteristics lend themselves perfectly to engaging students in the middle years in higher order thinking. The intellectual growth of middle years students must be acknowledged and supported by matching their dramatic changes in thinking ability with increased expectations of what they can achieve. The inclusion of higher order thinking skills as a middle years practice, in conjunction with other pedagogies, will greatly enhance the prospect of meeting middle years students' developing cognitive needs and will cognitively engage them at a deeper level.

It is also necessary to consider what is important for students to learn. Thinking skills and knowledge should be learned and used in an integrated way, rather than in isolation from one another. The deliberate development of higher order thinking skills is one link in a complex chain of curriculum, pedagogy and assessment that together can effectively address the learning needs of middle years students. Suggestions for how teachers can support these learning needs include focusing on creative-, critical- and complex-thinking skills. The first step towards achieving this requires an understanding of the importance of higher order thinking; however, any discussion of higher order thinking must begin by distinguishing it from ordinary thinking.

The nature of thinking
All human beings think, but thinking can occur with different levels of complexity. Definitions of thinking can be complicated. Cognitive scientists have defined

thinking as problem-solving, which begins with perception and recognition and is followed by a search for connections. Then, data are retrieved and transformed, and, lastly, progress towards problem resolution is assessed (Geertsen, 2003). Lower order thinking requires routine or simplistic applications of prior knowledge and involves memorising or reproducing information, which can result in students having fragmented knowledge that is not integrated or well connected (Jonassen, 2000). In addition, this form of thinking requires only surface-level cognitive engagement (Fredricks, Blumenfeld & Paris, 2004). Higher order thinking, on the other hand, incorporates much more.

Provocation 13.1 Thinking about thinking

To be able to teach thinking skills we must be aware of the variety of types of thinking.

 Think about your own thinking in recent days (think metacognitively). Give an example of how you used each of the types of thinking listed below:

- remembering
- knowledge reproduction
- information synthesis
- generalising
- explaining a complexity
- hypothesising
- problem-solving

- analysing
- evaluating
- thinking critically
- predicting
- reflecting
- thinking metacognitively.

The nature of higher order thinking

Higher order thinking challenges students to expand the use of their minds. For decades, there has been ongoing confusion in defining higher order thinking. According to Lewis and Smith (1993, p. 136), 'Higher order thinking occurs when a person takes new information and information stored in memory and interrelates and/or rearranges and extends this information to achieve a purpose or find possible answers in perplexing situations.' Several authors have attempted clarification by restricting higher order thinking to Bloom's (1956) analysis, synthesis and evaluation (Hopson, Simms & Knezek, 2001–02). However, Braggett (1997) maintained that such definitions exclude some higher order thinking skills important for middle years students, and he added critical thinking, relationships, predicting, hypothesising, problem-solving and reflective thinking. More recently, Gibbs and Poskitt (2010) described the deep levels of cognitive engagement employed during higher order thinking as including self-regulation, metacognition, strategising, constructing and producing knowledge and creating products and performances.

Ultimately, rather than being overwhelmed by the definitional debate that continues among theorists, it is important that educators focus on the value of higher order thinking. But some general definitions of higher order thinking may be useful. In attempting to summarise the multiple definitions, Yeung (2015, p. 556) concluded that higher order thinking involves lower order thinking in combination with the ability to transform or transfer knowledge to new 'uncharted contexts'. It involves thinking critically and reflectively to create new meanings (Queensland Curriculum and Assessment Authority, 2015).

Why teach higher order thinking skills in the middle years?

Throughout history, and in many facets of life, higher order thinking has been an attribute that enhanced an individual's possibility of success. The better hunters in a tribe, the better players in a team, the better employees in an organisation are those with that something extra. Many hunters, players and employees may have the basic skills to perform the required task, but the standout members of these groups are those who can analyse, synthesise and evaluate the circumstances in which they find themselves. It is their higher order thinking skills that give them the advantage. Unfortunately, it is not possible to say that schools always identify the better students by their higher order thinking skills. Instead, success is often measured by students' abilities to reproduce knowledge, rather than by their ability to create their own (Renzulli, 2000). The stories that abound of great achievers in our society who were deemed underachievers at school bear witness to incorrect judgements of student ability.

As children grow, their capacity to learn thinking skills increases, and so too must the levels of intellectual challenge offered to them in school. Research conducted by Lingard et al. (2001) found low levels of intellectual demand across the schools in the study. Subsequently, Luke et al. (2003) evaluated middle years education across Australia and argued for further emphasis to be placed on intellectual engagement and demand in middle years classrooms. In the United States, the National Middle School Association (2003), now called the Association for Middle Level Education, also emphasised the need for high expectations and intellectually challenging activities to be integrated into middle years education. Reis (1998) argued that some students who underachieve do so because the level of thinking required provides so little challenge that they choose not to participate as a matter of principle. She suggested that there is a need to address the mismatch between students' abilities and the thinking opportunities provided in the classroom. According to Hattie (2009), students are more highly engaged and demonstrate higher levels of achievement when they are able to use self-regulatory thinking strategies and metacognition. It is also known that students are more likely to be deeply engaged if they perceive their learning as inspiring and challenging (D. Brown et al., 2008).

Influences on teaching higher order thinking
Beyond the school
The modern world needs citizens who are competent at handling information, can continually solve problems in creative and collaborative ways and can communicate these solutions. There has been a shift in some high-profile companies in favour of recruiting employees who can demonstrate abilities to think analytically, creatively and holistically. Jalongo (2003) argued that educational systems need to do more than prepare students to be cogs in the machinery of commerce. Higher order thinking plays a major role in fulfilling these societal needs and in preparing students for their futures in the 21st century. In order to be effective in their futures and to function in a data-rich society that values intellectual capital, students must be able to continuously learn and use a repertoire of thinking skills (Costa & Kallick, 2008).

Unfortunately, there are also societal barriers to the development of higher order thinking skills in students. For example, the governments of some countries, to determine funding allocation to schools, have introduced high-stakes testing. This often hijacks the curriculum, as schools retreat to drilling students in knowledge reproduction in order to maintain funding or avoid being labelled as failing. High-stakes testing, and too often school-wide block testing, requires that teachers place emphasis on content. This forces teaching to become subject centred and students to rote learn facts and procedures. Little time is left for depth of thought. This approach is in conflict with the student-centred approach needed by middle years students and the imperative to engage them in higher order thinking. While society, government or education systems continue to have such priorities, a real, system-wide focus on the development of higher order thinking is difficult to achieve.

Middle years teachers need to be mindful that while it is important to engage students with the curriculum, students need multiple opportunities to transfer and integrate their knowledge to engage in challenging higher level thinking. In valuing and focusing on their students' critical- and creative-thinking skills, teachers can help to prepare them for active citizenship and their futures in a rapidly changing and diversifying world. Further, the curriculum often requires that teachers focus on the development of such skills. For example, in the Australian context, the Australian Curriculum identifies critical and creative thinking as one of seven general capabilities to be developed across all curriculum areas and year levels: 'In the Australian Curriculum, students develop capability in critical and creative thinking as they learn to generate and evaluate knowledge, clarify concepts and ideas, seek possibilities, consider alternatives and solve problems. Critical and creative thinking involves students thinking broadly and deeply using skills, behaviours and dispositions such as reason, logic, resourcefulness, imagination and innovation in all learning areas at school and in their lives beyond school' (Australian Curriculum, Assessment and Reporting Authority [ACARA], 2015b).

Within the school
The way a school is organised can affect the teaching of higher order thinking. For example, many secondary schools have lesson blocks from 40 to 70 minutes in length. Students may study a particular subject only two or three times each week. It takes time to engage in higher order thinking. Teachers need time to plan experiences that provide opportunities to learn and use higher order thinking skills, but often teachers have limited time or must plan alone because there is no common planning time. Administrators, through timetabling initiatives, can help facilitate the implementation of higher order thinking. Common planning time allows teachers to collaborate, differentiate the curriculum and discuss appropriate pedagogies for a single group of students. It also allows teachers of different subjects to plan integrated curriculum or multidisciplinary strategies that provide interconnected, authentic contexts in which students can further use higher order thinking skills.

The teaching of higher order thinking at the school level can be influenced by resourcing and school policies. Higher order thinking often leads students in diverse directions. This requires access to a range of resources, including information and communication technologies (ICT). If the resources are inadequate to support the learning, student interest and teacher enthusiasm are likely to diminish quickly. The ubiquity of ICT is leading to expanded opportunities for students to use higher order thinking and to express their thinking through diverse means. For example, there are many apps, such as Lego Movie, iMovie, Explain

Everything and Book Creator, that allow students to make their thinking visible, collaborate with others and share their thinking with their peers. It is also important to remember that not all learning or higher order thinking is best suited to the classroom. For example, there are many possibilities for excursions that have the potential for students to experience a full range of higher order thinking opportunities in a real-world context.

Adopting middle years pedagogical approaches provides opportunities for schools, particularly traditional secondary schools, to address the factors that influence the teaching of higher order thinking. For example, block scheduling, in which students are with the same teacher for an extended period of time or have the same teacher for more than one subject, provides students with more time to engage in active learning and problem-solving, and consequently to develop deeper knowledge. Individuals differ in the type of thinking they find challenging: a problem that challenges some students may not be a challenge for others. Having more regular classroom contact with fewer students allows teachers to develop a better understanding of the needs of individuals. Teachers who deal with large numbers of students may have little opportunity to analyse the prior knowledge, experiences and thinking skills of individuals. One approach to ensuring that students with differing needs and higher order thinking skills are able to engage with suitable learning experiences is for teachers to use ICT to provide differentiated activities for their students. Apps such as Showbie and iTunes U enable teachers to create a range of related activities targeted to individual students' diverse abilities and skill levels.

In the classroom

While it is common for the teaching of higher order thinking to be constrained by systemic imperatives and school structures, teachers' attitudes remain the most powerful influence. Teachers must believe that students want to think, and it takes time and energy to develop learning experiences that require students to think critically or creatively. McKendree et al. (2002, p. 58) cited critical-thinking studies which found that a 'lack of critical thinking skills meant that few students were able to apply appropriate reasoning beyond the superficial in order to reach solutions when presented with even moderately novel problems'. If the dominant classroom discourse involves the teacher presenting information to students, higher order thinking is unlikely to occur, as it requires students to be actively engaged. Teachers who value thinking skills do not simply dispense knowledge. They allow students to work productively with knowledge.

Other middle years approaches provide opportunities for the development of higher order thinking; for example:

- Thematic teaching and integrated curricula show students the interconnections across disciplines and provide opportunities to engage in experiences requiring higher order thinking.
- Constructivist approaches link learning to students' interests, prior knowledge and learning strategies.
- Authentic assessment allows for a variety of assessment instruments, such as performance-based tasks that are more relevant to students and more reflective of practitioners' work in the field.
- Cooperative learning supports higher order thinking, because students must discuss and defend their opinions and ideas when they work with other students.
- Home rooms allow teachers to create a learning environment that values thinking and thoughtfulness by providing stimulating physical surroundings and celebrating the products of students' learning.

Provocation 13.2 Higher order thinking

The use of higher order thinking in schools can be influenced from beyond the school, within the school and within the classroom.

 Create three T-charts titled 'Beyond the school', 'Within the school' and 'Within the classroom', each with a 'Plus' and a 'Minus' column, and use them to record examples of positive and negative influences on the use of higher order thinking in your own schooling experience. This might be from your own school life, your experiences on teaching practicum or your experience as a teacher in a school.

Middle years students are more likely to be engaged when their learning is challenging and relevant to their needs and interests. It is very important that this unique developmental stage is considered when planning programs for students in this age group. Recently, researchers have found that a great deal of change occurs in adolescent brains during this time, as discussed in Chapter 2. The teaching and integration of higher order thinking skills is a vital pedagogy to support cognitive development of middle years students.

Adolescent brain development and higher order thinking
Adolescent brains differ from adult brains neurochemically, anatomically and in terms of activity levels (Casey, Jones & Somerville, 2011; Fuller, 2003). A number of dramatic changes begin to occur in the brain in early adolescence. An understanding of these changes and their impact on learning and thinking can help teachers to better cater for middle years students. It can also help students to understand the changes that are occurring and respond accordingly. When students learn about brain development, they more clearly understand the influences of such choices as nutrition, physical activity, sleep patterns and substance abuse (Caskey & Ruben, 2003).

During adolescence the process of synaptic pruning begins, and to allow it to function more efficiently the brain removes certain connections that are seldom used. The decision about what to keep is dependent on an individual's experiences and environment (Strauch, 2003). This period is often referred to as the time to 'use it or lose it' (Caskey & Ruben, 2003). The brain grows by retaining connections that are most used and losing those that are least used. Activities in which students in this age group engage repeatedly have the greatest influence on the brain's developing circuitry (Nagel, 2013). According to B. Clark (2001), connections can be formed or maintained if stimulation is provided through learning experiences that require higher order thinking.

Processes such as synaptic pruning, myelination and dendritic arborisation that occur during this time allow the brain to finetune and strengthen connections (Casey, Jones & Somerville, 2011). The brain's capacity to reshape and reorganise its connections is known as neuroplasticity (Nagel, 2013). Experiences are known not only to shape this reorganisation but also to influence an individual's cognitive processes, including analytical reasoning. The consequences of such extensive brain development can include difficulty discerning important information, motivation and attention problems, independence seeking, novelty seeking, risk-taking and mood swings. This does not mean that middle years students are not capable of complex thought. Several authors have suggested a range of strategies to help students develop cognitively during this period. For example, middle years students often display poor cognitive performance in situations such as timed examinations. Fuller (2003) suggested that during this time, project-based assessment might be more appropriate. Caskey and Ruben (2003) extended this idea, adding that such learning experiences help students to form complex neural connections through higher order thinking processes.

The implication of brain research for teachers and students is that appropriately challenging activities will assist the brain's development. The brain deconstructs experiences as they enter it and reconstructs them when remembering. The more connections the brain has developed, the more effective the thinking and learning will be. Middle years students must be provided with in-depth understanding of concepts in a physically and psychologically safe learning environment that accounts for the neurobiological reality of adolescent brain development; otherwise, they may be unable to learn effectively or to transfer what they have learned (Nagel, 2013).

Teaching higher order thinking

Rather than asking how middle years students could learn about particular subjects (a subject-centred approach), Stringer (1997) suggested that teachers should ask how these subjects could help students learn (a student-centred approach). This demonstrates an immensely important shift in thinking and a vital step in middle years education. From this step, higher order thinking practices can be initiated.

A study by Torff (2003) found that as teachers develop from novice to expert, their classroom practices change from being content rich, curriculum centred and lean in higher order thinking to being lean in content, learner centred and rich in higher order thinking. Focusing students' learning experiences on their needs and interests rather than on the facts and knowledge of the subject or discipline is a significant aspect of middle years education. While this constructivist approach is the basis of many curricula, teachers must do more than change the content they teach. They must recognise that students need to learn content that is meaningful and, at the same time, learn skills to use the information for a range of purposes. Without higher order thinking skills, the content students learn is little more than a collection of unrelated or irrelevant facts.

According to Saavedra and Opfer (2012), teachers must explicitly teach students complex-thinking and communication skills. They emphasised that this is far more demanding than teaching rote skills and that teachers must recognise the essential need for these skills and to intentionally plan accordingly. In contrast with more traditional teaching approaches, this requires a shift to providing students with opportunities to practise applying knowledge in new contexts, communicating in complex ways and using new knowledge to solve problems or to think creatively. Schleicher (2012) also called for explicit teaching of higher order skills, stating that students may not develop them if they are not explicitly taught.

Developing higher order thinking skills

In contrast to learning in which students engage in teacher-directed lower order thinking, when students construct their own knowledge and engage in higher order thinking, the outcomes may not always be predictable. To facilitate the engagement of students in higher order thinking, teachers must de-emphasise some of the more traditional approaches of convergent, right or wrong, yes or no, factual thinking. Teachers must overcome some prevalent misconceptions about how thinking skills can be developed. Costa (1985) emphasised that learning how to think does not happen automatically, that students do not learn to think critically by themselves, and that asking students to think about something does not develop thinking skills. Some debate then arises as to how thinking skills and habits of mind should be taught. Should they be developed in isolation, taught as part of the wider curriculum or taught as a combination of these methods?

According to Saavedra and Opfer (2012), students should be taught lower and higher order thinking skills at the same time. The researchers added that other important strategies for teachers include:

- encouraging students to transfer their learning
- teaching students how to learn
- modelling metacognition and talking through their own thinking with students
- fostering creativity
- modelling misunderstandings and explicitly addressing them.

To aid the teaching of thinking skills, several models have been developed. Bloom (1956), through his Taxonomy of Cognitive Development, defined a hierarchy of thinking skills, from knowledge, comprehension and application to the accepted higher order thinking levels of analysis, synthesis and evaluation. L.W. Anderson and Krathwohl (2001) reordered and relabelled Bloom's cognitive dimensions as remembering, understanding, applying, analysing, evaluating and creating.

Contemporary influences on the teaching of thinking skills

Many strategies, approaches and theories exist that are useful for teaching students diverse thinking skills. Some have been used for many years and remain important and effective.

De Bono (1995) developed the Six Thinking Hats Framework that teachers and students can apply across the curriculum, although he suggested that initially the skills should be taught explicitly. Students become familiar with the Six Thinking

Provocation 13.3 Adapting a task to incorporate higher order thinking

This is an example of how a simple dice game, called Dice Difference, can be developed into an inquiry that incorporates higher order thinking. Steps to the game are as follows:

1. Group students in pairs: one is Player A and one is Player B.
2. In these pairs, players take turns to roll two dice twenty times.
3. The winner of each roll depends on the outcome of subtracting the lowest number from the highest number for each roll. Player A wins if the difference between the two numbers showing is 0, 1 or 2. Player B wins if the difference between the two numbers showing is 3, 4 or 5.
4. The players use a T-chart and tally marks to record who wins each of the twenty rolls.
5. Check around the class. Who won most games—Player A or B?

What usually occurs is that most, if not all, Player A's win. To students this seems strange, because their intuition says that the game is fair, as each player could score with three possible results: 0, 1 and 2 or 3, 4 and 5.

Take the students to deeper thinking now by asking them to create a table to answer the following questions in relation to this game:

- What differences between the numbers on the two dice can occur?
- What difference is likely to occur most frequently?
- What difference is likely to occur least frequently?
- Is the game fair?

In pairs, the students discuss what's going on. If they need help, Figure 13.1 could be used, empty to start with and filled in with the difference in each case. The students should be able to see that, out of the 36 possible combinations, there are 24 ways to get 0, 1 or 2, whereas there are only 12 ways to get 3, 4 or 5.

The final step is to have the students try to make the game fair. There are a number of ways this can be done, so students can find a number of correct outcomes and share their ideas with the class. It's also good fun to play some more games using the newer, fairer rules.

 Using the list below, identify where in the Dice Difference activity the various types of thinking are used.

- remembering
- understanding
- applying

- analysing
- evaluating
- creating.

 Think of an activity from your own teaching area. List the elements or steps of the activity and then extend the activity to include some higher order thinking.

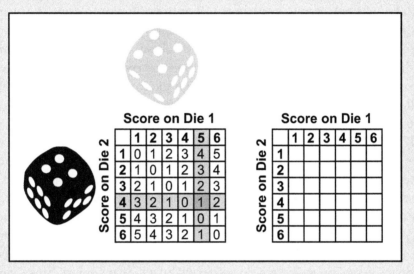

Figure 13.1 Dice Difference

Hats and learn to apply different perspectives to their thinking, leading to different possible solutions to questions posed. Other strategies developed by de Bono to assist thinking skills are Plus, Minus and Interesting (PMI), Other People's Viewpoint (OPV), and CoRT Thinking.

Gardner (1993), who through his Theory of Multiple Intelligences highlighted the diverse thinking strengths that a person may have, has encouraged teachers and students to value varying forms of intelligence as valid and human. Use of Gardner's theory allows teachers to focus on thinking skills in multiple curriculum areas and in real-world contexts. To further assist teachers of thinking skills, some innovative tools have been developed. For example, Bloom's (1956) levels of thinking can be cross-referenced with Gardner's multiple intelligences to create a planning matrix that caters for all styles and levels of thinking.

Buzan (2000) developed Mind Mapping as a way of representing thoughts and plans in graphic form, taking advantage of new understandings about the brain and memory. Mind maps are representations of what he calls 'radiant thinking'.

Software such as Inspiration has allowed for the simple and clear depiction of thoughts and plans through concept mapping, tree diagrams, flow charts and mind maps. Jonassen (2000) described ways that ICT can be utilised as cognitive tools, which he calls 'mindtools', to support higher order thinking. Using ICT as mindtools requires that they be employed as knowledge-building tools, as distinct from information-using tools. Examples include databases, spreadsheets, modelling and visualisation tools, multimedia publishing tools and conversation and conferencing software. Incorporating these frameworks and tools into thinking classrooms is an excellent method for teachers to scaffold the development of higher order thinking in students.

The notion of scaffolding is important in assisting students to develop higher order thinking. Vygotsky (1978) defined scaffolding as the support structure for learners engaged in activities just beyond their independent abilities (i.e., beyond their zone of proximal development). Asking students to function in this zone challenges them to think critically without overwhelming them (Marshall & Horton, 2011). Just because thinking is inherent in the structure of the brain, this cannot be used as an argument against making students conscious of their thought processes and practising to improve them (Sylwester, 2000). One cannot just think; one must think about something. Therefore, it is essential to integrate academic content with the teaching and learning of higher order thinking skills (Matters, 2004).

Teaching higher order thinking through discussion

Since higher order thinking skills could be applied to any teaching and learning situation, it would be impossible to give examples pertinent to all circumstances. However, O'Tuel and Bullard (1995) presented a very helpful framework that could guide the development of higher order thinking skills across the curriculum. This framework has three steps: the teaching of, for and about thinking skills.

Teaching *of* higher order thinking occurs when a specific thinking skill is explicitly taught and students have the chance to practise it. This involves explicit teaching through guided practice. For example, during discussion, thinking about other people's viewpoints and being able to articulate personal thoughts in an appropriate way require the higher order thinking skills of analysis and evaluation. To help students achieve this, specific higher order thinking skills can be taught and practised prior to the discussion. Some of these skills, with associated sentence starters, are shown in Table 13.1.

Table 13.1 A cognitive organiser to guide students' higher order thinking skills during class and group discussions

Skills	Sentence starters
Stating and defending points of view	I believe ... My point of view is ... I still maintain that ...
Concurring with or expanding ideas	I agree with ... I would like to add ... In addition I would like ...
Contradicting others' points of view	I disagree with ... I strongly oppose ... I believe this is unfounded ...
Noting self-contradictions of speakers	Previously you stated ... You have contradicted your previous ... You seem to have changed your ...
Re-evaluating one's own point of view	I see what you are saying ... I have reconsidered ... I still firmly believe ...

Source: Selected from Cam (1995). Used with permission from Hale & Iremonger.

The benefits of this can be contrasted with what happens if these skills are not taught. Cam (1995) stated that people who are unpractised at thinking skills often reject alternatives out of hand, show themselves to be unimaginative, are dogmatic and inflexible and do not make the most of their opportunities.

After some thinking skills and ways of expressing ideas have been taught, students move on to integrating these skills into broader activities. Teaching *for* higher order thinking occurs when an activity requires the use of the skill but the skill is not the focus of the lesson. Once students have developed familiarity with some of the discussion skills, teachers can encourage their use at any time. This may not always lead to comfortable situations for the teacher. When students begin to think critically about what they view, hear or read, and when they have the skill to participate in class and group discussions and the confidence to articulate their thoughts, a sedate and accepting group of knowledge recipients is replaced by an inquiring, dynamic group of thinkers.

Teaching *about* higher order thinking gives students opportunities to practise metacognition that allows them to evaluate their thinking. With targeted questioning a teacher can help students think about their own thinking. Cam (1995) illustrated some excellent examples of this type of questioning or prompting. Examples are shown in Table 13.2. At the conclusion of any discussion, students can be asked to reflect on the thinking skills used and the success of the group and individuals at using these skills and to articulate reasons why they have changed or maintained their points of view.

Table 13.2 Teacher prompts to assist students to think about their thinking

Thinking skills	Teacher prompts
Considering alternatives	Does anyone have a different idea? How else could we look at this?
Keeping your bearings	Does that help us with the problem we are looking at?
Appealing to criteria	Why (by what criteria) do you say that?
Seeing implications	What is being implied here? What could happen if . . .?
Consistency	Can you say both . . . and . . .?

Source: Selected from Cam (1995). Used with permission from Hale & Iremonger.

Provocation 13.4 Teaching higher order thinking through discussion

Reflect on your own learning and teaching experiences and ways that metacognition might be promoted.

 Add some further teacher prompts to the list in Table 13.2. Perhaps you could make them specific to your teaching areas.

 Think metacognitively when you are chatting with friends. Take note if they or you use prompts similar to these.

Using ICT to promote higher order thinking

As educational technologies permeate classrooms more and more, it is important that they be used to enhance higher order thinking; otherwise, they become simply another delivery system for information. Content-free ICT such as PowerPoint or video production are excellent for classroom use, as they are not restricted in their application and, as Wegerif (2002) believed, they can be used to create external representations of thought. Apps, which are continually being developed for mobile devices such as tablets, can also serve this function. Murphy (2003) stated that multimedia publishing tools afford opportunities for students to engage in critical thinking. As with all teaching tools, however, the context and the teacher's pedagogy will determine the level of effectiveness of the classroom application of these ICT (Rodrigues, 2006). For example, for students to effectively produce in-class digital videos, they must be allowed to work collaboratively, and, in so doing, their critical and creative thinking is enhanced (Kimber & Wyatt-Smith, 2006).

Once context and pedagogy conducive to eliciting the affordances of the ICT are in place, the unique nature of technology can further enhance higher order thinking. For example, when students are making videos in class, one of the key aspects of their production is the editing stage. Students working together to edit their productions have opportunities to evaluate, connect, make decisions about and synthesise their work, which in turn require the students to discuss and justify, leading to critical thinking—a component of higher order thinking (Hilton & Hilton, 2013). Similarly, Buckingham (2007) claimed that the ability to manipulate image and dialogue through editing gives students flexibility and control over their productions, which facilitates self-conscious reflection, also a key higher order thinking skill.

Engaging middle years students through thoughtful incorporation of technology in the classroom aligns with their broader interest in and use of ICT in their daily lives and takes advantage of styles of communication and learning that can enhance their higher order thinking. Dede (2005) argued that even using the internet can lead to valuable higher order thinking if teachers ask students to synthesise information, because this requires students to evaluate information, determine which sources are inconsistent or unreliable, filter relevant information and use only reliable sources to create new text or make new meanings.

Assessment of higher order thinking skills

Assessing higher order thinking is not an easy task. Proponents of teaching thinking skills in isolation from the main curriculum cite ease of evaluation as a major advantage to their method, as it does not get lost in the broader agenda. The fact that this approach does not relate to students' broader curriculum or middle years philosophy and therefore has little authenticity would seem to outweigh any assessment advantage. Dede suggested that assessment must become more complex, to measure higher order thinking rather than simply to measure regurgitated facts (cited in Hopson, Simms & Knezek, 2001–02). A more authentic assessment method is the development of rubrics, which scaffold and assess students' thinking skills development in the broader context of an integrated curriculum. Hurley and Weldon (2004) pointed out that this assists students in taking ownership and responsibility for their thinking and learning.

In the example given above of teaching higher order thinking through discussion, assessment could occur in a number of ways. First, as part of the overall process, the teacher could monitor performance using a checklist, taking note of the speaker and the skill used. Over a number of discussions, this tracking method would soon reveal patterns of participation and development of higher order thinking skills used by the speakers. Second, as students must reflect on their own participation in the discussion, as well as that of others, self-assessment and peer assessment are possible. Students could track their own performance by indicating on personal cognitive organisers when they used particular skills. Again, over time, patterns of their own performance would be revealed to them. Finally, student self-assessment might occur through reflections on conclusions reached in the discussion and on how thinking and ideas were reinforced or changed.

Another means of assessing students' higher order thinking is through the use of two-tiered test items (Hilton et al., 2013). The first tier assesses content knowledge,

Provocation 13.5 Providing choice

Two-tiered items can be a useful diagnostic assessment for teachers to identify students' prior understanding of a concept.

 Using the Australian Curriculum as a guide within your teaching area, select a topic you might assess using a two-tiered test. Develop an initial question that can be answered with true or false, and then develop four choices for students to explain the answer. Try to make each of these four choices represent a type of thinking specific to your topic.

George runs 100 metres in 20 seconds. If he runs the same distance at twice the speed, he will take twice as long.

☐   True   ☐   False

Because (choose the best reason):

☐	1.	Doubling the speed doubles the time.	(Incorrect understanding of relationship between distance and speed.)
☐	2.	Doubling the speed halves the time.	(Quantitative—correct inverse proportional thinking.)
☐	3.	The distance doesn't change.	(Absolute thinker, unaware of relationship between distance and speed.)
☐	4.	Running faster will take less time.	(Qualitative—correct understanding of relationship between distance and speed.)

To make a sticky mess, you need to mix 4 cups of sugar and 10 cups of flour. If you want to make a larger amount of this recipe with 6 cups of sugar, you need 15 cups of flour.

☐   True   ☐   False

Because (choose the best reason):

☐	1.	You don't need to change the amount of flour.	(Incorrect, unaware of the proportional relationship.)
☐	2.	You have 2 more cups of sugar so you need 2 more cups of flour.	(Incorrect, additive thinker.)
☐	3.	You increased the sugar by half so you need to increase the flour by half.	(Correct, multiplicative/proportional thinker).
☐	4.	You always need 6 more cups of flour than sugar.	(Incorrect, additive thinker.)

Figure 13.2 Examples of two-tiered test items

or lower order thinking, while the second tier requires students to provide a response that shows their reasoning. The second tier responses can be used to gain an insight into the students' deeper understanding of concepts. Examples of such items from middle years mathematics are shown in Figure 13.2.

In our rapidly changing world, middle years students are faced with an increasing array of knowledge sources and technologies. This fact, in conjunction with the developmental characteristics of middle years students, creates an imperative to fully exercise the intellectual capabilities of middle years students. For schooling to have relevance to these students, and for them to be informed participants in the real world, their intellectual engagement at school must match the increasingly sophisticated and complex nature of their thinking. The development of higher order thinking must be facilitated on many levels, from societal expectations to individual classroom practices. Pedagogies associated with higher order thinking can contribute to the requirement of increased intellectual demand on middle years students.

Chapter summary

This chapter makes the following key points:

- Higher order thinking requires engagement in complex forms of thought to transfer and transform knowledge and create new meaning or products.
- There is a need for higher order thinking skills in today's world and middle years students' future lives.
- Promoting higher order thinking is strongly aligned with adolescent brain development and middle years students' increased capacity to engage in more complex thought.
- There is a strong need to challenge middle years students and focus on depth of understanding.
- There must be an explicit teaching focus on higher order thinking in these years if it is to be developed effectively.

Chapter Fourteen

Positive behaviour management

MIA O'BRIEN

Learning intentions

In this chapter we will:
- explore four broad yet influential theoretical perspectives that shape perceptions of student behaviour and influence behaviour management approaches in contemporary education
- examine research-informed priorities for teaching and learning in the middle years
- consider the significance of positivity for managing behaviour
- identify and describe practices for managing behaviour positively, including the explicit development of positive learning identities, prosocial skills and values and genuine engagement in learning.

Perspectives of student behaviour

Consider the following statement made by Mendler (2005, p. 5): 'Essentially, kids who misbehave are telling us that their basic needs are not being met. Although we need to have specific, short-term strategies to handle inappropriate behaviour, good discipline is linked to our understanding of the motives that drive students to act inappropriately and the solutions that address these basic needs'. Mendler is not alone in this sentiment, and the view that managing an effective learning environment has much to do with acknowledging and understanding the needs of students is widely affirmed within contemporary discussions of classroom and behaviour management (Bilmes, 2012; Clarke & Pittaway, 2014; McDonald, 2013). In this opening section we will outline current theories and thinking about behaviour, approaches to managing behaviour and, indeed, the reasons why simplistic notions of managing behaviour are becoming outmoded. This view challenges us to think differently about what we see when we see students behaving (either appropriately or inappropriately). The aim of this section is to provide a research-informed, theoretically principled basis from which to interpret student behaviour not simply as compliance or non-compliance but as an authentic, personal response to the immediate intellectual, social and psychological environment as experienced within a complex personal and social setting. This shift in perspective, from behaviour as an indication of compliance to behaviour as an expression of needs and values, changes the way we think about and respond to our students' actions in the classroom.

Important distinctions in theories of human behaviour

The assumptions (or theories) that we hold about what drives human behaviour are important. Whether they are informed by research, influenced by others or shaped by experience (or all three), these theories entail distinctive ways of explaining what certain behaviours mean, why they are occurring and what should be done about them. What's important about these theories, even informal or personally derived folk theories, is the degree to which they are adequate and helpful in achieving our broader educational aims and values.

Provocation 14.1 Different needs drive different behaviours

Imagine for a moment that you are looking into a middle years classroom. There is nothing unusual about this classroom, in that it hosts a diverse cohort of Year 8 students sitting, or half sitting, at desks and chairs arranged in small clusters. There is a teacher roaming around the room, pausing occasionally to hover over a particular cluster and chat before moving on to the next one, and a teacher aide sitting adjacent to two students in a cluster on one side, offering direct support and guidance on an as-needed basis. Most of the students are busily working on what appears to be a group task involving an experiment conducted earlier. The results of that experiment are in a jar in the centre of each cluster, and the task itself requires completion of a worksheet that students must complete individually, including the development of diagrams to depict different stages of the experiment, with annotations, observations and explanatory notes.

You can't help but notice a degree of restlessness in the room. Some students are focused entirely on the task, stopping occasionally to show each other, or the teacher, their progress. There is an air of mild competition between them, and progress from moment to moment is marked by pseudo-silent air punches and cries of 'yessssss' accompanied by sideways glances around the room to ensure others are watching. These students visibly enjoy the inevitable affirmation offered by the teacher and return to work rubbing their hands in mock glee. Other students vacillate between working on the task and chatting surreptitiously when the opportunity presents itself. They smile quietly when corrected by the teacher, returning their attention to the task, at least until the teacher is out of earshot.

Lastly, there are two groups at the back of the room looking far from interested in the task. The first of these groups seems friendly enough, and its members are making an attempt to look busy—with heads down and pencils up as the teacher strolls by. However, when the teacher is not looking, they take turns dashing backward and forward between other groups, returning to their home group to whisper in low, conspiratorial tones while their peers scribble rapidly onto their worksheets in response. The second group is made up of what appear to be older, or perhaps more mature, students, mostly male, with one female. They make no bones about their lack of interest in the task and in fact go to great pains to show their nonchalance by engaging in moderately loud discussion about their plans for the weekend. Occasionally the teacher sends them a stern look or directive to hush— but they continue regardless.

 Describe and explain the different types of behaviour illustrated in this example.

Contrasting perspectives

It's important to note that there is a very wide array of theories that aim to describe and explain human behaviour, primarily in the fields of psychology and social psychology, and it is not within the remit of this chapter to review them. However, four overarching perspectives have been highly influential in educational thinking to date (McDonald, 2013), and the principles and heuristics that distinguish them are worth acknowledging, as they continue to shape practice and approaches to managing behaviour in classrooms and schools today. They are behaviourist perspectives, cognitive behavioural perspectives, humanist perspectives and situated, socio-cultural and ecological systems perspectives.

Behaviourist perspectives

Traditional behaviourism, in a nutshell, views behaviour as a response to stimuli and aims to manipulate behaviour by rewarding desired behaviour and discouraging non-desired behaviour. The behaviourist perspective is based on the extensive work of B.F. Skinner (1953), and its underlying assumption is that people either comply with the requirements of a particular setting and respond appropriately to stimuli or do not comply with the requirements and so respond inappropriately to stimuli.

Applied to the classroom scenario presented in Provocation 14.1, a behaviourist perspective would see those students who eagerly attend to the task as complying with the requirements or stimuli and would endorse the need to reward that behaviour, perhaps through affirmations from the teacher. Any explicit affirmation is designed to positively reinforce the desired behaviour, encouraging the students' continued commitment to the task. Those students who are not attending to the task would be seen as non-compliant, responding inappropriately to the stimuli and in need of correction.

Correction may take one of three forms. The first, parallel positive reinforcement, occurs via the teacher's endorsement of the desired behaviour of other students directed meaningfully at those students who need to redirect their behaviour accordingly, as in 'The group at the front has been working very productively all morning. Great work, guys! I'd like to see everyone else follow their lead.' In the second form of correction, negative reinforcement, the teacher may stand over a particular group of students until they work more productively on the task, moving away only when they are back on task. Finally, punishment may range from a verbal admonishment or an enforced consequence, such as separating a student from the group to work alone, to allocating extra work to complete or taking a more severe disciplinary action.

Research into behaviourism and methods for manipulating behaviour continue to build on Skinner's work (Woolfolk & Margetts, 2012). This view forms the foundation of a number of current approaches to discipline or managing behaviour, such as Applied Behavioural Analysis (Alberto & Troutman, 2013) and Assertive Discipline (Canter & Canter, 2001). However, the important point is this: behaviourist perspectives employ an arguably narrow focus on behaviour in their interpretation of managing learning in classroom settings (Hickey, 2003), given their emphasis on stimulus–response heuristics and an ongoing focus on conditioning behaviour as a path to encouraging compliance to external requirements.

Behaviourists see students in the classroom scenario as either complying with the requirements and norms of the classroom or not, to varying degrees. However, behaviourism does little to explain *why* some students appear to willingly attend to the task at hand or why some do not.

Cognitive behavioural perspectives

In a similar but slightly different vein, cognitive behavioural perspectives place an emphasis on the kinds of competencies that students may require to engage in learning effectively (J.S. Kaplan & Carter, 1995). This view includes acknowledging and developing the academic skills that learning tasks require, in addition to encouraging self-management skills, such as being self-directed and self-disciplined. The underlying assumption is that being disciplined is both managerial, creating order for learning, and educational, requiring independently deployed cognitive skills. When both are in place, motivation will follow. This approach values the explicit development of particular thinking skills and habits and encourages students to maintain control over emotions and behaviours. It continues to fuel enthusiastic research, particularly in relation to adolescent learning and motivation (Martin, 2013, 2015).

Applied to the classroom scenario in Provocation 14.1, this view would encourage the teaching of academic skills specific to the task at hand and would see student non-engagement in the task as an indication of lack of cognitive or emotional self-discipline (Martin, 2013). The restless group at the back of the classroom, from which each student takes turns to gather information from other, more on-task groups, is an illustration of how gaps in academic skill can manifest in mild misbehaviour. In such instances, the aim of the behaviour is simply to fill the gap (by gathering information from others) and complete the task.

An intervention might entail cognitive training (skills development, modelling and rehearsal) combined with some form of positive reinforcement. There are a number of similar theories and perspectives that fall within this more clinical perspective and approach, which are considered psychoanalytic in nature (McDonald, 2013), given the focus on cognitive skill and its link to internalised discipline and behaviour as stimulus–response.

Humanist perspectives

In contrast, humanist perspectives aim to promote a more holistic understanding of the human experience and the role of basic needs as influencers of action and behaviour. Maslow's (1943, 1954, 1968) Hierarchy of Needs is the most well known example of this theoretical stance. His original works, of 1943 and 1954, promoted the view that people are motivated to meet a certain set of needs that are structured in a systematic hierarchy. These needs were later refined and articulated, in 1968, to entail the following:

- basic biological and physiological necessities
- safety
- social contact, connection, acceptance and a sense of belonging with others
- achievement and self-mastery, which can be referred to as esteem
- intellectual and cognitive challenge
- aesthetic appreciation and aesthetically satisfying experiences
- realising personal potential
- experiences of transcendence of self, such as to be in the service of others.

Maslow's work has been widely applied to conceptualisations of behaviour in school and educational settings, and in particular to our understandings of motivation in learning (Woolfolk & Margetts, 2012). Indeed, the humanist perspective has developed extensively and encompasses the work of Carl Rogers (1969), Malcolm Knowles (1975) and contemporaries keen to highlight the role of individual intentionality and personal values in behaviour and the importance of human freedom, dignity, agency, meaning and potential. It is this view—that, for all humans, needs drive actions—that is at the centre of the humanist perspective and at the heart of Mendler's (2005) comment at the start of the chapter.

Applied to an analysis of the classroom scenario presented in Provocation 14.1, a humanist perspective would lead us to wonder about the degree to which the setting and the task were meeting the needs of the students. For example, the students engaging in the task consistently are finding the task personally valuable in some way, whereas those who are restless or disengaged from the task have needs that are not being met by the task alone; perhaps that is why some of the students are constantly seeking the teacher's attention or affirmation and others are not. For other students the task elicits needs that are not readily met, and so they seek to meet those needs elsewhere, such as by asking for advice and support from other students. And the needs of the small group of students at the back seem far better served through an explicit disregard for both the task and the setting, to the extent that they are willing to bear the brunt of the teacher's occasional admonishment, for that too serves some greater purpose personally.

In this way, a humanist perspective directs our focus to the rich array of human qualities and characteristics that require attention when we learn. The plethora of theories and approaches that sit within this perspective or build on Maslow's original work aim to extend the central principle: core needs, which form a complex and hierarchical system, drive behaviour, as we are constantly motivated to find ways to meet those needs (Woolfolk & Margetts, 2012).

Situated, socio-cultural and ecological systems perspectives
Contemporary educational practices embrace and reflect social views of learning and development (Woolfolk & Margetts, 2012). Social perspectives reach beyond the intrapsychological emphasis on the individual and inner mental processes to take account of the social, relational and participatory qualities of being human in the world (Gee, 2004; Lave, 1996; Vygotsky, 1978). This view acknowledges that learning and knowledge emerge from social interaction and participating in cultural activities (Bereiter & Scardamalia, 1989; Gee, 2004; Hickey, 2003; Wenger, 1999) while in some cases simultaneously incorporating a humanist perspective (McDonald, 2013).

In this perspective, both identity and context are essential to understandings of the student. Who the student is and how they choose to act are reflexive of the context in which they are enmeshed and who they are becoming. Understanding students requires that teachers consider the local, social and political circumstances and systems in which they are simultaneously situated (Bronfenbrenner, 1979). This ecological system includes:

- microsystem—a child's immediate daily interactions, such as the family, local community and school
- mesosystem—connections that are formed beyond the immediate circumstances, such as church groups, sporting groups and clubs
- exosystem—broader yet still impactful contexts, such as the child's father's workplace and the family-friendly initiatives that are either offered or not available
- macrosystems—attitudes and ideologies of culture and society, such as state and federal government policies regarding parental leave.

An ecological systems view highlights the integrative and influential nature of these contextual factors and sensitises us to how a child may act within or experience a particular setting. It reminds us that individual students bring a diverse array of experiences to school, and these experiences warrant our attention if we are to fully understand and create meaningful learning experiences for our students.

In this view, learning is phenomenological (Giles et al., 2012), in that it is a personal experience involving the student's lifeworld (Sandberg & Dall'Alba, 2009). It is an experience that is both epistemological, entailing what a person comes to know and be able to do, and ontological, entailing how a person learns to be (Heidegger, 1962). But it is also social and relational, and this integrative view requires attention to the complex ways in which teachers, students and curricula encounter each other in educational contexts (Giles et al., 2012; Kemmis et al., 2014; Turner & Meyer, 2000; Wenger, 1999).

To return to the scenario presented in Provocation 14.1, a socio-cultural perspective would encourage us to recognise the importance (and influence) of the people, circumstances and various life trajectories that comprise the lifeworlds of the students in the classroom. Primarily, this view reframes what we see: not simply behaviour, but varying levels of participation in, and valuing of, the social prac-tices of that particular classroom and school. And while we may still wonder about why students engage with different levels of enthusiasm, the social view reminds us, first, that the classroom presents a complex social and relational space that students are attempting to navigate and, second, that those students bring with them to the classroom other layers of meaning and complexity—the specific personal, social and cultural characteristics of their respective lifeworlds—which influence and shape what they value and how they see themselves. The challenge for teachers is to see beyond the immediate behaviour of students in classrooms and instead aim to understand who their students are and how they can engage them in learning.

Aspirations, values and intentions in managing behaviour

This section of the chapter will examine research-informed principles and prior-ities for middle years education and consider the meaning and significance of positivity in managing student behaviour. The aim of the section is to outline the now widely endorsed philosophy of positive education and to foreground its poten-tial for rethinking our approach and intentions in behaviour management practice. If we were to frame this section with a question, it might be 'What do we really value in middle years education, and to what extent does positive education, as a research-based approach, enable these aspirations and values to become a reality in classroom practice?'

Consider, for example, the emphasis on student engagement and motivation in the *Melbourne declaration on educational goals for young Australians*, which includes the following statement:

The middle years are an important period of learning, in which knowledge of fundamental disciplines is developed, yet this is also a time when students are at the greatest risk of disengagement from learning. Student motivation and engagement in these years is critical, and can be influenced by tailoring approaches to teaching, with learning activities and learning environments that specifically consider the needs of middle years students. Focusing on student engagement and converting this into learning can have a significant impact on student outcomes. Effective transitions between primary and secondary schools are an important aspect of ensuring student engagement. (Ministerial Council on Education, Employment, Training and Youth Affairs, 2008, p. 12)

Provocation 14.2 Positivity and behaviour management

'There is nothing as practical as a good theory.' This maxim, widely attributed to Kurt Lewin, promotes the practical value of theory. However, Lewin (1946, p. 35) also went on to say that 'the research needed for social practice can best be characterised as research for social management or social engineering. It is a type of action research, a comparative research of the conditions and effects of various forms of social action, and research leading to social action. Research that produces nothing but books will not suffice.'

The four broad theoretical perspectives reviewed in the preceding section all offer distinctive, research-informed approaches to interpreting and responding to student behaviour. However, Lewin's comment about the value of research is particularly apt for teaching, in that a theory is useful only if it serves our broader educative intentions (Kemmis et al., 2014).

Thinking back to your experiences of school, or to a school you have spent time in recently, perhaps for a professional experience placement, consider and discuss these questions:

 What do we value in middle years education? Why is positivity significant for managing behaviour?

Clearly, engagement and finding ways to interest middle years students in learning are priorities. Next to these is substantial research that outlines the complexity of biological, psychological, neurological and social changes students in the middle years navigate as part of the transition into adolescence (Groundwater-Smith & Mockler, 2015). The evidence in this research indicates that middle school students need support to:

- understand and manage their emotions;
- view and relate to themselves and to others;
- respond to emotional and social challenges; and
- establish a social identity and develop skills that will enable them to participate in, and contribute productively to, Australian society. (Australian Research Alliance for Children and Youth, 2011, in Groundwater-Smith & Mockler, 2015, p. 9)

In middle years education and in education more generally there is a distinctive turn towards the positive, and this reflects a global trend in education (Furlong, Gilman & Huebner, 2014; Green, Oades and Robinson, 2011). For example, in extending their discussion of considerations for working with middle years students, Groundwater-Smith and Mockler (2015) draw from research that identifies what is important to students in their learning, which includes having positive relationships with their teachers, the need for harmonious and engaging classroom management skills and opportunities to work collaboratively with other students (Durling, Ng & Bishop, 2010). Similarly, Groundwater-Smith and Mockler (2015) point to the work by Dinham and Rowe (2007) that highlights the need for age-appropriate pedagogy, which for middle years students would aspire to create:

- *Relevance*—personal meaning derived from middle-school curricula which engages students with the 'real world';
- *Responsibility*—appropriate self-control over learning, accountability and responsibility;
- *Belonging*—sense of acceptance and affirmation within a supportive and safe learning environment;
- *Awareness*—both self and social awareness, through appropriate curricula and learning;
- *Engagement*—defined here as meeting students' developmental needs through tasks which are motivating, challenging and invite affiliation;

- *Competence*—developing personal expertise and competencies, knowledge and skills;
- *Ethics*—ethical awareness facilitated; personal values developed; and
- *Pedagogy*—active rather than passive learning. (quoted in Groundwater-Smith & Mockler, 2015)

In a similarly positive style, the National Safe Schools Framework draws frequently on positivity literature and articulates 'positive behaviour management' as one of nine key characteristics essential in maintaining a safe and supportive learning environment (Ministerial Council on Education, Employment, Training and Youth Affairs, 2011). Within the framing of this approach, positive behaviour management is described as prioritising the teaching of positive values, prosocial skills and harmonious learning environments. There are other chapters in this book that delve more deeply into the aspirations, values and intentions of middle years education. However, the point is that, whether we are referring to the philosophy of middle years (Chadbourne & Pendergast, 2010), the body of evidence-based principles that identify the learning needs of middle school students (Groundwater-Smith & Mockler, 2015; Martin, 2015) or the kinds of values and practices that middle school students have identified first hand as significant and impactful (Poskitt, 2011), there is a very clear and explicit emphasis on the need to promote and enable positive experiences of learning as a signifying characteristic of middle school.

This emphasis is visible in contemporary approaches to behaviour management. See, for example, the shift from simply 'managing behaviour' to 'positive behaviour support' in the language and framing of relevant policies and initiatives by the majority of state-level education departments across Australia and New Zealand and internationally. This shift reflects a global turn in teaching, learning and educational research towards positive education (Furlong et al., 2014). It falls to teachers, school leaders and related professionals to consider the implications not only for pedagogy, but most particularly for how we conceptualise behaviour management positively.

Positivity in education

Positive education draws heavily from the innovations of positive psychology to shift attention from what goes wrong with students in school to what goes right (Furlong et al., 2014). The term was originally coined by positive psychology researchers working alongside educators to refer to the explicit teaching of skills and happiness (Seligman et al., 2009). More recent descriptions acknowledge that it is positive psychology applied to education settings which incorporates strategies and practices that foster psychological wellbeing, strengths and character as valued aspects of the learning experience (Green, Oades & Robinson, 2011).

Much of the positive education research integrates applied positive psychology interventions with the humanist perspective and ecological systems view (Peterson, 2006). In doing so, the field identifies protective factors that strengthen students' engagement in learning, such as optimism, resilience and valuing learning at home, and seeks to examine the potential impact of negative influences or risks, such as anxiety, trauma and low valuing of learning at home. Much of this work confirms the applicability of Martin Seligman's (2012) original framing of five essential elements that contribute to an individual's sense of satisfaction and flourishing in life: positive emotion, engagement in valued activity, positive relationships, meaningful life experiences and accomplishment. In complement to this work, Barbara Fredrickson (2001) describes the centrality of positive emotions, positive cognitions and positive, agentic action in achieving a lasting sense of wellbeing.

What is most salient about the positive education field is its capacity to build on and confirm the potential for teaching positivity and forms of positive (and empowering) emotion, cognition and behaviour to students in schools. School-based research in this field has demonstrated the beneficial development of positive psychological traits such as:

- resilience, optimism and hope (Boman & Mergler, 2014; Furlong, Gilman & Huebner, 2014; Linley & Proctor, 2013; Snyder & Lopez, 2005)
- strategies for increasing overall life satisfaction (Suldo, Savage & Mercer, 2013) and subjective wellbeing (Suldo et al., 2015)
- the cultivation of empathy, prosocial behaviour and positive orientations towards school (Spinrad & Eisenberg, 2015).

The significance of the above traits, in addition to positive teacher–student relationships, has been noted in achieving fewer incidences of behaviour management issues and improvements in student engagement (Furlong, Gilman & Huebner, 2014; B. Wilkins, Boman & Mergler, 2015). As these studies illustrate, there is a substantial evidence base to support the shift in schools from managing behaviour to directly cultivating positive experiences and dispositions in school (Furlong et al., 2013); and the benefits are both personal and social (Furlong, Gilman & Huebner, 2014).

The significance of learning identity in middle school

Despite the emergence of positivity as a widely accepted orientation to contemporary education, the challenges for middle schooling remain significant. In fact, in addressing this point in a recent work on the challenges of teaching and learning in the middle years, Groundwater-Smith and Mockler (2015, p. 5) pointedly chose the subtitle 'the challenges are considerable and ongoing'. Within that work the authors contend that 'the challenges of the middle years of schooling today are about *more* than transition issues. The policy contexts that frame the work of teachers and students in the middle years may have significant impact on practice, potentially narrowing both curriculum and pedagogy in ways previously unseen' (p. 12, emphasis added).

The challenges are indeed about more than transition. As the imposition of mandated curriculum and standardised testing continues to press down on teachers' work (Hardy, 2013; Thompson, 2015), there is an even greater imperative to ensure that practices related to managing classrooms and behaviour achieve much more than simple compliance. While there is an ever narrowing opportunity to impact practice through curriculum and pedagogy, behaviour will inevitably need to be managed. Therein lies our opportunity. This final section of the chapter identifies and describes practices that explicitly develop positive learning identities, prosocial skills and values and genuine engagement in learning.

Learning is an experience of identity development (M. O'Brien & Dole, 2012; M. O'Brien, Makar & Fielding-Wells, 2014; Wenger, 1999), and middle school is a time when most students are primarily concerned with who they are, how they are seen and how they learn to see themselves (A. Kaplan & Flum, 2012; Smith & Grootenboer, 2007). This is an invaluable window through which to consider behaviour management as an opportunity to engage young people in positive experiences of learning and positive perceptions of themselves as learners.

The term identity refers primarily to the sense of self formed by how we might know and describes ourselves (Danielewicz, 2001; Stryker & Burke, 2006). Identities can be transferable or contextual (Hoy, Demerath & Pape, 2001), and as individuals we can hold multiple and sometimes conflicting identities concurrently (Wenger, 1999). For example, we might see ourselves as being a confident, capable musician and a popular member of the church band while simultaneously seeing ourselves as an anxious, low-achieving and less popular student at school. We can have a musical identity, a learning identity and identities related to our role and position in the family (mother, daughter, wife or all three). Some propose that identity refers to the integrative engagement of students' cognitive, affective and psychomotor domains (Grootenboer & Marshman, 2016). However, the social view frames identity in terms of the lived experience of participating in the world, as ways of being in the world that relate to, and are reflexive of, the social relationships and cultural practices that we engage in, as well as our learning trajectories (Wenger, 1999). Identities are not stable but rather continuous and emergent (M. O'Brien & Dole, 2012; Wenger, 1999). This means that whenever students are engaged in learning, they are simultaneously developing a learning identity, and these learning identities can either enable or constrain the way they learn and positively or negatively shape their experience of being learners.

For most people, but particularly school-aged children, identity development is formatively reflexive of social experience and highly influenced by peers (Hoy, Demerath & Pape, 2001; Stryker & Burke, 2006). The significance of identity for middle years students cannot be overstated, given the centrality of identity formation in social and emotional development during this period (Bahr, 2005). Middle school is a time when students begin to align themselves more strongly with particular social and cultural groups (Smith & Grootenboer, 2007) and with specific ways of knowing and being in the world (A. Kaplan & Flum, 2012). School and learning in school significantly influence and are reflexive of students' identity development (A. Kaplan & Flum, 2012; Lannegrand-Willems & Bosma, 2006). Quite rightly, identity is a central construct in contemporary framings of middle school philosophy, principles and pedagogies (Australian Research Alliance for Children and Youth, 2011; Groundwater-Smith & Mockler, 2015; Ministerial Council on Education, Employment, Training and Youth Affairs, 2008).

It would be helpful, then, to have a clear conception of learning identity as a basis from which to build positive approaches to behaviour management. Drawing from recent research into positive learning identities with primary and middle years school students, the term learning identity is used here to refer to the self-perceptions, personal values, psychological dispositions and affective orientations, as well as to the personal knowledge and academic capabilities, that the learner brings to bear in order to participate in, and make meaning from, a specific learning setting (M. O'Brien, Blue & Rowlands, 2016; M. O'Brien, Makar & Fielding-Wells, 2014).

Practices for managing behaviour positively

Positive learning identities and engagement

Managing behaviour positively entails an approach and commitment to practices that foster positive learning identities and scaffold affirming experiences of learning. This view draws considerably from humanist and social or socio-cultural perspectives of human behaviour and unabashedly emphasises the importance of considering the needs, rights and individual perspectives of middle years students. It foregrounds positive behaviour management as practices that aim to deliberately scaffold the development of positive self-perceptions, positive valuing of learning, self and others, and positive and empowering psychological dispositions and affective orientations, as well as to enable agentic, intentional approaches to building personal knowledge and capability. Where the overarching aim of behaviour management is to build positive learning identities and to scaffold affirming and life-enhancing experiences of learning, the following areas of practice are worth considering.

Positive relationships

A recent study in the United States found that most teachers believe the secret to successful classroom management lies in the quality of the relationships between teacher and students (E. Sullivan & Keeney, 2008). Relationships matter, and there is a growing evidence base in positive education to affirm that relationships between teachers, students and other members of the school and related community have a significant influence on learning and engagement and that the quality of those relationships do much to effectively counter any risk factors that might otherwise negatively influence how students feel about learning (Furlong, Gilman & Huebner, 2014; Green, Oades & Robinson, 2011).

What does a quality teacher–student relationship look like? It is a professional working relationship, and it is most effective when there is a clear sense of trust, respect, accountability and empathy for student needs (McDonald, 2013). Achieving this relationship requires consistent attention to both how you act as a teacher and what you do.

In describing the somewhat nebulous area of pedagogical practice concerning how to act, van Menen and Li (2002, p. 217) use the term 'teacher pathic knowledge' to refer to 'discernible qualities such as personal presence, relational perceptiveness, tact for knowing what to say or do in contingent situations, thoughtful routines and practices, and other aspects of teacher knowledge that are pre-reflective, pre-theoretical, pre-linguistic'. Some refer to this area of practical wisdom as 'phronesis' (Giles, 2010). Teaching and learning occur in a constant flux of actions and interactions and comprise complex, nuanced cycles of sayings, doings and relatings (Kemmis et al., 2014). But, as with any interaction, the mood, personality and disposition of participants leave an indelible impression. Think about those short conversations with a colleague in the hallway or an acquaintance you might run into on the street. During the most inane conversations—even a chat about the weather—we can be surprised by their enthusiasm, flattered by their interest in us, concerned by their apparent lack of interest in the world, worried by their not-so-subtle aggravation or struck by any number of other impressions. The non-verbal cues we sense about how they are feeling or how they view us are explicit qualities of the message they convey—almost as explicit as the words they actually speak. In other words, teaching and learning are constantly conditioned by personal, relational, intentional and contingent factors that when coherent help to make the processes work well but when absent can significantly constrain and limit the experience for all.

In van Menen and Li's (2002) work these ideas are described as the 'experiential and lived sensibilities' of being in the world and comprise an important relational aspect of teacher expertise—that is, knowing how to appear fully attentive and empathetic as a student talks to you, perhaps remembering a few things about their life and interests out of school, knowing when there is concern on their face as you walk by and asking if they're feeling okay. Most importantly, this kind of knowing is about knowing your students well enough to calibrate how you react to different kinds of behaviour. Can a gentle smile soften an otherwise firm redirection to get on with the task at hand? Or is it time to stare a little more meaningfully? Are you able to tell, by the way one of your students has a slight slouch to his posture today, that something is a little off and you might suggest a quiet chat with him in the break? These are the kinds of things that students notice acutely about their relationships with teachers: what the teacher remembers, seems aware of, takes note of and is empathetic to (Giles, Smythe & Spence, 2012; van Menen & Li, 2002).

Giles (2010, p. 1511) argues that developing these kinds of pathic sensibilities is a critical priority for teachers, stating that relational expertise attunes teachers more closely to the needs of their students and enables them to respond more effectively 'beyond the rules of engagement'. Importantly, it draws our attention to a foundational principle in managing behaviour positively: relationships that purposefully cultivate trust, respect and mutual regard are an important way to affirm students' sense of belonging and value as learners.

In terms of what we do, or the actions that teachers can take to convey concern and build personal connections with students, McDonald (2013) offers some concrete and practical suggestions:

- Greet students as they come to class. Being at the door as students arrive is professional but also an opportunity to greet students and 'take the temperature' or gauge the mood as students enter.
- Smile and acknowledge students. Make them feel welcome and wanted and that they matter in your classroom; notice them.
- Acknowledge the return of a student if they have missed a class or lesson. This is another way to let students know that you notice them and that they matter.
- Be explicit about thanking students or appreciating various things they have done that show initiative, courtesy, kindness, support, fairness, consideration for others and so on. Again, it reinforces the fact that you're paying attention to them, but it also builds a positive classroom culture.
- Do an activity together, something that is extracurricular, like working together on a community service or social justice activity, or perhaps just playing a simple game of hangman to settle everyone into class after an exam or sports session. This provides different opportunities for students to get to know you and for you to get to know them.
- Be human, so that students can see you *are* human and are willing to share your vulnerability and personal story. Share an anecdote or a birthday, acknowledge a mistake or challenge, and so on.

Simple yet intentional actions by teachers can influence how students experience being in a learning environment (Demirdag, 2015; E. Sullivan & Keeney, 2008). Creating and consistently maintaining mutually respectful, professionally friendly relationships (where there is even a little personal knowledge and understanding shared between teacher and student) are essential bases from which to correct small misdemeanours or, when needed, to restore positivity and commitment following more significant fallouts.

Positive classroom culture

Creating a positive classroom culture will provide the infrastructure from which to maintain positive relationships when the business of learning is underway or needs to get underway (Demirdag, 2015). A positive classroom culture starts with a clear and shared understanding of the routines, expectations, procedures and qualities of behaviour that are established, reinforced and shared as norms or ways of working. In a general sense, many of these structures and routines are similar from classroom to classroom, in that they reflect common approaches to teaching, learning and organising learning environments across the globe. However, contemporary innovations in education are reshaping the look and feel of learning spaces (Lippman, 2010). Non-traditional spaces that include clusters of soft furnishings, different zones for different activities and spaces for connecting to and working with technology, as well as spaces for working together, are the new norms. There is no single best structure or routine, but rather there are principles for supporting quality learning in a range of environments (Clarke & Pittaway, 2014).

Within the positive education approach, a positive classroom culture entails routines, expectations, procedures and qualities of behaviour that are safe, supportive, accountable, inclusive and collegial (Demirdag, 2015; Evertson & Weinstein, 2006; McDonald, 2013; Prior, 2014). The core principle is that these aspects are explicit and consistently applied as means by which to organise and manage learning.

Classroom culture and the routines, procedures and expectations that create that culture play an important role in the middle years classroom. Classroom management processes that are positive and affirming—for example, taking the opportunity to reward effort and attitude even when academic outcome is in need of further attention (Hester, Gable & Manning, 2003)—will reinforce students' self-esteem (Demirdag, 2015). Most importantly, given the cognitive, social and psychological needs of middle years students, classroom management practices should prioritise opportunities for choice, autonomy, accountability, meaningful connections to learning, connection to others, encouragement of effort, and self-expression (Demirdag, 2015; McDonald, 2013; Prior, 2014).

There are a number of theories of classroom management that have at their core a philosophy that reflects particular theories of human behaviour, including those reviewed earlier in this chapter. Richmond (2007) summarises these along a continuum of four distinctive approaches:

1. *Authoritarian*—The teacher is in charge; control over behaviour is seen to lie outside the students, not within their own control.
2. *Behaviourist*—The teacher's role is to condition the behaviour of the students so that they develop appropriate self-control according to the external requirements for compliance.
3. *Democratic*—The students are seen as having greater potential to manage their own behaviour, so the teacher can work cooperatively with students to negotiate appropriate expectations and behaviour.
4. *Constructivist*—Control over behaviour lies entirely with the students, but they are therefore more accountable for their learning.

Reflecting Richmond's (2007) view, there is a move in contemporary approaches to classroom management to draw from a range of theoretical approaches and select practices that serve different purposes, at different times, with various students. There is also movement towards classroom management practices that may necessarily begin at, or draw from, the behaviourist end of the continuum but that confidently move towards the democratic and constructivist end of the continuum, where students value learning intrinsically and there is explicit regard for, and valuing of, student autonomy and their capacity to self-manage engagement in learning (Demirdag, 2015; McDonald, 2013; E. Sullivan & Keeney, 2008).

Redirecting, reinforcing and restoring engagement
Sometimes students lose their concentration, get distracted, feel a little disenchanted with the order of the day or bridle at an apparent lack of opportunity to be heard or represented. The relatively minor classroom misbehaviours that result are generally straightforward to deal with when there is a consistent commitment to positive teacher–student relationships; a strong culture that promotes negotiation, inclusivity and student agency; and clear, reasonable and age-appropriate rules for engagement in learning (McDonald, 2013; E. Sullivan & Keeney, 2008). This can particularly be the case when students themselves have an opportunity to contribute to the creation of that culture, at both the school and the classroom level (Groundwater-Smith, 2015), and have been invited to be valued citizens of the classroom community (Freiberg, 1999).

Active student involvement in learning is the first response to averting disengagement or misbehaviour (McDonald, 2013). In his recent research on learning and motivation, Martin (2013, 2015) highlights the importance of seeing disengagement as a combined, interrelated problem that has as its cause a possible gap in required academic skills in a particular area, which can have an influential effect on the will to engage. Over time the consequences of simple things like poor management or difficulty with new concepts or ways of working can erode the confidence and motivation levels of some students. Our task in these cases is to be alert to this fact and to identify how some behaviours are signals that the student has encountered a potential gap in their learning and needs assistance to get back on track. Usually, given the appropriate support coupled with a healthy dose of respect and encouragement, students can be redirected. Our task together is to rebuild both the intellectual skill needed and the efficacy and motivation to stay engaged.

When redirecting disengaged behaviour or reinforcing expectations, it is important to be consistent, maintain students' dignity, be aware of their need to maintain an impression in the presence of their peers, express unconditional respect regardless of the misdemeanour and have a clean slate policy so that everyone can move on (McDonald, 2013; Richmond, 2007; E. Sullivan & Keeney, 2008). However, occasionally there are students who display chronically challenging behaviours. Fortunately, these students are in the minority, and it is important to acknowledge that, in most cases, chronically challenging behaviour is the result of emotional and behavioural disorders (B. Rogers, 2015) or genuine personal trauma (McDonald, 2013). Influencing and changing chronically challenging behaviour are difficult and require regular support and longer term planning. As the statement from Mendler (2005) in the opening section of this chapter notes, inappropriate behaviour is primarily a signal that basic needs are not being met or that a student is seeking to meet them inappropriately.

Managing these students relies on a whole-school approach and should garner additional support through the allocation of professional resources. The school-wide positive behaviour support approach recently implemented in a number of schools across Australia and the United States is one example that provides key principles for managing challenging behaviour positively and safely (Sugai, 2009). These principles usually include:

- monitoring behaviour against a research-based continuum
- implementing a range of interventions designed to redirect behaviour
- utilising environmental arrangements that aim to prevent recurrences of problem behaviour
- teaching prosocial skills and behaviours
- implementing evidence-based behavioural practices
- screening and monitoring regularly student performance and progress on behavioural as well as academic goals (Sugai, 2009).

Similarly, restorative justice practices have become widely popular in schools across Australia, New Zealand, the United States and Europe. The value of these approaches for middle school settings is in the explicit positioning of students as valued members of a school and classroom community and in their active involvement in deliberations about what is fair, right and just in terms of the behaviour and expectations of all members (Vaandering, 2014).

When there is a clear and consistently implemented school-based approach to behavioural support, the teacher is more able to address and respond to challenging behaviours as they arise in the classroom. In general, these strategies respond to behaviours hierarchically, from low-level inappropriate behaviour to more challenging, defiant behaviours, and include the following approaches:

- Use preventative low-level responses. Use students' names and offer a firm redirect.
- Be aware of your own emotional state and remain neutral. Ensure you do not become angry, frustrated or aggressive; do not become personally involved.
- Do not take bait. Young people can be good at engaging others in conflict, through insults or defiant, belligerent body language and facial expressions. Ignore it.
- Take students aside for a private talk. Diffuse any engagement with peers and offer a face-saving opportunity by moving away from an audience.
- Listen, acknowledge, agree and defer. Ask the student what is bothering them, acknowledge their feelings and perspectives, and move to discuss this further after the lesson so that the disruption is minimised and the power of disruptive behaviour is minimal.
- Use the language of de-escalation. Show students you care about their wellbeing and are not taking the behaviour personally: 'You seem frustrated. Is everything okay?'
- Use de-escalating statements. 'I understand that you are frustrated, but this is something we should discuss after class.'
- Remove a student from the class or offer them a choice—stop or leave. But ensure there is somewhere safe for them to go, with someone responsible to meet or accompany them.
- Use one-on-one problem-solving. Model the appropriate way to address an issue or problem, through discussion and genuine problem-solving. Sometimes this can include asking the student to help you to help them (Demirdag, 2015; McDonald, 2013).

Finally, it is important to remember that even with students who display chronically challenging and defiant behaviour, our role as teachers is to understand that such behaviour reflects a deep-seated, unmet need, trauma or disorder (McDonald, 2013; B. Rogers, 2015) and to ensure that schools and classrooms offer a safe, supportive and potentially transformative environment in which those students can rebuild their relationship with you, others, learning and life (Freiberg, 1999; Furlong, Gilman & Huebner, 2014; Vaandering, 2014).

Chapter summary

This chapter makes the following key points:

- There are four broad yet influential theoretical perspectives that shape perceptions of behaviour and influence behaviour management approaches in contemporary education.
- The aims and priorities for middle years teaching and learning form a values-based framework from which to consider the potential of positive education for behaviour management.
- Managing behaviour can, with deliberation and intention, build positive learning identities and engage students positively and productively in learning.
- Contemporary approaches and practices for managing behaviour positively include the explicit development of positive learning identities, prosocial skills and values and genuine engagement in learning.

Chapter Fifteen

Using information and communication technologies

SARAH PRESTRIDGE and GLENN FINGER

Learning intentions

In this chapter we will:
- emphasise the need to address the disconnect between middle years students' personal use and formal classroom use of information and communication technologies (ICT) for learning
- stimulate thinking about how, when, where and why Australian middle years students use ICT in their increasingly connected worlds
- conceptualise a framework that can guide teachers to enable middle years students to learn about ICT and learn through using ICT.

Learning in a connected world

Throughout this chapter, we treat the term information and communication technologies as being synonymous with digital technologies, and therefore these terms are used interchangeably. That is, ICT refers to a plethora of existing digital technologies, such as mobile phones and social media, as well as emerging technologies, which are in various stages of development and use, such as enterprise and consumer 3D printing, virtual reality, augmented reality, wearable technologies, machine learning, brain–computer interfaces and ongoing innovation in artificial intelligence. Changes in technologies require us to reflect on those already in use and the potential of those we have available now and to imagine what future technologies might emerge. This requires thinking about the implications of those ICT for curriculum, pedagogy and assessment as you read through this chapter.

Middle years students are now living in a world where access to the internet and a range of digital devices is considered to be a necessity in their personal lives. Almost every endeavour which middle years students undertake is impacted upon by digital technologies. From organising their day to communicating with family and friends, undertaking shopping experiences, entertainment and a range of social experiences, students in the middle years are increasingly connected and can use these technologies anywhere and at a time of their own choosing. They can communicate and access information in synchronous and asynchronous ways. While there might be some locations where this access is not pervasive, students can connect and engage in those activities outside school (W. Clark et al., 2009; M. Ito et al., 2008; Luckin et al., 2009). Similarly, S. Wang et al. (2014) have suggested that technology ownership and access have become more pervasive for middle years students.

With an understanding of this increasing pervasiveness of digital technologies in the lives of middle years students, this chapter aims to achieve the three learning intentions through encouraging and adopting an evidence-informed approach with reference to relevant research literature. Importantly, this chapter relies upon a shared understanding of the relationships between these technologies and learning in order to provoke thinking about important implications for curriculum, pedagogy and assessment in using ICT in middle years classes. To illustrate, as students progress through the Australian Curriculum: Technologies, it is expected that 'they will begin to identify possible and probable futures, and their preferences for the future. They develop solutions to meet needs considering impacts on liveability, economic prosperity and environmental sustainability. Students will learn to recognise that views about the priority of the benefits and risks will vary and that preferred futures are contested' (Australian Curriculum, Assessment and Reporting Authority [ACARA], 2016c).

So, from the outset, we understand that technological change is dynamic and that technology and teaching form a wicked problem, as it is incomplete, contradictory, changing and occurring in complex and unique social contexts (Mishra & Koehler, 2006; Rittel & Weber, 1973). However, we encourage you to view this as also providing exciting possibilities and opportunities—perhaps even as a game changer—to motivate, engage and inspire students in the middle years to develop the digital capabilities needed.

Middle years students use ICT in their personal lives and for learning purposes in complex and interrelated ways. In understanding how students use ICT, students', teachers' and parents' voices and perspectives are of interest. The report *From print to pixel: the role of videos, games, animations and simulations within K-12 education* drew upon the views of students, teachers and community members from 7600 schools and 2600 districts in the United States and around the world (Project Tomorrow, 2016a, p. 2). This report affirmed that there is an 'increasing use [of] videos, games, animations and simulations across all segments of the population to support both informal learning and entertainment' and that 'students do not see learning as only happening from 8 to 2:30 each day' (p. 3). Moreover, the report found that, in comparing findings from 2012 with those from 2015, there was a complementary increase in teachers' use of digital content in the classroom. Examples included the increased use of videos found online, games, online curriculum, online textbooks, animations, virtual field trips, self-created videos, and simulations. Directly relevant to how, when, where and why middle years students use ICT in their increasingly connected worlds, the Speak Up findings presented the *Ten things everyone should know about K-12 students' digital learning* (Project Tomorrow, 2016b) and *What do parents really think about digital learning?* (Project Tomorrow, 2016c). These are summarised below.

Student voice summary

Ten things everyone should know about K–12 students' digital learning

#1   Learning via YouTube
38% of students are finding online videos to help with their homework and 27% say they regularly watch videos created by their teachers . . .

#2   Students are mobilists!
Personal access to mobile devices has reached several significant tipping points: 86% of 9–12th, 72% of 6–8th . . . graders are smartphone users now.

#3   More games please
Almost two-thirds of students want to use digital games for learning in school . . . 53% say they have received better grades by using technology within learning.

#4 Students want to code—especially girls!

Amongst girls . . . 50% [of] 6–8th graders want to code!

#5 Teacher—I have a question!

Students are regularly using digital tools outside of school to communicate with their teachers about school . . .

- 48% by email
- 15% by texting

#6 Tweet-tweet?

47% of 9–12th graders are Twitter users now . . . in 2011 . . . only 11% were tweet-tweeting.

#7 I'll take my learning mobile

76% of students think every student should have access to a mobile device during the school day to support learning . . .

#8 Watching online videos

74% of 6–8th graders say they watch online videos for schoolwork. And what class do they watch videos in the most? Science!

#9 Change in social media use

. . . 43% of students in grades 6–12 say they never use Facebook. But spending more time with content creation sites: 54% say they use YouTube all the time!

#10 Goodbye 1:1!

Different tasks = different tools! Laptops top students' lists for writing a report, taking online tests and working on group projects. Smartphones are #1 for connecting with classmates and accessing social media. (Project Tomorrow, 2016b)

Parent voice summary

What do parents really think about digital learning?

#1 Tech use in school is important

85% of parents say that the effective use of technology in school is important to student success.

#2   Surprise! Top parent concern about tech use
... Technology use in school varies from teacher to teacher ...

#3   Blended sounds great!
 ... 55% [of parents] chose a 'blended learning' model as the best for their child; in second place, the traditional classroom environment (42%).

#4   Learning on the go
Over 2/3rds of parents agree: it is important for students to use [ICT] during the school day [as they] extend learning beyond the school day.

#5   A mobile device in every backpack
41% of parents say they would buy a mobile for their child to use in school ... 11% have already done this!

#6   Joining the social media revolution
... 61% [of parents use Facebook] often or all the time. Up and coming for those new digital parents under 29: YouTube (43%), Pinterest (37%), Instagram (29%).

#7   Speaking of YouTube
... Parents say watching online videos can help with learning [including] re-watch[ing] videos as many times as needed ...

#8   Text me!
55% of parents say they want their child's teacher and school to communicate with them via text messaging to a mobile device ...

#9   The perfect school for my child would include ...
Schoolwide Internet access (55%), digital textbooks (50%), mobile apps for learning (48%), laptops for every child (46%) and online educational videos and games (41%).

#10 And I'm willing to help pay for that!
... 64% of parents say they would pay an annual technology fee to support class-room digital learning expenses. (Project Tomorrow, 2016c)

Provocation 15.1 A day in the life of a middle years student

This case study presents a day in the life of a teenage girl, Bella, who is in Year 8 and is fourteen years old.

Bella's story

I wake up and check my phone for any messages from my friends—Text Messenger, Instagram and Snapchat. If I have time, I will listen to music. On the way home from school on the bus, I usually check for messages again. I check it on and off again all afternoon, and then at night, in bed, I spend a while, at least three hours on YouTube to see what's trending. On YouTube, I watch Isaac's channel. He's a friend of my brother. I watch beauty gurus, cooking gurus, like *My Cupcake Addictions*, *Nerdy Nummie*, stuff that is popular and see what's happening, so I'm up to date and can talk to my friends about it tomorrow. I used to read (a book) before I went to bed, but now I just watch YouTube. YouTube is more entertaining than a book. It's easier to watch, and it's really hard to find a good book, so it's sort of mindless watching YouTube. YouTube is more interactive because you can leave a comment. It suggests other videos to watch. It's more accessible and more private. Also, the YouTube videos are quicker and shorter, so they hold your attention.

I look at some people's YouTube channel and laugh at them, as they're silly. I'm not interested in making my own as I can't cook and I don't know what to do. Even if I did, I know that I'd start off with zero likes, and then a year later, I would have say, one like, and that would be my mum!

In school, we are allowed to use our phones in history. We are allowed to take photos of the whiteboard which is full of writing but we really just take photos of each other. We also do an online safety module but we just check Instagram and Facebook. We are supposed to look up policy but no one does. Sometimes on the school laptop I go onto Putlocker to watch a movie if the class is boring.

 Do you agree or disagree with the following pedagogical insights from this case study? Justify why you agree or disagree.

- The majority of teenagers are consumers of technology rather than producers.
- High levels of self-consciousness exist for being trendy and cool (by number of likes), which poses limitations on how or if teenagers publish online and social currency.

- Social media provide entertainment and respond to teenagers' preference for multimodal text types that are delivered to them (suggestive content) with opportunity for a level of interaction (comments).
- Teenagers are very aware when there is no purpose for the use of digital technology in school work and they disengage.

ICT literacy in Australian students

While the previous section outlined important findings from a major American study, this section complements that data by summarising relevant findings from the *National Assessment Program—ICT literacy: Years 6 & 10*, conducted in Australia in a three-year cycle since 2005. This assessment program captured data about students' ICT knowledge, understanding and skills and their ability to use ICT creatively, critically and responsibly. The most recent report provided the 2014 results of 10,562 Australian students by state, territory and student subgroups, including details of their achievements on the test of ICT literacy (ACARA, 2015c). The report showed a concerning decline from 2011 to 2014 in ICT literacy performance for middle years learners, especially when the proficiency standards expected in this assessment were reasonable for Year 6 and Year 10 students. For example, Year 6 students were asked to search a website to find appropriate material, format a document, crop an image and create a short slideshow. Students in Year 10 were asked to design an online survey, use software to add two new levels to an online game and create a short animated video. All of these skills have been reflected in the ICT capability to be developed as a general capability across all learning areas of the Australian Curriculum (ACARA, 2016b). However, are these skills outdated, and do these skills truly represent what our current students' ICT literacy skills need to be? Perhaps the National Assessment Program should have been asking questions similar to those asked in Project Tomorrow (2016a), such as about using YouTube and changes in social media use.

The decline from 2011 to 2014 in ICT literacy performance for middle years learners occurred within the context of only 4 per cent of Year 6 students and only 2 per cent of Year 10 students having no computers at home. Interestingly, 52 per cent of Year 6 students and 66 per cent of Year 10 students reported having access to three or more devices (desktop, laptop or tablet) at home. Importantly, 56 per cent of Year 6 students and 77 per cent of Year 10 students reported that they used computers daily at home, while 34 per cent of Year 6 students and 65 per cent of Year 10 students reported using computers daily at school. An important implication outlined in this report is that 'we cannot expect students to become proficient on important employability and life skills, just by using computing devices for games and social interaction. They also need to be taught the relevant knowledge, understanding and skills' (ACARA, 2015c, p. xi). What is missing here is the important thinking that digital games and social interaction can be educational and that it is necessary for teachers to show students how to leverage these technologies for educational purposes.

Students were also asked to indicate the frequency with which they used ICT for a range of educational purposes. Year 6 and Year 10 students reported that they were using ICT at least once a week, or at least once a month but not every week, for assessment-related tasks and collaborating with other students, including collaborating with students from other schools. Approximately one in three Year 6 students reported using 'online learning programs such as Mathletics' (ACARA, 2015c, p. 92) at least once a week, while only one in ten Year 10 students reported using online programs at least once a week. Students also reported using ICT at least once a week, including preparing reports or essays, organising their program of work or topic using a learning management system, completing worksheets or exercises, data logging as part of an investigation and reflecting on their learning experiences. We need to be concerned that middle years students are using a only limited range of technologies mainly for consolidating learning. Rather, we suggest that they should also be using ICT as cognitive tools to assist in deep engagement in the conceptual development process.

Using ICT to engage students

Various researchers have investigated middle years students and their use of ICT in a range of curriculum learning areas. There are both enthusiasm and concerns about middle years students and ICT. Starting with the use of ICT to engage and enthuse middle years learners is a more purposeful beginning point. Research for over a decade has been centred on ways in which ICT might enhance or transform learning for curriculum purposes. More than a decade ago, C.J.P. Nolan & McKinnon (2003), in referring to New Zealand school education, went as far as saying that the middle years appeared to be in crisis, with research evidence suggesting challenges in relation to students being difficult to motivate, presenting behavioural problems and underachieving. In response, they implemented a research study focused on the development, implementation and evaluation of a computer-based integrated curriculum for Years 9 and 10 students. Their findings were presented in relation to three key elements of the project—that is, a set of integration strategies to accommodate diverse educational needs and purposes, a range of out-of-class activities to motivate students and provide them with experiences, data and information for follow-up in class studies and the use of integrated computer programs to facilitate integrated learning.

Similarly, Smith (2005) noted that middle years students often have a well-established relationship with media and that they play an important role in their lives and argued for curriculum which is relevant for middle years students. Research by Myhre, Popejoy and Carney (2006) examined the questions 'What characterises the teachers who choose to start using technology in their instructional practice?' and 'What does the technological and instructional context look like that allows for such changes to take place?' From their research on a technology and mathematics project involving more than 300 teachers, they reported that although certain institutional and organisational efforts were important, teachers formed their own support systems that enabled change processes. Myhre, Popejoy and Carney highlighted their observation that teachers enjoyed substantial autonomy when it related to making decisions about classroom teaching. Smith (2005) proposed components of a curriculum to develop critical media literacy. Subsequent research by McMillan (2007) envisioned that video production might enhance the relevance of a middle years arts curriculum and undertook an action research project. McMillan's findings suggested that video production activated student voice, imaginations and learning in a range of learning areas. While noting these positive findings, McMillan highlighted some issues which needed addressing, such as reduced student load, having a technician to support implementation and increased time allocation.

Research by Molyneux and Godinho (2012) involved the creation of a digital resource, the Venom Patrol website, to teach scientific concepts about Australia's venomous animals to students in Years 5–9. The study reported that the students were critical and insightful users of digital texts and responded positively to the non-linear structure of that resource. Elsewhere, in examining whether or not middle years students used the web in a superficial manner, Zhang and Quintana (2012) designed a software tool called Digital IdeaKeeper to support inquiry planning, information search, analysis and synthesis. They examined the differences between the work of Year 6 students who engaged in online inquiry without IdeaKeeper with that of students who used IdeaKeeper. They reported that IdeaKeeper supported online inquiry that was more integrated, efficient, continuous, metacognitive and focused. The effects of having laptops and science technology tools in middle school classes were studied by Yerrick and Johnson (2009), who found that there were positive differences in student achievement and responses to pedagogy and in the effectiveness of tools implemented by teachers over the course of the year.

In providing a synthesis of approximately fifteen years of research on the integration of new literacies in middle schools, Kist (2012) made the important suggestions that there were salient characteristics that made innovation more successful for middle school teachers and students and that the organisational plan of many middle schools was significant. It is acknowledged as well that teachers are required to assess student learning within standardised or formal school-based curriculum requirements. Interestingly, research by Beavis et al. (2014) found that forms of traditional assessment can be considered authentic within digital game–based teaching and learning units as well as in units based on STEM (science, technology, engineering and mathematics). However, additional authentic assessment was still considered part of the teaching and learning sequence in these technology-based units. For example, more formative-type assessment was drawn from student blogs, discussion forums, online feedback and comments made by students on peer work, small-group teacher and student dialogue and self-reflective assessment, which suggests a focus on valuing the *progress* of student learning. In this way students are assessed through multiple forms and are able to display a development of knowledge and skills rather than one product or skill. Authentic and student-driven assessment has been found to have a positive influence on student learning (Oliver & Herrington, 2003).

Promoting digital citizenship

There is a growing body of research literature related to concerns about middle years students and their use of ICT, such as the more public identification of the problem of cyberbullying (Burnham & Wright, 2012; Katz et al., 2014). Research has proposed a proactive approach to building students' understanding and etiquette online through a multipronged approach for both prevention and intervention actions (Katz et al., 2014). Katz et al. (2014) suggest that young people and their parents need to become better educated about appropriate online behaviour, and they also emphasise the value in changing young people's behaviours by targeting their decision-making processes.

Guidance for effective appropriation of ICT through improved awareness and education is provided by the Office of the Children's eSafety Commissioner relating to eSafety, including advice about 'balancing online time', 'cyberbullying', 'digital reputation', 'offensive or illegal content', 'online gaming', 'photos, videos and social media', 'protecting personal information', 'sexting', 'trolling' and 'unwanted contact'

(Australian Government Office of the eSafety Commissioner, 2016a, 2016b). A recommended approach is digital citizenship, which promotes confident and positive engagement with digital technology (Australian Government Office of the eSafety Commissioner, 2016c). Many school systems and many schools have developed ICT use policies relating to digital citizenship (Riddle, 2016a). Riddle (2016b) has defined and described the nine elements of digital citizenship:

1.   Digital Access: full electronic participation in society.
2.   Digital Commerce: electronic buying and selling of goods.
3.   Digital Communication: electronic exchange of information.
4.   Digital Literacy: process of teaching and learning about technology and the use of technology.
5.   Digital Etiquette: electronic standards of conduct or procedure.
6.   Digital Law: electronic responsibility for actions and needs.
7.   Digital Rights & Responsibilities: those freedoms extended to everyone in a digital world.
8.   Digital Health & Wellness: physical and psychological well-being in a digital technology world.
9.   Digital Security (self-protection): electronic precautions to guarantee safety.

These are important elements which can provide the basis for an educative and developmental approach for middle years students. There are numerous resources available for teachers—for example, the Australian Government Office of the eSafety Commissioner (2016c) lesson plans, which include plans for teaching digital citizenship for upper primary, lower secondary and middle secondary school students. Topics for these lesson plans include important considerations for middle years students, such as 'digital footprint', 'making safe, responsible, informed choices online', 'rights, responsibilities and benefits of digital citizenship' and 'measuring potential harm caused by actions online'.

A conceptual framework for ICT use

In this section, we propose a conceptual framework for middle years students and their ICT use. This framework is intended to help guide teachers in effectively designing teaching and learning environments and experiences for middle years students, who are increasingly connected through digital technologies within and beyond their formal schooling contexts.

We refer to an Australian context which can be used as a basis for the ways in which three main considerations might find expression in a range of other contexts. Those considerations are:

1. the renditions or frameworks which set out the expectations or standards for teachers—i.e., what capabilities teachers need to teach with ICT
2. the ways in which ICT might be presented as a subject area to be studied—i.e., learning about ICT
3. the ways in which ICT might be used for learning across curriculum areas—i.e., learning with and through technology.

Thus, while the following refers to an Australian context, you are encouraged to consider how ICT use finds its expression through your relevant curriculum in your context.

First, there are expectations of teachers in Australia which are expressed through the Australian Professional Standards for Teachers at the career stages of graduate, proficient, highly accomplished and lead teacher (Australian Institute for Teaching School Leadership, 2011a). ICT are considered in the professional knowledge, professional practices and professional engagement of teachers. The Teaching Teachers for the Future Project (Finger et al., 2013) built upon the standards for graduate teachers to formulate the ICT Elaborations for Graduate Teachers (Australian Institute for Teaching School Leadership, 2011b). The Teaching Teachers for the Future Project drew upon the Technological Pedagogical and Content Knowledge conceptualisation (Koehler & Mishra, 2009; Mishra & Koehler, 2006), and these elaborations made Technological Pedagogical and Content Knowledge capabilities more explicit in relation to the Australian Professional Standards for Teachers. Table 15.1 provides an example of ICT Elaborations for two of the Standard 2 focus areas and their descriptors. This illustrates how expectations for teachers include ICT use to demonstrate the standard of 'knowing the content and how to teach it'.

Second, there are expectations that ICT capability is a general capability to be taught and developed across all learning areas of the Australian Curriculum. The ICT capability is organised according to five interrelated organising elements:

Applying social and ethical protocols and practices when using ICT
This element involves students developing an understanding of how social and ethical protocols and practices are applied when using ICT . . .

Table 15.1 An example from the ICT Elaborations for Graduate Teachers

Standard 2	Know the content and how to teach it	
Focus area	Descriptor	ICT elaboration
2.1 Content and teaching strategies of the teaching area	Demonstrate knowledge and understanding of the concepts, substance and structure of the content and teaching strategies of the teaching area.	Demonstrate knowledge and understanding of ways that the use of digital resources and tools can complement teaching strategies and promote deep learning of, and engagement with, the content of specific teaching areas.
2.2 Content selection and organisation	Organise content into an effective learning and teaching sequence.	Demonstrate the ability to select and organise digital content in relation to relevant curriculum.

Source: Australian Institute for Teaching School Leadership (2011b, p. 2).

Investigating with ICT

This element involves students investigating questions, topics or problems using ICT.

Creating with ICT

This element involves students using ICT to realise creative intentions and create solutions to challenges and tasks.

Communicating with ICT

This element involves students understanding and using appropriate ICT to communicate with others.

Managing and operating ICT

This element involves students managing and operating ICT to investigate, create and communicate. (ACARA, 2016b)

Third, there is learning about digital technologies through the digital technologies subject area (ACARA, 2016d) within the Australian Curriculum: Technologies learning area (ACARA, 2016c). ACARA (2016c) makes the distinction between the digital technologies curriculum and the ICT general capability, explaining that 'the capability helps students to become effective *users* of digital technologies while the Digital Technologies curriculum helps students to become confident *developers* of digital solutions' (original emphasis). There are important understandings about the kinds of thinking to be developed in students—namely, systems thinking, design thinking and computational thinking. These considerations are critically important in understanding how middle years students learn about and with ICT.

Provocation 15.2 Middle years students and their use of ICT

In a Year 9 English class, the students were studying Indigenous rights as part of their development of persuasive text, specifically exploring the influence of digital media. The topic included how white Australians alienate Aboriginals and how, even today, Aboriginals feel that their culture is disrespected, uncelebrated and disenfranchised. Michael, one of the students, was interested in this topic but found the discussion quite boring, as he could not relate to it. He said that he needed to see how the Aboriginals were feeling; even though the teacher was really trying to make it interesting, he just sat in class, subdued.

That night he went home having remembered he had seen something posted on Facebook about Aboriginals reacting to an Australia Day celebration. He found the short video excerpt again and emailed the link to his teacher. The next day, the teacher used it in class, and afterwards there was a very active and engaged discussion. Michael felt valued for his contribution, and the class discussion was much more interesting, as everyone could see, 'for real', how the Aboriginals were passionate about their beliefs. Michael stated, 'I would rather watch a video to see the reaction as it is more real and relevant and you can put a face to the teacher's statements.'

 Do you agree or disagree with the following pedagogical insights from this case study? Justify why you agree or disagree.

- Classroom is a communal learning entity, not a teacher-controlled space.
- Greater engagement in curriculum is enabled for students when they have opportunities to contribute to the shared knowledge.
- Mutual respect is gained between teacher and learner when value is placed on the contributions of all in the shaping of learning pathways.
- The teacher is the pedagogue modelling how to interpret and leverage learning from social media.

The Australian Curriculum and the expectations for professional standards and teacher capabilities, as discussed earlier, provide a context for teachers to use ICT in learning and teaching with middle years students. However, greater clarity can be provided for teachers in how to use ICT with middle years learners so that they are used for learning purposes, in addition to middle years students using ICT for personal and social purposes, as established above. For instance, Bers (2006) suggested that some research attempts to understand what young people *are* doing with technologies, while other research focuses on what young people *could be* doing with technologies. To respond to pedagogical possibilities, Bers developed a framework for designing and evaluating technologically rich approaches that promote positive youth development. The categories or components of positive youth development which Bers referred to are competence, connection, character, confidence, caring and contribution. These middle years traits complement, and provide student-centred foundations for enabling, learning with ICT as a general capability and learning about ICT within the technologies learning area, which might find similar expression in other curricula and in other international educational contexts.

The Technological Pedagogical and Content Knowledge conceptualisation acknowledged the interplay of the content to be taught, how it is taught and how technology impacts upon content, pedagogy and integration (Koehler & Mishra, 2009). This framework also acknowledged that teachers need to know which digital tool is most effective for the given task, which pedagogies support student engagement through the use of the technologies at given points in the learning sequence and the different ways in which technology can reshape and represent content. From a 21st-century learning perspective, more effective student learning outcomes are enabled when constructivist ideologies encompass technology and content through collaborative inquiry-based learning. Hence, there is a range of complex processes here, such as students connecting, communicating, collaborating, validating, publishing, propagating, innovating and inspiring.

Teachers need to know how technologies can be best appropriated to leverage student learning. For teachers of middle years students, understanding this requires the added complication of understanding their connected world. As identified earlier in this chapter, the prevalence and pervasiveness of technologies in the lives of middle years students cannot be overlooked when considering how to position learning that makes it relevant, meaningful and useful to beyond-the-classroom contexts. Ignoring social media can be detrimental to learning for these students (Smith, 2005).

As illustrated in Bella's story presented in Provocation 15.1, as well as in research, such as that by Zhang and Quintana (2012), current use of technologies has been found to be superficial. To move beyond this, middle years teachers need to design and implement transdisciplinary units of work in which students are using technologies to collaborate, curate, computate and create. Greater connections should be made with real issues of social justice and political and social agendas, drawing on interests of students that have impacts on their lives. The goal of this approach is for teachers to scaffold students through complex real-world dilemmas, drawing upon authentic subject-based strategies that meld together in ways that help provide insights and processes for problem-solving. In this way, both the nuances and the specialised methods of each discipline domain can be leveraged by students in order to engage in critical inquiry. For middle years learners, the need for challenging collaborative thought work that draws upon and puts into action siloed knowledge and skills is considered by Kist (2012, 2014) to be an essential part of the learning process for students in these grade levels.

A problem-based approach and student-centred learning are not new and have been implemented in classrooms for some time. Additionally, these approaches have been identified widely in research relating to technology integration for increased student engagement and collaboration (ChanLin, 2008), 21st-century skills of information analysis and critique of multimodal texts (Trilling & Fadel, 2009) and design thinking to assist in engineering solutions (V. Jones, 2014). With regard to transdisciplinary approaches, ICT provide teachers with the opportunities to enable and encourage students to use a wide variety of digital tools; to collaborate within teams and beyond classrooms; to use digital tools to curate, manage and organise content; and to create digital solutions to real-world problems.

The conceptual framework presented in Figure 15.1 lists the elements that need to be considered for middle years students and ICT use. The two learning contexts outlined in this chapter—the connected world and the classroom—inform approaches to middle years students and their ICT use. The conceptual framework acknowledges the importance of teacher capabilities and contexts, which need to enable students to engage with ICT in ways that promote positive youth development. Collectively, those elements can inform teachers' rethinking of curriculum, pedagogy and assessment, and they can also be adapted to align with a diverse range of educational contexts to appropriately reflect the relevant curriculum of those contexts.

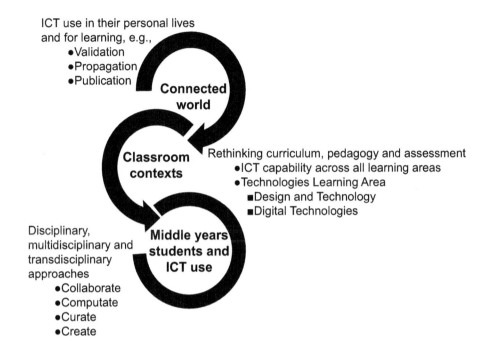

ICT use in their personal lives
and for learning, e.g.,
- •Validation
- •Propagation
- •Publication

Connected world

Rethinking curriculum, pedagogy and assessment
- •ICT capability across all learning areas
- •Technologies Learning Area
  - ■Design and Technology
  - ■Digital Technologies

Classroom contexts

Disciplinary,
multidisciplinary and
transdisciplinary
approaches
- •Collaborate
- •Computate
- •Curate
- •Create

Middle years students and ICT use

Figure 15.1 A conceptual framework for middle years students and their ICT use

Drawing on the understanding that middle years students use technologies to seek new comprehensions and new knowledge, to validate their growing realisations and to propagate and publish their ideas, a reciprocal relationship needs to exist where inside-classroom learning informs and reforms learning through social media and digital technologies as middle years students operate within their digital ecosystems. This relationship means that students need to become part of the decision-making with regard to the topics, the pathways for learning, the digital tools used and even the curriculum materials under study. Teachers should draw on the technological expertise of middle years students, knowing that they are guiding and supporting student engagement in learning.

Consider how this conceptual framework might stimulate your thinking about designing learning experiences, and, as shown through the examples provided in Table 15.2, how it might assist you in identifying the ICT tools which you might use for enabling students to collaborate, computate, curate and create. These tools are

Table 15.2 Ideas for enabling middle years students to supplement the curriculum for productivity outcomes, to augment or enrich the existing curriculum and to leverage opportunities for transformative practices with ICT use

Processes	Tool descriptions	Example ICT tools	Supplement	Augment	Leverage
Collaborate	Collaborative spaces	Google Docs, wikis, Padlet	Teacher–student or student–student administrative email	Teacher-directed collaboration on project topic	Student purpose-built spaces for project collaboration within and beyond classroom
	Synchronous, real-time chat	Skype, Google Hangouts			
	Asynchronous chat	Google forums, Edmodo, email			
	Online repositories	Weebly, LMS, Ning, Blackboard			
Computate	Digital construction	Minecraft	Step-by-step teacher-led coding lesson	Students engaged in coding activities	Student-created digital game using programming tools
	Game making and coding	Scratch			
	Robotics	Lego Mindstorms, Lego Dash & Dot			
	Electronic invention	Makey Makey			
Curate	Content management	Diigo	Teacher-made mind map to represent topic	Teacher-led mind map on topic as a class representation	Student ongoing development of mind map over period of unit
	Graphic organisation	Mind Maps, Inspiration			
	Research and literacy organisation	Read & Write Gold			
	Image collation	Flickr, Instagram			
Create	Movie and animation creation	iMovie, Movie Maker, PowToon	Teacher-made tutorial to reinforce mathematics concept	Student-created multimedia on class topic	Collaborative student multimedia artefact representative of authentic investigation beyond classroom for peer review
	Interactive blackboards and screen capture	ShowMe, Explain Everything			
	Design	Google Drawings, SketchUp			
	Website building	Wix, Google Sites			

Provocation 15.3 IMPACT Learning Framework

The IMPACT (Inspire, Model, Practise, Connect and Transform) Project, formerly known as Project 600, uses a networked learning community involving students, teachers, school leaders, parents and caregivers, the IMPACT Centre and a teaching team of literacy and numeracy experts. By February 2016, the online delivery model had enabled this to be scaled up to directly deliver literacy, numeracy, critical thinking, STEM and other initiatives to approximately 45,000 students from over 600 primary and secondary schools, including middle years students in Years 6–9, in Queensland. The project allows students to experience rich pedagogical approaches through the use of virtual classrooms and web conferencing in subject areas that might not be available in the mainstream classroom (Watt et al., 2014).

Teachers implement their learning sequences in online synchronous spaces using the IMPACT pedagogical framework, which is a dynamic, overarching common language for teaching and learning. IMPACT aims to develop learners with a growth mindset (Dweck, 2008). Teachers and school leaders use the five elements—inspire, model, practise, connect and transform—when designing, delivering, reviewing and improving learning programs. The themes evident throughout student and teacher responses about their involvement in IMPACT relate strongly to:

- improved computing skills, with many of the responses highlighting that the students were not the digital natives that their generation is often assumed to comprise

- immersion in an online learning environment, with many of the students outlining that this was their first exposure to an online teaching delivery model

- feedback from students and teachers suggesting that the students enjoyed the experience and developed solutions to issues that emerged when they were learning online.

Do you agree or disagree with the following pedagogical insights from this case study? Justify why you agree or disagree.

- Online learning enables networked learning communities through enhanced communication and collaboration opportunities and functionalities.
- IMPACT can be the basis for an appropriate learning framework for teaching and learning online with middle years students.

- Middle years students benefit from engaging in online learning experiences such as virtual classrooms and web conferencing in addition to conventional, formal, face-to-face teaching and learning.
- This case study provides examples of instances in which ICT are used to supplement, augment or leverage the curriculum opportunities for students.

listed here to provide some guidance for thinking about different ways students can use ICT for learning purposes and as cognitive tools. However, the important factor about effective use of any tool lies with how the teacher appropriates it for learning in the classroom and beyond. Categories for such technological appropriation have emerged from research showing that teachers are using ICT to supplement the curriculum for productivity outcomes such as using ICT to motivate, reinforce or practise subject skills; to augment or enrich the existing curriculum in which ICT are considered tools for teaching content, collaboration and higher order thinking; and to leverage opportunities for transformative practices with ICT in which new ways of working with ICT are driven by students equally with curriculum requirements (Ertmer et al., 2012; Prestridge, 2012; Prestridge & de Aldama, 2016). Therefore, in rethinking curriculum, pedagogy and assessment, can you identify examples of how the ICT tools suggested in Table 15.2 might be used to supplement, augment and leverage curriculum?

Chapter summary

This chapter makes the following key points:

- There should be connections between middle years students' use of ICT for a range of purposes in their personal lives and for learning purposes.
- Teachers are encouraged to have the competencies and dispositions to capitalise upon the opportunities which are being presented by ICT available now and to be able to design learning experiences which capitalise upon future technological changes. Our current middle years students are likely to be working in new kinds of jobs and in different ways from those we currently know.
- Being digitally literate, as defined by ACARA (2015c), reflects a functional or skills-based perception. However, we must remind ourselves that the

contributions and agency of middle years students matter. Therefore, using ICT to leverage relevant, meaningful learning for middle years students matters.

- The chapter provided a conceptual framework for middle years students and their ICT use to give guidance to educators in designing the use of ICT. Through ICT being used for modification and redefinition, it is possible to rethink curriculum, pedagogy and assessment.
- We know that education is a human endeavour and that in this increasingly connected world middle years students can have agency to use ICT appropriately and effectively. It is people—including middle years students—who can do more than consume content. Middle years students can reproduce it and construct it and can shape the future.

Chapter Sixteen

Parent and community engagement

DONNA PENDERGAST

Learning intentions

In this chapter we will:
- develop an understanding of the importance of parent and community engagement in the context of the middle years learner and its benefits for student achievement
- consider strategies to enhance parent and community engagement.

The importance of parent and community engagement

Parents tend to be more actively engaged in their children's schooling during the primary school years compared to the secondary years. The Australian Child Wellbeing Project investigated this phenomenon through more than 100 discussions and a national survey of 5400 young people in schools in Years 4, 6 and 8. They report that in Australia this pattern is consistently reflected, with reduced parental engagement in schools as students progress into the secondary years of schooling and when comparing Year 4 to Years 6 and 8 (Redmond et al., 2016). The reason for this decline in parent involvement is likely to be partly due to developmental issues, as adolescent students are attempting to create their own identities independent of their parents. It may also be a cultural pattern related to the shift from primary to secondary schooling or related to the practical realities that secondary schools are typically much larger than primary schools and engagement with parents is more challenging because of this scale. This phenomenon is not new, and the decrease in the engagement of parents and also the community, such as grandparents and members of the public, as students move through school is one of concern regarding student wellbeing. Importantly, it is not the quantum of time or frequency but the nature of the involvement of parents and the community that has the potential to make an impact on middle years students.

The decrease in parent and community engagement is the antithesis of what is advocated in relevant policy related to middle years education. For example, one of the signature practices for effective teaching and learning in middle years schooling is the development of relevant curricula through meaningful family, school and community linkages and partnerships (Middle Years of Schooling Association [MYSA], 2008). Developing a sense of community and developing productive learning communities are also key elements of successful middle years education. Without a focus on community, it would be difficult to argue that a school or system could implement reforms in education for the middle years in a sustainable manner. Creating connections from which intellectual rigour can grow and providing opportunities for developing a sense of belonging and cohesion are critical elements in the middle schooling ethos. Hence, the study of middle years education would be incomplete without a focus on the role and value of parent and community engagement, its potential benefits and effective strategies for its development.

In this chapter, we use the term parents to represent the families with whom students live, whether they be couples, including same-sex couples, single parents, grandparents, aunts and uncles, older siblings, adoptive or foster parents or a range of other groups. These parents may participate in their children's learning at school in a wide variety of familiar ways, including:

- helping with homework
- accompanying classes on excursions
- attending parent information nights
- participating in parents' and citizens' associations
- volunteering in the school tuckshop
- attending school functions
- being involved in school productions
- helping students with mathematics or reading

- attending parenting sessions
- attending award ceremonies, assemblies and special events.

We use the term community in this chapter to apply to groups that might be within or external to the school. The Australian literature around community and middle schooling produces multidimensional understandings of community. In some cases, community is constructed around geographical or proximity criteria, so it becomes community within schools and community extending beyond the boundaries of the school. This reconfiguring incorporates two understandings of community: community in the sense of connectedness and belonging, of shared venture and collaboration; and learning community or community of learners as a curriculum organiser. Communities typically incorporate collective features, including a common or shared purpose, interest or geography; collaboration, partnership and learning; a respect of diversity; and contribution to enhanced potential and outcomes (S. Kilpatrick, Barrett & Jones, 2003).

What do parent, family and community partnerships look like? How do parents, families and communities work with middle years students to make learning meaningful? Why are the notions of family and community partnerships and learning communities particularly relevant for the middle years? What roles should parents and communities play in ensuring effective transition from childhood to the middle years? It is to these questions the chapter now turns, always in the context of the middle years learner.

The *Position paper* of the Middle Years of Schooling Association (MYSA, 2008), now named Adolescent Success, foregrounds two concepts of community that support young adolescents as they experience a range of significant physical, emotional, social and moral changes. It is proposed that the development of small learning communities of students will provide students with sustained, personalised attention to their needs, interests and achievements. These small student communities may also support the establishment of a safe and positive learning environment for students and an environment that encourages innovative teaching and learning practices. The relationships between schools and the wider community are also viewed as a vital component of middle schooling approaches. The MYSA suggests that involving parents and members of the community in student learning and positioning schooling as an important component in the community are aspects of the interconnected approach that it has developed to enhance middle years learning and teaching.

The introduction of the new junior secondary phase of education in Queensland is based on the six Junior Secondary Guiding Principles developed by the Australian Council for Educational Research (ACER, 2012). These principles are intended to provide challenging educational offerings that engage young adolescents while at the same time giving them a sense of belonging and support during the changes they face. One of the guiding principles—parent and community involvement—is explicit to the topic of this chapter, serving as a firm commitment for approaches that help to keep parents connected with their children's learning when they enter high school (ACER, 2012). School leaders are required to audit their processes around this principle and to develop strategies to keep parents engaged in appropriate ways and to widen community participation. As a guiding principle, it is now assumed that all state schools in Queensland teaching Years 7–8 have intentional strategies in place to focus on continuously optimising parent and community involvement.

When looking beyond Australian shores, the trend for aligning community and middle schooling is consistent with these frameworks. For example, the 2010 position paper *This we believe: keys to educating young adolescents*, developed by the American National Middle School Association (now the Association for Middle Level Education), includes many references to community. It is based on a revised model for success which incorporates four essential attributes comprising sixteen characteristics, and it is delivered in three domains: curriculum, instruction and assessment; leadership and organisation; and culture and community. Two of the six characteristics of culture and community directly align with parent and community partnerships: 'The school actively involves families in the education of their children' and 'The school includes community and business partners' (National Middle School Association, 2010). These elements are argued to facilitate stronger bonds within, and extending beyond, the school and to aid in the creation of learning environments in which students are motivated to take on challenging learning activities. It is rationalised that this leads to higher levels of achievement and improved student behaviour. Concomitant with these intellectual- and engagement-related benefits is the utilisation of organisational structures that support and assist in the building of meaningful relationships. In addition to drawing on the intellectual capital that community members can bring to student learning, it is argued, student involvement in community activities can also support the emotional, psychological and moral development of young adolescents. Working with members of their community is said to develop the students' sense of belonging and combat the sense of disengagement or alienation that students often feel during these years.

Provocation 16.1 Parent and community involvement in the middle years

The professional associations representing the advancement of middle years education, including the Association for Middle Level Education and the MYSA, promote the need for strong parent and community involvement with young people in the middle years.

 Reflect on a school you have been involved with as a student or staff member and provide responses, including explanations and descriptions, to the following questions:

- How does the school actively involve families in the education of their children?
  - How are families in the school encouraged to become involved in meaningful ways in the life of the school?
  - What specific programs are in place to promote parental involvement?
  - Does the school reach out to the families in the school, particularly to those families who are reluctant to come to the school?
  - Do parents have opportunities to be involved in decision-making groups?

- How does the school include community and business partners?
  - How is the school proactive in seeking community and business partnerships?
  - Do community members partner with the school to provide specific learning experiences for students?
  - Do students become involved in apprenticeships with community and business partners?
  - Does the school participate in community service learning initiatives?

The benefits of parent and community engagement

Benefits of enhanced parent and community involvement can include, but are not limited to, benefits to students' learning outcomes. They can also support the social and cultural development of students and their understanding of options for employment and further education and training. Parents and community members help develop, understand and support a clear and common focus on core academic, social and personal goals contributing to improved student performance and have a meaningful and authentic role in achieving these goals. The school community works together to actively solve problems.

Mentoring and outreach programs provide for two-way learning between students and community or business members (State Education Resource Center, 2014). Epstein (1996) suggests that such connections serve to improve school programs and school climate, provide family services and support, increase parents' skills and leadership in school matters, connect families with others in the school and in the community, help teachers with their work and increase ownership and commitment to the school by the community. Research has further demonstrated that strong links between schools and the community can enhance the culture of the school and have a positive influence on student retention and behaviour (Boethel, 2003; Falbo, Lein & Amador, 2001; A.T. Henderson & Mapp, 2002; Saulwick Muller Social Research, 2006).

While involving parents in school activities may have an important community and social function, it is the engagement of parents in learning in the school and in the home that brings about positive changes in children's academic attainment, via their support for academic achievement, early intervention in academic and social difficulties and facilitation of successful student transitions (Falbo, Lein & Amador, 2001).

The literature related to parent and community engagement is extensive, and it points to an important difference between simply involving parents in schooling and engaging parents in learning. It is the latter that has been shown to have the greatest positive impacts on academic achievement in young adolescent learners.

Families, schools and communities contribute in unique ways to the learning process. Understanding and measuring the interdependence of these factors can assist in progressing strategies to improve levels of parental engagement. One way of considering the effect is to consider the work of Hattie (2003), who synthesised over 500,000 studies to analyse the effects of influences on student achievement. He deduced that almost all things we do in the name of education have a positive effect on achievement. By way of summary of the size of the effect of influences, he reported that the major sources of variance are six-fold: students (50 per cent), teachers (30 per cent), home (5–10 per cent), schools (5–10 per cent), principals (5–10 per cent) and peers (5–10 per cent). In this case, home, which accounts for about 5–10 per cent of the variance, is in addition to the effects already accounted for by the attributes of the student. The home effects are additional and are related to the parental involvement, expectations and encouragement of students.

Parents' involvement in school-based activities is most likely to have a positive influence in the early years of schooling, when children require additional support to adjust to a new learning environment and to develop a sense of belonging. As children get older, parental involvement in school-based activities may affect student outcomes indirectly through ensuring school attendance and by reinforcing appropriate behaviour. Shifting from involvement to effective parental engagement practices is a must as children grow and develop. The early years of education provide opportunities for parents to learn about effective ways to converse with their children about learning and become comfortable talking with teachers and other staff about their children's academic and social development. For this reason, it is important that, from the beginning, parents feel comfortable participating in activities on school grounds and consider the school as a partner in their children's learning. As the child grows into an adolescent, the already established patterns of their parent discussing and engaging in learning processes and conversations and modelling effective communication with teachers and school personnel reinforce positive expectations and keep open dialogue that will assist with learning practices.

Strategies for engaging parents and communities

Most jurisdictions will have a set of principles or beliefs that guide parent and community engagement in student learning. For example, the Department of Education, Training and Employment (2014b) in Queensland has developed the Parent and Community Engagement Framework to help schools, parents and the community to work together to maximise student learning. The framework identifies what schools can do to strengthen learning outcomes for students, through effective partnerships between principals, teachers, students, parents and the community. A range of strategies typically exist in relation to parent and community involvement. These include:

- providing consistent research-based information for parents about adolescent development
- working collaboratively with parent bodies such as parents' and citizens' groups to develop and implement supportive approaches to involving parents in student learning
- actively seeking feedback from parents on programs and activities in the school

Provocation 16.2 Assisting parents to remain engaged

The parents of Jacob and Henry took a very active role in the early years of their schooling. Their mum attended reading support sessions twice a week for the entire seven years of the twins' journey through primary school, and when she could she attended meet-the-principal and other events held at the school. There were often events during school time as well, including those during which her children and others performed and contributed to assembly. One of the parents usually walked the boys to class each morning and greeted their teacher, often updating them with details of family events, minor health ailments, challenges with homework or play-ground interactions the boys were encountering. Each term the parents attended parent–teacher meetings in the classroom and viewed the twins' folios of work, usually spending twenty minutes discussing each son in turn. They sometimes emailed the teacher to clarify expectations about homework projects.

As transition to the secondary school, located at the same campus of the P–12 school, approached, there was more focus on preparing the boys for Year 7 and for the secondary school environment. One of the parent information evenings emphasised the need for parents to continue to be actively involved and provided information about subjects the boys would be studying. It was at this time that the parents became a little less confident about their role and how to support the boys during their high school years. Both found the message confusing: 'It is time to let go of your sons so they can mature, but at the same time it is important to remain closely connected so they are supported.' The parents were also concerned about their ability to help with some of the subject-matter.

 What advice would you give Jacob and Henry's parents about their involve-ment and, importantly, their engagement with the school, with a particular focus on ways that would lead to increasing the boys' academic achievement?

- seeking relationships with social workers and other support agencies in the community
- seeking to build high-quality collaborative relationships with business partners in the community.

Strategies vary depending on the school context, the desired outcomes and the age groups of students. Building working relationships with parents and community members is an investment on the part of schools. A variety of strategies are available, including approaches to communicating in two directions: gathering input and information from parents and keeping them informed of what is going on in the school. Building collaborative relationships with companies, societies and social support services is also important.

In addition to strategies for enhancing community within schools, there are at least three important strategies for establishing community that extends beyond the perimeter of the school. These can be categorised as full service schools, service learning and vocational programs. In Australian middle school settings currently, there is a focus on service learning and to a growing degree full service school models as forms of community partnerships. Vocational programs provide the opportunity for students to participate in paid and unpaid internships and to assume job responsibilities under the guidance of workplace mentors. Though aimed at the age group beyond middle schooling, this may have an impact on the later middle years students.

Full service schools

The term full service school is borrowed from the United States, where many such schools have been established over the last decade or more. In Australia, they are a relatively recent phenomenon. There are several models of full service schools, but most share the idea that schools are the centre for the development of community and the logical site for linking services needed by students and their families (Groundwater-Smith et al., 2001). This approach is evident in the growing number of extended services schools in England, which provide a range of services to the local community, including childcare, access to school facilities and access to specialist parenting programs (Caldwell & Harris, 2008). A national evaluation of extended services schools in England has indicated that these schools improved at twice the national average rate between 2005 and 2006 in key indicators of school performance, including the rate of student exclusions and students' academic achievements (Department of Children, Schools and Families, 2007). Activities that may typically be undertaken as part of full service schools include:

- individual counselling and family support
- specialised curriculum development for the context—e.g., vocational focus for local employment
- breakfast programs and recreation programs
- community projects—e.g., development of a code of practice for student use of the local shopping centre, negotiated with security guards

- local agency networks for student referrals
- student housing submissions.

There are many issues to consider in the establishment and ongoing support of full service schools in Australia, including the important question of who benefits from the model, but they are seen as a trend for the future.

Service learning

Service learning is the introduction of directly linked community projects into the school context or curriculum. Mutual gains and developing a sense of belonging are direct benefits of this approach, along with enhancing relevance and authenticity. For students, the opportunity to participate in authentic learning experiences serves to increase their engagement and to develop transferable skills, along with the development of resilience and leadership traits. For teachers, new teaching approaches, ideas for professional development and ready access to tools and resources to maximise learning outcomes can be achieved through school–community links. For communities, increased community commitment to young people and a revitalising of community building occur. Service learning projects typically offer students the opportunity to practise citizenship while meeting community needs.

Vocational programs

Connecting with the community via a range of vocationally orientated programs is common in schools, especially in the senior years. For the middle years, early exposure to a range of work settings is important for establishing aspirations and motivating students. Importantly, the MYSA's (2008) Signifying Practices of middle years education point to the need for a curriculum that is relevant and connected, with assessment practices that feature authenticity as a core element. The building of community through vocational programs enables both practices to be achieved, setting the scene for improved pedagogy across the quantum of learning. Other benefits of engaging in vocational activities include obtaining practical experience from work, gaining familiarity with how workplaces operate, developing employability skills, developing and improving interpersonal skills and facilitating exploration of potential career paths.

From the perspective of the wider community engaging with students through vocational programs, the benefits include contributing to the next generation of their vocation, an opportunity to contribute to the individual and school culture and an opportunity to shape future aspirants.

Epstein (1996) provided a useful framework outlining six types of involvement parents can have in partnerships with schools. More recently, this model has been utilised as the basis to develop the seven key dimensions that form the basis of Australia's Family–Schools Partnerships Framework (Department of Education, Employment and Workplace Relations, 2008). These seven key dimensions have been incorporated in the Emerson et al. (2012, pp. 28–9) report conducted on behalf of the Australian Research Alliance for Children and Youth for the Family–School and Community Partnerships Bureau. The seven dimensions and examples are presented below:

1. Communicating—This key dimension emphasises that effective communication:
    *   is active, personal, frequent, culturally appropriate and multidimensional
    *   is open to families' needs and attitudes
    *   is a two-way exchange between families and schools that involves not only an exchange of information, but also opportunities for schools and families to learn from each other
    *   makes clear that families are genuine partners and can help solve big problems.
2. Connecting learning at home and at school—This key dimension emphasises families and schools understanding:
    *   the overlap between the home and school environments
    *   the connection between successful partnerships and children's learning, including the importance of high expectations from both teachers and parents to children's success at school
    *   the importance of families and schools working together to create positive attitudes to learning, and of parents working with teachers in the educational decision-making process for their children
    *   the benefits of schools being venues and agents to parental self-growth, learning and the development of new skills.
3. Building community and identity—This key dimension emphasises:
    *   activities that improve the quality of life in a community while honouring the culture, traditions, values and relationships in that community
    *   that the work of schools includes aspects of the social, emotional, moral and spiritual development of young people
    *   that schools can act as a focal point for communities to come together and engage in capacity building.
4. Recognising the role of the family—This key dimension emphasises that as primary educators of their children, parents and families have a lasting

Provocation 16.3 Building mutual benefits

We return now to Jacob and Henry and their parents' engagement with the school. The boys are in their second year at high school, and their parents drop the boys at school in the car park and find they need to refer to student information on the school website to locate the names of some of the teachers, because they have little to do with them regularly. The parents always attend parent–teacher meetings, but with seven teachers to meet and discuss both Jacob's and Henry's progress, the meetings are usually focused on providing marks on particular assessment pieces and broad coverage of progress. They are in frequent contact with the pastoral care teachers of each boy and make contributions to the school when possible, such as at community events hosted by the school. Both parents are keen and willing to engage more but feel inadequate to provide advice about subject-matter. They also see teachers as the learning experts and do not want to be thought of as interfering parents. They are feeling more distant from the school and, importantly, more distant from the learning their boys are involved in.

This scenario highlights some of the challenges for parents in maintaining an appropriate balance of connection with the school yet facilitating a gradual release of responsibility so they clearly demonstrate to their child that they have confidence in their capacity to make decisions and take greater control.

 Drawing from the seven strategies presented in the final section of the chapter, draw up an action plan for Jacob and Henry's parents outlining what they could do to rebuild engagement, as well as involvement, in the school. Then, draw up an action plan for the school leaders and teachers using the same seven strategies, so that the process is mutually aligned.

influence on their children's attitudes and achievements at school. They can encourage their children's learning in and out of school and are also in a position to support school goals, directions and ethos. Parents look to schools to provide secure and caring environments for their children.

5. Consultative decision-making—This key dimension emphasises that parents are entitled to be consulted and to participate in decisions concerning their children. An inclusive approach to school decision-making and parental involvement/engagement creates a shared responsibility among parents, community members, teachers and school leaders.

6. Collaborating beyond the school—This key dimension emphasises identifying, locating and integrating community resources which can strengthen and support schools, students and their families, and opportunities for schools, students and families to assist the community in return.
7. Participating—This key dimension emphasises that families' time, energy and expertise can support learning and school programs in multiple ways and that all contributions are valuable. This may involve:
   - working with students on learning activities in classrooms
   - participating in other school activities outside the classroom
   - participating in activities outside the school itself
   - supporting and valuing teachers
   - ensuring that parental involvement/engagement is a recognised topic of staff meetings, professional development and in the induction of new staff.

Chapter summary

This chapter makes the following key points:

- Parent and community engagement is a key priority for effective middle years education.
- The occurrence of parent and community engagement is typically lower in the middle years compared to the primary years of schooling.
- The nature of parent and community engagement should be responsive to the age and stage of the student.
- The benefits of parent and community engagement are broad and important factors contributing to academic achievement.
- Strategies vary depending on the school context, desired outcomes and age groups of students. Building working relationships with parents and community members is an investment on the part of schools.

Acknowledgements

I wish to acknowledge Peter Renshaw and Jessica Harris for their contributions to earlier versions of this chapter published in the first and second editions of this book.

Part Four

Assessment practices in the middle years

Chapter Seventeen

Assessment

CLAIRE M. WYATT-SMITH, LENORE ADIE, FABIENNE VAN DER KLEIJ and J. JOY CUMMING

Learning intentions

In this chapter we will:
- develop an understanding of the common concepts underlying assessment theory and practice
- consider assessment from the perspective of external standardised testing as well as classroom assessment
- elaborate on hallmarks of quality assessment in middle years assessment practice.

Assessment concepts and definitions

Socio-cultural perspectives of assessment and understandings from the field of meta-cognition and learning frame the discussions in this chapter. This combination reflects the view of assessment as situated practice. Put simply, context matters. Assessment occurs in socio-political and historical contexts: available choices for teachers and students and decisions about assessment priorities are therefore circumscribed by educational, socio-economic and political values dominant in those contexts at particular points in time. What may be taken as natural or accepted as good assessment practice in one context or era may appear as unfamiliar, strange or even inappropriate in other contexts or eras.

Against a background of internationally diverse education contexts, assessment is defined generally as the collection and analysis of evidence of student learning used for a range of purposes. Rowntree (1977), in his seminal text with the provocative title *Assessing students: how shall we know them?*, and numerous other writers including Weeden, Winter and Broadfoot (2002), has elaborated the range of assessment purposes. These are typically inclusive of the long-standing distinction between assessment for learning improvement purposes and assessment for measurement purposes. This division reflects the traditional goals of assessment for improvement on the one hand and, on the other, assessment for accountability. We ask readers to consider how the division is potentially limiting in developing new assessment mindsets. Instead, we offer two unifying notions: fitness for purpose and intelligent accountability. Campbell and Rozsnyai (2002, p. 132) define fitness for purpose as 'one of the possible criteria for establishing whether or not a unit meets quality, measured against what is seen to be the goal of the unit'. Crooks (2003) notes six criteria for intelligent accountability, including improving trust between key stakeholders; involving participants in the process; promoting constructive contributions; counteracting performance indicator distortion; providing functional feedback; and, finally, stakeholders becoming more engaged and committed in their work. Taken together, these open the space for examining how the assessments that students undertake contribute to their learning, to the evidence teachers use to improve their teaching and to longitudinal data of students' learning histories from kindergarten through the middle years and into senior schooling.

The middle years of schooling have been under intense focus for accountability for some years. In Australia, this is evident in the move to census testing and reporting systems through, for example, the National Assessment Program—Literacy and Numeracy in Years 3, 5, 7 and 9; sample testing in science and information and communication technologies (ICT) literacies and in civics and citizenship; and the more recent move to introduce testing of young children on school entry. The intensity of accountability assessment is also evident through international comparative studies, such as the Progress in International Reading Literacy Study, the Trends in International Mathematics and Science Study and the Programme for International Student Assessment. These collectively assess reading, mathematics and science for nine- to fifteen-year-old students.

Evidence from recent research identifies the importance of the intersection between assessment and student learning (Baird et al., 2014). Assessment as an ongoing process can inform teachers about next stages in teaching to address students' learning needs. It should also inform students about where they are in their learning in relation to expected goals. This enables students to understand their progress, self-regulate their learning and identify new targets. Assessment can play an enabling role in teaching and learning (Wyatt-Smith & Klenowski, 2014) but can also have unintended and negative consequences for teaching and learning (Baird et al., 2014). These include the impact of external high-stakes assessments on narrowing the curriculum and teaching to the test (Lingard, Thompson & Sellar, 2016; Nichols & Berliner, 2007) and demotivation of students who have repeated low performance or, in contrast, who lack learning challenges (Masters, 2013).

Within the complexity of modern society, students in the middle years of schooling present with a great range of diversity. While some students may disengage during secondary school, others embrace learning and 'make great strides in educational attainment' (Dinham & Rowe, 2008, p. 21). The middle years is a time when students' rates of physical, social, emotional, intellectual and moral development occur differentially, creating great diversity within this group. The middle years of schooling are a critical stage in students' learning journeys. Students have attained basic curriculum knowledge and skills to embark on wider learning adventures. Both the nature of the learning and the diversity of expectations on students continue to increase in demand and volume. At the same time, students' lives outside school are becoming more complex and distracting. Families, friendships, extracurricular activities, sports and technologies compete with the school for student attention. There is potential for students in these years to disengage from schooling and become at risk of underachieving or even of becoming early school leavers (Gemici & Lu, 2014). Analyses of the most recently published National Assessment Program—Literacy and Numeracy writing results reveal how, in each state and territory in Australia, increasing numbers of students across Years 3 to 9 are underachieving insofar as they are failing to reach the national minimum benchmarks (Wyatt-Smith & Jackson, in press).

It is well recognised that narrowly construed assessments can reinforce a sense of failure and diminish self-esteem. Teachers need to employ strategies that will support students in these critical years to engage with their learning and become effective learners. These strategies include assessment that provides the critical links between what is valued as learning, ways of learning and thinking, ways of identifying need and improvement and, perhaps most significantly, ways of bridging school and other communities of practice. Assessment is a powerful factor shaping learning growth.

As the following discussion shows, effective instruction and fit-for-purpose assessment for the middle years need not only to accommodate the characteristics of the middle years learner but also to recognise the rapidly changing environment in which schooling now takes place.

Formative, diagnostic and summative purposes

Assessments can be described as formative, diagnostic or summative. Rather than the distinct type of the assessment, it is the purpose of the assessment that is the critical feature. Assessment information can be used for decision-making at different levels of education—for example, at the level of student, class, school or country (Brookhart & Nitko, 2008; Wiliam, Kingsbury & Wise, 2013).

- Assessment is formative when it is intended to inform or make changes to teaching and learning.
- Assessment is diagnostic when it is intended to identify specific learning needs.
- Assessment is summative when it is used to sum up and report information on a student's achievement at some terminal point in time or course of study.

Some discussions about the distinctions between formative and summative assessment have focused on the timing of the assessment; formative assessment is said to occur during the learning process, and summative assessment occurs after the learning has taken place. However, a distinction between formative and summative assessment based on time-related characteristics is not useful (Bennett, 2011; Sadler, 1989; Stobart, 2008). Although the distinction between formative and summative assessment indicates their intended uses, summative and formative assessments are not mutually exclusive in their purposes: they can coexist as the primary and secondary purposes of the same assessment (Bennett, 2011). Further, an assessment can be categorised as formative until a decision is taken to use it for summative purposes.

The primary issue is the difference between the purpose and the function of an assessment. The purpose relates to the goal of the assessment design, while the way in which assessment results are actually used determines their function. Sometimes assessments can be used to different ends, even though they were designed to serve only one particular purpose (Stobart, 2008). For example, some assessments are intended to make pass or fail decisions about students at the end of a course (summative). However, when they are accompanied by qualitative feedback (intended for formative or learning improvement purposes), the same assessments could inform students about the quality of their work and areas in which they need to improve. Teachers could also use the results to modify their teaching practices.

Assessment *of*, *for* and *as* learning

Assessment has also been described as being *of* learning, *for* learning and *as* learning. Assessment of learning relates to the summative purpose of assessment. Assessment for learning describes the formative purpose and was introduced by the Assessment Reform Group to specifically focus on student learning and the role of the student in the learning process. The Assessment Reform Group (2002, p. 2) defined assessment for learning as 'the process of seeking and interpreting evidence for use by learners and their teachers to decide where the learners are in their learning, where they need to go and how best to get there'. A more recent definition of assessment for learning stresses the continuous nature of assessment interactions to inform daily practice. Klenowski (2009, p. 264) stated that assessment for learning is 'part of everyday practice by students, teachers and peers that seeks, reflects upon and responds to information from dialogue, demonstration and observation in ways that enhance ongoing learning'. The Assessment Reform Group (2002, p. 2) identified ten principles of assessment for learning, stating that assessment:

- is part of effective planning
- focuses on how students learn
- is central to classroom practice
- is a key professional skill
- is sensitive and constructive
- fosters motivation
- promotes understanding of goals and criteria
- helps learners know how to improve
- develops the capacity for self-assessment
- recognises all educational achievement.

Assessment as learning is commonly understood as students understanding themselves as learners at a metacognitive level. This is related to students' strategies for the regulation of their learning and the decision-making processes this involves (Birenbaum, Kimron & Shilton, 2011; Earl, 2003).

Assessment dependability

Validity and reliability are both necessary to ascertain quality assessment. Dependability of assessments relates to 'maximum validity and optimal reliability' (Mansell, James & Assessment Reform Group, 2009).

Validity
Validity is the most important indicator of quality in assessment (Newton & Shaw, 2014). It is generally defined as the extent to which an assessment measures what it claims to measure. However, the concept of validity is widely contested, and different researchers emphasise different elements of validity. Three commonly used categories of validity are:

1. construct validity—the extent to which the assessment evidence provides an accurate representation of the learning domain
2. face validity—the extent to which the assessment seems fit for purpose at face value
3. consequential validity (Messick, 1989, 1994)—the interpretation of assessment evidence and its subsequent uses.

Construct validity implies that the assessment activity and evidence gathered should be closely aligned with the knowledge and skills that are expected to be learned and the focus of instruction. Face validity implies that the assessment seems fit for purpose at face value; for example, a multiple choice test may not be a valid method to assess a learner's ability in a practical skill such as cooking. Consequential validity implies that assessment results obtained for one purpose should not be used for a purpose for which they were not intended and which they do not suit; for example, standardised test scores intended to provide a measure of core literacy skills should not be used as a measure of school quality. Overall, how assessment evidence is used determines the appropriate method of validation (Kane, 2016).

Reliability
Reliability is the extent to which an assessment provides consistent results under consistent conditions and the extent to which one or multiple assessors reach the same agreement. Thus, it relates to the consistency of the assessment results and judgement decisions (Harlen, 2007). For psychometrically developed tests, reliability is directly related to test length; the more information that is gathered about a student's learning, the more reliably this will support a decision. This also extends to the use of assessment evidence from multiple sources to support low- and high-stakes decisions about students; multiple pieces of evidence need to be drawn on to support a reliable decision.

To be fair to students, who marks an assignment or examination should not have a substantial impact on their results. In order to reach acceptable agreement between multiple assessors and some degree of objectivity in assessment, a clear shared understanding of the assessment criteria and scoring rules is necessary. As we discuss later, in classroom assessments, moderation processes among teachers can assist in developing consistency on judgements.

Provocation 17.1 Dimensions of quality assessment

In the process of collaboratively designing your assessment task, you have been asked to explain the essential aspects of reliability and validity to your colleagues.

What are the main issues of reliability and validity of assessments for class-room teachers?

Assessment paradigms

Since the 1990s, accountability policies of governments in several countries including Australia have resulted in the introduction of external testing programs in the middle years. Differences between external standardised testing and class-room assessments are both practical and theoretical. A major practical difference between classroom-based assessments and external tests for summative purposes is that the former can be based on a range of activities and formats with recorded outcomes built up over a period of time, while the latter tend to be one-off stand-ardised assessments. Different theoretical models and philosophies underpinning different types of assessments can be visualised on a continuum with psychometric models at one end and contextualised classroom assessment at the other (Gipps & Stobart, 2003).

External standardised testing

Psychometric measurement has derived from the application of principles of scien-tific certainty to educational assessment. The focus is usually on inference from a test score of the degree to which a student has achieved in some underlying trait or ability, such as reading literacy. In keeping with the scientific approach and a focus on comparability, psychometric test development and implementation focus on reliability and standardisation. For psychometric purposes, the most reliable test that can be used is a multiple choice test that can be machine scored. However, most modern external tests allow open-ended items (where students have to supply a response of some type) to structured questions. Raters are given a range of possible student responses and appropriate scoring schema. The format and administration of the test are still sufficiently constrained to be highly standardised, and the nature of responses that can occur is restricted by the question focus and structure.

Most external tests are developed using psychometric or measurement principles. These tests are sometimes called standardised tests, because test scores have been converted to one standardised scale of student achievement, which allows objective comparison of student performance. Student performance is usually reported as a score on a dimension; while a student's score can be described in terms of what a typical student with that score can do, it can also be reported in terms of other students' scores in the school, across the state and even internationally. The descriptive interpretation is usually an inference of an overall proficiency based on the types of items the student has been able to successfully complete. For example, for the results for the Programme for International Student Assessment 2012 reading literacy test, a fourteen-year-old student who achieved at Level 2, one of the lower levels, is described as being able to recognise the main idea in a text, make low-level inferences, compare and contrast single features of a text and make connections between the text and the outside world.

Clearly, it is unfair to ask students to undertake any form of assessment without some preparation in the kinds of tasks and conditions (e.g., time, location and access to resources) in which they will be expected to perform. However, the potential for standardised external or school-derived tests to regulate learning possibilities needs to be avoided. Some standardised assessments can have a narrowing effect on teaching and learning (Cumming, Wyatt-Smith & Colbert, 2016). This is especially the case when teachers feel constrained in their practice to teach to the test (Lingard, Thompson & Sellar, 2016; Nichols & Berliner, 2007), spending considerable classroom time rehearsing students for test-taking.

Classroom assessment

The major focus of assessment for middle years students should be developing quality classroom assessment. This assessment is situated in the local context and can take a variety of forms, such as tests, performances, reports, presentations and the construction of artefacts. Classroom assessments predominantly focus on multiple contexts of performance—for example, in English, constructing different text types, drafting and revision skills as elements that create the effective writer rather than as intimations of underlying attributes or traits such as writing skills.

In a true learning culture, assessment activities become productively inter-woven with learning and teaching, so that assessment is continuous (rather than an end point or terminal) in nature. This is not to suggest that students are continu-ously being assessed. Instead, assessment is understood as integral to teaching and learning activities, when teachers observe limitations as well as strengths in particular achievements (Wyatt-Smith & Klenowski, 2014).

When classroom assessment is aligned with the curriculum and with the knowledge and skills expected to be learned, validity is high; however, the subjec-tive nature of teacher judgement can reduce the reliability. To maintain and strengthen public confidence in teacher assessment practices it is necessary to incorporate a range of strategies aimed at supporting teacher judgements and interpretations of assessment data. Five actions that support the dependability of teacher judgements are:

1. careful specification of the assessment tasks
2. specification of the criteria and standards
3. teacher training
4. opportunities for teachers to share interpretations of criteria and standards through moderation
5. development of an assessment community within the school (Harlen, 2004).

For example, the Australian Curriculum is based on a system of standards refer-encing. This means that assessment design and judgements of quality are based on established achievement standards, which provide external reference points for informing judgements and are pivotal for achieving comparability (Harlen, 2004; Sadler, 1989; Wyatt-Smith & Castleton, 2005; Wyatt-Smith, Klenowski & Gunn, 2010). Performance is judged as meeting the standard or as being above or below the standard, usually in the form of A to E grades. In order to achieve high reliability while preserving validity in the design of assessment tasks, it is important for teacher assessors to develop common understandings of mandated standards and reach 'similar recognition of performances that demonstrate those standards' (G. Maxwell, 2001, p. 6). Research has identified that professional cap-ability in assessment, including designing appropriate and challenging assessment tasks, is an area where teachers often request professional development (Wyatt-Smith & Looney, 2016).

Assessment in practice

We identify the hallmarks of quality assessment in the middle years as assessment that makes provision for:

- connectedness and responsiveness—taking account of students' interests, capabilities and repertoires of practice both inside and outside school, including the actual and virtual communities in which students live
- explicit recognition of the increasing autonomy of middle years students as learners—providing students with a role in negotiating selection of goals and the timing and manner of reaching these through to assessment
- a tailored, diverse and yet balanced range of learning and assessment options and modes—ensuring students can extend their knowledge and existing strengths in working with particular combinations of knowledge, modes and resources while encouraging risk-taking beyond this
- teacher and student discussion and other interactions around quality—enabling students to engage productively in self-assessment in relation to relevant features of quality
- the deliberate integration of a mix of new, emerging and traditional technologies in assessment practices—to facilitate communication and learning between teacher and students and among peers
- an explicit focus on developing students' metacognitive capabilities relating to learning how to learn—enabling students to develop know-how in the processes they rely on in learning and self-monitoring over time.

Alignment

As a starting point, the alignment of curriculum, assessment and pedagogy is essential to ensure that assessment practices are valid (Bennett, 2011; Popham, 2011). The curriculum and any stated achievement standards identify the valued knowledge and skills that will be evident in assessment tasks and inform teaching practice. In this model, assessment is planned at the beginning of the semester, before teaching commences. This is referred to as 'backwards design' (Wiggins & McTighe, 2011) or 'front-ending assessment' (Wyatt-Smith & Bridges, 2007). Teaching and learning activities are developed last, to ensure that the valued knowledge and skills evident in the curriculum and assessment tasks will be taught, providing students with optimal learning opportunities. Following the principles of Universal Design for Learning (see www.cast.org/our-work/about-udl.html), teachers design the assessments and learning activities to ensure maximum participation for all students.

The Meeting in the Middle Project investigated the impact of such alignment on the engagement of educationally disadvantaged students in the middle phase of schooling, and it found that 'in-depth consideration of assessment before the unit began had a significant impact on the quality of the pedagogy, and thus on student outcomes'. In the study, the researchers developed and applied the concept of front-ending assessment and task design processes as the anchor for curriculum planning and teaching. The authors emphasised that assessment should not be viewed as 'an endpoint or terminal activity, something tacked on the end of the unit, or done after teaching and learning' are concluded (Wyatt-Smith & Bridges, 2007, p. 46). Collaborative planning among teachers facilitates conversations about the standards and the valued qualities in student work that will evidence learning. This practice results in teachers developing shared understandings of the achievement standards before teaching commences. This understanding informs teaching and learning activities, including the feedback provided to students.

Designing assessment tasks

One of the critical factors in engaging students across the middle years of schooling is the increased demand and authenticity of learning and assessment activities in order to create real and meaningful challenges for students (Cumming & Maxwell, 1999). These learning and assessment activities are often transdisciplinary in the middle years, allowing students to connect knowledge from a range of key learning areas and as much as possible with community and other practices.

A number of key features have been identified to guide the design of quality assessments. Alignment, as discussed in the previous section, is pivotal to the development of valid assessments. However, other critical features in assessment design empirically developed in the middle years study referred to earlier (Wyatt-Smith & Bridges, 2007) include consideration of the task's:

- intellectual challenge and how students will engage with it
- scope and demand
- communication language
- requirements regarding curriculum literacy
- performance contexts, including the resources required for successful completion and the schedule of feedback
- opportunities for student self-assessment, including how students come to know and understand the expected standard of performance

- intended purposes regarding use of assessment information (Klenowski & Wyatt-Smith, 2014).

To promote student autonomy in the middle years, learning goals and activities to support learning can be collaboratively developed. In some cases a range of activities may be provided, with students able to exercise choice. Throughout the middle years it is not necessarily the case that all students need to complete the same learning and assessment activities simultaneously.

Criteria sheets and rubrics

At this stage of the planning phase, statements of assessment criteria and standards descriptors can also be developed. Commonly referred to as criteria sheets or rubrics, these statements are representations of quality descriptors: they make explicit the criteria that are the valued elements or features to be assessed and describe the different standards of performance. The essence of good assessment is to make explicit the expectations that you hold as a teacher for successful demonstration of learning (Sadler, 1989). This involves two key stages. First, what are the elements of learning that you are hoping to observe? Second, what type of demonstration is sufficient to show that the student has indeed learned? In developing the second stage, exploration of qualitative descriptors and use of informing words are important. Rather than being measured by quantitative terms—none, some and good, or no references, fewer than five references and more than five references—quality learning is distinguished by depth. Here, the distinctive qualitative standard is degree of independence or depth of thinking.

Quality assurance

However, standards, as written descriptors, remain open to interpretation, and other systems are required to develop common understandings of achievement standards to enhance reliability. Sadler (1989) argued that exemplars or samples of student work provide concrete referents for illustrating standards that otherwise remain abstract mental constructs. He made the point that the stated standards and exemplars work together to show different ways of satisfying the requirements of, say, an A or a C standard.

Moderation, or social moderation, is another activity that is used to increase the reliability of teacher judgement of student work (Adie, 2013). Moderation is described as a 'form of quality assurance for delivering comparability in evidence-based judgements of student achievement' (G. Maxwell, 2007, p. 2). In social moderation, teachers meet to discuss judgements of student work to reach consensus on the quality of the performance. Such processes allow diversity of assessment tasks to suit contexts.

Assessment and classroom pedagogic practice

Recent research in assessment shows that the most powerful assessment that occurs for students is assessment used for formative purposes—sharing learning intentions and success criteria with learners, rich questioning, feedback that progresses learning and student peer assessment and self-assessment (Wiliam, 2011).

Learning intentions and success criteria

Informing students of the learning intentions and success criteria of a lesson enables them to self-assess and develop their own learning goals. Learning intentions can be discussed at any point of a lesson, dependent on the type of learning; for example, in an inquiry lesson, the learning intention may not be discussed until the end of the lesson, whereas in other lessons, this may be discussed at the beginning. When discussing learning intentions and success criteria it is important that students understand all the terms and also develop a shared understanding of the expected standard. Teachers support students to develop these skills by including them in activities such as ordering work samples or developing standards descriptors.

Questioning

Teachers' questioning needs to be conducted in such a way as to gauge student understanding and reasoning about a topic. Questioning is a key skill used by teachers to gain an understanding of the depth of student knowledge and skills. This understanding then informs how the lesson progresses—that is, whether the lesson continues as planned, a topic needs to be retaught or students need to be provided with differentiated activities. It is important that teachers gain the maximum number of student responses and depth of information through their questioning strategies. This may be accomplished by using strategies such as personal whiteboards, showing a number of fingers in response to a multiple choice question or using a range of technologies (e.g., tablets for instantly collecting individual student responses to a question). Teachers can also encourage all students to be engaged in the class discussion through strategies such as Wait Time and Think, Pair, Share.

Feedback

Feedback in education is generally defined as 'information provided by an agent (e.g., teacher, peer, book, parent, self, experience) regarding aspects of one's perform-ance or understanding' (Hattie & Timperley, 2007, p. 81). Quality feedback has been identified as one of the most powerful influences on student learning. Feedback can help students identify where they are in their learning in relation to their goals, what they need to work on to improve and strategies to achieve their goals. In order for feedback to be useful and effective for learning, at least three conditions have to be met:

1. The learner needs the feedback.
2. The learner receives the feedback and has time to use it.
3. The learner is willing and is able to use the feedback (Stobart, 2008).

There is no one way to provide feedback that will be effective for all students. How students engage with feedback and the effect feedback has on learning relates to, for example, their motivation, self-regulation and current achievement level (Bangert-Drowns et al., 1991; Kluger & DeNisi, 1996; Shute, 2008). Research generally suggests that, to be effective, feedback needs to be substantial, construct-ive and focused on the learning task (Heitink et al., 2016). It is important to focus feedback on the student's work and not on the student as a person, as the latter is not informative for student learning (Hattie & Timperley, 2007). Feedback can have substantial positive or negative effects on student motivation for learning. It is not effective for learning and can be demotivating when it does not help the student understand why something was wrong and how they can improve (Hattie & Timperley, 2007; Shute, 2008). For example, feedback that tells the student only whether a task was completed successfully or not has limited value for learning. Differences in student expertise with a topic also affect their response to feed-back. For example, students who already have a deep understanding of a topic may become frustrated when feedback spells out exactly what they need to do (E. Hargreaves, 2013; Kay & Knaack, 2009); rather, giving hints can be more effective, allowing students to have agency in making decisions about which steps to take next in their learning. For example, for middle years students, feedback that is overly wordy may inhibit rather than support comprehension of the next steps. It is also important to realise that providing feedback to students ideally occurs in dialogue between teacher and student, with both teacher and student asking questions to understand each other's perspective. Following up on feedback is a good idea, to ensure that students have understood the feedback, which will enable them to use it to improve their learning.

Peer and self-assessment

Complementing the assessment information gathered by the teacher is the information that students themselves provide as they participate in peer assessment and self-assessment activities. Supporting students to become self-directed learners requires much assessment to be in their hands also; 'if formative assessment is to be effective, pupils should be trained . . . so that they can understand the main purposes of their learning and thereby grasp what they need to do to achieve' (Black & Wiliam, 1998, p. 8).

Teachers can provide self-monitoring guidelines, scales and checklists that students can use to consider their progress (Gibbons, 2002). It is through actively engaging students in reflecting on their learning that you can access key assessment insights not otherwise available. For example, a study by Cumming and Van der Kleij (2016) reported that by having students take screenshots of online activities during the learning process provided a substantial evidence base about their learning process and outcomes and also increased their engagement in their learning. This evidence was judged to be of better quality than evidence normally collected by the teacher or teacher aides.

Encouraging metacognition

The majority of students will require strategies and practice to clearly articulate their thinking. Think Alouds are one strategy to encourage students to verbalise their thoughts as they carry out a task such as performing actions or reading. While they can be used in instruction, the focus here is on illuminating student understanding. The evidence obtained using Think Alouds is metacognitive; that is, it reveals strategies and misconceptions.

It may be best to introduce students to Think Alouds through teacher demonstration—for example, reading a section of text and carrying out a task such as writing a letter, navigating a website (displayed on a large screen) or assembling some apparatus for an experiment. Another approach is to provide a list of probes (e.g., 'What does that mean?', 'Why do you do this next?', 'Why did this happen?' and 'What do you remember from last week?') and then to ask students to verbalise or jot down thoughts as they carry out a task. If it is text based, red dots can be placed strategically to prompt Think Alouds. Such metacognitive bookmarks can be used to help students assess their own understanding; for example, they can note the page or paragraph where they used each strategy and later can reflect on how the strategy used helped them (Block & Israel, 2004).

Collecting and collating evidence

In addition to assessment tasks and other measures of student learning, a robust body of evidence can be collected through:

- observations—both planned and incidental
- consultations—including with students, individually and in small groups, as well as with other teachers, parents and education and health professionals, as appropriate
- focused analysis—of work in progress or final versions of completed work
- anecdotal records and checklists (see Forster & Masters [1996a, 1996b] for examples).

Observation notes or anecdotal records regarding student learning can be written or oral and supplemented with paper or digital evidence. Their advantage is that they allow you to observe learning and 'record a wide range of actual . . . experiences' (Boyd-Batstone, 2004, p. 230). The techniques are commonly practised by early years teachers but are gaining recognition for their usefulness for older students due to their effective ways of providing rich, contextualised information. Time to talk with students individually in conferences, for example, enhances the quality of these records. Through ongoing observation, teachers can be monitoring student understanding and development in a systematic way.

Observations must be recorded as soon as possible if they are to capture important qualitative and quantitative information and impressions that may need to be confirmed later. To do this, it is necessary target about a fifth of the students each lesson or day. Records can be made using a small notebook, sticky labels or digitally (with the date and the student's initials). Boyd-Batstone (2004) describes a series of steps that can be simply implemented by teachers. Although she writes in terms of literacy, her method is easily extended across the curriculum. More detailed records can be developed after the lesson that identify actions to be followed in terms of student learning. These records can be used to develop a performance profile of student growth over time. Such profiles are based on identified achievement standards and developmental continua.

Portfolios

A way to organise learning evidence and to demonstrate progression over a semester or year is to have students amass and organise evidence of their learning outcomes into hard copy or digital portfolios. While it is relatively easy for students to collect such evidence, much can be gained by having them develop their own frameworks for presenting the portfolio evidence showcasing learning achievement through a range of media. While there is often a focus on best work, it can be helpful for students to use a developmental approach, so they can reflect on and illustrate how their mastery has grown. This could be through inclusion of early plans, drafts and final 'published' writing or through photographs or other records indicating activities along the way to completion of an activity or product. For self-assessing growth, students should be able to use grids showing suggested ways of assessing dimensions of personal quality assurance and engagement with a task and others (Cumming, 2004). Where students have no previous experience of working with portfolios, they may need careful explanation and frequent feedback about their developing portfolios, as well as examples of finished products. Many schools arrange a learning expo for students to present their portfolios to parents and peers and ideally to a wider community audience.

Assessing for diversity

The diversity of student cohorts in today's classrooms is well recognised. The undeniable fact is that students come to school with existing knowledge and skills, as well as with repertoires of practice in literacy and numeracy that cover a wide range, in terms of both how they are constituted and stages of development. By the middle years the range of students' repertoires has broadened, not narrowed.

Working collaboratively with guidance and support staff can enhance middle years teachers' understanding of students' needs. Difficulties in basic areas of learning, such as literacy and numeracy, need keen attention during these years of schooling. It is important for classroom teachers to become familiar with diagnostic tools in literacy and numeracy. It is also vital for teachers to know some of the indicators of learning difficulties so they can support as needed or request advice and assistance. These often show up in students' written work as spelling, grammatical and organisational problems and in subjects where they need to use mathematical concepts, such as science, practical arts and geography.

It is important to monitor individual student understanding of the meta-language of a subject area and their fluency with the reading, writing and speaking demands of the subject, through attention to:

- subject terminology and specific vocabulary
- symbolic codes and other representational forms
- relationships between common everyday language and subject-specific terminology
- the language of the processes of the subject, such as scientific or mathematical processes
- the match between the language of instruction and the language of formal assessment requirements
- the literacies of the classroom and the social interactions within which curricular learning is to occur.

In many countries such as Australia and the United States, legislation mandates that adjustments to assessments should be provided for students with a disability to allow optimal demonstration of their learning. However, developing fair and equitable adjustments can be challenging for teachers (Forlin, Keen & Barrett, 2008; Pearce, Campbell-Evans & Gray, 2010). Adjustments may relate to various categories, including motivational and setting adjustments; assistance with learning and with, during and prior to assessment; adjustments to equipment and assistive technology; and adjustments to formats of assessment and learning tasks (Davies, Elliot & Cumming, 2016). Examples of modifications using assistive technology include allowing a student with dyslexia the use of a computer for essay writing and

Provocation 17.2 Assessment for learning

To be an effective middle years teacher, you need to know your students and know how they are progressing in their learning.

 Provide responses with defensible arguments to the following questions:

- What assessment helps you to see how your students are learning and where they are having difficulty?
- What is the link between the desired learning outcomes, the pedagogical practices and the development of systematic (but not necessarily formal) assessment processes?
- What information might you expect or want to collect from what students do as they complete teacher-generated learning and assessment activities?

Provocation 17.3 Developing an assessment identity

Designing quality assessment tasks requires knowledge of the curriculum, the content and skills to be taught, learning progressions in a subject, as well as local knowledge of the community and the learners within your class. Developing expertise in assessment involves teachers becoming assessment literate and assessment capable.

 What activities will you undertake to increase your own understanding and expertise in educational assessment?

providing modified representations of assessment materials by using multimedia, enlarged texts or videos.

Effective assessment—cognisant of the nature of learners, of implicit cultural and literate practices of the curriculum and of demonstrated ways in which assessment can inform and report on learning—plays a very significant role in education. The approach to assessment outlined in this chapter adopts what we refer to as an intelligent accountability. It recognises assessment as being at the heart of learning and teaching. Key concepts of alignment and front-ending assessment ensure that assessments are designed to cover the prescribed curriculum as well as to respond to student interests. We propose that the notion of fitness for purpose provides a reference point for interrogating the assessments students are required to complete. From a socio-cultural perspective, and building on Rowntree (1977), the two new questions of all assessments are 'Whose interests are they serving?' and 'How do we extend beyond how teachers know students as learners to how students know themselves as learners?' In answering these questions, if education systems can assure that assessments advance student progress, enhance the quality of teaching that occurs and provide useful reports about how education is benefiting young people, then intelligent accountability could be said to be achieved.

Chapter summary

This chapter makes the following key points:

• Assessment concepts and the definitions underlying assessment theory and practice include the multiple interconnected dimensions of formative, diagnostic and summative purposes of assessment, as well as measures of validity and reliability.

- The two key assessment paradigms that you will meet when teaching in the middle years include assessment for measurement purposes (psychometrics and external standardised testing), and assessment for improvement purposes.
- The hallmarks of quality in middle years assessment practice are evident within assessment design and use, assessment and classroom pedagogic practice, the collection and collation of evidence, and differentiating assessment to address diverse student cohorts.
- It is imperative that all assessments are framed within consideration of fitness for purpose and intelligent accountability.

Part Five

Middle years education in action

Chapter Eighteen

School reform and sustainable practice

DONNA PENDERGAST

Learning intentions

In this chapter we will:

- explore the benefits and challenges of sustainable middle school reform
- develop an appreciation of the roles of teachers and school leaders to ignite, resource and continue to commit to reform in order to achieve cultural change and sustainable practice
- develop an understanding of the Educational Change Model for middle schools
- investigate examples of authentic practice which exemplify the core variables for each of the three stages in the Educational Change Model.

Sustainable middle years education reform

The need to continue to reform schools and systems to intentionally employ approaches to middle years teaching and learning remains firmly on the agenda. Evidence of the dip in academic achievement, the persistence of transition challenges and the increases in psychosocial and other challenges for young adolescent learners affirms this position. While many schools adopt sophisticated middle years strategies, others may not yet have commenced their journey of reform or may be at the very beginning; the duration of this journey is longer than most would expect if a sustainable change in culture is to be ensured. This is all the more challenging as systems and schools are multifaceted, with starting points that are different, as well as system leaders who must face multiple choices and combinations of decisions along the reform path (Mourshed, Chijioke & Barber, 2010). However, the imperative remains. Underpinning most educational reform initiatives is the purpose of improving student learning outcomes (Organisation for Economic Co-operation and Development [OECD], 2015a), and explicit approaches to middle years learning and teaching are no exception.

However, the experience of reform fatigue is very salient within education, at both school and systems levels. When teachers, school leaders and the wider community are introduced to changes in curriculum or pedagogy they can respond in varying ways. Some embrace change and look forward to new ideas and challenges, while others hold fast to old ways of doing and prefer a regular and predictable program over time. Those who prefer the latter can become difficult and resistant to change. This can occur for a number of reasons, including a sense of loss of control or a loss of status, or it can lead to a feeling of impending chaos, a sense of unpredictability and uncertainty. But any change can result in some degree of chaos in order to rejuvenate and transform practice. Major changes can in many instances force individuals to redefine themselves and in some cases to reinvent what they do. In this way change is a stimulus for re-energising and re-imagining what might be possible (Mourshed, Chijioke & Barber, 2010).

This chapter aims to bring to life the middle years education concepts outlined in this book by providing authentic examples of middle years reform in action. It is framed around two organisers: the *Position paper* of the Middle Years of Schooling Association (MYSA, 2008), now named Adolescent Success, and the Educational Change Model for middle years reform (Pendergast, 2006; Pendergast et al., 2014a). Examples taken from a range of settings are presented to provide insights into selected initiatives that are part of some of our schools today and will ideally be part of many more in the future.

The MYSA's position statement

In 2008 in Australia, the MYSA (2008) launched its first national position paper on middle schooling, defining middle schooling as an 'intentional approach to teaching and learning that is responsive and appropriate to the full range of needs, interests and achievements of middle years students in formal and informal

Provocation 18.1 Can individuals make a difference?

Can one person make a difference? According to Dinham (2008), in his book *How to get your school moving and improving*, there are four broad and interdependent fundamentals underpinning student success and achievement in schools, including in middle years contexts:

1   a central focus on students, both as learners and people
2   quality teaching
3   professional learning
4   educational leadership.

In this sense you have considerable opportunity as an individual teacher or school leader to be part of initiating, developing and sustaining reform.

 Using these four fundamentals for student success and achievement, reflect on what you have learned in this book. Draw a concept map with yourself in the centre. For each of the four fundamentals, map the strengths you bring to reforming middle years education.

schooling contexts'. Furthermore, it specified three essential elements of middle schooling:

1.   Clear philosophy relevant to the context [see Figure 18.1].
2.   Comprehensive range of signature practices [see Figure 18.2] ...
3.   Evidence-based approach.

Initiatives in middle years education reform are not exclusively Australian, and they have drawn on decades of international research, implementation scenarios and policy development (Dinham & Rowe, 2009; George, 2008–09; Jackson & Davis, 2000; National Middle School Association, 2001; Pendergast et al., 2007). This chapter provides examples of reform in which the three essential elements— philosophy, practices and approach—as advocated by the MYSA (2008) are being attended to in authentic scenarios. Furthermore, the examples shared are mapped according to a reform-based model which proceeds through three phases: initiation, development and consolidation.

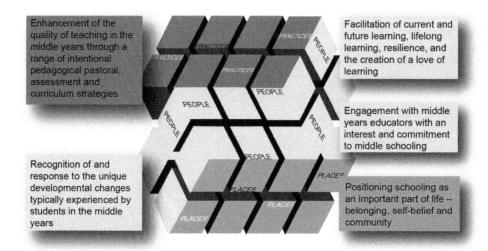

Enhancement of the quality of teaching in the middle years through a range of intentional pedagogical pastoral, assessment and curriculum strategies

Facilitation of current and future learning, lifelong learning, resilience, and the creation of a love of learning

Engagement with middle years educators with an interest and commitment to middle schooling

Recognition of and response to the unique developmental changes typically experienced by students in the middle years

Positioning schooling as an important part of life – belonging, self-belief and community

Figure 18.1 MYSA Middle Schooling Model: People, practices and places

Source: MYSA (2008).

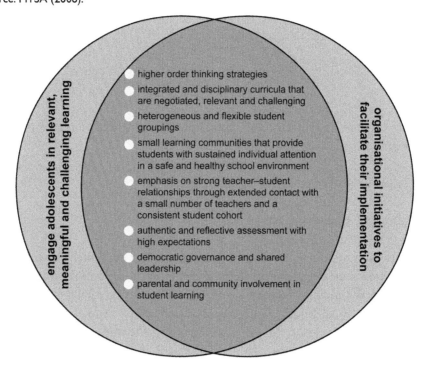

engage adolescents in relevant, meaningful and challenging learning

organisational initiatives to facilitate their implementation

- higher order thinking strategies
- integrated and disciplinary curricula that are negotiated, relevant and challenging
- heterogeneous and flexible student groupings
- small learning communities that provide students with sustained individual attention in a safe and healthy school environment
- emphasis on strong teacher–student relationships through extended contact with a small number of teachers and a consistent student cohort
- authentic and reflective assessment with high expectations
- democratic governance and shared leadership
- parental and community involvement in student learning

Figure 18.2 The MYSA's Signifying Practices

Source: Adapted from MYSA (2008).

Sustaining reform in schools and systems

According to Mourshed, Chijioke and Barber (2010, p. 72), who explored how twenty education systems around the world improved their performance and how they went about sustaining the changes,

> for a system's improvement journey to be sustained over the long term, the improvements have to be integrated into the very fabric of the system pedagogy. We have identified three ways that improving systems do this: by establishing collaborative practices, by developing a mediating layer between the schools and the center, and by architecting tomorrow's leadership. Each of these aspects of sustaining improvement is an interconnected and integral part of the system pedagogy.

The three ways in which systems achieve change as listed above will now be explored.

Establishing collaborative practices

The concept of a teacher as an active agent of school reform and development has historically been central to educational practices and policies. The bottom-up initiation and implementation of educational innovations involve active and collaborative learning and development of new practices for those teachers concerned. Allowing individuals to work together and have collective responsibility to improve practice is seen as a positive, whereas a lack of agency has been recognised as a problem in school development. The challenge during the reform process is to shift from viewing the teaching and learning process as merely a transmission of knowledge to taking a more active role in the process of knowledge construction through individual and collaborative efforts. In his synthesis of over 50,000 studies and 800 meta-analyses of student achievement, John Hattie (2003, p. 86) drew one major conclusion: 'The remarkable feature of the evidence is that the biggest effects on student learning occur when teachers become learners of their own teaching.' This is the essence of collaborative practice: teachers jointly engaged in an empirical, routine and applied study of their own profession.

To be active and effective agents in the implementation of a reform, teachers need to take time to discuss, negotiate and develop a common understanding of the goals of the reform, in terms of new pedagogies, human mix or organisational models. Collaborative practice is all about teachers and school leaders working together to develop effective instructional practices, studying what works well in the classroom and doing this both with rigorous attention to detail and with a commitment to improving not only one's own practice but that of others. Collaborative practice is the method by which a school system hardwires the values and beliefs implicit in its system into a form manifest in day-to-day teaching practice. Fullan (2001) referred to this as a 'theory of changing', whereby there is a shared belief around how changes can be brought about. An effective and sustained junior secondary reform requires the focus to move from the student to the teacher as the subject and agent of implementing the reform.

Developing a middle layer

A middle layer between school delivery and the system plays a critical mediating role. It may take the form of a geographic, school cluster or subject-based mediating layer, among others. This middle layer is beneficial in providing targeted support and in ameliorating challenges to schools, as well as in monitoring compliance, facilitating communication between schools and systems, encouraging inter-school collaboration and buffering community resistance to change.

Building the future leadership

For sustainable reform, middle years leaders and teachers are required to be both the subjects and the agents of change (Main, 2013). This type of reform requires a style of leadership that will enhance the individual and collective problem-solving capacities of its teachers. It also demands a focused investment by policy-makers through teacher training programs and professional development opportunities to build the human capital necessary to sustain the intended reform.

In school systems, the system leaders secure such continuity by ensuring that the system's inherent explicit and implicit pedagogical aspects are transferred to future generations of leadership. The most successful examples of leadership continuity noted by Mourshed, Chijioke and Barber (2010, p. 89) were in systems able to develop their future leaders from within their system:

> Each of these improving systems has written a consistent story of improvement by ensuring the leaders who shepherd the system share the experience and ownership of the system's pedagogy. When pivotal leadership roles are filled, these systems have usually been able to identify leaders from within their system with the required capabilities and experience to fill them. That they were able to find such leaders is no mere accident—these systems deliberately set about architecting for tomorrow's leaders. As a result, the improvement journey of these systems has been evolutionary—not halting, nor inconsistent, and not repeatedly disrupted.

Teachers as the subjects and agents of change

Main and Bryer (2005b) identified acceptance, effectiveness and sustainability as the staged process for the successful implementation of middle years education initiatives and for reform or change efforts, especially with regard to teachers and their work (see Table 18.1). Within these stages, in each of which 'teachers are at the centre of the solution for sustainable reform' (Main, 2016b), a number of areas were identified as necessary foci to ensure the success of reform:

- [increase] informed acceptance by all stakeholders including administrators (local, district, State, National), teachers, students and the wider community as part of the planning process
- strengthen the effectiveness of recommended teacher practice ... through ... training for teachers intending to work in this area and continuing and targeted in-service training (professional development) for experienced teachers working in this area
- clarify policy issues such as training, certification, placement, and staffing that affect sustainability, as part of evaluating alternative practice.

Issues regarding teachers' acceptance, effective practice, training and enhanced theoretical understanding highlight the need to focus on building the human capital as the subject of change. Acceptance and assumed responsibility for the reform among all stakeholders could be viewed as the single most important factor for the success of a new junior secondary program. This focus also aligns with the empirical evidence that points to the teacher as the key determinant of student engagement, motivation and progress during the critical developmental years of early adolescence (Dinham & Rowe, 2007).

Many of the reform efforts for middle years education in Australia have been imposed through a top-down reform process. This approach has seen school leaders and administrators set up the physical structures that align with the notion of middle schools (e.g., teams, block scheduling and small communities of learners) with the expectation that middle schooling will take place. Stevens (2004, p. 389) noted that 'teachers tend to implement in their classrooms what they know and understand, in spite of whatever innovation may be adopted by the school'. With this in mind, for a middle years reform to be accepted, effective and sustained, teachers working in this area must know and understand junior secondary practices.

With strong evidence that the quality of teaching far outweighs other associated factors in influencing student achievement outcomes (Dinham & Rowe, 2007),

Table 18.1 Research agenda for middle school practice

Practice criteria	Teachers	Students	Community and School as community
Acceptance	• Informed consent: Choice to teach • Access to training • Awareness of the benefits (data driven) • Supportive leadership	• Informed consent: Voice • Learning based on students' interests, preferred teaching and learning styles, and assessment models	• Informed consent: Involvement in consultation process

Effectiveness	• Relationships:
	  Teacher-Students
	  Teacher-Teacher
	  Teacher-Others
	• Access to training
	• Networking through middle school organisations and other middle schools
	• Supportive leadership
	• Essential skills:
	  Curriculum and pedagogy
	  Sense of efficacy
	  Alternative classrooms
		• Relationships:
		  Student-Student
		  Student-Teacher
		• Curriculum:
		  Exploratory
		  Safe environment
		  Autonomy
			• Relationships:
			  School-Parents
			  School-Community
			• Ongoing community partnerships demonstrating a democratic ideology

Sustainability	• Teacher support is derived from improved student outcomes in both attentive and academic domains (evidence is data-based) • Access to training • Supportive leadership • Avoiding labels such as 'experimental' or 'rigid orthodoxy'	• Improved student outcomes occur in both affective (behavioural and socioemotional) and academic domains (evidence is data-based)	• Policy support is derived from improved student outcomes in both affective and academic domains (evidence is data-based) • State-wide supportive leadership combining both 'top-down' and 'bottom-up' approaches

Source: Main & Bryer (2007).

teachers working within this age group are faced with tension points between the acceptance, effectiveness and sustainability of a suite of practices that are generally foreign to their training and work histories. The breadth of teachers' knowledge of the curriculum, effective pedagogical skills and interpersonal and communication skills affect other practice indicators for effective junior secondary schools, such as building small communities of learners and delivering a challenging, integrated and negotiated curriculum. Teachers' knowledge and understanding of middle years practice and their resultant sense of efficacy on these indicators are directly related to curriculum delivery for students and whether the program is authentically responsive to students' needs and achieves the intended result of improved student outcomes. Ongoing training on the *how* of middle years practices may improve teachers' acceptance and sense of efficacy in implementing these practices. This in turn may augment their practice effectiveness and may increase its sustainability from one year to the next. As the expectant agents of change, teachers also need to be the subjects of change. Hence, for reforms to be effective, change is firmly positioned in the classroom.

Provocation 18.2 Middle years school reform

Middle years reform processes and schools are being well positioned to continue to improve their practice.

 Using Table 18.1 as a reference, discuss the questions below:

- What aspects of acceptance, effectiveness and sustainability are evident in your school?
- How are teachers in your school being supported as the subjects and agents of change?

The Educational Change Model for middle schools

More than a decade ago a national project funded by the Australian Ministerial Council on Education, Employment, Training and Youth Affairs set out to explore the practices, processes, strategies and structures that best promote lifelong learning and the development of lifelong learners in the middle years (Pendergast et al., 2005). The study successfully achieved this research task, along with mapping the

Educational Change Model, a three-phase model for effective and sustainable middle years reform. The model was developed from the extensive analysis of 25 innovative schools around Australia and provides a unique insight into the desirable sequences and time spent achieving reforms, along with typical pitfalls that lead to a regression in the reform process. The phased model indicates that programs of reform were established in three phases, gradually introducing particular core component changes and spanning a total of about eight to seventeen years, depending on circumstances (see Table 18.2). The three broad phases of reform can be mapped onto any major reform initiative and feature indications of time taken to achieve each phase, with the initiation phase typically occupying a year or two, the development phase the next two to five years and the consolidation phase a further five to ten years. Each phase is characterised by a series of core components that should be achieved before moving to the next phase, providing a road map to the logical progression of components across the reform period.

This model was employed in 2014 to facilitate professional learning for school leaders in all government schools in Queensland, where Year 7 was to become part of secondary school from 2015 and the introduction of junior secondary was to be implemented for Years 7–9 (Queensland Government, 2015). In 2014, all 259 public secondary school leadership teams across Queensland participated in a multifaceted program known as the Leading Change Development Program (Pendergast et al., 2014b). The program aimed to build school leader capacity to direct effective change processes in schools, specifically in preparation for the transition of Year 7 and the consolidation of the new approach to teaching Years 7–9. The program was conceptually built around the Educational Change Model (Pendergast et al., 2005).

The model serves as a useful guide for schools at any stage of middle years education reform. The original study reported that it was typical for schools to experience a dip in the reform process, often the result of predictable events, such as the loss of middle schooling champions, changes to leadership, teacher team breakdown and failure to establish protocols for determining the efficacy of the reform process. Importantly, the reform process can be less traumatic and achieved in the most expedient time when certain key factors, listed below as enablers, are aligned and sustained. This provides optimal or fast-track conditions implementation. Possible inhibitors of reform are shown in the following list.

- Enablers:
  - team membership across several years
  - congenial, philosophically aligned dynamics among team members

Table 18.2 The Educational Change Model phases and their core components

Phases			Core components	Time (years)
1. **Initiation**	1.1	School vision and visioning processes	Introduce new language, philosophy	1–2
	1.2	Student transitions and transitioning procedures	Focus on transition	
	1.3	Connectedness of student learning to the world outside the school	Establish leadership model	
	1.4	Teacher teaming	Develop knowledge base around junior secondary learners	
	1.5	Innovative leadership	Establish quality teaching model with structures, protocols and practices	
	1.6	Social and academic outcomes	Plan and establish evidence principles	
2. **Development**	2.1	Improved alignment of curriculum, pedagogy and assessment systems	Implement and refine junior secondary quality teaching model	2–5
	2.2	Enhanced pedagogies, especially the provision of greater intellectual challenge	Encourage emerging leadership	
	2.3	Sustainable innovation	Facilitate learning communities for teachers	
	2.4	Linking school culture change with innovative structures	Use and extend evidence sources	
	2.5	Professional learning communities, with teachers as learners	Develop support structures to enable sustainability of reform	
	2.6	Evidence-based policy development processes	Plan and implement, revise and renew	

(continues)

Table 18.2 *continued*

Phases				Core components	Time (years)
3. **Consolidation**	3.1		Changing social and economic conditions demanding a broader skill set	Refine quality teaching practice	5–10
	3.2		Learner- and learning-focused programs	Lead and support others	
	3.3		Student engagement in learning	Build capacity, ownership and sustainable practices	
	3.4		Meeting greater diversity in adolescent needs and capacities	Learning how to learn	

- – sensitive and sustained leadership
- – early adoption and shared risk-taking among members, who challenge each other to extend themselves
- – a strong emphasis on team problem-posing and problem-solving
- – effective use of research in evidence-based planning.
- Inhibitors:
  - – weak or inconsistent, or insufficient dispersal of, leadership
  - – poorly conceived or poorly expressed vision statement
  - – uncooperative, non-supportive or inadequately trained staff
  - – discontinuity of staff
  - – rigid traditionalism among staff majority
  - – failure to provide an appropriate support structure or to redirect and redefine the school culture
  - – insufficient funding to provide essential equipment or to finance innovations
  - – resistance from the community
  - – dramatic upward or downward trends in student population
  - – impatience or loss of enthusiasm resulting from slow progress in the process of renewal (Pendergast et al., 2005).

While the three-phase model is not intended to be a formula for middle years education reform, it has the potential to serve as a valuable guide and comparative base for schools undertaking reform and seeking direction, particularly with regard to the core components, potential inhibitors and enablers and timelines involved (see Table 18.2). Importantly, while there is no single, *right* way to undertake teaching and learning in the middle years, typically there is progression through three phases that involves the systematic linking of many components of a school's operation.

Provocation 18.3 Applying the Educational Change Model to a school setting

Evaluation of middle years reform implementation can be made against key elements of the Educational Change Model, using the timeframes as a guide. Table 18.2 provides the basis for an audit tool for consideration of any school in terms of the three phases in the Educational Change Model. The occurrence and evidence of the core components in each phase can be recorded through their progressive stages of completeness, from 1 to 5, or from 'beginning' through 'intermediate' to 'advanced'.

Using Table 18.2 as a guide, create an audit tool listing the phases, core components and stage levels, and consider a school you are familiar with. At what stages do you consider the school to be in terms of the Educational Change Model? Explain your reasoning.

Authentic middle years education in practice

The next section of the chapter is structured on the three phases of reform proposed by the Educational Change Model and gives information about each stage, illustrated by scenarios of practices providing real examples (though the names of the schools have not been provided) of the core change variables in action. The examples are not exhaustive; nor do they necessarily represent best practice; but they are illustrations of some of the ways in which middle years initiatives have been the focus of reform.

Phase 1 Initiation

The first phase of reforming the middle years typically lasts from one to two years. The initiation phase is important for establishing a firm foundation from which complex signifying practices, evidence-based initiatives and sustainable reforms can be built, with a view to providing the best environment for achieving implementation success and longevity.

1.1 School vision and visioning processes
Conceptualising a holistic vision for learning is important in providing both strategic directions for the whole school and a firm foundation for middle years initiatives. Within this vision, the values, beliefs and intentions of reforming the middle years should be explicit. In the examples that follow, three different school scenarios and the way the schools' visions and philosophies around middle schooling were determined are shared.

Combining schools to create a P–12 cluster
In a traditional high school and three feeder primary schools, one year of planning and professional development is undertaken prior to any changes in practices in the middle years. Key staff members are identified as the core team for the process, and a consultant is employed for half a day per month to assist with planning, monitor progress and provide feedback. Key school personnel meet to revise middle schooling philosophy and principles, consider existing models and possibilities for the school and gain ideas for the action plan for the remainder of the year. Before the meeting they receive readings for consideration, and a process is followed at the meeting through which the group forms a consensus around the following questions:

- What are the non-negotiables of middle schooling for our context?
- What are the key potential benefits of undertaking middle years reform in our school and cluster context?
- What are our beliefs about teaching and learning in the middle years?

Those teachers wishing to be involved in the middle years initiatives in the future can attend a six-session professional development program on a voluntary basis. The core team meets regularly to review and plan, and the school commences implementation the following year. A middle years committee is established to support the ongoing process.

Improving outcomes for middle school students
A plan is formulated in a traditional high school incorporating the identification and implementation of short-, medium- and long-term goals to reflect the school's middle years vision. To achieve this, key staff with middle schooling experience and expertise and a desire to focus their teaching and leadership in the middle years are appointed through a rigorous external interview process. These staff include

primary-trained teachers with expertise in the middle years, which is not usual practice in secondary schools. Those involved in the middle schooling project can take part in professional readings, visits to schools where middle years reform is underway and professional development run by external experts. Short-, medium- and long-term goals are developed with the facilitation of the school leadership team and key teachers subsequent to steady growth in confidence by the teachers of their capacities for the middle years. The staff reconceptualise the curriculum design and commence collaborative writing of units of work based around signifying practices such as negotiated and integrated curriculum. Changes are made to some buildings to enable preferred pedagogies, such as team teaching, and outside environments are modified to support identified practices to be implemented. A further enabler of this process is the redesign of the school timetable, which is usually driven by the senior subject allocations.

Creating a new middle school
In a P–12 school, the school community collaborates on a research-based vision of beliefs and values to shape its educational philosophy. The vision for the entire school is then interpreted into the vision for the middle school, providing a seamless connection across the early, middle and senior years of the school structure. The leadership team is involved in the design of the middle school from conception, collaborating with architects and builders for a purpose-built facility.

Planning identifies actions to align with the various aspects of the vision. The visioning process incorporates emphasis on a culture of innovation and response to change. Constant reflection occurs on vision and goals, with review and response central to the ongoing sustainability of the philosophy of the middle school. The beliefs adopted are summed up in the phrase 'rights, responsibil- ities and trust', while the values are collaboration, independence, consultation, cooperation, empowerment, ownership, relationships, fun and reflection. The staff organise the classroom to reflect the beliefs and values, and they set in place structures that provide the students with parameters while allowing them freedom of choice, which is important for responsibility and ownership. These structures may include an inquiry approach, an integrated and negotiated curriculum, cooperative and independent learning through learning centres, and assessment and evaluation processes that align with the beliefs and values. Having an explicit overarching and shared philosophy promotes the alignment of what is taught, how it is taught and how it is assessed.

1.2 Student transitions and transitioning procedures
In formal schooling contexts learners typically experience a number of transitions. These transitional moments can lead to instability and changing levels of confidence in learners, possibly leading to disengagement from learning. Transitions for learners may include those from home to early institutional care settings and to preschool and early school learning, from primary to secondary school settings and to senior schooling within secondary levels, and from school to post-school education, further training and work. There are a number of possible transitions in the middle years, such as from primary to secondary school or, within a P–10 or P–12 structure, from early to middle years. An intentional focus on transition programs can build a sense of community while responding to the needs and concerns of the schools' particular students, thereby diminishing the possible negative effects of transitional moments. Transitional arrangements are typically multifaceted and include structures and procedures to sustain the program.

Creating connections between schools
A situation that occurs quite often is a co-location but lack of connection between a feeder primary school and a secondary school, as is the case in this example, despite the schools being located side by side. An intentional transition program is put in place. The upper primary teachers meet with heads of departments from the secondary school to share resources, discuss similarities and differences and plan collaborative activities for Semester 2 of the school year. Using a paired mentoring approach, Year 7 students from the primary school combine with Year 8 students for a session each of English, science and studies of society and environment. This is followed up with a buddy day, where each Year 7 student shadows a Year 8 student for half a day, attending classes, using lockers, ordering lunch and so on. This allows students to develop cultural awareness of the transition ahead of them, and this alleviates fear of the unknown as a possible factor leading to problems in transition. A parent information evening, including the dissemination of a student survey to identify possible issues, is conducted.

Creating a cluster model
A cluster, also known as a coalition, is formed with a group of primary schools and their local secondary school which aims to provide a seamless curriculum for students in the transition from primary to secondary schooling. The focus is on uniformity and continuity of learning content and pedagogical approaches. Task groups are established in core key learning areas and in life skills. These groups

guide the planning and implementation of integrated units of work. Topics and content are selected to provide continuous development of concepts and understandings. Resources are shared, including material, human, technological, plant, location and site resources. To ensure consistency of teacher judgements in assessment, moderation of student work samples is undertaken between all schools. Opportunities for professional development are provided for the cluster, so all those involved are learning together, developing common understandings and practices.

Provocation 18.4 Moderating student performance

Numerous education systems in Australia have adopted an approach for moderating student performance, both within and across schools, that has a focus on attaining a consistency of judgement with teachers across year levels. This is a particularly useful strategy for a cluster of teachers from upper primary and early secondary to gain an understanding of standards over the two settings. Teachers meet in groups of five or six to share unit plans, student work samples and assessment practices to moderate their interpretations of learning against set standards. Prior to meeting, teachers use annotated work samples and criteria to make judgements about demonstrated standards of performance. Assessment samples are selected to represent a range of standards to share at moderation.

 Investigate other examples of ways that consistency can be achieved.

Personal passports

In this college, the passport, or folio, program runs for up to one hour per week for ten weeks in Term 4. The three middle years teachers each take three weekly sessions with all Year 6 students. There is time for reflection on the primary school experience and thinking about secondary school (e.g., 'How I'm feeling about coming to secondary school: fears, questions, etc.'). A passport document is compiled by each student. It is a comprehensive document in which the students record their thoughts and feelings, their fears, their strengths and weaknesses, their ambitions, and any concerns or queries they may have about the secondary school or the transition process. This forms part of the communication link which is established between the students and the Year 7 coordinator. Parents are involved in feedback surveys and sharing thoughts and concerns with their children.

During the first two weeks of secondary school, each student spends fifteen minutes with their pastoral care teacher to share their passport. This is vital, as it provides the secondary teacher with insights into the student that may take a year to evolve in the usual classroom setting. The passport is continually developed and shared as appropriate; it may help contribute to the creation of a résumé in Year 9 or 10.

Teacher exchange, shadowing and looping
With teacher exchanges, a primary teacher and a secondary or middle years teacher exchange positions for a period—a week, month, term or year. Teacher exchange may occur as a permanent or a temporary arrangement. With looping, a primary teacher might move on to secondary school with their students, staying with them for the full year, after which they return to the primary school and start with another cohort of students. With teacher shadowing, a teacher observes a colleague from a different school or sub-school to gain insights and understandings.

Transition from middle to senior years
At this college there is a celebration at the end of Year 9, acknowledging the importance of a formal transition to senior years, with an evening designed by the students that focuses on themselves and on what they have to say about themselves. This may be portrayed in music, poetry, drama, art and so on, integrated into a theme for the evening. Year 9 leaders present a farewell speech. In Term 4, students from Year 10 talk to Year 9 students about their experiences the year before. Year 12 school leaders also share with them their experiences of the previous three years, providing a starting and ending point for the senior years of schooling. Year 12 students spend some lunch breaks with Year 9 during Semester 2. House coordinators talk to Year 9 students about procedural and logistical matters. For transition issues related to the curriculum, information nights are held for parents and students. Transition meetings are conducted between Year 9 core teachers and senior school staff who are involved in vocational education, careers advising and special education. These are held prior to subject selection, to assist in finding appropriate pathways for each student.

1.3 Connectedness of student learning to the world outside the school
Connectedness is important if change is to be sustained. There must be an emphasis on making relevant connections for students between theoretical underpinnings and real-life experiences, with consistent efforts made to maximise experiential

learning. Learners in the middle years respond to a curriculum that is relevant, integrated and negotiated. Students also need to be connected to teachers as mentors and, where possible, to other adult mentors within the school or broader community. Examples of connection may include those discussed below.

Community projects
A particular area or need in the local community is identified as a possible project which middle years students embrace. Examples include local park regeneration, environmentally challenged areas such as creeks or river banks, market gardens, local hall renovations, design of community facilities and establishing a thrift shop one day per week. The project may be the core of an integrated unit of work, engaging students over an extended period of time.

Volunteer groups
Students in pairs or small groups spend an allocated time each week over an extended period of time working with a volunteer organisation. Examples include Meals-on-Wheels, animal welfare, sporting clubs and information centres.

Enterprise Education programs
These are usually experiential, involve teamwork, develop ownership and control of the learning for the student and incorporate a learning cycle that includes design, planning, production, marketing, review and reflection. The emphasis is on the enterprise skills developed, both extrinsically and intrinsically. Links are made with people in commerce, business and industry to support the programs in the school and provide real-life learning experiences for the students in real settings. Examples of programs include health campaigns, food product development, school shops, building projects, motorbike restoration, cafés, fashion and design, school vineyards, musical productions, art galleries, CD or DVD production and recycling campaigns.

1.4 Teacher teaming
The development and use of cooperative and collaborative teacher teams are important signifying practices of intentional reform in the middle years. Teachers, as members of semi-autonomous work groups, undertake collaborative planning for year levels, for example, or they collaborate in transdisciplinary teams, in subject groups or in key learning areas. These teams also reflect on program outcomes (e.g., the impact of behaviour management strategies and pastoral care programs) and

on the quality of student learning (e.g., the moderation of assessment standards). Teacher teaming is sometimes discussed as if it is a universal good, but there are often issues which can be vexed questions for resolution in practice, relating to the capacity and experience of individual team members, the quality of relationships and interpersonal dynamics and the team leadership.

Teacher and student teams
In this college 4 teachers and 120 students work together in pods for most of the week. The teachers organise their own timetable (block scheduled), determining who will teach what group of students when and for which learning areas. An integrated curriculum approach is utilised with the subjects that connect best for particular units of work. The teachers have common planning time when students have specialist teachers. Heterogeneous student teams may be across one year level or multi-age, or they may be constructed around interests in topics and achievement levels.

Two-teacher teams
Two teachers at this college share a double classroom space with a bi-fold door in between. One teacher has the students for two or three key learning areas, and the other has the same group for two or three different key learning areas. They plan common units of work, sometimes undertake two separate units with the same overarching concept or incorporate links in areas such as skills and processes. They periodically choose to design some common assessment tasks. On occasions they team teach, or one may take both classes for some direct instruction. Students go to specialist teachers for the remaining learning areas.

1.5 Innovative leadership
Innovative organisational structures and dispersal of leadership among staff within broader professional learning communities are important in establishing the conditions for ongoing sustained reform in the middle years. Innovative leaders in the middle years have unique characteristics (see Figure 18.3).

Positions of leadership
Standard models of leadership are replaced in this school by a more flexible model built around present needs. In addition to the principal, there is a deputy principal with classroom responsibilities and ten other classroom teachers, four of whom are in positions of leadership, with roles that are negotiated on an ongoing basis.

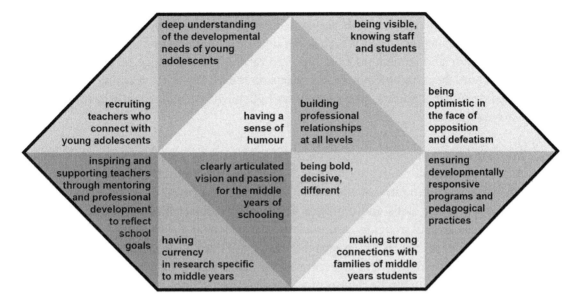

Figure 18.3 Innovative leadership characteristics

Five specialist teachers and three teacher assistants (aides) complete the team. Professional learning teams are in place for numeracy, religious education, integrated studies and welfare. The student welfare committee consists of a core group of staff members who identify and monitor support for students experiencing difficulty in the areas of behaviour, learning and social or emotional development.

Middle years leadership
The advisory committee at this school provides advice on major items of discussion which is adopted by the school after consensus is achieved. The committee comprises members of the community, education experts, teachers, students and other interested nominees, and it has shaped a new leadership model with genuine leadership at this committee level. Operationally, each of the four phases of learning (early, junior, middle and senior years) has a leader responsible for oversight of the curriculum, pedagogy and assessment practices across the phase. The school principal's role is framed as supportive, providing administrative assistance to the phase leaders.

1.6 Social and academic outcomes
A sustained focus on developing the whole person requires attention to the full range of possible outcomes from schooling. In addition to the obvious academic

achievement outcomes, schools also provide opportunities to develop and refine many social outcomes. Even if such social outcomes are more difficult to measure and monitor and sometimes exist more precariously on the edge of the formal curriculum, they can have powerful impacts on the quality of the learning experienced by students and on their motivation to be involved subsequently in formal learning situations.

Learning Journeys Program

At this college, all students undertake common core subjects: English, mathematics, science and physical education (PE), with the Learning Journeys Program drawing together skills and concepts across other subject areas which include history, geography, religion and society, and personal development. Elective subjects in areas such as art, languages, music and drama complete the curriculum offering for Year 9. This structure enables a balance to be achieved between specific preparation for the rigours of senior secondary schooling and the development of the life skills required to be an active and contributing member of society. The Learning Journeys are structured with a focus on extending content from the individual and their place in the community to an exploration of national and international issues and influences. The Learning Journeys Program has explored topics such as:

- sustainability—a local response to drought through planned approaches to reducing the school's water consumption
- national identity—the diversity of Australia's population and the key influences in the formation of a nation through activity related to four broad themes:
  1. immigration and family backgrounds
  2. images of Australia's development
  3. welfare and approaches to responding to community needs
  4. Indigenous issues
- United Nations Week—role play and simulations of the workings of the United Nations, including exploring the interests of individual countries within General Assembly and Security Council meetings, juxtaposed with the workings of commissions in areas such as human rights, terrorism, climate change, HIV/AIDS, disarmament, education, refugees, water, poverty and nuclear energy
- design—considering design processes from the perspective of the fashion industry, motor vehicles, landscape gardening and set production.

Students also have the opportunity to develop their own learning journey, a discrete activity during the course of the year in which they are encouraged to set learning goals, undertake planning, record their learning and nominate assessment criteria.

Social and emotional competencies
A cluster of schools instigates programs based on developing specific competencies, including self-awareness, responsible decision-making, social awareness and self- and relationship management. For example, the peer support program operates in Term 1 each year to help smooth the transition from primary to secondary school. Students in Year 9 undergo a leadership training program at the end of the Year 9 and another at the beginning of Year 10. They then work in groups of two or three and lead small groups of Year 7 students through activities that focus on topics such as friendships, self-esteem, peer group pressure and identifying and labelling bullying behaviour.

Farm skills project
The students at this boys school participate in compulsory farm residential camps for two weeks in Year 8 and four weeks in Year 9. The experience aims to develop social and emotional outcomes that are identified by the school as desirable, fundamental outcomes for boys in the middle years. The sequential farm experiences lead students to explore and reflect upon their social and emotional maturity in the following areas:

- confidence and self-image—participation, attitude
- self-awareness—emotional awareness, honest self-assessment
- self-management—self-organisation, motivation, emotional management, independence
- social competence—communication, conflict management, collaboration and cooperation, empathy, contribution to positive group culture
- leadership.

Phase 2 Development
The second phase lasts from two to five years. Once the foundations in the initiation phase are in place, including a clear philosophy, teacher teams, innovative leadership and effective transitions, it is possible to move to the more complex areas of reform. These include signifying practices such as negotiated curriculum, integration,

enhancing intellectual demand and sustainable evidence-based processes. Phase 2 is where changes to practices are particularly evident.

2.1 Improved alignment of curriculum, pedagogy and assessment systems

To sustain reform in schools, there is a need to balance and link changes in the three key instructional message systems of curriculum, pedagogy and assessment. Reducing curriculum content clutter, or overload, and providing opportunities for deeper cross-disciplinary or transdisciplinary problem-solving are key strategies to assist in realigning the three key message systems.

Integrated curriculum

This school's approach to integrated studies incorporates all key learning areas and religious education into the various units of work over a two-year cycle. Units are usually of one term's duration. The school realises that equal coverage in each key learning area in each unit of study is not always possible; nor is it necessarily best practice, as it may lead to a superficial coverage. Instead, one or two branches of learning become the central focus, and the other key learning areas are included where relevant. This is more likely to bring desired depth to the learning activities, rather than breadth. This emphasis is negotiated with students. Teacher team planning is an essential feature of the program. This ensures that there is no unnecessary repetition of content, all key learning areas are included over time and in appropriate proportion and there is potential to incorporate a variety of teaching and learning styles. The integrated modules are more accurately described as connected curriculum.

Students undertake a rich task project which extends for the duration of the module and has a culminating performance, artefact or submission as the major assessment. In this way assessment is for learning, not focused on an end point. Module titles have included:

- Sharing Our Stories
- Choices: Responsible Participation
- Think Global, Act Local—Project Island Connection
- Images of Me, God and Everyone Else
- Live It Up!
- Space Invaders.

The school has adopted a comprehensive approach to monitoring student learning. In addition to implementing government-mandated assessment and reporting processes, teachers use a range of assessment strategies to measure and monitor student learning. Within the middle years program, assessment rubrics are a key component of the approach to gather data and monitor student learning. The assessment rubrics are complementary to planning materials, which guide student activity and subsequent learning across two domains: self-evaluation of learning activities and peer assessment of learning. Students contribute information about their own learning and that of their peers through an evaluative activity which requires individual reflection across four areas:

- what I learned
- what I did well
- my oral and written presentation
- ways I could improve.

Peer assessments of the presentations cover five areas:

- quality of information
- what they did well
- how they spoke
- general comments
- what could be improved.

2.2 Enhanced pedagogies, especially the provision of greater intellectual challenge
There is a need both to increase the range of pedagogical repertoires available to teachers and to improve the systems by which knowledge and skills are shared with others and put into practice. These might include, for example, the approaches discussed below.

Philosophy in Schools
Philosophy in Schools is a systematic approach to classroom discussions on philosophical questions such as justice, truth, morality and reality. Students and teachers are co-participants in a community of inquiry—a class group where members listen carefully to each other, build on each other's ideas, challenge the opinions of others and respect the input of all. A philosophical discussion features reasoning and inquiry, concept formation and meaning making. There are numerous commercial resources available to assist teachers with building a community of inquiry, including a selection of suitable material and tools for exploring concepts, reasoning

skills and processes. The approach is developmentally responsive to the needs of young people in the middle years of schooling as they confront and explore the problematic aspects of their experiences.

Simulation programs
Many software and online programs are available that provide middle years students with the opportunity to create and participate in, for example, a business or a management plan where they make decisions and respond to information as they might in a real-world setting.

Higher order thinking models
Many schools have implemented school-wide thinking skills models that allow for ongoing development of skills, complexities and reinforcement across year levels and in all learning contexts. Together these form the basis of a whole-school thinking culture that is embedded in curriculum planning and supported by resources and professional development.

2.3 Sustainable innovation
There is a need to acknowledge and plan for whole-school organisational reform as a long-term commitment by all participants, even if funding priorities and accountabilities and system imperatives act to overwhelm the overall energy levels of staff. Feedback loops built into school systems as they are reformed can both redirect and interrupt habitual practices, preventing the need for extensive over-hauls and supporting an evolutionary approach to reform. Succession planning and staff proofing of key initiators are crucial to sustain an innovation, as are effective management systems and ongoing analysis of evidence of impact. Signposts for success in sustainable innovation are listed below with examples:

- Shared philosophy, beliefs and values around how middle years students learn:
    - creating a teacher professional community within the school.
- Strategic direction and planning:
    - identifying current practices that align with the philosophy as a starting point (but always challenging these)
    - connecting practice and theory
    - adopting an *add in*, not an *add on*, approach
    - integrating ideas from across the entire school
    - maintaining an holistic approach

- – going deeper, then wider, then longer in implementing innovations
- – setting short-, medium- and long-term goals that are achievable and sustainable.
- The human factor:
  - – identifying a driver who will take a major role in change and implementation but will do so in collaboration with a team for shared responsibility to create ownership (without collaboration, if the driver leaves the school, the initiative is likely to collapse)
  - – beginning with those who are converted to the philosophy and practices of middle schooling, who can mentor others.
- Avenues of support:
  - – accessing these from expertise within the school and from communication and collaboration through networking with relevant resources—e.g., material, human and technological.

2.4 Linking school culture change with innovative structures

Change in school culture driven by sustained leadership and the development of innovative organisational procedures is a key way of establishing and maintaining the conditions for effective school reform. Any innovation must systematically address all elements that relate to its function in a school context. Important levers for sustaining reform in schools include innovative ways of blocking time, efficient and effective use of space and other resources and strategies which deepen relationships and enhance the sense of responsibility and accountability to others. Providing inspiration and support for risk-taking staff and celebrating their learning achievements can be important motivators of sustained action.

Many professionals argue that there is a distinct difference between the culture that traditionally exists in a primary school and that in a secondary setting. In recent years, teachers have discussed this perception and endeavoured to identify what the differences and similarities are and how each can learn from the other. A middle years environment tends to be another culture again—perhaps incorporating aspects of each, but predominantly responding to the unique phase of development of young adolescents. When a perception of middle schooling is negative, it is generally due to either lack of deep understanding about what it is or a negative past experience. Successful middle years settings often include teachers with primary and secondary training or experience.

The implementation of middle schooling philosophy, principles and practices looks different in different schools, even though the basic premises may be consistent. Schools need to consider the characteristics, needs and interests of their particular students, together with the community in which they live. Staff areas of experience and expertise also factor in the design of innovative structures that reflect the learning needs of their students. Additionally, available and possible resources, buildings and the environment need to be considered. Professional development that supports an innovative design includes staff visiting other schools that have been though the process, talking to the teachers about teaching and learning practices, then designing a model that suits their own school community based on the aspects observed.

2.5 Professional learning communities, with teachers as learners
Investment in the establishment and maintenance of professional learning of staff is essential for effective and sustained school reform. In part, this involves a philosophical repositioning around the importance of the middle years of schooling and of the development of students as lifelong learners. But for this to translate into changes in values and beliefs about teaching and learning and into changed pedagogic practices, concerted and committed professional learning has to occur among teachers in groups and as a whole staff; otherwise, commitment to the reform will rest with too few staff. In addition, if teachers are not developing as learners themselves, they will be limited role models for students attempting to become lifelong learners.

Teaching teams as learning communities
This college includes a middle school within a P–12 environment, where there is autonomy for middle years teachers within a whole-school philosophy. Professional learning communities are formed as teams who share, review, reflect, revise and plan together. Features of these communities include:

- stated beliefs and values which are reflected upon and revisited regularly
- curriculum that is shaped by the stated beliefs and values
- a flat leadership structure
- a culture of innovation within the school
- professional learning opportunities for all staff, identified by the staff according to both their own needs and in response to school and system initiatives
- developing professional and community partnerships.

Sustained teams have a commitment to ongoing improvement and innovation to enhance student learning outcomes.

Student learning communities also exist. Typically, each learning community comprises 120 students, and diversity is supported through mixed-ability classes. Each community has four or five home groups, a sub-school coordinator and a collaborative team of seven to nine multidiscipline teachers. Teacher pairs spend more time with partner home groups and follow these students through to transition into senior school, promoting long-term student–teacher–parent relationships and communications. This structure promotes prosocial behaviour, and students develop trusting relationships with each other and a small number of teachers. Each learning community demonstrates that every student is important as a person and as a learner, and acknowledged learning extends beyond the classroom to include people, sites and experiences within both local and global contexts.

Teacher networks are also crucial for the learning community. Middle years teachers in the local area meet once a term, on each occasion at a different member's school. The focus of the networks is for shared practice and improved outcomes for students. These after-school gatherings have included:

- sharing units of work and resources
- directed discussion and reflection around various pedagogical practices
- collaborative problem-solving
- assessment moderation
- guest speakers
- online learning
- collaboration with a nearby university for future research.

2.6 *Evidence-based policy development processes*

Reforming schools over recent times have emphasised building capacity and specific mechanisms to collect, analyse, review and provide feedback on key data related to school progress, student engagement and attainment and perceptions of quality held by teachers, students and parents. The major purpose of collecting this evidence is to ensure that practices are aligned with policies and that implementation effort is expended in the directions likely to have maximum pay-off for the school as it attempts to generate and sustain reform. This evidence needs to increase the integration of data from within and beyond the school, from system-wide evaluations and school-based indicators.

School reviews

After five years of implementation, this school contracts an external consultant to appraise current middle schooling principles and practices and to explore possibilities for future development, including the enhancement of existing elements that are proving to be effective in the implementation process. The focus is the extent to which middle schooling philosophy is reflected in the middle years curriculum, pedagogy, relationships and organisation of the school. After numerous visits to the school, examining school documents and participating in various learning activities and discussion groups with staff, students and parents, the consultant presents a report to the staff for validation before the final submission. The report details commendations and recommendations in the identified focus areas of the review.

Action learning

A cluster of primary and secondary schools works together on projects characterised by and reflected in the collaborative, participative and reflective features of the action learning process. In addition to the generally accepted four stages of an action research cycle—plan, act, observe and reflect—a further two stages are included in these projects, with seminars throughout the year providing a stimulus through which participants are able to review their current beliefs and practices. Action learning is an ongoing strategy, with the cycle repeated, so the evidence of change is recorded as the project progresses. All participants build on their current expertise and experience and are framed within the context of the particular culture of their school. The foci for school projects include:

- developing a vision for shared beliefs and values about middle schooling
- transition from primary to secondary school
- strategies to promote independent and collaborative learning
- active participation and student voice.

Phase 3 Consolidation

The final phase requires a further five to ten years and is a period of finetuning of reforms. After the Phase 2 initiatives have been implemented, there is an opportunity to reflect and refine, drawing on the evidence-based outcomes. Revisiting the philosophical base and facilitating diversity to a greater degree are the broad aims of this phase.

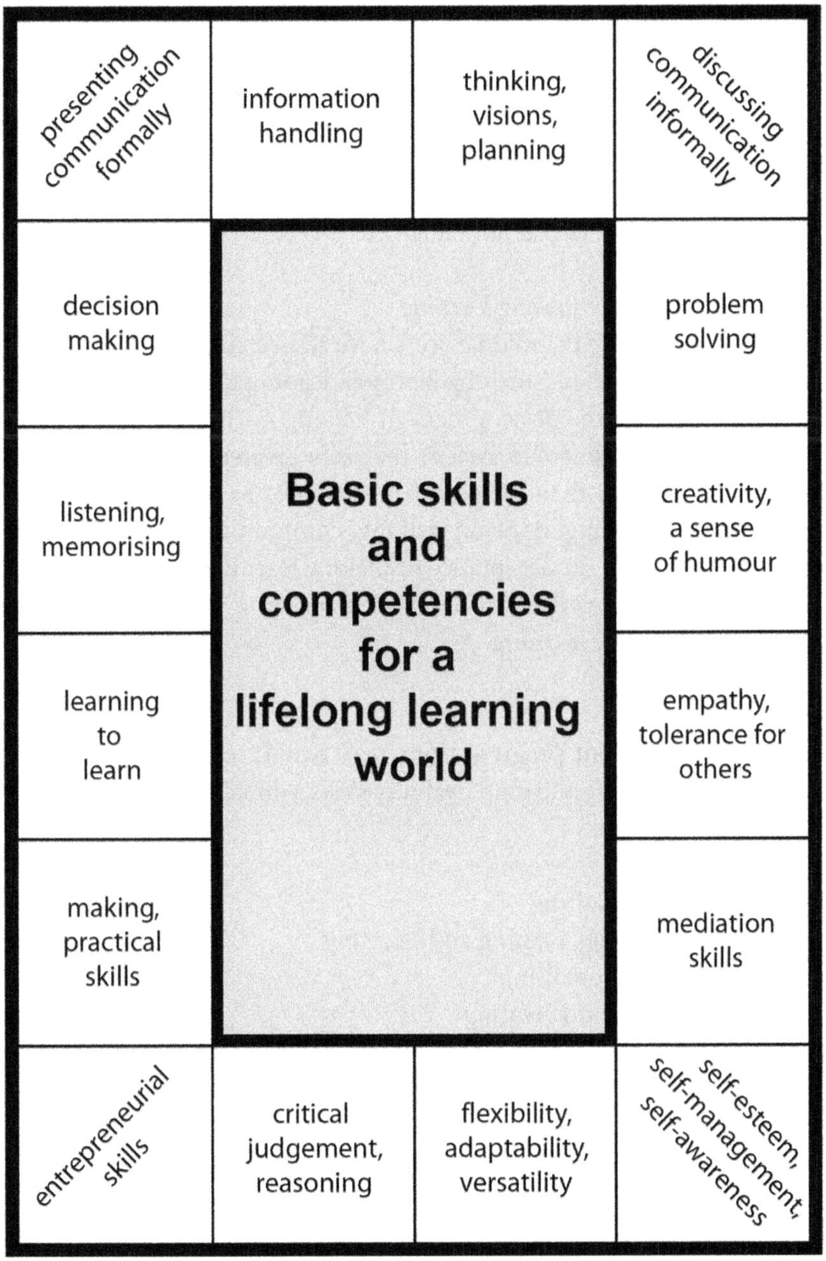

presenting communication formally	information handling	thinking, visions, planning	discussing communication informally
decision making			problem solving
listening, memorising	**Basic skills and competencies for a lifelong learning world**		creativity, a sense of humour
learning to learn			empathy, tolerance for others
making, practical skills			mediation skills
entrepreneurial skills	critical judgement, reasoning	flexibility, adaptability, versatility	self-esteem, self-management, self-awareness

Figure 18.4 Skills and competencies for lifelong learning

3.1 Changing social and economic conditions demanding a broader skill set
The economic, technological, social and cultural contexts for student learning have changed significantly over recent times. There is a need for a broader set of basic or essential skills that are conceptualised to embrace the multiliteracies based in information and communication technologies (ICT) increasingly demanded in knowledge-based economies and societies but that move beyond them into cultural, interpersonal and intrapersonal domains.

Skills and competencies for lifelong learning
At this college, teachers in the middle years have all been intensively trained in both middle schooling culture and lifelong learning, leading to a teaching and learning culture with a focus on the development of lifelong learning attributes. The focus has moved from a single value system that sets greater store on academic and intellectual performance than on personal attributes to other higher order skills (e.g., information handling, decision-making, communicating and thinking) that enhance self-esteem and the acceptance of lifelong learning. In Figure 18.4, middle schooling beliefs and practices are embodied within a framework of skills and competencies for lifelong learning.

Global Learnings
This college maps student progress from Year 1 to 12 using Global Learnings, a hybrid of lifelong learning and employability skills. Global Learnings for the middle school are:

- researching and consulting
- analysing, synthesising, relating and selecting
- negotiating and personalising
- planning, designing and creating
- judging and deciding
- operating, making and acting
- evaluating and revising
- presenting, performing, explaining and communicating.

Students' school-based assessment of Global Learnings uses the standards of developing, consolidating, proficient and exemplary.

3.2 Learner- and learning-focused programs

The organisation of learning incorporates recognition of difference, which leads to a student-driven, as opposed to a content-driven, approach to learning. Young people in the middle years respond best to pedagogical practices that take into consideration the characteristics of their unique stage of development. Certain approaches to learning are imperative if teachers are to effectively engage these learners. Imperatives include:

- Relationships for learning are the core business.
- Independence and interdependence skills are developed and incorporated.
- Physical activity and active participation are the basis of the learning process.
- ICT are tools for learning.
- Critical and creative thinking are planned, and planned for, within the unit of work.
- Authentic contexts for learning provide relevance and links to real life and the community.

3.3 Student engagement in learning

The reform literature has long attested to the fundamental importance of student engagement as a motivator for learning, and student disengagement and alienation from learning as key symptoms of failure in the design and implementation of learning programs (see Chapter 3). At the same time as there is a need to up the ante intellectually in schools there is a need for the learning to be engaging, interesting and connected to things that matter in the world of students. Increasingly, fun is seen as an important if accidental by-product of programs, and pleasure and satisfaction can and should be derived from sustained engagement in interesting learning activities. Negotiation of the curriculum, as well as of assessment and pedagogical practices—the how, what and why of learning—increases student engagement. Student voice can lead to democratic processes and a negotiated curriculum, setting in place a strategy to enhance student engagement in learning. This process is described further below.

Student voice

Authentic democratic processes provide students with a genuine and respected voice in their learning environment. Examples include situations in which:

- students have a vested interest in and shared control over their learning
- learning is both a process and a performance, with real-world, real-work relevance

- learning is integrative and collaborative
- the environment is respectful, caring, supportive, safe and comfortable
- the teacher is mentor and guide, modelling desired behaviours and attitudes
- parents and the wider community are integral parts of the learning process.

Democratic processes
Creating a democratic community with middle years students is a direct response to their stage of development. Features of this environment may include:

- students as active participators
- concern for the welfare of others, plus the common good
- care for the dignity and rights of all
- faith in the individual and the collective capacity of people to create possibilities for resolving problems
- authentic and deep participation
- responsible and self-managed classrooms with rights, responsibilities and consequences
- social curriculum
- social interaction
- class charters and meetings, and school councils.

Negotiated curriculum
This model provides an explicit process for holistic negotiation that identifies students' interests, questions and concerns, which form the units of work for that class. The process has the students identifying, individually at first, their questions and concerns, which they then share to find what is common. The process is repeated to identify world questions. General themes tend to emerge around personal and social issues that are meaningful to the students. In middle years classrooms, the most common include human body, change, environment, conflict, world peace, futures, justice and universe.

3.4 Meeting greater diversity in adolescent needs and capacities
School learning programs were traditionally organised with end points or transitions built in. Now continuity matters, and all (or most) students stay at school longer. There is a need to recognise that the clientele of schools has changed, along with students' social, cultural and economic contexts. Recognition of difference, both within groups and with regard to individual learners, reveals a learning environment

of greater complexity for teachers. Identification of special requirements for some learners is now expected practice. In addition, the majority of learners now demand more experience of active, self-directed and negotiated learning, featuring increased depth of experience and involvement in the development of new knowledge.

Learning to learn
Students in their first year of this middle school participate in a unique unit of work for the first six weeks. The aim is for them to learn about themselves as learners, become familiar with the school and build relationships with their peers and the staff. The students are involved in various activities to identify their dominant learning style, as well as modes that are not as strong. They learn how to utilise the school resource centre and available ICT and develop various research skills. Also included in the unit are learning activities to develop communication skills. The unit of work assists the students' transition into a new setting and provides them with the opportunity to develop new processes, skills and understandings at the very beginning of their adventure into middle school.

Given their judgement of what will be the most effective and productive for their students, teachers can differentiate on a number of dimensions:

- content—what the students know and are able to do, and the resources used to support their learning
- process—the strategies employed by individuals or groups of students that will assist them in accessing information and making sense of their learning
- product—how students will demonstrate, and provide evidence of, their learning.

Factors to be considered in differentiation include:

- learning styles
- pace of learning
- prior knowledge and experience
- thinking processes and ways of organising information
- cultural backgrounds and values
- developmental characteristics.

• • •

These examples, drawn from learning sites in Australia and around the world, provide snapshots of what is happening in learning contexts in the middle years. What should be apparent from this chapter is that changing school structures does not stand out as the panacea by which effective middle years teaching and learning can be enabled. Indeed, the most influential aspects of middle years reform are associated with teachers and teaching. This position is also argued by Dinham and Rowe (2009, p. 2), who note that, with respect to the middle years, 'the most important factors for high-quality education are quality teaching and learning provision; teaching standards; and ongoing teacher professional learning focused on evidence-based teaching practices that are demonstrably effective in maximising students' engagement, learning outcomes and achievement progress'.

The use of the Educational Change Model as the underpinning platform of reform enables a realistic view of the time taken to achieve effective and sustainable school reform (Pendergast, 2006). Importantly, a recent report presented by the OECD (2015a) entitled *Education policy outlook 2015: making reforms happen* reveals the scale and scope of education reforms being undertaken in OECD member countries and details more than 450 separate initiatives that have taken place in the past seven years. One of the most important points to note from this analysis is that 'once new policies are adopted, there is little follow-up. Only 10% of the policies considered in this dataset have been evaluated for their impact. Measuring policy impact more rigorously and consistently will not only be cost effective in the long run, it is also essential for developing the most useful, practicable and successful education policy options' (OECD, 2015a, p. 20).

Chapter summary

This chapter makes the following key points:

- The Educational Change Model has been specifically developed for the middle years and has been employed as a framework for reform at a systems level.
- Teachers and school leaders are important in their roles to ignite, resource and commit to reform in order to achieve cultural change and sustainable practice.
- Shifting the culture of schools is a long-term sustainability project requiring ongoing commitment.

Acknowledgements

The editors wish to thank Joy Reynolds for her administrative contribution to this book. We thank the reviewers for their insightful comments and the publishers for their confidence in this project.

References

ACARA (Australian Curriculum, Assessment and Reporting Authority) (2012). *General capability: literacy*. Australia: ACARA.

ACARA (Australian Curriculum and Assessment Reporting Authority) (2015a). *Australian Curriculum: Health and Physical Education (AC:HPE)*, version 8.1. Retrieved from www.australiancurriculum.edu.au/health-and-physical-education/rationale.

ACARA (Australian Curriculum, Assessment and Reporting Authority) (2015b). *Critical and creative thinking: introduction*. Retrieved from www.australiancurriculum.edu.au/generalcapabilities/critical-and-creative-thinking/introduction/introduction.

ACARA (Australian Curriculum, Assessment and Reporting Authority) (2015c). *National Assessment Program—ICT literacy: Years 6 & 10; report 2014*. Retrieved from www.nap.edu.au/verve/_resources/D15_8761__NAP-ICT_2014_Public_Report_Final.pdf.

ACARA (Australian Curriculum, Assessment and Reporting Authority) (2015d). *Personal and social capability: key ideas*. Retrieved from www.australiancurriculum.edu.au/generalcapabilities/personal-and-social-capability/introduction/key-ideas.

ACARA (Australian Curriculum, Assessment and Reporting Authority) (2016a). *The Australian Curriculum: Mathematics*. Retrieved from www.australiancurriculum.edu.au/mathematics/rationale.

ACARA (Australian Curriculum, Assessment and Reporting Authority) (2016b). *Information and communication technology (ICT) capability*. Retrieved from www.australiancurriculum.edu.au/generalcapabilities/information-and-communication-technology-capability/introduction/key-ideas.

ACARA (Australian Curriculum, Assessment and Reporting Authority) (2016c). *Technologies: learning area*. Retrieved from www.australiancurriculum.edu.au/technologies/key-ideas.

ACARA (Australian Curriculum, Assessment and Reporting Authority) (2016d). *Digital technologies: curriculum*. Retrieved from www.australiancurriculum.edu.au/technologies/digital-technologies/curriculum/f-10?layout=1.

ACER (Australian Council for Educational Research) (2012). *Junior secondary: theory and practice*. Brisbane: Queensland Department of Education and Training.

Active Healthy Kids Australia (2015). *The road less travelled: the 2015 Active Healthy Kids Australia progress report card on active transport for children and young people*. Adelaide: Active Healthy Kids Australia.

Adie, L. (2013). The development of teacher assessment identity through participation in online moderation. *Assessment in Education: Principles, Policy & Practice, 20*, 91–106.

REFERENCES

Ahmed, S.P., Bittencourt-Hewitt, A. & Sebastian, C.L. (2015). Neurocognitive bases of emotion regulation development in adolescence. *Developmental Cognitive Neuroscience, 15,* 11–25.

Ajaja, O.P. & Eravwoke, O.U. (2010). Effects of cooperative learning strategy on junior secondary school students achievement in integrated science. *Electronic Journal of Science Education,* 14(1), 1–18.

Alberto, P. & Troutman, A. (2013). *Applied behavior analysis for teachers,* 9th edn. Upper Saddle River, NJ: Pearson.

Albiero, P., Matricardi, G., Speltri, D. & Toso, D. (2009). The assessment of empathy in adolescence: a contribution to the Italian validation of the 'Basic Empathy Scale'. *Journal of Adolescence, 32*(2), 393–408.

Alessandri, G., Eisenberg, N., Vecchione, M., Caprara, G.V. & Milioni, M. (2016). Ego-resiliency development from late adolescence to emerging adulthood: a ten-year longitudinal study. *Journal of Adolescence, 50,* 91–102.

Alexander, P.A., Murphy, P.K. & Woods, B.S. (1996). Of squalls and fathoms: navigating the seas of educational innovation. *Educational Researcher, 25,* 31–6.

Alfaro, E.G., Umana-Taylor, A.J., Gonzales-Backen, M.A., Bamaca, M.Y. & Zeiders, K.H. (2009). Latino adolescents' academic success: the role of discrimination, academic motivation, and gender. *Journal of Adolescence, 32*(4), 941–62.

Alghamdi, R. & Gillies, R.M. (2013). The impact of cooperative learning in comparison to traditional learning (small groups) on EFL learners' outcomes when learning English as a foreign language. *Asian Social Science, 9*(13), 19–27.

Alloway, N., Gilbert, P., Gilbert, R. & Muspratt, S. (2004). *Factors impacting on student aspirations and expectations in regional Australia.* Retrieved from www.dest.gov.au/archive/highered/eippubs/eip04_1/eip_04_01.pdf.

Anderson, C. (2013). *Young entrepreneurs: 8 teenage millionaires.* Retrieved from smartbusinesstrends.com/young-entrepreneurs-8-teenage-millionaires.

Anderson, K.M. (2007). Differentiating instruction to include all students. *Preventing School Failure, 51*(3), 49–54.

Anderson, L.W. & Krathwohl, D.R. (eds) (2001). *A taxonomy for learning, teaching and assessing: a revision of Bloom's taxonomy of educational objectives.* New York: Longman.

Anderson, L.W., Krathwohl, D.R., Airasian, P., Cruikshank, K.A., Mayer, R.E., Pintrich, P.R., Raths, J. & Wittrock, M.C. (2005). *A taxonomy for learning, teaching, and assessing: a revision of Bloom's taxonomy of educational objectives,* complete edn. New York: Pearson.

Anfara, V.A. Jr, Andrews, P.G., Hough, D.L., Mertens, S.B., Mizelle, N.B. & White, G.P. (2008). *Research and resources in support of* This we believe. Westerville, OH: Association for Middle Level Education.

Angus, M., McDonald, T., Ormond, C., Rybarcyk, R., Taylor., A. & Winterton, A. (2009). *Trajectories of classroom behaviour and academic progress: a study of student engagement with learning.* Mount Lawley: Edith Cowan University.

Anstey, M. (2002). *Literate futures: reading, 2002.* Australia: Education Queensland and AccessEd.

Apple, M. (1990). *Ideology and curriculum,* 2nd edn. New York: Routledge.

Apple, M. & Beane, J. (2007). *Democratic schools: lessons in powerful education,* 2nd edn. Portsmouth, NH: Heinemann.

Arnett, J.J. (1998). Learning to stand alone: the contemporary American transition to adulthood in cultural and historical context. *Human Development, 41,* 295–315.

Arnett, J.J. (2006a). Emerging adulthood: understanding a new way of coming of age. In J.J. Arnett & J.L. Tanner (eds), *Emerging adults in America: coming of age in the 21st century* (pp. 3–19). Washington, DC: American Psychological Association.

Arnett, J.J. (2006b). The psychology of emerging adulthood: what is known, and what remains to be known? In J.J. Arnett & J.L. Tanner (eds), *Emerging adults in America: coming of age in the 21st century* (pp. 303–30). Washington, DC: American Psychological Association.

Arnett, J.J. (2007). Emerging adulthood: what is it, and what is it good for? *Child Development Perspectives, 1*, 68–73.

Arnett, J.J. (2014). *Adolescence and emerging adulthood*. New York: Pearson Education.

Arnett, J.J. (ed.) (2015). *The Oxford handbook of emerging adulthood*. Oxford: Oxford University Press.

Arnett, J.J. & Fishel, E. (2013). *When will my grown-up kid grow up? Loving and understanding your emerging adult*. New York: Workman Publishing.

Arnold, J. (1997). High expectations for all. *Middle School Journal, 28*(3), 51–3.

Arnold, J. (2016). A literacy data cycle story about people, not numbers. A presentation at the ALEA/ AATE annual conference, Adelaide.

Arnold, R. (2000). *Middle years literature review including list of references*. Sydney: Office of Board of Studies.

Ashman, A. (2015). *Education for inclusion and diversity*. Melbourne: Pearson.

Assessment Reform Group (2002). *Assessment is for learning: 10 principles; research-based principles to guide classroom practice*. Retrieved from assessmentreformgroup.files.wordpress. com/2012/01/10principles_english.pdf.

Atkins, S., Bunting, M., Bolger, D.J. & Dougherty, M. (2012). Training the adolescent brain: neural plasticity and the acquisition of cognitive abilities. In V. Reyna, S. Chapman, M. Dougherty & J. Confrey (eds), *The adolescent brain: learning, reasoning, and decision making* (pp. 211–41). Washington, DC: American Psychological Association.

Atuyambe, L., Mirembe, F., Annika, J., Kirumira, E.K. & Faxelid, E. (2009). Seeking safety and empathy: adolescent health seeking behavior during pregnancy and early motherhood in central Uganda. *Journal of Adolescence, 32*(4), 781–96.

Australian Association of Mathematics Teachers (1997). *Numeracy = everyone's business*. Report of the Numeracy Education Strategy Development Conference. Adelaide: Australian Association of Mathematics Teachers.

Australian Bureau of Statistics (2012). *Sports and physical recreation: a statistical overview, Australia, 2012*, cat. no. 4156.0 Canberra: Australian Government.

Australian Bureau of Statistics (2015). *Participation in sport and physical recreation, Australia, 2013–14*. Canberra: Australian Government.

Australian Council for Educational Research *see* ACER.

Australian Council for Health, Physical Education and Recreation (2014). *Report card on physical activity for children and young people*. Retrieved from www.achper.org.au/ associationnews/2014-report-card-on-physical-activity-for-children-and-young-people.

Australian Curriculum, Assessment and Reporting Authority *see* ACARA.

Australian Government Office of the eSafety Commissioner (2016a). *About the office*. Retrieved from www.esafety.gov.au/about-the-office.

Australian Government Office of the eSafety Commissioner (2016b). *eSafety information*. Retrieved from www.esafety.gov.au/esafety-information.

Australian Government Office of the eSafety Commissioner (2016c). *Digital citizenship*. Retrieved from www.esafety.gov.au/education-resources/classroom-resources/digital-citizenship-ms/ classroom-resources.

Australian Institute for Teaching and School Leadership (2011a). *The Australian Professional Standards for Teachers*. Retrieved from www.aitsl.edu.au/australian-professional-standards-for-teachers.

Australian Institute for Teaching and School Leadership (2011b). *ICT Elaborations for graduate teachers*. Retrieved from acce.edu.au/national-professional-standards-teachers-ict-elaborations-graduate-teachers.

Australian Institute of Health and Welfare (2011a). *Australian Burden of Disease Study: impact and causes of illness and death in Australia 2011*. Australian Burden of Disease Study Series no. 3., cat. no. BOD 4. Canberra: Australian Institute of Health and Welfare.

REFERENCES

Australian Institute of Health and Welfare (2011b). *Young Australians: their health and wellbeing*. Cat. no. PHE 140. Canberra: Australian Institute of Health and Welfare.

Australian Institute of Health and Welfare (2014). *Daily physical activity guidelines for adults*. Retrieved from www.aihw.gov.au/diabetes-indicators/exercise.

Australian Research Alliance for Children and Youth (2011). *Betwixt and between: a report on the ARACY's middle years project*. Canberra: Australian Research Alliance for Children and Youth.

Ausubel, D.P. (1954). *Theory and problems of adolescent development*. New York: Grune & Stratton.

Bahr, N. (2005). The middle years learner. In D. Pendergast & N. Bahr (eds), *Teaching middle years: rethinking curriculum, pedagogy and assessment* (pp. 48–64). Sydney: Allen & Unwin.

Bahr, N. & Crosswell, L. (2011). Contesting lost ground for the middle years in Australia: using the case study of Queensland. *Middle Years of Schooling Association Journal, 11*(2), 12–19.

Baiocco, R., Laghi, F. & D'Alessio, M. (2009). Decision-making style among adolescents: relationship with sensation seeking and locus of control. *Journal of Adolescence, 32*(4), 963–76.

Baird, J., Hopfenbeck, T., Newton, P., Stobart, G. & Steen-Utheim, A. (2014). *State of the field review: assessment and learning*. Retrieved from taloe.up.pt/wp-content/uploads/2013/11/FINALMASTER2July14Bairdetal2014AssessmentandLearning.pdf.

Balfanz, R. (2009). *Putting middle grades students on the graduation path: a policy and practice brief*. Westerville, OH: National Middle School Association.

Balsano, A.B., Phelps, E., Theokas, C., Lerner, J.V. & Lerner, R.M. (2009). Patterns of early adolescents' participation in youth development programs having positive youth development goals. *Journal of Research on Adolescence, 19*(2), 249–59.

Bandura, A. (1993). Perceived self-efficacy in cognitive development and functioning. *Educational Psychologist, 28*(2), 117–48.

Bandura, A. (1977). *Social learning theory*. Englewood Cliffs, NJ: Prentice Hall.

Bandura, A. (2001). Social cognitive theory: an agentic perspective. *Annual Review of Psychology, 52*, 1–26.

Bandura, A. (2012). On the functional properties of perceived self-efficacy revisited. *Journal of Management, 38*(1), 9–44.

Bangert-Drowns, R.L., Kulik, C.C., Kulik, J.A. & Morgan, M.T. (1991). The instructional effect of feedback in test-like events. *Review of Educational Research, 61*, 213–38.

Barclay, K. & Myrskylä, M. (2015). *Advanced maternal age and offspring outcomes: causal effects and countervailing period trends*. No. WP-2015-009. Rostock, Germany: Max Planck Institute for Demographic Research.

Barton, G.M. (2014). The arts and literacy: interpretation and expression of symbolic form. In G.M. Barton (ed.), *Literacy in the arts: retheorising learning and teaching* (pp. 3–20). Switzerland: Springer International Publishing.

Barton, G.M., Arnold, J. & Trimble-Roles, R. (2015). Writing practices today and in the future: multimodal and creative text composition in the 21st century. In J. Turbill, G.M. Barton & C. Brock (eds), *Looking back to look forward: teaching writing in today's classrooms* (pp. 241–61). South Australia: ALEA Occasional Publication.

Battista, M.T. (1999). The mathematics miseducation of America's youth: ignoring research and scientific study in education. *Phi Delta Kappan, 80*(6), 424–33.

Bayraktar, G. (2011). The effect of cooperative learning on students' approach to general gymnastics course and academic achievements. *Educational Research and Reviews, 6*(1), 62–71.

Beane, J. (1990). *A middle school curriculum: from rhetoric to reality*. Columbus, OH: National Middle School Association.

Beane, J. (1991). The middle school: the natural home of the integrated curriculum. *Educational Leadership, 49*, 9–13.

Beane, J. (1997). *Curriculum integration: designing the core of democratic education*. New York: Teachers College Press.

Beane, J. (2005). *A reason to teach: creating classrooms of dignity and hope*. Portsmouth, NH: Heinemann.

Beane, J. (2013). A common core of a different sort: putting democracy at the center of the curriculum. *Middle School Journal, 44*(3), 6–14.

Beavis, C., Rowan, L., Dezuanni, M., McGillivray, C., O'Mara, J., Prestridge, S., Steiler-Hunt, C., Thompson, R. & Zagami, J. (2014). Teachers' beliefs about the possibilities and limitations of digital games in classrooms. *E-learning and Digital Media, 11*(6), 568–80.

Bell, A. (1993). Principles for the design of teaching. *Educational Studies in Mathematics, 24*(1), 5–34.

Bennett, R.E. (2011). Formative assessment: a critical review. *Assessment in Education: Principles, Policy & Practice, 18*, 5–25.

Benson, P.L. (1997). *All kids are our kids: what communities must do to raise caring and responsible children and adolescents*. San Francisco, CA: Jossey-Bass.

Bereiter, C. & Scardamalia, S. (1989). Intentional learning as the goal of instruction. In L.B. Resnick (ed.), *Knowing, learning, & instruction: essays in honor of Robert Glaser* (pp. 361–85). Hillsdale, NJ: Erlbaum.

Bers, M. (2006). The role of new technologies to foster positive youth development. *Applied Developmental Science, 10*(4), 200–19.

Berten, H. & Van Rossem, R. (2009). Doing worse but knowing better: an exploration of the relationship between HIV/AIDS knowledge and sexual behavior among adolescents in Flemish secondary schools. *Journal of Adolescence, 32*(5), 1303–19.

Bilmes, J. (2012). *Beyond behavior management: the six life skills children need*, 2nd edn. St Paul, MN: Redleaf Press.

Birenbaum, M., Kimron, H. & Shilton, H. (2011). Nested contexts that shape assessment for learning: school-based professional learning community and classroom culture. *Studies in Educational Evaluation, 37*, 35–48.

Blachowicz, C.L.Z., Fisher, P.J.L., Ogle, D. & Watts-Taffe, S. (2006). Vocabulary: questions from the classroom. *Reading Research Quarterly, 41*, 524–39.

Black, P. & Wiliam, D. (1998). *Inside the black box: raising standards through classroom assessment*. London: School of Education, Kings College.

Blackwell, L.S., Trzesniewski, K.H. & Dweck, C.S. (2007). Implicit theories of intelligence predict achievement across an adolescent transition: a longitudinal study and an intervention. *Child Development, 78*, 246–63.

Block, K.C. & Israel, S.E. (2004). The ABCs of performing highly effective think-alouds. *Reading Teacher, 58*, 154–67.

Bloom, B. (1956). *Taxonomy of educational objectives*. New York: Longman.

Boethel, M. (2003). *Diversity: school, family and community connections*. Annual Synthesis. Austin, TX: National Center for Family and Community Connections with Schools, Southwest Educational Development Laboratory.

Boman, P. & Mergler, A.G. (2014). Optimism: what it is and its relevance in the school context. In M.J. Furlong, R. Gilman & E.S. Huebner (eds), *Handbook of positive psychology in schools*, 2nd edn (pp. 51–66). Oxfordshire and New York: Routledge.

Boomer, G., Lester, N., Onore, C. & Cook, J. (1992). *Negotiating the curriculum*. London: Falmer Press.

Boyd-Batstone, P. (2004). Focused anecdotal records assessment: a tool for standards-based, authentic assessment. *Reading Teacher, 58*, 230–9.

Braggett, E. (1997). *The middle years of schooling: an Australian perspective*. Australia: Hawker Brownlow Education.

Brand, S., Hatzinger, M., Beck, J. & Holsboer-Trachsler, E. (2009). Perceived parenting styles, personality traits and sleep patterns in adolescents. *Journal of Adolescence, 32*(5), 1189–207.

Bray, B. & McClaskey, K. (2013). A step-by-step guide to personalize learning. *Learning & Leading with Technology, 40*(7), 12–19.

REFERENCES

Braz, P.H., Frey, E., da Cruz, M.R., Camargo, M.E. & Olea, P.M. (2011). Consumption of Generation 'Z' stratified from human Maslow's needs. *International Journal of Management and Administrative Sciences*, 1(2), 1–8.

Brennan, M. & Sachs, J. (1998). Integrated curriculum for the middle years. In J. Cumming (ed.), *Extending reform in the middle years of schooling: challenges and responses* (pp. 18–24). Deakin West: Australian Curriculum Studies Association.

Brighton, K. (2007). *Coming of age: the education & development of young adolescents*. Westerville, OH: National Middle School Association.

Brookhart, S.M. & Nitko, A.J. (2008). *Assessment and grading in classrooms*. Upper Saddle River, NJ: Pearson Education.

Bronfenbrenner, U. (1979). *The ecology of human development: experiments by nature and design*. Cambridge, MA: Harvard University Press.

Brown, D., Reumann-Moore, R., Hugh, R., Christman, J.B. & Riffer, M. (2008). *Links to learning and sustainability: year three report of the Pennsylvania High School Coaching Initiative*. Retrieved from 8rri53pm0cs22jk3vvqna1ub-wpengine.netdna-ssl.com/wp-content/uploads/2015/10/Links_to_Learning_and_Sustainability.pdf.

Brown, J. & Duguid, P. (2000). *The social life of information*. Boston, MA: Harvard Business School Press.

Brown, M. (2005). Foreword. In B. Steel, D. Baker & A. Tomlin (eds), *Navigating numeracies: home/school numeracy practices* (pp. vii–xviii). Dordrecht: Springer.

Brown, R. (2010). Collaborative learning. In D. Pendergast & N. Bahr (eds), *Teaching middle years: rethinking curriculum, pedagogy and assessment*, 2nd edn (pp. 223–37). Sydney: Allen & Unwin.

Brown, T. (2013). 'In, through and about' movement: is there a place for the Arnoldian dimensions in the new Australian Curriculum for health and physical education? *Asia Pacific Journal of Health, Sport and Physical Education*, 4(2), 143–57.

Bruner, J.S. (1996). *The culture of education*. Cambridge, MA: Harvard University Press.

Buckingham, J. (2003). Class size and teacher quality. *Educational Research for Policy and Practice*, 2, 71–86.

Buckingham, D. (2007). Media education goes digital: an introduction. *Learning, Media and Technology*, 32(2), 111–19.

Buckskin, P. (2015). Engaging Indigenous students: the important relationship between Aboriginal and Torres Strait Islander students and their teachers. In S. Groundwater-Smith & N. Mockler (eds), *Big fish, little fish: teaching and learning in the middle years* (pp. 155–74). Port Melbourne, Vic: Cambridge University Press.

Burnham, J.J. & Wright, V.H. (2012). Cyberbullying: what middle school students want you to know. *Alabama Counseling Association Journal*, 38(1), 3–12.

Buzan, T. (2000). *The mind map book*. London: BBC.

Cabrera, A.F., Crissman, J.L., Bernal, E.M., Nora, A., Terenzini, P.T. & Pascarella, E.T. (2002). Collaborative learning: its impact on college students' development and diversity. *Journal of College Student Development*, 43(1), 20–34.

Caglar, E. (2009). Similarities and differences in physical self-concept of males and females during late adolescence and early adulthood. *Adolescence*, 44(174), 407–20.

Caldwell, B.J. & Harris, J. (2008). *Why not the best schools?* Melbourne: ACER.

Callanan, G.A. & Perri, D.F. (2006). Teaching conflict management: using a scenario-based approach. *Journal of Education for Business*, 81(3), 131–9.

Cameron, A. (2004). I'll never grow up, not me! *Macleans*, 117(31), 56–7.

Cam, P. (1995). *Thinking together: philosophical inquiry for the classroom*. Sydney: PETA and Hale & Iremonger.

Campbell, C. & Rozsnyai, C. (2002). *Quality assurance and the development of course programmes*. Papers on Higher Education Regional University Network on Governance and Management of Higher Education in South East Europe. Bucharest: UNESCO.

Canter, L. & Canter, M. (2001). *Assertive discipline: positive behavior management for today's classroom*. Los Angeles, CA: Canter & Associates.

Carrington, V. (2006). *Rethinking middle years: early adolescents, schooling and digital culture*. Sydney: Allen & Unwin.

Carroll, J.S., Badger, S., Willoughby, B.J., Nelson, L.J., Madsen, S.D. & McNamara Barry, C. (2009). Ready or not? Criteria for marriage readiness among emerging adults. *Journal of Adolescent Research*, 24(3), 349–75.

Carter, R., Jaccard, J., Silverman, W.K. & Pina, A.A. (2009). Pubertal timing and its link to behavioral and emotional problems among 'at-risk' African American adolescent girls. *Journal of Adolescence*, 32(3), 467–81.

Casey, B.J., Jones, R.M. & Somerville, L.H. (2011). Braking and accelerating of the adolescent brain. *Journal of Research on Adolescence*, 21(1), 21–33.

Caskey, M.M. & Anfara, V. (2014). *Research summary: developmental characteristics of young adolescents*. Retrieved from www.amle.org/BrowsebyTopic/Research/ResDet/TabId/198/ArtMID/696/ArticleID/455/Developmental-Characteristics-of-Young-Adolescents.aspx.

Caskey, M.M. & Ruben, B. (2003). Research for awakening adolescent learning. *Education Digest*, 69(4), 36–8.

Cefai, C. (2004). Pupil resilience in the classroom: a teacher's framework. *Emotional Behavioural Difficulties*, 9(3), 149–70.

Centers for Disease Control and Prevention (2016). *Child development: young teens*. Retrieved from www.cdc.gov/ncbddd/childdevelopment/positiveparenting/adolescence.html.

Chadbourne, R. (2001). *Middle schooling for the middle years: what might the jury be considering?* Victoria: Australian Education Union.

Chadbourne, R. (2004). A typology of teacher collaboration in middle schools. *Australian Journal of Middle Schooling*, 4(1), 9–16.

Chadbourne, R. & Harslett, M. (eds) (1998). *Case studies in middle schooling planner's guide*. East Perth: Education Department of Western Australia.

Chadbourne, R. & Pendergast, D. (2010). The philosophy of middle schooling. In D. Pendergast & N. Bahr (eds), *Teaching middle years: rethinking curriculum, pedagogy and assessment*, 2nd edn (pp. 23–49). Sydney: Allen & Unwin.

Chan, G.H. & Lo, T.W. (2016). The effect of negative experiences on delinquent behavior of youth in a social withdrawal situation. *Journal of Adolescence*, 50, 69–80.

ChanLin, L. (2008). Technology integration applied to project-based learning in science. *Innovation Education Technology International*, 45(1), 55–65.

Chi, M.T.H. & Ceci, S.J. (1987). Content knowledge: its role, representation, and restructuring in memory development. *Advances in Child Development and Behavior*, 20, 91–142.

Chi, M.T.H., Glaser, R. & Rees, E. (1982). Expertise in problem solving. In R. Sternberg (ed.), *Advances in the psychology of human intelligence* (vol. 1, pp. 7–75). Hillsdale, NJ: Lawrence Erlbaum.

Chown, D. (2013). Tackling controversy in the classroom: the introduction of senior health education in an Islamic school context. *Active & Healthy Magazine*, 20(1), 14–17.

Christie, F. & Derewianka, B. (2008). *School discourse*. London: Continuum.

Clark, B. (2001). Some principles of brain research for challenging gifted learners. *Gifted Education International*, 16, 4–10.

Clarke, M. & Pittaway, S. (2014). *Marsh's becoming a teacher*, 6th edn. Sydney: Pearson.

Clark, W., Logan, K., Luckin, R., Mee, A. & Oliver, M. (2009). Beyond Web 2.0: mapping the technology landscapes of young learners. *Journal of Computer Assisted Learning*, 25(1), 56–69.

Coffey, A. Berlach, R. & O'Neill, M. (2013). Transitioning Year 7 primary students to secondary settings in Western Australian Catholic schools: how successful was the move? *Research in Middle Level Education*, 36(10), 1–15.

REFERENCES

Collins, R. (2014). *Skills for the 21st century: teaching higher-order thinking*. Retrieved from www.curriculum.edu.au/leader/teaching_higher_order_thinking,37431.html?issueID=12910.

Cooper, K.S. (2014). Eliciting engagement in the high school classroom: a mixed-methods examination of teaching practices. *American Educational Research Journal, 51*(2), 363–402.

Cope, B. & Kalantzis, M. (eds) (2000). *Multiliteracies: literacy learning and the design of social futures*. London and New York: Routledge.

Corkindale, C., Condon, J.T., Russell, A. & Quinlivan, J.A. (2009). Factors that adolescent males take into account in decisions about an unplanned pregnancy. *Journal of Adolescence, 32*(4), 995–1008.

Cormack, P. (1991). *The nature of adolescence: a review of literature and other selected papers*. Adelaide: Education Department of South Australia.

Cormack, P. & Cumming, J. (1995). *From alienation to engagement: opportunities for reform in the middle years*. Canberra: Australian Curriculum Studies Association.

Costa, A.L. (ed.) (1985). *Developing minds*. Alexandria, VA: Association for Supervision and Curriculum Development.

Costa, A.L. & Kallick, B. (2008). *Learning and leading with habits of mind: 16 essential characteristics for success*. Alexandria, VA: Association for Supervision and Curriculum Development.

Côté, J. (2000). *Arrested adulthood: the changing nature of maturity and identity*. New York: New York University Press.

Covington, M.V. & Omelich, C.L. (1992). The influence of expectancies and problem-solving strategies on smoking intentions. In R. Schwarzer (ed.), *Self-efficacy: thought control of action* (pp. 263–83). New York: Routledge.

Crooks, T. (2003). Some criteria for intelligent accountability applied to accountability in New Zealand. Presented to the annual meeting of the American Educational Research Association, Chicago, IL.

Crowther, G. (1959). *15 to 18: a report of the Central Advisory Committee for Education (England)*. (Crowther Report). London: Her Majesty's Stationery Office.

Cumming, J. (Jim) (ed.) (1998). *Extending reform in the middle years of schooling: challenges and responses*. Canberra: Australian Curriculum Studies Association.

Cumming, J.J. (J. Joy) (2004). Assessing and reporting all learning. Paper presented at the conference of the Association for Commonwealth Examination and Accreditation Boards, Fiji.

Cumming, J.J. (J. Joy) & Maxwell, G.S. (1999). Contextualising authentic assessment. *Assessment in Education: Principles, Policy and Practice, 6*, 177–94.

Cumming, J.J. (J. Joy) & Van der Kleij, F.M. (2016). Effective enactment of assessment for learning and student diversity in Australia. In D. Laveault & L. Allal (eds), *Assessment for learning: meeting the challenge of implementation* (pp. 55–74). Dordrecht: Springer.

Cumming, J.J. (J. Joy), Wyatt-Smith, C. & Colbert, P. (2016). Students at risk and NAPLAN: the collateral damage. In B. Lingard, G. Thompson & S. Sellar (eds), *National testing in schools: an Australian assessment*. (pp. 126–38). Local/Global Issues in Education. London: Routledge.

Damasio, A. (2005). *Descartes' error: emotion, reason, and the human brain*, 2nd edn. New York: Penguin.

Damon, W. (1988). *The social world of the child*. San Francisco, CA: Jossey-Bass.

Danielewicz, J. (2001). *Teaching selves: identity, pedagogy, and teacher education*. Albany, NY: State University of New York Press.

Darling-Hammond, L. (2002). *Redesigning schools: what matters and what works; 10 features of good small schools*. Stanford, CA: School Redesign Network, Stanford University.

Darling-Hammond, L. (2008). *Powerful learning: what we know about teaching for understanding*. San Francisco, CA: Jossey-Bass.

Davies, M., Elliott, S.N. & Cumming, J. (2016). Documenting support needs and adjustment gaps for students with disabilities: teacher practices in Australian classrooms and on national tests. *International Journal of Inclusive Education, 20*(12), 1252–69. doi:10.1080/13603116.2016.1159256.

Day, G., Hazzard, D. & Locke, J. (2002). *Productive pedagogies strategies kit*. Brisbane: Queensland Department of Education.

de Bono, E. (1995). *Six thinking hats*. Melbourne: Hawker Brownlow Education.

Dede, C. (2005). Planning for neomillennial learning styles. *EDUCAUSE Quarterly*, *28*(1), 7–12.

Demirdag, S. (2015). Classroom management and students' self-esteem: creating positive classrooms. *Educational Research and Reviews*, *10*(2), 191–7.

Department of Children, Schools and Families (2007). *Extended schools: building on experience*. Nottingham: Department of Children, Schools and Families, United Kingdom Government.

Department of Education (2000). *Literate futures: report of the literacy review for Queensland state schools*. Brisbane: Queensland Department of Education.

Department of Education (2001). *The Queensland School Reform Longitudinal Study*. Brisbane: Queensland Department of Education.

Department of Education, Employment and Workplace Relations (2008). *Family–school partnerships framework: a guide for schools and families*. Canberra: Australian Government.

Department of Education, Training and Employment (2014a). *Year 7 pilot schools: insights guide for principals*. Brisbane: Queensland Department of Education, Training and Employment.

Department of Education, Training and Employment (2014b). *Parent and Community Engagement Framework: working together to maximimise student learning*. Brisbane: Queensland Department of Education, Training and Employment.

Department of Education, Training and Youth Affairs (2000). *Numeracy, a priority for all: challenges for Australian schools*. Canberra: J.S. McMillan Printing Group.

Department of Health (2014). *Australia's physical activity and sedentary behaviour guidelines*. Retrieved from www.health.gov.au/internet/main/publishing.nsf/content/health-pubhlth-strateg-phys-act-guidelines#apa1317.

Derewianka, B.M. (2012). Knowledge about language in the Australian Curriculum: English. *Australian Journal of Language and Literacy*, *35*(2), 127–46.

Deutsch, A.R. & Crockett, L.J. (2016). Gender, generational status and parent–adolescent sexual communication: implications for Latino/a adolescent sexual behavior. *Journal of Research on Adolescence*, *26*(2), 300–15.

Devís-Devís, J., Peiró-Velert, C., Beltrán-Carrillo, V.J. & Tomás, J.M. (2009). Screen media time usage of 12–16-year-old Spanish school adolescents: effects of personal and socioeconomic factors, season and type of day. *Journal of Adolescence*, *32*(2), 213–31.

Dewey, J. (1900). *The school and society*, 2nd edn. Chicago, IL: University of Chicago Press.

Dewey, J. (1916). *Democracy and education*. New York: Macmillan.

Dewey, J. (1931). The way out of educational confusion. In R. Archambault (ed.), *John Dewey on education: selected writings* (pp. 422–26). New York: Random House.

Dewey, J. (1936). The theory of the Chicago experiment. In K. Mayhew & A. Edwards (eds), *The Dewey school* (pp. 463–77). New York: Atherton.

Dhariwal, A., Connolly, J., Paciello, M. & Caprara, G.V. (2009). Adolescent peer relationships and emerging adult romantic styles: a longitudinal study of youth in an Italian community. *Journal of Adolescent Research*, *24*(5), 579–600.

Dillabough, J., McLeod, J. & Mills, M. (2008). In search of allies and others: 'troubling' gender and education. *Discourse: Studies in the Cultural Politics of Education*, *29*(3), 301–10.

Dinham, S. (2008). *How to get your school moving and improving: an evidence-based approach*. Melbourne: ACER.

Dinham, S. & Rowe, K. (2007). *Teaching and learning in middle schooling: a review of the literature*. A report to the New Zealand Ministry of Education. Wellington, New Zealand: ACER.

Dinham, S. & Rowe, K. (2008). Fantasy, fashion and fact: middle schools, middle schooling and student achievement. Paper presented at BERA, Edinburgh.

Dinham, S. & Rowe, K. (2009). Middle schooling: what's the evidence? *Research Developments*, *21*(3), 1–2.

REFERENCES

Doig, B. (2001). *Summing up: Australian numeracy performances, practices, programs and possibilities.* Melbourne: ACER.

Dole, S. (2003). Questioning numeracy programs for at-risk students in the middle years of schooling. In L. Bragg, C. Campbell, G. Herbert & J. Mousley (eds), *Mathematics education research: innovation, networking, opportunity. Proceedings of the twenty-sixth annual conference of the Mathematics Education Research Group of Australasia* (pp. 278–85). Geelong: Deakin University.

Dossel, S. (1993). Maths anxiety. *Australian Mathematics Teacher, 49*(1), 4–8.

Dowden, T. (2007). Relevant, challenging, integrative and exploratory curriculum design: perspectives from theory and practice for middle level schooling in Australia. *Australian Educational Researcher, 34*(2), 51–72.

Dowden, T. (2012). Implementing curriculum integration: three easy lessons from past practice. *Set: Research Information for Teachers, 3*, 25–31.

Dowden, T. (2014). Challenging, integrated, negotiated and exploratory curriculum in the middle years of schooling: designing and implementing high quality curriculum integration. *Australian Journal of Middle Schooling, 14*(1), 16–27.

Dubinsky, E. (2000). Mathematical literacy and abstraction in the 21st century. *School Science and Mathematics, 100*(6), 289–97.

Dumontheil, I. (2016). Adolescent brain development. *Current Opinion in Behavioral Sciences, 10*, 39–44.

Duncan, S. & Barrett, L. (2007). Affect is a form of cognition: a neurobiological analysis. *Cognition and Emotion, 21*(6), 1184–211.

Durlak, J.A., Weissberg, R.P. & Pachan, M. (2010). A meta analysis of after school programs that seek to promote personal and social skills in children and adolescents. *American Journal of Community Psychology, 45*(3–4), 294–309.

Durlak, J.A., Weissberg, R.P., Dymnicki, A.B., Taylor, R.D. & Schellinger, K.B. (2011). Enhancing students' social and emotional development promotes success in school: results of a meta-analysis. *Child Development, 82*, 405–32.

Durling, N., Ng, L. & Bishop, P. (2010). *Education of Years 7–10 students: a focus on their teaching and learning needs; summary report.* Retrieved from www.educationcounts.govt.nz/publications/schooling/75765.

Dweck, C.S. (2006). *Mindset: the new psychology of success.* New York: Random House.

Dweck, C.S. (2008). Can personality be changed? The role of beliefs in personality and change. *Association for Psychological Science, 17*(6), 391–4.

Dweck, C.S. (2010). Even geniuses work hard. *Educational Leadership, 68*(1), 16–20.

Earl, L.M. (2003). *Assessment as learning: using classroom assessment to maximize student learning.* Thousand Oaks, CA: Corwin.

Education Queensland (2000). *New Basics Project technical paper: version 3 April 2000.* Brisbane: Education Queensland.

Education Queensland (2001). *Years 1–10 curriculum framework for Education Queensland schools.* Brisbane: Education Queensland.

Effandi, Z. & Zanaton, I. (2007). Promoting cooperative learning in science and mathematics education: a Malaysian perspective. *Eurasia Journal of Mathematics, Science & Technology Education, 3*(1), 35–9.

Effeney, G., Carroll, A. & Bahr, N. (2013). Self-regulated learning: key strategies and their sources in a sample of adolescent males. *Australian Journal of Educational & Developmental Psychology, 13*, 58–74.

Emerson, L., Fear. J., Fox, S. & Sanders, E. (2012). *Parental engagement in learning and schooling: lessons from research.* Report for the Family–School and Community Partnerships Bureau. Canberra: Australian Research Alliance for Children and Youth.

Engström, L.-M. (2008). Who is physically active? Cultural capital and sports participation from adolescence to middle age—a 38-year follow-up study. *Physical Education and Sport Pedagogy*, *13*(4), 319–43.

Enright, E. & O'Sullivan, M. (2012). Physical education 'in all sorts of corners': student activists transgressing formal physical education curricular boundaries. *Research Quarterly in Exercise and Sport, 83*(2), 255–67.

Epstein, J. (1996). Advances in family, community and school partnerships. *New Schools: New Communities, 12*(3), 5–13.

Erb, T.O. & Doda, N.M. (1989). *Team organization: promise-practices and possibilities.* Washington, DC: National Education Association.

Erickson, A.G., Noonan, P., Carter, K.S., McGurn, L. & Purifoy, E. (2015). The team functioning scale: evaluating and improving effectiveness of school teams. *International Journal of Educational Research, 69*, 1–11.

Erikson, E. (1963). *Childhood and society.* New York: W.W. Norton.

Ernest, P. (2000). Empowerment in mathematics education. In M.A. Clements, H.H. Tairab & W.K. Yoong (eds), *Energising science, mathematics, and technical education for all: proceedings of the Conference Brunei* (pp. 79–93). Bandar Seri Begawan: University of Brunei Darussalam.

Ertmer, P.A, Ottenbreit-Leftwich, A.T., Sadik, O., Sendurur, E. & Sendurur, P. (2012). Teacher beliefs and technology integration practices: a critical relationship. *Computers & Education, 59*, 423–35.

Evangelou, M., Taggart, B., Sylva, E.M., Sammons, P. & Siraj-Blatchford, I. (2008). *What makes a successful transition from primary to secondary school?* London: Institute of Education, University of London.

Evertson, C.M. & Weinstein, C.S. (2006). *Handbook of classroom management: research, practice and contemporary issues.* Mahwah, NJ: Lawrence Erlbaum.

Eyers, V. (1992). *Report of the junior secondary review.* Adelaide: Education Department of South Australia.

Falbo, T., Lein, L. & Amador, N.A. (2001). Parental involvement during the transition to high school. *Journal of Adolescent Research, 16*(5), 511–29.

Felner, R.D., Jackson, A.W., Kasak, D., Mulhall, P.F., Brand, S. & Flowers, N. (1997). The impact of school reform for the middle years: longitudinal study of a network engaged in *Turning Points*–based comprehensive school transformation. *Phi Delta Kappan, 78*(7), 528–32, 541–50.

Finger, G., Albion, P., Jamieson-Proctor, R., Cavanagh, R., Grimbeek, P., Lloyd, M., Fitzgerald, R., Bond, T. & Romeo, G. (2013). Teaching Teachers for the Future (TTF) Project TPACK survey: summary of the key findings. In Teaching Teachers for the Future project, ed. T. Downes, special issue, *Australian Educational Computing, 27*(3), 13–25.

Fleming, N.D. & Mills, C. (1992). Not another inventory, rather a catalyst for reflection. *To Improve the Academy, 11*, 137–45.

Flowers, N., Mertens, S. & Mulhall, P. (1999). The impact of teaming: five research-based outcomes of teaming. *Middle School Journal, 31*(2), 57–60.

Flowers, N., Mertens, S. & Mulhall, P. (2000). What makes interdisciplinary teams effective? *Middle School Journal, 31*(4), 53–6.

Flowers, N., Mertens, S. & Mulhall, P. (2002). *What makes interdisciplinary teams effective?* Retrieved from http://middleschooleducators.com/wp-content/uploads/2013/06/What-Makes-Interdisciplinary-Teams-Effective.pdf.

Forlin, C., Keen, M. & Barrett, E. (2008). The concerns of mainstream teachers: coping with inclusivity in an Australian context. *International Journal of Disability, Development and Education, 55*, 251–64.

Forster, M. & Masters, G. (1996a). *Performances.* Melbourne: ACER.

Forster, M. & Masters, G. (1996b). *Portfolios.* Melbourne: ACER.

Francis, B. (2008). Engendering debate: how to formulate a political analysis of the divide between genetic bodies and discursive gender. *Journal of Gender Studies, 17*(3), 211–23.

Francombe-Webb, J., Rich, E. & De Pian, L. (2014). I move like you . . . but different: biopolitics and embodied methodologies. *Cultural Studies—Critical Methodologies, 14*(5), 471–82.

Fredricks, J.A., Blumenfeld, P.C. & Paris, A.H. (2004). School engagement: potential of the concept, state of the evidence. *Review of Educational Research, 74*(1), 59–109.

Fredrickson, B.L. (2001). The role of positive emotions in positive psychology: the broaden-and-build theory of positive emotions. *American Psychologist, 56*, 218–26.

Freebody, P. (2016). *Australian Curriculum: English*. Retrieved from www.australiancurriculum.edu. au/english/rationale.

Freebody, P., Chan, E. & Barton, G.M. (2013). Literacy and curriculum: language and knowledge in the classroom. In T. Cremin, B. Comber, K. Hall & L. Moll (eds), *International handbook of research in children's literacy, learning and culture* (pp. 304–18). Maiden, MA: Wiley-Blackwell.

Freiberg, H.J. (1999). *Beyond behaviorism: changing the classroom management paradigm*. Boston, MA: Allyn & Bacon.

Freire, A. & Macedo, D. (eds) (2000). An introduction. In A. Freire & D. Macedo (eds), *The Paulo Freire reader* (pp. 4–44). New York: Continuum International.

Freire, P. (1971). *Pedagogy of the oppressed* (trans. M.B. Ramos). New York: Herder & Herder.

Freire, P. & Macedo, D. (1987). *Literacy: reading the word and the world*. New York: Bergin & Garvey.

Freud, A. (1968). *The ego and the mechanisms of defence*. London: Hogarth Press and Institute of Psycho-Analysis.

Freyberg, R.J. (2009). Quantitative and qualitative measures of behavior in adolescent girls. *Adolescence, 44*(173), 33–55.

Froh, J.J., Yurkewicz, C. & Kashdan, T.B. (2009). Gratitude and subjective well-being in early adolescence: examining gender differences. *Journal of Adolescence, 32*(3), 633–50.

Fullan, M. (1993). *Change forces: probing the depths of educational reform*. Bristol, PA: Falmer Press.

Fullan, M. (1997). Emotion and hope: constructive concepts for complex times. In A. Hargreaves & R. Evans (eds), *Beyond educational reform: bringing teachers back in* (pp. 216–33). Buckingham, United Kingdom: Open University Press.

Fullan, M. (1999). *Change forces: the sequel*. London and Philadelphia, PA: Falmer Press.

Fullan, M. (2001). *The new meaning of educational change*, 3rd edn. New York: Teachers College Press.

Fullan, M. (2003). *Change forces with a vengeance*. London: RoutledgeFalmer.

Fuller, A. (1998). *From surviving to thriving: promoting mental health in young people*. Melbourne: ACER.

Fuller, A. (2002). *Raising real people: creating a resilient family*, 2nd edn. Melbourne: ACER.

Fuller, A. (2003). *Don't waste your breath: an introduction to the mysterious world of the adolescent brain*. Retrieved from andrewfuller.com.au/wp-content/uploads/2014/08/Dont-waste-your-breath-an-introduction-to-the-adolescent-brain.pdf.

Furlong, M.J., Gilman, R. & Huebner, E.S. (eds) (2014). *Handbook of positive psychology in schools*, 2nd edn. Oxfordshire and New York: Routledge.

Furlong, M.J., You, S., Renshaw, T.L., O'Malley, M.D. & Rebelez, J. (2013). Preliminary development of the Positive Experiences at School Scale for elementary school children. *Child Indicators Research, 6*(4), 753–75.

Furlong, M.J., You, S., Renshaw, T.L., Smith, D.C. & O'Malley, M.D. (2014). Preliminary development and validation of the Social and Emotional Health Survey for secondary school students. *Social Indicators Research,117*(3), 1011–32.

Gard, M. (2009). Friends, enemies and the cultural politics of critical obesity research. In J. Wright & V. Harwood (eds), *Biopolitics and the 'obesity epidemic': governing bodies* (pp. 32–45). London: Routledge.

Gard, M. & Wright, J. (2005). *The obesity epidemic: science, morality and ideology*. London: Routledge.

Gardner, H. (1993). *Multiple intelligences: the theory in practice*. New York: Basic Books.

Garmezy, N., Masten, A.S. & Tellegen, A. (1984). The study of stress and competence in children: a building block for psychopathology. *Child Development, 55*, 97–111.

Garrick, B. & Keogh, J. (2010). Differentiated learners. In D. Pendergast & N. Bahr, *Teaching middle years: rethinking curriculum, pedagogy and assessment*, 2nd edn (pp. 68–85). Sydney: Allen & Unwin.

Garrick, B., Pendergast, D. & Geelan, D. (2017). *Theorising personalised education: electronically mediated higher education.* Singapore: Springer.

Gee, J.P. (2004). *Situated language and learning: a critique of traditional schooling.* New York: Routledge.

Geertsen, H.R. (2003). Rethinking thinking about higher-level thinking. *Teaching Sociology, 31*(1), 1–19.

Gehrke, N. (1998). A look at curriculum integration from the bridge. *Curriculum Journal, 9*(2), 247–60.

Geiger, V., Goos, M. & Dole, S. (2015). The role of digital technologies in numeracy teaching and learning. *International Journal of Science and Mathematics Education, 13*(5), 1115–37.

Gemici, S. & Lu, T. (2014). *Do schools influence student engagement in the high school years?* Adelaide: National Centre for Vocational Education Research.

George, P. (2008–09). *Special report: the status of programs in Florida middle schools.* Florida: Florida League of Middle Schools.

Giannotta, F., Ciairano, S., Spruijt, R. & Spruijt-Metz, D. (2009). Meanings of sexual intercourse for Italian adolescents. *Journal of Adolescence, 32*(2), 157–69.

Gibbons, M. (2002). *The self-directed learning handbook: challenging adolescent students to excel.* San Francisco, CA: Jossey-Bass.

Gibbs, R. & Poskitt, J. (2010). *Student engagement in the middle years of schooling (Years 7–10): a literature review.* Report to the Ministry of Education. New Zealand: Ministry of Education.

Giedd, J.N. (1999). Brain development IX: human brain growth. *American Journal of Psychiatry, 156*(1), 4.

Giedd, J.N. (2012). The digital revolution and adolescent brain evolution. *Journal of Adolescent Health, 51*(2), 101–5.

Giles, D. (2010). Developing pathic sensibilities: a critical priority for teacher education programmes. *Teaching and Teacher Education, 26*, 1511–19.

Giles, D., Smythe, E. & Spence, D. (2012). Exploring relationships in education: a phenomenological inquiry. *Australian Journal of Adult Learning, 52*(2), 214–36.

Gillies, R.M. (2003). Structuring cooperative group-work in classrooms. *International Journal of Educational Research, 39*(1), 35–49.

Gillies, R.M. (2008). The effects of cooperative learning on junior high school students' behaviours, discourse and learning during a science-based learning activity. *School Psychology International, 29*(3), 328–47.

Gillies, R.M. (2016). Cooperative learning: review of research and practice. *Australian Journal of Teacher Education, 41*(3), 39–54.

Gillies, R.M. & Boyle, M. (2008). Teachers' discourse during cooperative learning and their perceptions of this pedagogical practice. *Teaching and Teacher Education, 24*(5), 1333–48.

Gillies, R.M. & Boyle, M. (2010). Teachers' reflections on cooperative learning: issues of implementation. *Teaching and Teacher Education, 26*(4), 933–40.

Gillies, R.M. & Boyle, M. (2011). Teachers' reflections of cooperative learning (CL): a two-year follow-up. *Teaching Education, 22*(1), 63–78.

Gipps, C. & Stobart, G. (2003). Alternative assessment. In T. Kellaghan & D. Stufflebeam (eds), *International handbook of educational evaluation* (pp. 549–75). Dordrecht: Kluwer.

Giroux, H. (2001). *Theory and resistance in education: towards a pedagogy for the opposition.* London: Bergin & Garvey.

Giroux, H. (2003). Critical theory and educational practice. In A. Darder, M. Baltodano & D. Torres (eds), *The critical pedagogy reader* (pp. 27–56). London: RoutledgeFalmer.

Giroux, H. & McLaren, P. (1989). *Critical pedagogy, the state and cultural struggle.* Albany, NY: SUNY Press.

REFERENCES

Goede, I.H.A.D., Branje, S.J.T. & Meeus, W.H.J. (2009). Developmental changes and gender differences in adolescents' perceptions of friendships. *Journal of Adolescence*, *32*(5), 1105–23.

Goldsworthy, C. (2010). *Linking the strands of language and literacy: a resource manual*. San Diego, CA: Plural Publishing.

Goos, M. (2007). Developing numeracy in the learning areas (middle years). Keynote address delivered at the South Australian Literacy and Numeracy Expo, Adelaide.

Goos, M., Dole, S. & Geiger, V. (2012). Numeracy across the curriculum. *Australian Mathematics Teacher*, *68*(1), 3–7.

Goos, M., Geiger, V. & Dole, S. (2014). Transforming professional practice in numeracy teaching. In Y. Li, E. A. Silver & S. Li (eds), *Transforming mathematics instruction: multiple approaches and practices* (pp. 81–102). New York: Springer.

Goos, M., Mills, M., Gilbert, R., Gowlett, C., Wright, T., Renshaw, P., Pendergast, D., Nichols, K., McGregor, G., Khan, A., Keddie, A. & Honan, E. (2008). *Longitudinal Study of Teaching and Learning in Queensland State Schools (Stage 1)*. Brisbane: Queensland Department of Education, Training and the Arts.

Graber, J.A., Brooks-Gunn, J. & Petersen, A.C. (1996). *Transitions through adolescence: interpersonal domains and contexts*. Mahwah, NJ: Erlbaum.

Green, S., Oades, L. & Robinson, P. (2011). *Positive education: creating flourishing students, staff and schools*. Retrieved from www.psychology.org.au/publications/inpsych/2011/april/green.

Groenke, S.L., Haddix, M., Glenn, W.J., Kirkland, D.E., Price-Dennis, D. & Coleman-King, C. (2015). Disrupting and dismantling the dominant vision of youth of color. *English Journal*, *104*(3), 35–40.

Grootenboer, P. & Marshman, M. (2016). *Mathematics, affect and learning: middle school students' beliefs and attitudes about mathematics education*. Singapore: Springer.

Groundwater-Smith, S. (2015). A fair go and student agency in the middle years classroom. In S. Groundwater-Smith & N. Mockler (eds), *Big fish, little fish: teaching and learning in the middle years* (pp. 63–75). Melbourne: Cambridge University Press.

Groundwater-Smith, S., Brennan, M., McFadden, M. & Mitchell, J. (2001). *Secondary schooling in a changing world*. Sydney: Harcourt.

Groundwater-Smith, S. & Mockler, N. (2015). Challenges for teaching and learning in middle years. In S. Groundwater-Smith & N. Mockler (eds), *Big fish, little fish: teaching and learning in the middle years*. (pp. 3–13). Melbourne: Cambridge University Press.

Guan, S.A. & Fuligni, A.J. (2016). Changes in parent, sibling, and peer support during the transition to young adulthood. *Journal of Research on Adolescence*, *26*(2), 286–99.

Guskey, T.R. & Passaro, P.D. (1994). Teacher efficacy: a study of construct dimensions. *American Educational Research Journal*, *31*(3), 627–43.

Haager, D. & Klingner, J.K. (2005). *Differentiating instruction in inclusive classrooms*. Columbus, OH: Merrill.

Haeckel, E. (1868). *Natürliche Schöpfungsgeschichte* [Natural history of creation]. Berlin: George Reimer.

Haerens, L., Kirk, D., Cardon, G. & De Bourdeaudhuij, I. (2011). Toward the development of a pedagogical model for health-based physical education, *Quest*, *63*(3), 321–38.

Hajkowicz, S., Cook, H., Wilhelmseder, L. & Boughen, N. (2013). *The future of Australian sport: megatrends shaping the sports sector over coming decades*. Retrieved from www.ausport.gov.au/__data/assets/pdf_file/0019/523450/The_Future_of_Australian_Sport_-_Full_Report.pdf.

Hall, G.S. (1904). *Adolescence* (2 vols). Englewood Cliffs, NJ: Prentice Hall.

Halliday, M.A.K. (1973). *Explorations in the functions of language*. London: Edward Arnold Publishers.

Halliday, M.A.K. & Hasan, R. (1985). *Language, context, and text: aspects of language in a social-semiotic perspective*. Oxford: Oxford University Press.

Halpern, D.F. (2000). *Sex differences in cognitive abilities*, 3rd edn. Mahwah, NJ: Lawrence Erlbaum.

Hamada, M. & Ebrary, I. (2013). *Active and collaborative learning: practices, problems and prospects.* Hauppauge, NY: Nova Science Publishers.

Hamburg, B. (1974). Early adolescence: a specific and stressful stage of the life cycle. In G. Coelho, D.A. Hamburg & J.E. Adams (eds), *Coping and adaptation* (pp. 101–25). New York: Basic Books.

Hardy, I. (2013). A logic of appropriation: enacting national testing (NAPLAN) in Australia. *Journal of Education Policy*, 29(1), 1–18.

Hargreaves, A. & Dawe, R. (1990). Paths of professional development: contrived collegiality, collaborative culture, and the case of peer coaching. *Teaching and Teacher Education*, 6(3), 227–41.

Hargreaves, A. & Earl, L. (1990). *Rights of passage: a review of selected research about schooling in the transition years.* Toronto, Canada: Queen's Printer.

Hargreaves, A. & Fullan, M. (2012). *Professional capital: transforming teaching in every school.* New York: Teachers College, Columbia University.

Hargreaves, D.H. (1994). The new professionalism: the synthesis of professional and institutional development. *Teaching and Teacher Education*, 10(4), 423–38.

Hargreaves, E. (2013). Inquiring into children's experiences of teacher feedback: reconceptualising assessment for learning. *Oxford Review of Education*, 39, 229–46.

Harlen, W. (2004). Can assessment by teachers be a dependable option for summative purposes? Paper presented at the General Teaching Council for England conference, London.

Harlen, W. (2007). *Assessment of learning.* London: Sage.

Harper, D. (2001). *Online etymology dictionary.* Retrieved from www.etymonline.com.

Hascher, T. & Hagenauer, G. (2010). Alienation from school. *International Journal of Educational Research*, 49(6), 220–32.

Hattie, J. (2003). *Teachers make a difference: what is the research evidence?* Sydney: ACER.

Hattie, J. (2009). *Visible learning: a synthesis of over 800 meta-analyses relating to achievement.* London: Routledge.

Hattie, J. & Timperley, H. (2007). The power of feedback. *Review of Educational Research*, 77, 81 112.

Hayes, D., Mills, M., Christie, P. & Lingard, B. (2006). *Teaching and schooling making a difference: productive pedagogies and performance.* Sydney: Allen & Unwin.

Hayward, K. (2013). 'Life stage dissolution' in Anglo American advertising and popular culture: kidults, lil'britneys and middle youths. *Sociological Review*, 61(3), 525–48.

Haywood, K.M. & Getchell, N. (2009). *Life span motor development*, 5th edn. Champaign, IL: Human Kinetics.

Heidegger, M. (1962). *Being and time* (trans. J. Macquarrie & E. Robinson). New York: SCM Press.

Heitink, M.C., Van der Kleij, F.M., Veldkamp, B.P, Schildkamp, K. & Kippers, W.B. (2016). A systematic review of prerequisites for implementing assessment for learning in classroom practice. *Educational Research Review*, 17, 50–62.

Hembree, R. (1990). The nature, effects and relief of mathematics anxiety. *Journal for Research in Mathematics Education*, 21(1), 33–46.

Henderson, A.T. & Mapp, K.L. (2002). *A new wave of evidence: the impact of school, family, and community connections on student achievement.* Annual Synthesis. Austin, TX: National Center for Family and Community Connections with Schools, Southwest Educational Development Laboratory.

Henderson, R. & Lennon, S. (2014). A conversation about research as risky business: making visible the invisible in rural research locations. In S. White & M. Corbett (eds), *Rural methodologies* (pp. 119–34). New York: Routledge.

Hennessey, A. & Dionigi, R. (2013). Implementing cooperative learning in Australian primary schools: generalist teachers' perspectives. *Issues in Educational Research*, 23(1), 52–68.

Herrman, H., Stewart, D.E., Diaz-Granados, N., Berger, E.L., Jackson, B. & Yuen, T. (2011). What is resilience? *Canadian Journal of Psychiatry*, 56(5), 258–65.

REFERENCES

Hester, P., Gable, R.A. & Manning, M.L. (2003). A positive learning environment approach to middle school instruction. *Childhood Education, 79*(3), 130–6.

Hickey, D.T. (2003). Engaged participation vs. marginal non-participation: a stridently sociocultural model of achievement motivation. *Elementary School Journal, 103*, 401–29.

Hill, P. (1995). *The middle years of schooling.* Melbourne: Centre of Applied Research, University of Melbourne.

Hill, S. (2012). *Developing early literacy: teaching and assessment,* 2nd edn. Melbourne: Eleanor Curtain Publishers.

Hilton, A. & Hilton, G. (2013). Incorporating digital technologies into science classes: two case studies from the field. *International Journal of Pedagogies and Learning, 8*(3), 153–68.

Hilton, A., Hilton, G., Dole, S. & Goos, M. (2013). Development and application of a two-tier diagnostic instrument to assess middle years students' proportional reasoning. *Mathematics Education Research Journal, 25*, 523–45.

Hoffnung, M., Hoffnung, R.J., Seifert, K.L., Bruton Smith, R., Hine, A., Ward, L. & Pause, C. (2010). *Lifespan development: a chronological approach,* 2nd edn. Brisbane: John Wiley & Sons.

Holtmann, M., Pörtner, F., Duketis, E., Flechtner, H-H., Angst, J. and Lehmkuhl, G. (2009). Validation of the Hypomania Checklist (HCL-32) in a nonclinical sample of German adolescents. *Journal of Adolescence, 32*(5), 1075–88.

Hong, Z. (2010). Effects of a collaborative science intervention on high achieving students' learning anxiety and attitudes toward science. *International Journal of Science Education, 32*(15), 1971–88.

Hoover, J. & DiSilvestro, R.P. (2005). *The art of constructive confrontation.* Hoboken, NJ: John Wiley & Sons.

Hopson, M.H., Simms, R.L. & Knezek, G.A. (2001–02). Using a technology-enriched environment to improve higher-order thinking skills. *Journal of Research on Computing in Education, 34*(2), 109–19.

Hopwood, B., Hay, I. & Dyment, J. (2016). The transition from primary to secondary school: teachers' perspectives. *Australian Educational Research, 43*: 289–307.

Hoy, A.W., Demerath, P. & Pape, S. (2001). Teaching adolescents: engaging developing selves. In T. Urdan & F. Pajares (eds), *Adolescence and education: general issues in the education of adolescence* (pp. 119–61). Greenwich, CT: Information Age.

Hoy, A.W. & Spero, R.B. (2005). Changes in teacher efficacy during the early years of teaching: a comparison of four measures. *Teacher and Teacher Education, 21*, 343–56.

Hu, J. & Liden, R.C. (2011). Antecedents of team potency and team effectiveness: an examination of goal and process clarity and servant leadership. *Journal of Applied Psychology, 96*(4), 851–62.

Hummer, T.A., Wang, Y., Kronenberger, W.G., Dunn, D.W. & Mathews, V.P. (2015). The relationship of brain structure to age and executive functioning in adolescent disruptive behavior disorder. *Psychiatry Research: Neuroimaging, 231*(3), 210–17.

Hunter, L. & Forrest, N. (2010). Negotiated curriculum. In D. Pendergast & N. Bahr (eds), *Teaching middle years: rethinking curriculum, pedagogy and assessment,* 2nd edn (pp. 205–20). Sydney: Allen & Unwin.

Hurley, G. & Weldon, E. (2004). A culture for thinking and learning. *Education Views, 13*, 8.

Inhelder, B. & Piaget, J. (1958). *The growth of logical reasoning from childhood to adolescence.* New York: Basic Books.

Ito, J.K. & Brotheridge, C.M. (2008). Do teams grow up one stage at a time? Exploring the complexity of group development models. *Team Performance Management, 14*(5–6), 214–32.

Ito, M., Horst, H.A., Bittanti, M., Boyd, D., Herr-Stephenson, B., Lange, P.G., Pascoe, C.J. & Robinson, L. (2008). *Living and learning with new media: summary of findings from the digital youth project.* Retrieved from digitalyouth.ischool.berkeley.edu/report.

Jackson, A.W. & Davis, G.A. (2000). *Turning Points 2000: educating adolescents in the 21st century.* Columbus, OH: National Middle Schools Association.

Jacobs, J.E., Lanza, S., Osgood, D.W., Eccles, J.S. & Wigfield, A. (2002). Changes in children's self-competence and values: gender and domain differences across grades one through twelve. *Child Development*, 73(2), 509–27.

Jakobsson, B.T., Lundvall, S., Redelius, K. & Engström, L.-M. (2012). Almost all start but who continue? A longitudinal study of youth participation in Swedish club sports. *European Physical Education Review*, 18(1), 3–18.

Jalongo, M.R. (2003). The child's right to creative thought and expression. *Childhood Education*, 79, 218–28.

Jarzabkowski, L.M. (2001). The primary school as an emotional arena: a case study in collegial relationships. Unpublished PhD thesis. Canberra: Canberra University.

Jaworska, N. & MacQueen, G. (2015). Adolescence as a unique developmental period. *Journal of Psychiatry & Neuroscience: JPN*, 40(5), 291–3.

Jenkins, J.R., Jewell, M., Leicester, N., O'Connor, R.E., Jenkins, L.M. & Troutner, M.N. (1994). Accommodations for individual differences without classroom ability groups: an experiment in school restructuring. *Exceptional Children*, 60, 344–68.

Jensen, B. (2014). *Making time for great teaching.* Retrieved from grattan.edu.au/wp-content/uploads/2014/03/808-making-time-for-great-teaching.pdf.

Jewitt, C. (2008). Multimodality and literacy in school classrooms. *Review of Research in Education*, 32(1), 241–67.

Johnson, D.W., & Johnson, R.T. (1999). Making cooperative learning work. *Theory into practice*, 38(2), 67–73.

Johnson, D.W. & Johnson, R.T. (2002). Learning together and alone: overview and meta-analysis. *Asia-Pacific Journal of Education*, 22, 95–105.

Johnson, D.W. & Johnson, R.T. (2009). An educational psychology success story: social interdependence theory and cooperative learning. *Educational Researcher*, 38(5), 365–79.

Johnson, D.W., Johnson, R.T. & Smith, K. (2007). The state of cooperative learning in postsecondary and professional settings. *Educational Psychology Review*, 19(1), 15–29.

Johnson, D.W., Maruyama, G., Johnson, R.T., Nelson, D. & Skon, L. (1981). Effects of cooperative, competitive, and individualistic goal structures on achievement: a meta-analysis. *Psychological Bulletin*, 89, 47–62.

Jonassen, D.H. (2000). *Computers as mind tools for schools: engaging critical thinking*, 2nd edn. Upper Saddle River, NJ: Prentice Hall.

Jones, J.E. & Bearley, W.L. (2001). Facilitating team development: a view from the field. *Group Facilitation*, 3 (spring), 56–66.

Jones, V. (2014) Teaching STEAM: 21st century skills. *Child Technology English*, 18(4), 11–13.

Kane, M.T. (2016). Explicating validity. In Validity, ed. P.E. Newton & J.-A. Baird, special issue, *Assessment in Education: Principles, Policy & Practice*, 23, 198–211.

Kaplan, A. (Avi) & Flum, H. (2012). Identity formation in educational settings: a critical focus for education in the 21st century. *Contemporary Educational Psychology*, 37, pp. 171–5.

Kaplan, A.M. (Andreas M.) & Haenlein, M. (2010). Users of the world, unite! The challenges and opportunities of social media. *Business Horizons*, 53(1), 59–68.

Kaplan, J.S. & Carter, J. (1995). *Beyond behavior modification: a cognitive-behavioral approach to behavior management*, 3rd edn. Austin, TX: Pro-Ed.

Katzenbach, J.R., Smith, D.K. & Douglas, K. (1993). *The wisdom of teams.* Boston, MA: Harvard Business Press.

Katz, I., Keeley, M., Spears, B., Taddeo, C., Swirski, T. & Bates, S. (2014). *Research on youth exposure to, and management of, cyberbullying incidents in Australia: synthesis report.* SPRC Report 16/2014. Sydney: Social Policy Research Centre, University of New South Wales.

REFERENCES

Kavas, A.B. (2009). Self-esteem and health-risk behaviors among Turkish late adolescents. *Adolescence*, *44*(173), 187–99.

Kay, R. & Knaack, L. (2009). Exploring the use of audience response systems in secondary school science classrooms. *Journal of Science Education and Technology*, *18*, 382–92.

Keddie, A. & Mills, M. (2007). *Teaching boys: developing classroom practices that work*. Sydney: Allen & Unwin.

Keith, J. (1985). Age in anthropological research. In R.H. Binstock & E. Shanus (eds), *Handbook of aging and the social sciences*, 2nd edn (pp. 231–63). New York: Van Nostrand Reinhold.

Keller, F.S. (1968). 'Good-bye, teacher . . .' *Journal of Applied Behavior Analysis*, *1*, 79–89.

Kemmis, S., Wilkinson, J., Edwards-Groves, C., Hardy, I., Grootenboer, P. & Bristol, L. (2014). *Changing education, changing practices*. Singapore: Springer.

Keshavan, M.S., Giedd, J., Lau, J.Y., Lewis, D.A. & Paus, T. (2014). Changes in the adolescent brain and the pathophysiology of psychotic disorders. *Lancet Psychiatry*, *1*(7), 549–58.

Kilpatrick, J. (2001). Understanding mathematical literacy: the contribution of research. *Educational Studies in Mathematics*, *47*(1), 101–16.

Kilpatrick, S., Barrett, M. & Jones, T. (2003). Defining learning communities. Paper presented at the annual Joint AARE/NZARE conference, Auckland.

Kimber, K. & Wyatt-Smith, C. (2006). Using and creating knowledge with new technologies: a case for students-as-designers. *Learning, Media and Technology*, *31*(1), 19–34.

Kimmel, D.C. & Weiner, I.B. (1985). *Adolescence: a developmental transition*. Hillsdale, NJ: Lawrence Erlbaum.

Kinnunen, J.M., Lindfors, P., Rimpelä, A., Salmelo-Aro, K., Rathmann, K., Perelman, J., Federico, B., Richter, M., Kunst, A.E. & Lorant, V. (2016). Academic well-being and smoking among 14- to 17-year-old schoolchildren in six European cities. *Journal of Adolescence*, *50*, 56–64.

Kist, W. (2012). Middle schools and new literacies: looking back and moving forward. *Voices from the Middle*, *19*(4), 17–21.

Kist, W. (2014). *The global school: connecting classrooms and students around the world*. Bloomington, IN: Solution Tree Press.

Klassen, R.M., Tze, V.M., Betts, S.M. & Gordon, K.A. (2011). Teacher efficacy research, 1998–2009: signs of progress or unfulfilled promise? *Educational Psychology Review*, *23*(1), 21–43.

Klenowski, V. (2009). Assessment for learning revisited: an Asia-Pacific perspective. *Assessment in Education: Principles, Policy & Practice*, *16*, 263–8.

Klenowski, V. & Wyatt-Smith, C. (2014). *Assessment for education: standards, judgement and moderation*. Thousand Oaks, CA: Sage.

Kline, L.W. (1995). A baker's dozen: effective instructional strategies. In R.W. Cole (ed.), *Educating everybody's children: diverse teaching strategies for diverse learners* (pp. 21–45). Alexandria, VA: Association for Supervision and Curriculum Development.

Kloep, M., Güney, N., Çok, F. & Simsek, O.F. (2009). Motives for risk-taking in adolescence: a cross-cultural study. *Journal of Adolescence*, *32*(1), 135–51.

Kluger, A.N. & DeNisi, A. (1996). The effects of feedback interventions on performance: a historical review, a meta-analysis, and a preliminary feedback intervention theory. *Psychological Bulletin*, *119*, 254–84.

Kluth, P. & Danaher, S. (2010). *From tutor scripts to talking sticks: 100 ways to differentiate instruction in K–12 inclusive classrooms*. Baltimore, MD: Brookes Publishing.

Knowles, A.-M., Niven, A.G., Fawkner, S.G. & Henretty, J.M. (2009). A longitudinal examination of the influence of maturation on physical self-perceptions and the relationship with physical activity in early adolescent girls. *Journal of Adolescence*, *32*(3), 555–66.

Knowles, M.S. (1975). *Self-directed learning: a guide for learners and teachers*. Englewood Cliffs, NJ: Prentice Hall.

Kochanska, G. & Murray, K.T. (2000). Mother–child mutually responsive orientation and conscience development: from toddler to early school age. *Child Development*, *71*, 417–31.

Koehler, M.J. & Mishra, P. (2009). What is technological pedagogical content knowledge? *Contemporary Issues in Technology and Teacher Education, 9*(1), 60–70.

Kohlberg, L. (1986). A current statement on some theoretical issues. In S. Modgil & C. Modgil (eds), *Lawrence Kohlberg: consensus and controversy* (pp. 485–586). Philadelphia, PA: Falmer.

Kolb, B. (2013). *Brain plasticity and behavior.* New Jersey: Lawrence Erlbaum Associates.

Konza, D. (2014). Why the 'fab five' should be the 'big six'. *Australian Journal of Teacher Education, 39*(12), doi:10.14221/ajte.2014v39n12.10.

Kose, S., Sahin, A., Ergun, A. & Gezer, K. (2010). The effects of cooperative learning experience on eighth grade students' achievement and attitude toward science. *Education, 131*(1), 169–82.

Krieger, N., Kiang, M.V., Kosheleva, A., Waterman, P.D., Chen, J.T. & Beckfield, J. (2015). Age at menarche: 50-year socioeconomic trends among US-born black and white women. *American Journal of Public Health, 105*(2), 388–97.

Kronborg, L. & Plunkett, M. (2008). Curriculum differentiation: an innovative Australian secondary school program to extend academic talent. *Australasian Journal of Gifted Education, 17*(1), 19–29.

Kulik, J.A., Kulik, C.L.C. & Cohen, P.A. (1979). A meta-analysis of outcome studies of Keller's personalized system of instruction. *American Psychologist, 34*(4), 307–18.

Kwok Lai, S.Y.C. & Shek, D.T.L. (2009). Social problem solving, family functioning, and suicidal ideation among Chinese adolescents in Hong Kong. *Adolescence, 44*(174), 391–407.

Laal, M. & Ghodsi, S. (2012). Benefits of collaborative learning. *Procedia—Social and Behavioral Sciences, 31,* 486–90.

Laban-Eurolab (n.d.). *Laban/Bartenieff Movement Studies Theory.* Retrieved from www.laban-eurolab.org/english/lbms/theory/.

Langberg, J., Epstein, J., Altaye, M., Molina, B., Arnold, L. & Vitiello, B. (2008). The transition to middle school is associated with changes in the developmental trajectory of ADHD symptomatology in young adolescents with ADHD. *Journal Clinical Child Adolescent Psychology, 37*(3): 651–63.

Langton, T.W. (2007). Applying Laban's movement framework in elementary physical education. *Journal of Physical Education, Recreation and Dance, 78*(1), 17–53.

Lannegrand-Willems, L. & Bosma, H.A. (2006). Identity development-in-context: the school as an important context for identity development. *Identity: An International Journal of Theory and Research, 6*(1), 85–113.

Lave, J. (1996). Teaching, as learning, in practice. *Mind, culture, and activity, 3*(3), 149–64.

Layard, R. (2007). Happiness and the teaching of values. *CentrePiece, 12*(1), 18–23.

Layne, T. & Hastie, P. (2015). A task analysis of a sport education physical education season for fourth grade students. *Physical Education and Sport Pedagogy, 20*(3), 314–28.

Leahy, D., O'Flynn, G. & Wright, J. (2013). A critical 'critical inquiry' proposition in health and physical education. *Asia-Pacific Journal of Health, Sport and Physical Education, 4*(2), 175–87.

Lee, Y.-C. & Sun, Y.C. (2009). Using instant messaging to enhance the interpersonal relationships of Taiwanese adolescents: evidence from quantile regression analysis. *Adolescence, 44*(173), 199–209.

Lefrancois, G.R. (1976). *Adolescents.* Belmont, CA: Wadsworth.

Legault, L., Green-Demers, I. & Pelletier, L. (2006). Why do high school students lack motivation in the classroom? Toward an understanding of academic amotivation and the role of social support. *Journal of Educational Psychology, 98*(3), 567–82.

Lennon, S. (2009). A one year journey in the life of a literacy project officer: learning about boys and motivating others. *Literacy Learning: The Middle Years, 17*(2), 46–52.

Lennon, S. (2015) *Unsettling research: using critical praxis and activism to create uncomfortable spaces.* Critical Qualitative Research. New York: Peter Lang.

Lenroot, R.K. & Giedd, J. (2006). Brain development in children and adolescents: insights from anatomical magnetic resonance imaging. *Neuroscience and Behavioral Reviews, 30*(6), 718–29.

REFERENCES

Lerner, R.M. & Benson, P.L. (2003). *Developmental assets and asset building communities: implications for research, policy, and practice.* Norwell, MA: Kluwer Academic.

Letendre, G.K. (2000). *Learning to be adolescent.* New Haven, CT: Yale University Press.

Levin, D. & Mee, M. (2016). *Achieving the vision of 'This we believe': how middle schools can meet the essential attributes of middle level education.* Retrieved from www.amle.org/BrowsebyTopic/WhatsNew/WNDet/TabId/270/ArtMID/888/ArticleID/615/Achieving-the-Vision-of-This-We-Believe.aspx.

Lewin, K. (1946). Action research and minority problems. *Journal of Social Issues, 2*(4), 34–46.

Lewis, A. & Smith, D. (1993). Defining higher order thinking. *Theory into Practice, 32*(3), 131–7.

Li, M.P. & Lam, B.H. (2013). *Cooperative learning.* Retrieved from www.ied.edu.hk/aclass/Theories/cooperativelearningcoursewriting_LBH%2024June.pdf.

Lin, E. (2006). Cooperative learning in the science classroom. *Science Teacher, 73*(5), 34–9.

Lingard, B., Ladwig, J.A., Mills, M., Bahr, N., Chant, D. & Warry, M. (2001). *Queensland School Reform Longitudinal Study.* Brisbane: Education Queensland.

Lingard, B., Thompson, G. & Sellar, S. (2016). National testing from an Australian perspective. In B. Lingard, G. Thompson & S. Sellar (eds), *National testing in schools: an Australia assessment* (pp. 1–17). Oxfordshire: Routledge.

Linley, P.A. & Proctor, C. (2013). *Research, applications, and interventions for children and adolescents: a positive psychology perspective.* Dordrecht and New York: Springer.

Lippman, P.C. (2010). *Evidence-based design of elementary and secondary schools.* New York: Wiley.

Liu, J., Raine, A., Wuerker, A., Venables, P.H. & Mednick, S. (2009). The association of birth complications and externalizing behavior in early adolescents: direct and mediating effects. *Journal of Research on Adolescence, 19*(1), 93–111.

Lounsbury, J.H. (1997). Foreword. In J.L. Irvin (ed.), *What current research says to the middle level practitioner* (p. xi). Columbus, OH: National Middle School Association.

Luckin, R., Clark, W., Graber, R., Logan, K., Mee, A. & Oliver, M. (2009). Do Web 2.0 tools really open the door for learning? Practices perceptions and profiles of 11–16-year-old students. *Learning, Media and Technology, 34*(2), 87–104.

Luke, A. (2002). Beyond science and ideology critique: developments in critical discourse analysis. *Annual Review of Applied Linguistics, 22*, 96–110.

Luke, A., Elkins, J., Weir, K., Land, R., Carrington, V., Dole, S., Pendergast, D., Kapitzke, C., van Kraayenoord, C., Moni, K., McIntosh, A., Mayer, D., Bahr, M., Hunter, L., Chadbourne, R., Bean, T., Alverman, D. & Stevens, L. (2003). *Beyond the middle: a report about literacy and numeracy development of target group students in the middle years of schooling* (Vol. 1). Brisbane: J.S. McMillan Printing Group.

Luke, A. & Freebody, P. (1999a). *Further notes on the four resources model.* Retrieved from www.reading-online.org/past/past_index.asp?HREF=/research/lukefreebody.html.

Luke, A. & Freebody, P. (1999b). A map of possible practices: further notes on the four resources model. *Practically Primary, 4*(2), 5–8.

Lupton, D. (2012). M-health and health promotion: the digital cyborg and surveillance society. *Social Theory and Health, 10*, 229–44.

Luthar, S.S. & Zelazo, L.B. (2003). Research on resilience: an integrative view. In S.S. Luthar (ed.), *Resilience and vulnerability: adaptation in the context of childhood adversities* (pp. 104–29). Cambridge, United Kingdom: Cambridge University Press.

Lyons, Ford & Slee 2014

McCandless, B.R. (1970). *Adolescents.* Hinsdale, IL: Dryden.

McCuaig, L., Quennerstedt, M. & Macdonald, D. (2013). A salutogenic, strengths-based approach as a theory to guide HPE curriculum change. *Asia Pacific Journal of Health, Sport and Physical Education, 4*(2), 109–25.

Macdonald, D. (2011). Like a fish in water: physical education policy and practice in the era of neoliberal globalization. *Quest, 63*(1), 36–45.

Macdonald, D. (2013). The new Australian health and physical education curriculum: a case of/for gradualism in curriculum reform? *Asia Pacific Journal of Health, Sport and Physical Education, 4*(2), 95–108.

Macdonald, D. (2014). Is global neo-liberalism shaping the future of physical education? *Physical Education and Sport Pedagogy, 19*(5), 494–9.

McDonald, T. (2013). *Classroom management: engaging students in learning.* 2nd edn. Australia: Oxford University Press.

McEwin, C. & Greene, M. (2011). *The status of programs and practices in America's middle schools: results from two national studies.* Westervill, OH: Association for Middle Level Education.

McInnerney, J.M. & Roberts, T.S. (2004). Collaborative or cooperative learning? In T.S. Roberts (ed.), *Online collaborative learning: theory and practice* (pp. 203–14). Hershey, PA: Information Science Publishing.

McKendree, J., Small, C., Stenning, K. & Conlon, T. (2002). The role of representation in teaching and learning critical thinking. *Educational Review, 54*(1), 57–67.

McLaine, J. & Dowden, T. (2011). Accommodating environmental controversies in the classroom curriculum: too hot to handle or opportunities for deep learning? *Social Educator, 29*(2), 22–9.

McMahon, F.R. (2007). *Not just child's play: emerging tradition and the lost boys of Sudan.* Jackson, MS: University Press of Mississippi.

McMillan, I. (2007). The irresistible art of video: implementing digital video in middle years art. Master's thesis. Manitoba: University of Manitoba.

McTighe, J. & O'Connor, K. (2005). Seven practices for effective learning. *Educational Leadership, 63*(3), 10–17.

Magnifico, A., Lammers, J. & Curwood, J. (2015). Analyzing the contributions of reviewers to online fanfiction writing. Paper presented at the annual meeting of the American Educational Research Association, Chicago, IL.

Main, K. (2007). A year long study of the formation and development of middle school teaching teams. Unpublished PhD thesis. Brisbane: Griffith University.

Main, K. (2012). Effective middle school teacher teams: a ternary model of interdependency rather than a catch phrase. *Teachers and Teaching: Theory and Practice, 18*, 75–88.

Main, K. (2013). Australian middle years reform: a focus on teachers and leaders as the subjects and agents of change. In I.R. Haslam, M.S. Khine & I.M. Saleh (eds), *Large scale reform and social capital building: the professional development imperative* (pp. 180–97). London: Routledge.

Main, K. (2016a). Cooperative learning. In S. Mertens, M. Caskey & N. Flowers (eds), *The encyclopaedia of middle grades education,* 2nd edn (p. 106). Charlotte, NC: Information Age Publishing.

Main, K. (2016b). Australian middle years reform. In I.R. Haslam & M.S. Khine (eds), *Leveraging social capital in systemic education reform* (pp. 97–113). Rotterdam: SensePublishers.

Main, K. & Bryer, F. (2005a). What does a 'good' teaching team look like in a middle school classroom? In B. Bartlett, F. Bryer & D. Roebuck (eds), *Stimulating the 'action' as participants in participatory research. Proceedings of the 3rd International Conference on Cognition, Language, and Special Education* (pp. 196–204). Brisbane: Griffith University.

Main, K. & Bryer, F. (2005b). Researching middle school: an Australian perspective. In D. Pendergast & N. Bahr (eds), *Teaching middle years: rethinking curriculum, pedagogy and assessment* (pp. 88–99). Sydney: Allen & Unwin.

Main, K. & Bryer, F. (2007). A framework for research into Australian middle school practice. *Australian Educational Researcher, 34*(2), 91–105.

Main, K., Bryer, F. & Grimbeek, P. (2004). Forging relationships: an integral feature of middle schooling practice. *Australian Journal of Middle Schooling, 4*(2), 8–17.

Main, K. & Whatman, S. (2016). Building social and emotional efficacy to (re) engage young adolescents: capitalising on the 'window of opportunity'. *International Journal of Inclusive Education, 20(10),* 1–16.

Malti, T. & Ongley, S.F. (2014). The development of moral emotions and moral reasoning. In M. Killen & J.G. Smetana (eds), *Handbook of moral development*, 2nd edn (pp. 163–83). New York: Psychology Press.

Manning, L. (1993). *Developmentally appropriate middle level schools*. Olney, MD: Association for Childhood Education International.

Mansell, W., James, M. & Assessment Reform Group (2009) *Assessment in schools. Fit for purpose? A commentary by the Teaching and Learning Research Programme*. London: Teaching and Learning Research Programme, Economic and Social Research Council.

Marcia, J.E. (1980). Identity in adolescence. In J. Adelson (ed.), *Handbook of adolescent psychology* (pp. 159–87). New York: John Wiley.

Marks, M.A., Mathieu, J.E. & Zaccaro, S.J. (2001). A temporally based framework and taxonomy of team processes. *Academy of Management Review, 26*(3), 356–75.

Marshall, J.C. & Horton, R.M. (2011). The relationship of teacher-facilitated, inquiry-based instruction to student higher-order thinking. *School Science and Mathematics, 111*(13), 93–101.

Marsh, H., Craven, R. & Debus, R. (2000). Separation of competency and affect components of multiple dimensions of academic self-concept: a developmental perspective. *Merril Palmer Quarterly, 45*, 567–601.

Martin, A.J. (2013). *From will to skill: the psychology of motivation, instruction and learning in today's classroom*. Retrieved from www.psychology.org.au/inpsych/2013/december/martin.

Martin, A.J. (2015). Teaching academically at risk students in middle school: the roles of explicit instruction and guided discovery learning. In S. Groundwater-Smith & N. Mockler (eds), *Big fish, little fish: teaching and learning in the middle years* (pp. 29–39). Melbourne: Cambridge University Press.

Martin, A.J. & Dowson, M. (2009). Interpersonal relationships, motivation, engagement, and achievement: yields for theory, current issues, and educational practice. *Review of Educational Research, 79*(1), 327–65.

Maslow, A.H. (1943). A theory of human motivation. *Psychological Review, 50*(4), pp. 370–96.

Maslow, A.H. (1954). *Motivation and personality*. New York: Harper & Row.

Maslow, A.H. (1968). *Toward a psychology of being*. New York: D. Van Nostrand.

Mason, M.J. & Korpela, K. (2009). Activity spaces and urban adolescent substance use and emotional health. *Journal of Adolescence, 32*(4), 925–39.

Masten, A.S. (1999). Resilience comes of age: reflections on the past and outlook for the next generation of research. In M.D. Glantz & J.L. Johnson (eds), *Resilience and development: positive life adaptations* (pp. 281–96). New York: Kluwer Academic.

Masten, A.S. (2003). Commentary: developmental psychopathology as a unifying context for mental health and education models, research, and practice in schools. *School Psychology Review, 32*(2), 169–74.

Masters, G.N. (2013). *Reforming educational assessment: imperatives, principles and challenges*. Retrieved from research.acer.edu.au/cgi/viewcontent.cgi?article=1021&context=aer.

Matters, G. (2004). Variations on a theme by Paganini. *Curriculum Perspectives, 24*(1), 58–60.

Maxwell, G. (2001). *Moderation of assessments in vocational education and training*. Brisbane: Queensland Department of Employment and Training.

Maxwell, G. (2007). *Implications for moderation of proposed changes to senior secondary school syllabuses*. Paper commissioned by the Queensland Studies Authority. Brisbane: Queensland Studies Authority.

Maxwell, J. (1983). Failures in mathematics: causes and remedies. *Mathematics in School, 12*(2), 8–11.

Mead, M. (1935). *Sex and temperament in three primitive societies*. New York: William Morrow.

Meckbach, J., Gibbs, B., Almqvist, J. & Quennerstedt, M. (2014). Wii teach movement qualities in physical education. *Sport Science Review, 23*(5), 241–66.

Mendler, A. (2005). *Power struggles: successful techniques for educators*. Bloomington, IN: Solution Tree.

Merrell, K.W. & Gimpel, G. (2014). *Social skills of children and adolescents: conceptualization, assessment, treatment.* New York: Psychology Press.

Mertens, S.B., Flowers, N., Anfara, V.A. Jr & Caskey, M.M. (2010). Common planning time. *Middle School Journal*, 41(5), 50–7.

Mesch, G.S. (2009). Social bonds and internet pornographic exposure among adolescents. *Journal of Adolescence*, 32(3), 601–18.

Messick, S. (1989). Validity. In R.L. Linn (ed.), *Educational measurement*, 3rd edn (pp. 13–103). New York: Macmillan.

Messick, S. (1994). The interplay of evidence and consequences in the validation of performance assessment. *Educational Researcher*, 23(2), 13–23.

Meyer, M. & Fennema, E. (1992). Girls, boys and mathematics. In T.R. Post (ed.), *Teaching mathematics in grades K–8: research-based methods* (pp. 443–64). Boston, MA: Allyn & Bacon.

Middle Years of Schooling Association *see* MYSA.

Mills, K.A. (2015). *Literacy theories for the digital age: social, critical, multimodal, spatial, material and sensory lenses.* Bristol, United Kingdom: Multilingual Matters.

Ministerial Council on Education, Employment, Training and Youth Affairs, Student Learning and Support Services Taskforce (2008). *Melbourne declaration on educational goals for young Australians.* Canberra: Ministerial Council on Education, Employment, Training and Youth Affairs.

Ministerial Council on Education, Employment, Training and Youth Affairs (2011).

Mishra, P. & Koehler, M. (2006). Technological pedagogical content knowledge: a framework for teacher knowledge. *Teachers College Record*, 108(6), 1017–54.

Moje, E.B. (2002). Re-framing adolescent literacy research for new times: studying youth as a resource. *Reading Research and Instruction*, 41(3), 211–28.

Moje, E.B., Luke, A., Davies, B. & Street, B. (2009). Literacy and identity: examining the metaphors in history and contemporary research. *Reading Research Quarterly*, 44(4), 415–37.

Moje, E.B., McIntosh Ciechanowski, K., Kramer, K., Ellis, L., Carrillo, R. & Collazo, T. (2004). Working toward third space in content area literacy: an examination of everyday funds of knowledge and discourse. *Reading Research Quarterly*, 39(1), 38–71.

Moll, L.C., Amanti, C., Neff, D. & Gonzalez, N. (1992). Funds of knowledge for teaching: using a qualitative approach to connect homes and classrooms. In Qualitative issues in educational research, ed. S. Chandler, special issue, *Theory into Practice*, 31(2), 132–41.

Molyneux, P. & Godinho, S. (2012). 'This is my thing!' Middle years students' engagement and learning using digital resources. *Australasian Journal of Educational Technology*, 28(8), 1466–86.

Monahan, K.C. & Booth-LaForce, C. (2016). Deflected pathways: becoming aggressive, socially withdrawn, or prosocial with peers during the transition to adolescence. *Journal of Research on Adolescence*, 26(2), 9–12.

Money, J. & Ehrhardt, A. (1972). *Man and woman, boy and girl.* Baltimore, MD: Johns Hopkins University Press.

Moshman, D. (2005). *Adolescent psychological development: rationality, morality, and identity.* Hillsdale, NJ: Laurence Erlbaum.

Mourshed, M., Chijioke, C. & Barber, M. (2010). *How the world's most improved school systems keep getting better.* Retrieved from mckinseyonsociety.com/how-the-worlds-most-improved-school-systems-keep-getting-better.

Murphy, C. (2003). *Literature review in primary science and ICT (no. 5).* Bristol, United Kingdom: Futurelab.

Myhre, O., Popejoy, K. & Carney, J. (2006). Conditions for technology acceptance in intermediate and middle school mathematics. In C. Crawford, R. Carlsen, K. McFerrin, J. Price, R. Weber & D. Willis (eds), *Proceedings of Society for Information Technology & Teacher Education International Conference 2006* (pp. 1001–5). Chesapeake, VA: Association for the Advancement of Computing in Education.

MYSA (Middle Years of Schooling Association) (2008). *MYSA position paper: middle schooling; people, practices and places*. Brisbane: MYSA.

Nagata, K. & Ronkowski, S. (1998). *Collaborative learning: differences between collaborative and cooperative learning*. Santa Barbara, CA: Office of Instructional Consultation, University of California, Santa Barbara.

Nagel, M.C. (2007). Cognition, emotion, cognitive commotion: understanding the interplay of emotion stress and learning in adolescents. *Australian Journal of Middle Schooling, 7*(2), 11–16.

Nagel, M.C. (2013). Student learning. In R. Churchill, P. Ferguson, S. Godinho, N.F. Johnson, A. Keddie, W. Letts & J. Mackay (eds), *Teaching: making a difference*, 2nd edn (pp. 74–111). Sydney: John Wiley & Sons.

Nagel, M.C. (2014). *In the middle: the adolescent brain, behaviour and learning*. Melbourne: ACER.

Nalkur, P. (2009). Adolescent hopefulness in Tanzania. *Journal of Adolescent Research, 24*(6), 668–90.

National Middle School Association (2001). *This we believe—and now we must act*. Westerville, OH: National Middle School Association.

National Middle School Association (2003). *This we believe: successful schools for young adolescents*. Westerville, OH: National Middle School Association.

National Middle School Association (2010). *This we believe: keys to educating young adolescents*. Westerville, OH: National Middle School Association.

National Reading Panel (2000). *Teaching children to read: an evidence-based assessment of the scientific research literature on reading and its implications for reading instruction*. Washington, DC: National Institute of Child Health and Human Development.

Natsuaki, M.N., Biehl, M.C. & Xiaojia, G. (2009). Trajectories of depressed mood from early adolescence to young adulthood: the effects of pubertal timing and adolescent dating. *Journal of Research on Adolescence, 19*(1), 47–74.

Neill, A. (1960). *Summerhill: a radical approach to child-rearing*. London: Penguin.

Nesin, G. & Lounsbury, J. (1999). *Curriculum integration: twenty questions—with answers*. Atlanta, GA: Georgia Middle School Association.

Newton, P.E. & Shaw, S.D. (2014). *Validity in educational and psychological assessment*. London: Sage.

Nichols, S.L. & Berliner, D.C. (2007). *Collateral damage: how high-stakes testing corrupts America's schools*. Cambridge, MA: Harvard Education Press.

Nitzberg, J. (2012). A community education approach to youth work education. In D. Fusco (ed.), *Advancing youth work: current trends, critical questions* (pp. 190–203). New York: Routledge.

Niu, H.-J. & Wang, Y.-D. (2009). Work experience effect on idolatry and the impulsive buying tendencies of adolescents. *Adolescence, 44*(173), 233–44.

Noble, T., Wyatt, T., McGrath, H., Roffey, S. & Rowling, L. (2008a). *Scoping study into approaches to student wellbeing: final report*. Canberra: ACU and Erebus International.

Noble, T., Wyatt, T., McGrath, H., Roffey, S. & Rowling, L. (2008b). *Scoping study into approaches to student wellbeing: literature review*. Canberra: ACU and Erebus International.

Nolan, C.J.P. & McKinnon, D.H. (2003). Enhancing the middle in a New Zealand secondary school: integration, experiential learning, and computer use. *International Journal of Educational Reform, 12*(3), 230–43.

Nolan, P., Brown, M., Stewart, D. & Beane, J. (2000). Middle schools for New Zealand: a direction for the future. *Median, 6*, 4–6.

Noss, R. (1998). New numeracies of a technological culture. *For the Learning of Mathematics, 18*(2), 2–12.

O'Brien, M., Blue, L. & Rowlands, D. (2016). My best possible learning self: primary school children's perspectives on happiness and success in the classroom. Unpublished manuscript.

O'Brien, M. & Dole, S. (2012). Pre-service learning and the (gentle) disruption of emerging teaching identity. In J. Faulkner (ed.), *Disrupting pedagogies in the knowledge society: countering conservative norms with creative approaches* (pp. 161–73). Hershey, PA: IGI Global.

O'Brien, M., Makar, K. & Fielding-Wells, J. (2014). Characterising positive learner identities in inquiry mathematics classrooms. Paper presented at the annual Joint AARE/NZARE conference, Brisbane.

O'Brien, T.C. (1999). Parrot math. *Phi Delta Kappan, 80*(6), 434–8.

O'Connor, J. (2015). *Putting the propositions into practice.* Retrieved from www.achper.org.au/blog/blog-putting-the-propositions-into-practice.

O'Connor, K.L., Dolphin, L., Fitzgerald, A. & Dooley, B. (2016). Modelling problem behaviors in a nationally representative sample of adolescents. *Journal of Adolescence, 50*, 6–15.

OECD (Organisation for Economic Co-operation and Development) (2000). *Special needs education: statistics and indicators.* Paris: OECD Centre for Educational Research and Innovation.

OECD (Organisation for Economic Co-operation and Development) (2004). *Learning for tomorrow's world: first results from PISA 2003.* Paris: OECD.

OECD (Organisation for Economic Co-operation and Development) (2011). *Building a high-quality teaching profession: lessons from around the world.* Retrieved from dx.doi.org/10.1787/9789264113046-en.

OECD (Organisation for Economic Co-operation and Development) (2015a). *Education policy outlook 2015: making reforms happen.* Retrieved from www.oecd-ilibrary.org/education/education-policy-outlook-2015_9789264225442-en.

OECD (Organisation for Economic Co-operation and Development) (2015b). *Skills for social progress: the power of social and emotional skills.* OECD Skills Studies. Paris: OECD Publishing.

Offer, D. & Schonert-Reichl, K.A. (1992). Debunking the myths of adolescence: findings from recent research. *Journal of the American Academy of Child and Adolescent Psychiatry, 31*(6), 1003–14.

Öhman, M., Almqvist, J., Meckbach, J. & Quennerstedt, M. (2014). Competing for ideal bodies: a study of exergames used as teaching aids in schools. *Critical Public Health, 24*(2), 196–209.

Oliver, R. & Herrington, J. (2003). Exploring technology-mediated learning from a pedagogical perspective. *Interactive Learning Environments, 11*(2), 111–16.

Organisation for Economic Co-operation and Development *see* OECD.

O'Tuel, F.S. & Bullard, R.K. (1995). *Developing higher order thinking in the content areas K–12.* Highett: Hawker Brownlow Education.

Padilla-Walker, L.M. & Bean, R.A. (2009). Negative and positive peer influence: relations to positive and negative behaviors for African American, European American, and Hispanic adolescents. *Journal of Adolescence, 32*(2), 323–37.

Palmer, J.A, (2001). *Fifty modern thinkers of education.* New York: Routledge.

Pang, B. (2014). Promoting physical activity in Hong Kong Chinese young people: factors influencing their subjective task values and expectancy beliefs in physical activity. *European Physical Education Review, 20*(3), 385–97.

Pang, B. & Macdonald, D. (2016). Understanding young Chinese Australian's (dis)engagement in health and physical education and school sport. *Physical Education and Sport Pedagogy, 21*(4), 441–58.

Park, S., Kim, H. & Kim, H. (2009). Relationships between parental alcohol abuse and social support, peer substance abuse risk and social support, and substance abuse risk among South Korean adolescents. *Adolescence, 44*(173), 87–100.

Parr, N.J., Zeman, J., Braunstein, K. & Price, N. (2016). Peer emotion socialization and somatic complaints in adolescents. *Journal of Adolescence, 50*, 22–30.

Payton, J., Weissberg, R.P., Durlak, J.A., Dymnicki, A.B., Taylor, R.D., Schellinger, K.B. & Pachan, M. (2008). *The positive impact of social and emotional learning for kindergarten to eighth-grade students: findings from three scientific reviews.* Technical report. Chicago, IL: Collaborative for Academic, Social, and Emotional Learning (NJ1).

Pearce, M., Campbell-Evans, G. & Gray, J. (2010). Capacity to be inclusive: secondary teachers' perspective. *Special Education Perspectives, 19*(1), 15–27.

Pendergast, D. (2005). The emergence of middle schooling. In D. Pendergast & N. Bahr (eds), *Teaching middle years: rethinking curriculum, pedagogy and assessment* (pp. 3–20). Sydney: Allen & Unwin.

Pendergast, D. (2006). Fast-tracking middle schooling reform: a model for sustainability. *Australian Journal of Middle Schooling, 6*(2), 13–18.

Pendergast, D. (2015). Teacher identity in the middle years. In S. Groundwater-Smith & N. Mockler (eds), *Big fish, little fish: teaching and learning in the middle years* (pp. 207–19). Sydney: Cambridge University Press.

Pendergast, D. & Bahr, N. (eds) (2010). *Teaching middle years: rethinking curriculum, pedagogy and assessment*, 2nd edn. Sydney: Allen & Unwin.

Pendergast, D., Flanagan, R., Land, R., Bahr, M., Mitchell, J., Weir, K., Noblett, G., Cain, M., Misich, T., Carrington, V. & Smith, J. (2005). *Developing lifelong learners in the middle years of schooling*. Canberra: Ministerial Council on Education, Employment, Training and Youth Affairs.

Pendergast, D. & Garvis, S. (2015). Early and middle years of schooling. In A. Ashman (ed.), *Education for inclusion and diversity*, 5th edn (pp. 300–31). Kuala Lumpur, Malaysia: Pearson.

Pendergast, D. & Main, K. (2013). The Middle Years of Schooling Association's representations of young adolescents: particularising the adolescent. *Social Alternatives, 32*(2), 25–30.

Pendergast, D., Main, K., Kanasa, H., Barton, G., Hearfield, S., Geelan, D. & Dowden, T. (2014a). *Junior Secondary Leading Change Development Program: digital resource package*. Brisbane: Griffith University.

Pendergast, D., Main, K., Kanasa, H., Barton, G., Hearfield, S., Geelan, D. & Dowden, T. (2014b). *An ongoing journey: evaluation of the Junior Secondary Leading Change Development Program*. Brisbane: Queensland Department of Education and Training.

Pendergast, D., Nichols, K. & Honan, E. (2012). Integrated curriculum: building an evidence base of effectiveness in middle year classrooms. *Australian Journal of Middle Schooling, 12*(1), 12–20.

Pendergast, D., Whitehead, K., De Jong, T., Newhouse-Maiden, L. & Bahr, N. (2007). Middle years teacher education: new programs and research directions. *Australian Educational Researcher, 34*(2), 73–90.

Penney, D. & Chandler, T. (2000). Physical education: what future(s)? *Sport, Education and Society, 5*, 71–87.

Perry, B. & Fulcher, J. (2003). A whole school approach to the provision of mathematics for low-achieving girls in a secondary school. In L. Bragg, C. Campbell, G. Herbert & J. Mousley (eds), *Mathematics education research: innovation, networking, opportunity. Proceedings of the twenty-sixth annual conference of the Mathematics Education Research Group of Australasia* (pp. 570–8). Geelong: Deakin University.

Perry, B. & Howard, P. (2000). *Evaluation of the impact of the Counting On Program: final report*. Sydney: NSW Department of Education and Training.

Petersen, J.L. & Hyde, J.S. (2009). A longitudinal investigation of peer sexual harassment victimization in adolescence. *Journal of Adolescence, 32*(5), 1173–88.

Peterson, C. (2006). *A primer in positive psychology*. New York: Oxford University Press.

Petrie, K. (2016). Architectures of practice: constraining or enabling PE in primary schools. *Education 3-13*, doi:10.1080/03004279.2016.1169484.

Piaget, J. (1955). *The construction of reality in the child* (trans. M. Cook). London: Routledge & Kegan Paul.

Piaget, J. (1964). Part I: cognitive development in children: Piaget development and learning. *Journal of research in science teaching, 2*(3), 176–86.

Popham, J. (2011). *Transformative assessment in action: an inside look at applying the process*. Alexandria, VA: Association for Supervision and Curriculum Development.

Portzky, G., Audenaert, K. & van Heeringen, K. (2009). Psychosocial and psychiatric factors associated with adolescent suicide: a case–control psychological autopsy study. *Journal of Adolescence, 32*(4), 849–62.

Poskitt, J. (2011). New Zealand intermediate school student insights about engagement in learning. *Australian Journal of Middle Schooling*, *11*(1), 12–20.

Pounder, D.G. (1999). Teacher teams: exploring job characteristics and work-related outcomes of work group enhancement. *Educational Administration Quarterly*, *35*(3), 317–48.

Prensky, M. (2014). The world needs a new curriculum. *Educational Technology*, *54*(4), 3–15.

Prestridge, S. (2012). The beliefs behind the teacher that influences their ICT practices. *Computers & Education*, *58* (1), 449–58.

Prestridge, S. & de Aldama, C. (2016). A classification framework for exploring technology-enabled practice-frame TEP. *Journal of Educational Computing Research*. doi:10.1177/0735633116636767.

Prior, J. (2014). Love, engagement, support, and consistency: a recipe for classroom management. *Childhood Education*, *90*(1), 68–70.

Project Tomorrow (2016a). *From print to pixel: the role of videos, games, animations and simulations within K–12 education*. Retrieved from www.tomorrow.org/speakup/pdfs/SU15AnnualReport. pdf.

Project Tomorrow (2016b). *Ten things everyone should know about K–12 students' digital learning*. Retrieved from www.tomorrow.org/speakup/pdfs/10things_students2015.pdf.

Project Tomorrow (2016c). *What do parents really think about digital learning?* Retrieved from www. tomorrow.org/speakup/pdfs/10things_students2015.pdf.

Puzio, K. & Colby, G. (2013). Cooperative learning and literacy: a meta-analytic review. *Journal of Research on Educational Effectiveness*, *6*(4), 339–60.

Queensland Curriculum and Assessment Authority (2015). *Higher-order thinking*. Retrieved from www.qcaa.qld.edu.au/p-10/transition-school/continuity-curriculum-pedagogies/higher-order-thinking.

Queensland Government (2015). *Year 7 is moving to high school*. Retrieved from www.qld.gov.au/education/schools/programs/pages/year7.html.

Quennerstedt, M. (2010). Physical education in New Zealand and Sweden: good or bad for students' health? *New Zealand Physical Educator*, *43*(2), 7–11.

Radencish, M.C. & McKay, L.J. (1995). *Flexible grouping for literacy in the elementary grades*. Boston, MA: Allyn & Bacon.

Ramirez, J.M. (2003). Hormones and aggression in childhood and adolescence. *Aggression and Violent Behavior*, *8*(5), 621–44.

Redmond, G., Skattebol, J., Saunders, P., Lietz, P., Zizzo, G., O'Grady, E., Tobin, M., Thomson, S., Maurici, V., Huynh, J., Moffat, A., Wong, M., Bradbury, B. & Roberts, K. (2016). *Are the kids alright? Young Australians in their middle years: final report of the Australian Child Wellbeing Project*. Retrieved from australianchildwellbeing.com.au/sites/default/files/uploads/ACWP_Final_Report_2016_Full.pdf.

Reigeluth, C.M., Aslan, S., Chen, Z., Dutta, P., Huh, Y., Lee, D., Lin, C.-Y., Lu, Y.-H., Min, M., Tan, V., Watson, S.L. & Watson, W.R. (2015). Personalized integrated educational system technology functions for the learner-centered paradigm of education. *Journal of Educational Computing Research*, *53*(3), 459–96.

Reigeluth, C.M. & Karnopp, J.R. (2013). *Reinventing schools: it's time to break the mold*. Lanham, MD: Rowman & Littlefield.

Reis, S.M. (1998). Underachievement for some—dropping out with dignity for others. *ITAG News* (Iowa Talented and Gifted Association Newsletter), *23*(4), 12–15.

Reis, S.M., Eckert, R.D., McCoach, D.B., Jacobs, J.K. & Coyne, M. (2008). Using enrichment reading practices to increase reading fluency, comprehension, and attitudes. *Journal of Educational Research*, *101*(5), 299–315.

Rennie, J. & Ortlieb, E. (2013). Diverse literacy learners: deficit versus productive pedagogies. In E. Ortlieb & E. Cheek (eds), *School-based interventions for struggling readers, K–8* (pp. 203–18). Bingley, United Kingdom: Emerald Publishers.

REFERENCES

Rennie, L., Venville, G. & Wallace, J. (2012). *Knowledge that counts in a global community: exploring the contribution of integrated curriculum*. Abingdon, United Kingdom: Routledge.

Renzulli, J.S. (2000). Raising the ceiling for all students: school improvement from a high-end perspective. In A.L. Costa (ed.), *Teaching for intelligence: a collection of 11 articles* (pp. 151–77). Sydney: Skylight-Hawker Brownlow.

Richmond, C. (2007). *Teach more, manage less*. Sydney: Scholastic Australia.

Riddle, M. (2016a). *Welcome to the Digital Citizenship website*. Retrieved from www.digitalcitizenship.net/Home_Page.html.

Riddle, M. (2016b). *Nine elements*. Retrieved from www.digitalcitizenship.net/Nine_Elements.html.

Rittel, H. & Webber, M. (1973). Dilemmas in a general theory of planning. *Policy Sciences, 4*(2), 155–69.

Robbins, S.P., Millett, B. & Waters-Marsh, T. (2004). *Organisational behaviour*. Sydney: Pearson Australia.

Roberts, R.E., Ramsay Roberts, C. & Duong, H.T. (2009). Sleepless in adolescence: prospective data on sleep deprivation, health and functioning. *Journal of Adolescence, 32*(5), 1045–57.

Robinson, K. (2006). *Do schools kill creativity?* Retrieved from www.ted.com/talks/ken_robinson_says_schools_kill_creativity?language=en.

Rock, M.L., Gregg, M., Ellis, E. & Gable, R.A. (2008). REACH: A framework for differentiating classroom instruction. *Preventing School Failure: Alternative Education for Children and Youth, 52*(2), 31–47.

Rodrigues, S. (2006). Pedagogic practice integrating primary science and e-learning: the need for relevance, recognition, resource, reflection, readiness and risk. *Technology, Pedagogy and Education, 15*(2), 175–89.

Rodriguez, A. (2012). *An analysis of elementary school teachers' knowledge and use of differentiated instruction*. Retrieved from digitalcommons.olivet.edu/edd_diss/39.

Rogers, B. (2015). *Classroom behaviour: a practical guide to effective teaching, behaviour management and colleague support*. London: Sage.

Rogers, C. (1969). *Freedom to learn: a view of what education might become*. Columbus, OH: Charles Merill.

Rogoff, B. (1998). Cognition as a collaborative process. In W. Damon (ed.), *Handbook of child psychology*, 5th edn (vol. 2, pp. 679–744). New York: Wiley.

Romero, C., Master, A., Paunesku, D., Dweck, C.S. & Gross, J.J. (2014). Academic and emotional functioning in middle school: the role of implicit theories. *Emotion, 14*(2), 227–34.

Romo, L.F., Mireles-Rios, R. & Hurtado, A. (2016). Cultural, media, and peer influences on body beautiful perceptions of Mexican American adolescent girls. *Journal of Adolescent Research, 31,* 474–501.

Roorda, D.L., Koomen, H.M., Spilt, J.L. & Oort, F.J. (2011). The influence of affective teacher–student relationships on students' school engagement and achievement: a meta-analytic approach. *Review of Educational Research, 81*(4), 493–529.

Roseth, C., Johnson, D.W. & Johnson, R.T. (2008). Promoting early adolescents' achievement and peer relationships: the effects of cooperative, competitive, and individualistic goal structures. *Psychological Bulletin, 134,* 223–46.

Rowntree, D. (1977). *Assessing students: how shall we know them?* London: Harper & Row.

Rumble, P. & Aspland, T. (2010). The four attributes model of the middle school teacher. *Australian Journal of Middle Schooling, 10*(1), pp. 4–15.

Rumble, P. & Smith, C. (2016). What matters most when working with young adolescents: the teacher! *Curriculum Perspectives, 36*(1), 1–10.

Rutter, L. (2012). *Continuing professional development in social care*. Thousand Oaks, CA: Sage.

Rutter, M. (1985). Resilience in the face of adversity: protective factors and resistance to psychiatric disorders. *British Journal of Psychiatry, 147,* 589–611.

Ryan, M.E. & Barton, G.M. (2014). The spatialized practices of teaching writing: shaping the discoursal self. In Diversity and international writing assessment, ed. M. Poe, *Research in the Teaching of English*, special issue, *48*(3), 303–29.

Saavedra, A.R. & Opfer, V.D. (2012). Learning 21st-century skills requires 21st-century teaching. *Phi Delta Kappan*, *94*(2), 8–13.

Sadler, D.R. (1989). Formative assessment and the design of instructional systems. *Instructional Science*, *18*(2), 119–44.

Sallis, E. (2014). *Total quality management in education*. New York: Routledge.

Sandberg, J. & Dall'Alba, G. (2009). Returning to practice anew: a lifeworld perspective. *Organisation Studies*, *30*(12), pp. 1349–68.

Sandholtz, J.H. (2000). Interdisciplinary team teaching as a form of professional development. *Teacher Education Quarterly*, *27*(3), 39–55.

Santrock, J.W. (2003). *Adolescence*, 9th edn. Boston, MA: McGraw-Hill.

Saulwick Muller Social Research (2006). Family–School Partnerships Project: a qualitative and quantitative study. Report prepared for the Department of Education, Science and Training, the Australian Council of State School Organisations and the Australian Parents Council, Commonwealth of Australia. Canberra: Department of Education, Science and Training.

Schaefer, M.B., Malu, K.M. & Yoon, B. (2016). An historical overview of the middle school movement, 1963–2015, *RMLE Online*, *39*(5), 1–27.

Schlechty, P.C. (2001). *Shaking up the schoolhouse*. San Francisco, CA: Jossey-Bass.

Schlechty, P.C. (2002). *Working on the work: an action plan for teachers, principals, and superintendents*. Jossey-Bass Education. San Francisco, CA: Jossey-Bass.

Schleicher, A. (ed.) (2012). *Preparing teachers and developing leaders for the 21st century: lessons from around the world*. Paris: OECD.

Schoen, H.L., Fey, J.T., Hirsch, C.R. & Coxford, A.F. (1999). Issues and options in the math wars. *Phi Delta Kappan*, *80*(6), 444–53.

Schoon, I. (2006). *Risk and resilience: adaptations in changing times*. Cambridge, United Kingdom: Cambridge University Press.

Schoor, C., Narciss, S. & Körndle, H. (2015). Regulation during cooperative and collaborative learning: a theory-based review of terms and concepts. *Educational Psychologist*, *50*(2), 97–119.

Schulz, L., Kushnir, T. & Gopnik, A. (2007). Learning from doing: intervention and causal inference in children. In A. Gopnik & L. Schulz (eds), *Causal learning: psychology, philosophy, computation* (pp. 67–85). New York: Oxford University Press.

Schumm, J. & Vaughn, S. (1995). Meaningful professional development in accommodating students with disabilities: lesson learned. *Remedial and Special Education*, *16*, 344–53.

Schwartz, K. (2015). *Harnessing the incredible learning potential of the adolescent brain*. Retrieved from ww2.kqed.org/mindshift/2015/12/21/harnessing-the-incredible-learning-potential-of-the-adolescent-brain.

Selfhout, M.H.W., Branje, S.J.T., ter Bogt, T.F.M. & Meeus, W.H.J. (2009). The role of music preferences in early adolescents' friendship formation and stability. *Journal of Adolescence*, *32*(1), 95–107.

Seligman, M.E.P. (2012). *Flourish*. New York: Simon & Schuster.

Seligman, M.E.P., Ernst, R.M., Gillham, J., Reivich, K. & Linkins, M. (2009). Positive education: positive psychology and classroom interventions. *Oxford Review of Education*, *35*(3), 293–311.

Selman, R. (1980). *The growth of interpersonal understanding*. New York: Academic Press.

Shachar, H. & Fisher, S. (2004). Cooperative learning and the achievement of motivation and perceptions of students in 11th grade chemistry classes. *Learning and Instruction*, *14*(1), 69–87.

Shaffer, D.R. (2002). *Developmental psychology: childhood and adolescence*, 6th edn. Belmont, CA: Wadsworth.

Shaffer, D.R. & Kipp, K. (2010). *Developmental psychology: childhood and adolescence*, 8th edn. Belmont, CA: Wadsworth, Cengage Learning.

Shaw, P., Greenstein, D., Lerch, J., Clasen, L., Lenroot, R., Gogtay, N., Evans, A., Rapoport, J. & Geidd, J. (2006). Intellectual ability and cortical development in children and adolescents. *Nature, 440*, 676–9.

Shek, D.T.L., Tang, V.M.Y. & Lo, C.Y. (2009). Evaluation of an internet addiction treatment program for Chinese adolescents in Hong Kong. *Adolescence, 44*(174), 359–74.

Shute, V.J. (2008). Focus on formative feedback. *Review of Educational Research, 78*, 153–89.

Siemon, D., Virgona, J. & Corneille, K. (2001). *The middle years numeracy research project: 5–9; final report.* Retrieved from www.education.vic.gov.au/Documents/school/teachers/teaching-resources/discipline/maths/mynumfreport.pdf.

Sigelman, C.K. & Waitzman, K.A. (1991). The development of distributive justice orientations: contextual influences on children's resource allocations. *Child Development, 62*, 1367–78.

Silverman, R., Speece, D.L., Harring, J.R. & Ritchey, K. (2013). Fluency has a role in the simple view of reading. *Scientific Studies of Reading, 17*(2), 108–33.

Simpkins, S.D., Bouffard, S.M., Dearing, E., Kreider, H., Wimer, C., Caronongan, P. & Weiss, H.B. (2009). Adolescent adjustment and patterns of parents' behaviors in early and middle adolescence. *Journal of Research on Adolescence, 19*(3), 530–57.

Sirsch, U., Dreher, E., Mayr, E. & Willinger, U. (2009). What does it take to be an adult in Austria? Views of adulthood in Austrian adolescents, emerging adults, and adults. *Journal of Adolescent Research, 24*(3), 275–92.

Skinner, B.F. (1953) *The possibility of a science of human behavior.* New York: Free House.

Skinner, B.F. (1963). Operant behavior. *American Psychologist, 18*(8), 503–15.

Skinner, B.F. (1984). Selection by consequences. *Behavioral and Brain Sciences, 7*(4), 477–510.

Skinner, E., Furrer, C., Marchand, G. & Kindermann, T. (2008). Engagement and disaffection in the classroom: part of a larger motivational dynamic? *Journal of Educational Psychology, 100*(4), 765–81.

Sklad, M., Diekstra, R., Ritter, M.D., Ben, J. & Gravesteijn, C. (2012). Effectiveness of school-based universal social, emotional, and behavioral programs: do they enhance students' development in the area of skill, behavior, and adjustment? *Psychology in the Schools, 49*, 892–909.

Smith, E. (2005). Critical media literacy in our middle schools. *Educational Perspectives, 38*(2), 17–18.

Smith, T. & Grootenboer, P.J. (2007). Mathematics in the middle school years. In S. Knipe (ed.), *Middle years of schooling: reframing adolescence* (pp. 171–86). Melbourne, Vic: Pearson.

Snapp, J. (2006). *Implementing curriculum integration in standards-based middle schools: the principal's role.* Westerville, OH: National Middle School Association.

Snyder, C.R. & Lopez, S.J. (2005). *Handbook of positive psychology.* New York: Oxford University Press.

So, H. & Brush, T.A. (2008). Student perceptions of collaborative learning, social presence and satisfaction in a blended learning environment: relationships and critical factors. *Computers & Education, 51*, 318–36.

Song, H., Ross, A., Thompson, R.A. & Ferrer, E. (2009). Attachment and self-evaluation in Chinese adolescents: age and gender differences. *Journal of Adolescence, 32*(5), 1267–86.

Spinrad, T.L. & Eisenberg, N. (2015). *Effortful control. Emerging trends in the social and behavioral sciences: an interdisciplinary, searchable, and linkable resource,* 1–11. DOI: 10.1002/9781118900772.etrds0097.

State Education Resource Center (2014). *Best practices in education.* Retrieved from www.sde.ct.gov/sde/lib/sde/pdf/talent_office/ctequityplan.pdf.

Steen, L.A. (1999). Numeracy: the new literacy for a data-drenched society. *Educational Leadership, 57*(2), 8–13.

Steen, L.A. (2001). The case for quantitative literacy. In L. Steen (ed.), *Mathematics and democracy: the case for quantitative literacy* (pp. 1–22). Princeton, NJ: National Council on Education and the Disciplines.

Steinberg, L. (2005). Cognitive and affective development in adolescence. *Trends in Cognitive Sciences*, *9*(2), 69–74.

Steinberg, L. & Lerner, R.M. (2004). The scientific study of adolescence: a brief history. *Journal of Early Adolescence*, *24*(1), 45–54.

Stevens, R.J. (2004). Why do educational innovations come and go? What do we know? What can we do? *Teaching and Teacher Education*, *20*, 389–96.

Stobart, G. (2008). *Testing times: the uses and abuses of assessment*. Abingdon, United Kingdom: Routledge.

Strauch, B. (2003). *The primal teen: what the new discoveries about the teenage brain tell us*. New York: Double Day.

Stride, A. (2014). Let US tell YOU! South Asian, Muslim girls tell tales about physical education. *Physical Education and Sport Pedagogy*, *19*(4), 398–417.

Stringer, B. (1997). Better connections. *EQ Australia*, *1*, 21–3.

Stryker, P. & Burke, P. (2006). The past, present and future of an identity theory. *Social Psychology Quarterly*, *63*, 284–97.

Sugai, G. (2009). *What is school-wide positive behavioral interventions and supports?* Retrieved from www.pbis.org/common/cms/files/pbisresources/What_is_SWPBS.pdf.

Suldo, S.M., Hearon, B.V., Bander, B., McCullough, M., Garofano, J., Roth, R.A. & Tan, S.Y. (2015). Increasing elementary school students' subjective well-being through a classwide positive psychology intervention: results of a pilot study. *Contemporary School Psychology*, *19*(4), 300–11.

Suldo, S.M., Savage, J. A. & Mercer, S.H. (2013). Increasing middle school students' life satisfaction: efficacy of a positive psychology group intervention. *Journal of Happiness Studies*, *15*(1), 19–42.

Sullivan, A., Johnson, B., Owens, L. & Conway, R. (2014). Punish them or engage them? Teachers' views of unproductive student behaviours in the classroom. *Australian Journal of Teacher Education*, *39*(6), pp. 43–56.

Sullivan, E. & Keeney, E. (2008). *Teachers talk: school culture, safety and human rights*. New York: National Economic and Social Rights Initiative and Teachers Unite.

Sultan, S. & Hussain, I. (2012). Comparison between individual and collaborative learning: determining a strategy for promoting social skills and self-esteem among undergraduate students. *Journal of Educational Research*, *15*(2), 35–43.

Sumter, S.R., Bokhorst, C.L., Steinberg, L. & Westenberg, M.P. (2009). The developmental pattern of resistance to peer influence in adolescence: will the teenager ever be able to resist? *Journal of Adolescence*, *32*(4), 1009–21.

Sussman, D., Leung, R.C., Chakravarty, M.M., Lerch, J.P. & Taylor, M.J. (2016). *Developing human brain: age related changes in cortical, subcortical, and cerebellar anatomy*. Retrieved from onlinelibrary.wiley.com/doi/10.1002/brb3.457/full.

Swanson, D.P., Beale Spencer, M. & Petersen, A. (1998). *The adolescent years: social influences and educational challenges*. Chicago, IL: University of Chicago Press.

Sylwester, R. (2000). On teaching brains to think: a conversation with Robert Sylwester. *Educational Leadership*, *57*(7), 72–5.

Theriot, S. (2009). *Research summary: service-learning*. Retrieved from www.amle.org/BrowsebyTopic/Research/ResDet/TabId/198/ArtMID/696/ArticleID/323/Service-Learning.aspx.

Thomas, G. (1992). *Effective classroom teamwork: support or intrusion?* New York: Routledge.

Thompson, G. (2015). The challenges of testing accountability: understanding limitations and negotiating consequences. In S. Groundwater-Smith & N. Mockler (eds), *Big fish, little fish: teaching and learning in the middle years* (pp. 126–37). Melbourne: Cambridge University Press

Thurston, A., Topping, K.J., Tolmie, A., Christie, D., Karagiannidou, E. & Murray, P. (2010). Cooperative learning in science: follow-up from primary to high school. *International Journal of Science Education*, *32*(4), 501–22.

Tieso, C. (2005). The effects of grouping practices and curricular adjustments on achievement. *Journal for the Education of the Gifted, 29*(1), 60–89.

Tillett, G. (1999). *Resolving conflict: a practical approach*, 2nd edn. Melbourne: Oxford University Press.

Tinning, R. & Fitzclarence, L. (1992). Postmodern youth culture and the crisis in Australian secondary school physical education. *Quest, 44*, 287–303.

Tinto, V., Goodsell, A. & Russo, P. (1993). Collaborative learning and new college students. *Cooperative Learning and College Teaching, 3*(3), 9–10.

Tomlinson, C.A. (1999). Mapping a route toward differentiated instruction. *Educational Leadership, 57*, 12–17.

Tomlinson, C.A. (2000). Reconcilable differences: standards-based teaching and differentiation. *Educational Leadership, 58*(1), 6–13.

Tomlinson, C.A. (2005). The differentiated classroom: responding to the needs of all learners. Upper Saddle River, NJ: Pearson and Merrill Prentice Hall.

Tomlinson, C.A., Callahan, C.M., Tomchin, E.M., Eiss, N., Imbeau, M. & Landrum, M. (1997). Becoming architects of communities of learning: addressing academic diversity in contemporary classrooms. *Exceptional Children, 63*(2), 269–82.

Tomlinson, C.A. & Imbeau, M.B. (2010). *Leading and managing a differentiated classroom*. Alexandria, VA: Association for Supervision and Curriculum Development.

Tomlinson, C.A., Kaplan, S., Renzulli, J., Purcell, J., Leppien, J. & Byrne, D. (2002). *The parallel curriculum: a design to develop high potential and challenge high-ability learners*. Thousand Oaks, CA: Corwin Press.

Torff, B. (2003). Developmental changes in teachers' use of higher order thinking and content knowledge. *Journal of Educational Psychology, 95*, 563–9.

Toshalis, E. & Nakkula, M.J. (2012). Motivation, engagement, and student voice. *Education Digest, 78*(1), 29–35.

Trilling, B. & Fadel, C. (2009). *21st century skills: learning for life in our times*. San Francisco, CA: Jossey-Bass.

Tschannen-Moran, M. & Woolfolk-Hoy, A.W. (2001). Teacher efficacy: capturing an elusive construct. *Teaching and Teacher Education, 17*(7), 783–805.

Tuckman, B.W. (1965). Developmental sequence in small groups. *Psychological Bulletin, 63*(6), 384–9.

Tuisku, V., Pelkonen, M., Kiviruusu, O., Karlsson, L., Ruuttu, T. & Marttunen, M. (2009). Factors associated with deliberate self-harm behavior among depressed adolescent outpatients. *Journal of Adolescence, 32*(5), 1125–36.

Turner, J.C. & Meyer, D.K. (2000). Studying and understanding the instructional contexts of classrooms: using our past to forge our future. *Educational Psychologist, 90*, 730–45.

Ungar, M., Ghazinour, M. & Richter, J. (2013). Annual research review: what is resilience within the social ecology of human development? *Journal of Child Psychology and Psychiatry, 54*(4), 348–66.

Upadyaya, K. & Salmela-Aro, K. (2013). Development of school engagement in association with academic success and well-being in varying social contexts. *European Psychologist, 18*(2), 136–47.

Vaandering, D. (2014). Implementing restorative justice principles in schools: what pedagogy reveals. *Journal of Peace Education, 11*(1), 64–80.

Van Dat, T. (2013). Theoretical perspectives underlying the application of cooperative learning in classrooms. *International Journal of Higher Education, 2*(4), 101–26.

Van de Vliert, E. (1997). *Complex interpersonal conflict behaviour: theoretical frontiers*. Hove, United Kingdom: Psychology Press.

Vangrieken, K., Dochy, F. & Raes, E. (2015). Team learning in teacher teams: team entitativity as a bridge between teams-in-theory and teams-in-practice. *European Journal of Psychology of Education, 31*, 1–24.

Vangrieken, K., Dochy, F., Raes, E. & Kyndt, E. (2015). Teacher collaboration: a systematic review. *Educational Research Review, 15*, 17–40.

van Kraayenoord, C.E. & Paris, S.G. (1997). Australian students' self-appraisal of their work samples and academic progress. *Elementary School Journal*, *31*, 523–37.

van Menen, M. & Li, S. (2002). The pathic principle of pedagogical language. *Teaching and Teacher Education*, *18*, 215–24.

Van Tassel-Baska, J., Zuo, L., Avery, L.D. & Little, C.A. (2002). A curriculum study of gifted-student learning in the language arts. *Gifted Child Quarterly*, *46*(1), 30–44.

Vars, G. (2000). Common learnings: a 50 year quest. *Journal of Curriculum and Supervision*, *16*(1), 70–89.

Voltz, D. & Fore, C. (2006). Urban special education in the context of standards-based reform. *Remedial and Special Education*, *27*, 329–36.

von Soest, T. & Wichstrøm, L. (2009). Gender differences in the development of dieting from adolescence to early adulthood: a longitudinal study. *Journal of Research on Adolescence*, *19*(3), 509–29.

Vygotsky, L.S. (1962). *Thought and language*. Cambridge, MA: MIT Press.

Vygotsky, L.S. (ed.) (1978). *Mind in society: the development of higher psychological processes*. Cambridge, MA: Harvard University Press.

Walker, C.O. & Greene, B.A. (2009). The relations between student motivational beliefs and cognitive engagement in high school. *Journal of Educational Research*, *102*(6), 463–72.

Wallhead, T.L. & Buckworth, J. (2004). The role of physical education in the promotion of youth physical activity. *Quest*, *56*, 285–301.

Wang, M.-T. & Eccles, J.S. (2011). Adolescent behavioral, emotional, and cognitive engagement trajectories in school and their differential relations to educational success. *Journal of Research on Adolescence*, *22*(1), 31–9.

Wang, M.-T. & Fredricks, J.A. (2014). The reciprocal links between school engagement, youth problem behaviors, and school dropout during adolescence. *Child Development*, *85*(2), 722–37.

Wang, S., Hsu, H., Campbell, T., Coster, D. & Longhurst, M. (2014). An investigation of the middle year school science teachers and students use of technologies inside and outside of the classroom: considering whether digital natives are more technology savvy than their teachers. *Educational Technology Research and Development*, *62*: 637–62.

Ward, G. & Quennerstedt, M. (2016). Transactions in primary physical education in the UK: a smorgasbord of looks-like-sport. *Physical Education and Sport Pedagogy*, *21*(2), 137–52.

Watson, J.B. (1913). Psychology as the behaviorist views it. *Psychological Review*, *20*, 158–77.

Watson, J.B. (1925). *Behaviorism*. New York: Norton.

Watt, G., Finger, G., Smart, V. & Banjer, F. (2014). Project 600: inspire, connect and transform. Paper presented at the ACEC 2014 Now It's Personal conference, Adelaide.

Weare, K. & Gray, G. (2003). *What works in developing children's emotional and social competence and wellbeing?* London: Department for Education and Skills, United Kingdom Government.

Weeden, P., Winter, J. & Broadfoot, P. (2002). *Assessment: what's in it for schools?* London: Routledge.

Wegerif, R. (2002). *Literature review in thinking skills, technology and learning (no. 2)*. Bristol, United Kingdom: Futurelab.

Weinstein, E.C., Selman, R.L., Thomas, S., Kim, J., White, A.E. & Dinakar, K. (2016). How to cope with digital stress: the recommendations adolescents offer their peers online. *Journal of Adolescent Research*, *31*, 415–41.

Wenger, E. (1999). *Communities of practice: learning, meaning, and identity*. Cambridge, United Kingdom: Cambridge University Press.

West, M. & Schwerdt, G. (2012). The middle school plunge. *Education Next*, *12*(2), n.p.

Wheelan, S.A. (2005). *Faculty groups: from frustration to collaboration*. Thousand Oaks, CA: Corwin Press.

Wheeler, S., Yeomans, P. & Wheeler, D. (2008). The good, the bad and the wiki: evaluating student-generated content for collaborative learning. *British Journal of Educational Technology*, *39*(6), 987–95.

REFERENCES

White, R., Wyn, J. & White, R. (2013). *Youth and society*, 3rd edn. Melbourne: Oxford University Press.

White, S.H. (1968). The learning–maturation controversy: Hall to Hull. *Merrill-Palmer Quarterly, 14*, 187–96.

White, S.H. (1994). G. Stanley Hall: from philosophy to developmental psychology. In R.D. Parke, P.A.J. Ornstein, J. Relser & C. Zahn-Waxler (eds), *A century of developmental psychology* (pp. 204–25). Washington, DC: American Psychological Association.

Whitehouse, A.J.O., Durkin, K., Jaquet, E. & Ziatas, K. (2009). Friendship, loneliness and depression in adolescents with Asperger's Syndrome. *Journal of Adolescence, 32*(2), 309–22.

Wiggins, G. & McTighe, J. (2011). *The understanding by design guide to creating high-quality units*. Alexandria, VA: Association for Supervision and Curriculum Development.

Wiliam, D. (2011). What is assessment for learning? *Studies in Educational Evaluation, 37*, 3–14.

Wiliam, D., Kingsbury, G. & Wise, S. (2013). Connecting the dots: formative, interim, and summative assessment. In R.W. Lissitz (ed.), *Informing the practice of teaching using formative and interim assessment: a systems approach* (pp. 1–19). Charlotte, NC: Information Age.

Wilkins, B., Boman, P. & Mergler, A. (2015). Positive psychological strengths and school engagement in primary school children. *Cogent Education, 2*(1), doi:10.1080/2331186x.2015.1095680.

Williams, W.V. (1988). Answers to questions about math anxiety. *School Science and Mathematics, 88*(2), 95–103.

Willis, J. (2007). Cooperative learning is a brain turn-on. *Middle School Journal, 38*(4), 4–13.

Willms, J. (2003). *Student engagement at school: a sense of belonging and participation; results from PISA 2000*. Paris: OECD.

Willms, J. & Friesen, S. (2012). *What did you do in school today? Research Series report 2: the relationship between instructional challenge and student engagement*. Toronto, Canada: Canadian Education Association.

Windle, G. (2011). What is resilience? A review and concept analysis. *Reviews in Clinical Gerontology, 21*(2), 152–69.

Winstock, Z. (2009). From self-control capabilities and the need to control others to proactive and reactive aggression among adolescents. *Journal of Adolescence, 32*(3), 455–66.

Wood, D., Bruner, J.S. & Ross, G. (1976). The role of tutoring in problem-solving. *Journal of Child Psychology and Psychiatry and Allied Disciplines, 17*, 89–100.

Woolfolk, A. & Margetts, K. (2012). *Educational psychology*, 3rd edn. Sydney: Pearson.

Woolley, G. (2011). *Reading comprehension: assisting children with learning difficulties*. Netherlands: Springer.

World Health Organization (1986). *Ottawa charter for health promotion*. Retrieved from www.who.dk/policy/Ottawa.htm.

Wright, J. & Harwood, V. (eds) (2009). *Biopolitics and the 'obesity epidemic': governing bodies*. London: Routledge.

Wright, J., Macdonald, D., Wyn, J. & Kriflik, L. (2005). Becoming somebody: changing priorities and physical activity. *Youth Studies Australia, 24*(1), 16–21.

Wyatt-Smith, C.M. & Bridges, S. (2007). *Meeting in the middle: assessment, pedagogy, learning and students at educational disadvantage; final evaluation report for the Department of Education, Science and Training on literacy and numeracy in the middle years of schooling*. Brisbane: Queensland Department of Education, Science and Training.

Wyatt-Smith, C.M. & Castleton, G. (2005). Examining how teachers judge student writing: an Australian case study. *Journal of Curriculum Studies, 37*(2), 131–54.

Wyatt-Smith, C.M. & Jackson, C. (in press). NAPLAN test data on writing: a picture of accelerating negative change. *Australian Journal of Language and Literacy*.

Wyatt-Smith, C.M. & Klenowski, V. (2014). Elements of better assessment for the improvement of learning. In C. Wyatt-Smith, V. Klenowski & P. Colbert (eds), *Designing assessment for quality learning* (vol. 1, pp. 195–210). Netherlands: Springer Science & Business Media.

Wyatt-Smith, C.M., Klenowski, V. & Gunn, S. (2010). The centrality of teachers' judgement practice in assessment: a study of standards in moderation. *Assessment in Education: Principles, Policy & Practice, 17*, 59–75.

Wyatt-Smith, C.M., Klenowski, V. & Gunn, S. (2010). The centrality of teachers' judgement practice in assessment: a study of standards in moderation. *Assessment in Education: Principles, Policy and Practice, 17*, 59–75.

Wyatt-Smith, C.M. & Looney, A. (2016). Professional standards and the assessment work of teachers. In D. Wise, L. Hayward & J. Pandya (eds), *The Sage handbook of curriculum, pedagogy and assessment* (pp. 805–20). London: Sage.

Yeager, D.S. & Dweck, C.S. (2012). Mindsets that promote resilience: when students believe that personal characteristics can be developed. *Educational Psychologist, 47*(4), 302–14.

Yerrick, R. & Johnson, J. (2009). The impact of digital tools on middle school science literacy. *Contemporary Issues in Technology and Teacher Education, 9*(3), 280–315.

Yeung, S.-Y.S. (2015). Conception of teaching higher order thinking: perspectives of Chinese teachers in Hong Kong. *Curriculum Journal, 26*(4), 553–78.

Zevenbergen, R. (2005). The construction of mathematical 'habitus': implications of ability grouping in the middle years. *Journal of Curriculum Studies, 37*(5), 607–19.

Zhang, M. & Quintana, C. (2012). Scaffolding strategies for supporting middle school students' online inquiry processes. *Computers & Education, 58*(1), 181–96.

Zins, J.E., Weissberg, R.P., Wang, M.C. & Walberg, H.J. (eds) (2004). *Building academic success on social and emotional learning: what does the research say?* New York: Teachers College Press.

Index